CONTENTS

GW00514854

TOWN PLAN SECTION
Legend and Key Plan - Page 2

The figure in brackets is the Main Map page number on w

AREA MAP SECTION
Legend and Key Plan - Page 29

(Detailed enlargements of specific areas)

MAIN MAP SECTION

Complete road map of Southern, Central and East Africa in page by page format

INDEX SECTION

STRIP ROUTE SECTION

Easy to use diagrams of road routes between specified towns

ISBN 1-86809-228-3

TOWN PLAN SECTION
STADSKAARTGEDEELTE

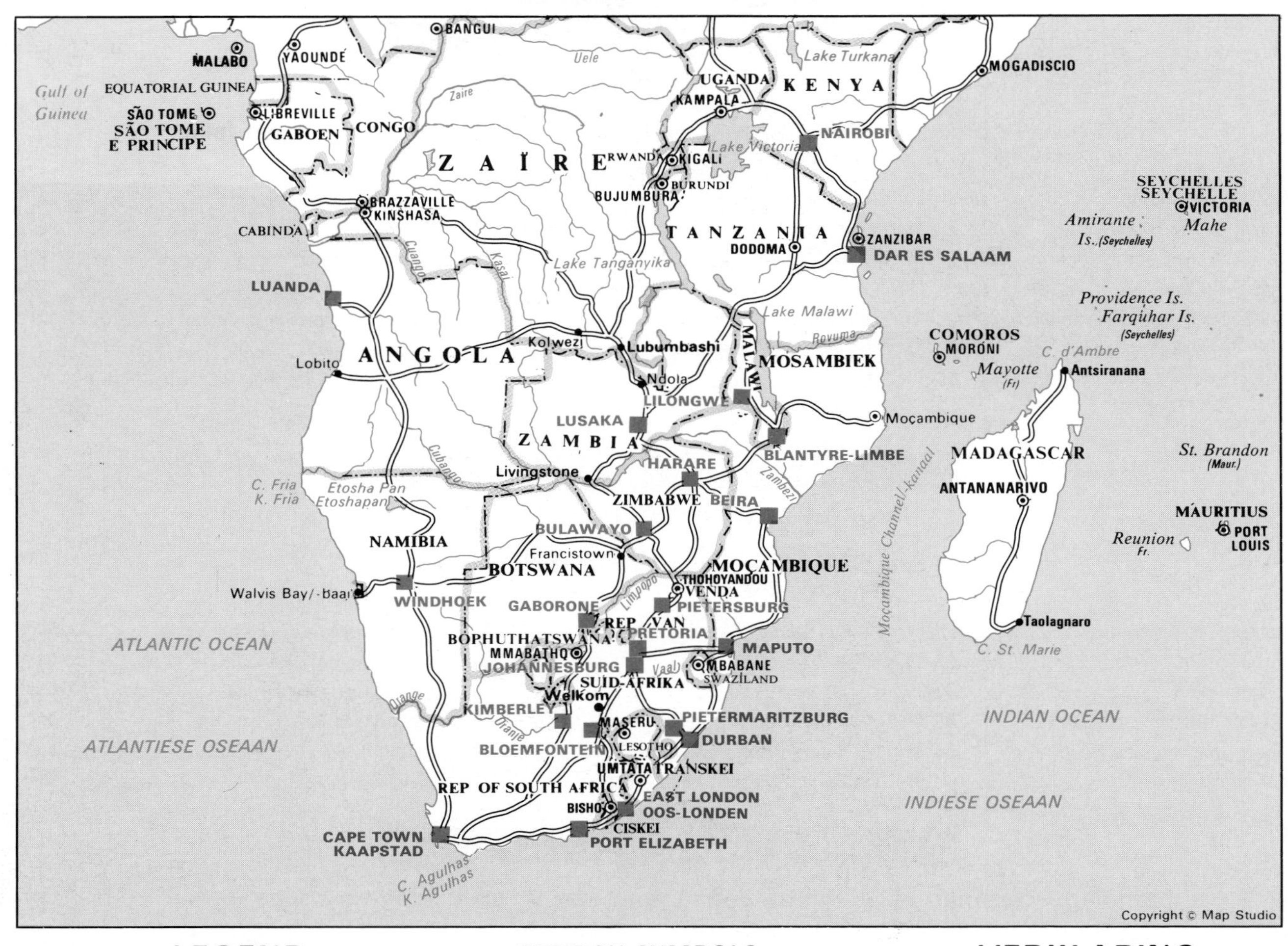

LEGEND

▬▬▬	Freeways / Deurpaaie
▬▬▬	National/Main Through Routes / Nasionale/Hoof-deurroetes
→	One-way Streets / Eenrigtingstrate
N1 M4 8 R101	Route Markers / Roete-aanwysers
───	Railways / Spoorweë
~~	Rivers / Riviere
• ▲	Places of Interest / Besienswaardige Plekke
⊡ L	Libraries / Biblioteke
🏛	National Monuments / Nasionale monumente
S	Schools / Skole
H	Hotels / Hotelle

CHURCH SYMBOLS
KERKSIMBOLE

†	Anglican / Anglikaanse	☾	Moslem
⚶	Apostolic Faith / Apostoliese Geloof		Nederduitse Gereformeerde Kerk
	Baptist / Baptiste		Presbyterian / Presbiteriaanse
	Congregational	†	Roman Catholic / Rooms-Katoliek
	Christian Science	®	Russian Orthodox / Russies-Ortodoks
	Gereformeerde Kerk		Seventh Day Adventist / Sewende Dag-Adventiste
	Greek Orthodox / Grieks-Katolieke	✡	Synagogue / Sinagoge
	Hervormde Kerk		Union
☽	Hindu / Hindoe		Church of England in S.A.
⚜	Lutheran / Lutheraanse		Full Gospel / Volle Evangelie
	Methodist / Metodiste		Pentecostal Protestant / Pinkster Protestante

VERKLARING

⬡	Parks / Parke	
	Caravan Parks / Woonwaparke	🚐
	Tourist Information / Toeriste-inligting	i
	Lighthouses / Ligtorings	⚐
	Hospitals / Hospitale	⊕
	Parking Areas / Parkeerplekke	🚗
	Post Offices / Poskantore	T
	Police Stations / Polisiestasies	●
	Drive-in Cinemas / Inryteaters	★
	Cinemas / Bioskope	▰
	Theatres / Teaters	🎭

SPORT SYMBOLS
SPORTSIMBOLE

●	Bowls/Rolbal	Cricket	🏛	Krieket	
H	Rugby/Rugby	Motor Racing		Motorwedrenne	
⛳	Golf/Gholf	Soccer		Sokker	
				Swimming/Swem	▱
				Tennis/Tennis	⚲
				Turf Racing/Perdewedrenne	⚲

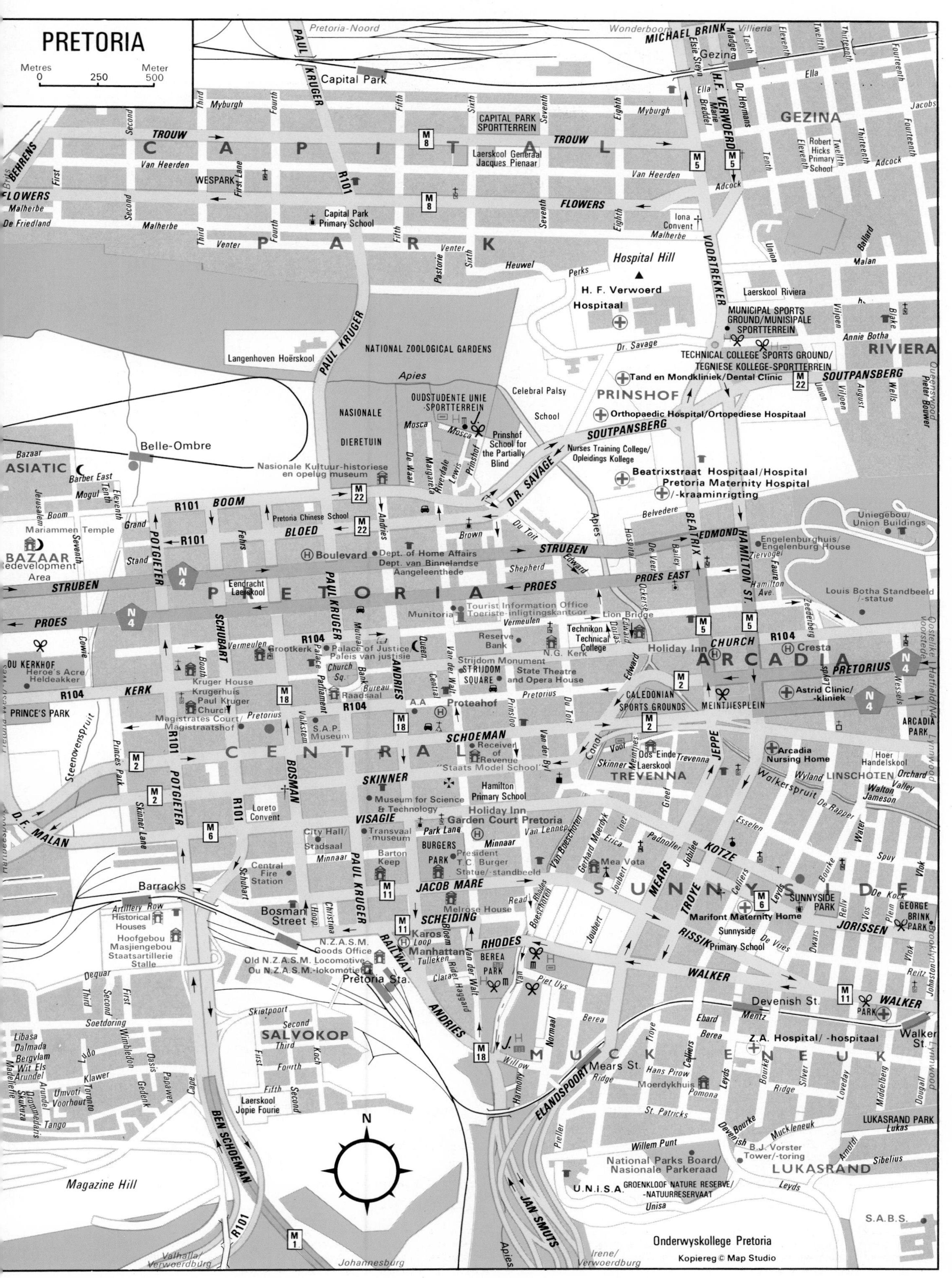

PRETORIA
Metres
Meter
0
250
500
Pretoria-Noord
Wonderboom
Villieria
MICHAEL BRINK
PAUL KRUGER
Capital Park
Gezina
H.F. VERWOERD
Myburgh
CAPITAL PARK SPORTTERREIN
GEZINA
TROUW
C A P I T A L
Van Heerden
Laerskool Generaal Jacques Pienaar
Robert Hicks Primary School
Adcock
WESPARK
First Lane
R101
FLOWERS
Malherbe
De Friedland
Capital Park Primary School
Iona Convent
Venter
P A R K
Heuwel
Hospital Hill
Perks
H. F. Verwoerd Hospitaal
VOORTREKKER
Laerskool Riviera
Malan
MUNICIPAL SPORTS GROUND/MUNISIPALE SPORTTERREIN
Annie Botha
RIVIERA
Dr. Savage
TECHNICAL COLLEGE SPORTS GROUND/ TEGNIESE KOLLEGE-SPORTTERREIN
Tand en Mondkliniek/Dental Clinic
SOUTPANSBERG
Langenhoven Hoërskool
NATIONAL ZOOLOGICAL GARDENS
Apies
NASIONALE DIERETUIN
OUDSTUDENTE UNIE -SPORTTERREIN
Celebral Palsy School
PRINSHOF
Orthopaedic Hospital/Ortopediese Hospitaal
Prinshof School for the Partially Blind
Nurses Training College/ Opleidings Kollege
Beatrixstraat Hospitaal/Hospital
Pretoria Maternity Hospital /-kraaminrigting
Belle-Ombre
Bazaar
ASIATIC
Barber East
Nasionale Kultuur-historiese en opelug museum
D.R. SAVAGE
Mogul
Boom
R101 BOOM
Pretoria Chinese School
Mariammen Temple
BLOED
Brown
Belvedere
BEATRIX
EDMOND
HAMILTON ST.
Uniegebou/ Union Buildings
Engelenburghuis/ Engelenburg House
BAZAAR
Redevelopment Area
Stand
Boulevard
Dept. of Home Affairs
Dept. van Binnelandse Aangeleentheede
STRUBEN
Shepherd
PROES EAST
STRUBEN
Eendracht Laerskool
P R E T O R I A
PROES
Louis Botha Standbeeld /-statue
PROES
Munitoria
Tourist Information Office
Toeriste-inligtingskantoor
Lion Bridge
Vermeulen
Reserve Bank
Technikon Technical College
N.G. Kerk
R104
CHURCH
Holiday Inn
Cresta
ARCADIA
OU KERKHOF
Heroe's Acre/ Heldeakker
Grootkerk
Palace of Justice Paleis van justisie
Church Sq.
Strijdom Monument
STRIJDOM SQUARE
State Theatre and Opera House
PRETORIUS
KERK
R104
Kruger House
Krugerhuis
Paul Kruger Church
Raadsaal
CALEDONIAN SPORTS GROUNDS
MEINTJIESPLEIN
Astrid Clinic/ -kliniek
PRINCE'S PARK
Magistrates Court/ Magistraatshof
Pretorius
S.A.P. Museum
Proteahof
SCHOEMAN
ARCADIA PARK
Receiver of Revenue
"Staats Model School"
C E N T R A L
Os Einde Laerskool
Trevenna
TREVENNA
Arcadia Nursing Home
Hoer Handelskool
Steenovenspruit
SKINNER
Hamilton Primary School
Walkerspruit
LINSCHOTEN
Orchard
Walton Jameson
Museum for Science & Technology
Holiday Inn Garden Court Pretoria
Loreto Convent
VISAGIE
D.F. MALAN
Skinner Lane
POTGIETER
BOSMAN
City Hall/ Stadsaal
Transvaal -museum
Park Lane
BURGERS PARK
Barton Keep
Minnaar
President T.C. Burger Statue/ -standbeeld
Mea Vota
KOTZE
Central Fire Station
JACOB MARE
S U N N Y S I D E
Barracks
Artillery Row
Historical Houses
Hoofgebou Masjiengebou Staatsartillerie Stalle
Bosman Street
Melrose House
SCHEIDING
MEARS
TROYE
SUNNYSIDE PARK
Marifont Maternity Home
JORISSEN
GEORGE BRINK PARK
N.Z.A.S.M. Goods Office
Old N.Z.A.S.M. Locomotive
Ou N.Z.A.S.M.-lokomotief
Pretoria Sta.
Karos Manhattan
RHODES
BEREA PARK
RISSIK
Sunnyside Primary School
WALKER
Tulleken
Piet Uys
Devenish St.
WALKER
Walker St.
Dequar
Soetdoring
Skietpoort
SALVOKOP
ANDRIES
Berea
Ebard
Z.A. Hospital/ -hospitaal
Libasa
Dalmada
Bergvlam
Wit Els
Arundel
Umvoti
Voorhout
Klawer
Laerskool Jopie Fourie
Willow
M U C K L E N E U K
Mears St.
Hans Pirow
Moerdykhuis
Pomona
Ridge
ELANDSPOORT
St. Patricks
LUKASRAND PARK
Muckleneuk
B.J. Vorster Tower/-toring
Willem Punt
National Parks Board/ Nasionale Parkeraad
LUKASRAND
Sibelius
Magazine Hill
BEN SCHOEMAN
N
U.N.I.S.A.
GROENKLOOF NATURE RESERVE/ -NATUURRESERVAAT
Unisa
S.A.B.S.
JAN SMUTS
Onderwyskollege Pretoria
Valhalla/ Verwoerdburg
Johannesburg
Irene/ Verwoerdburg
Apies
Kopiereg © Map Studio

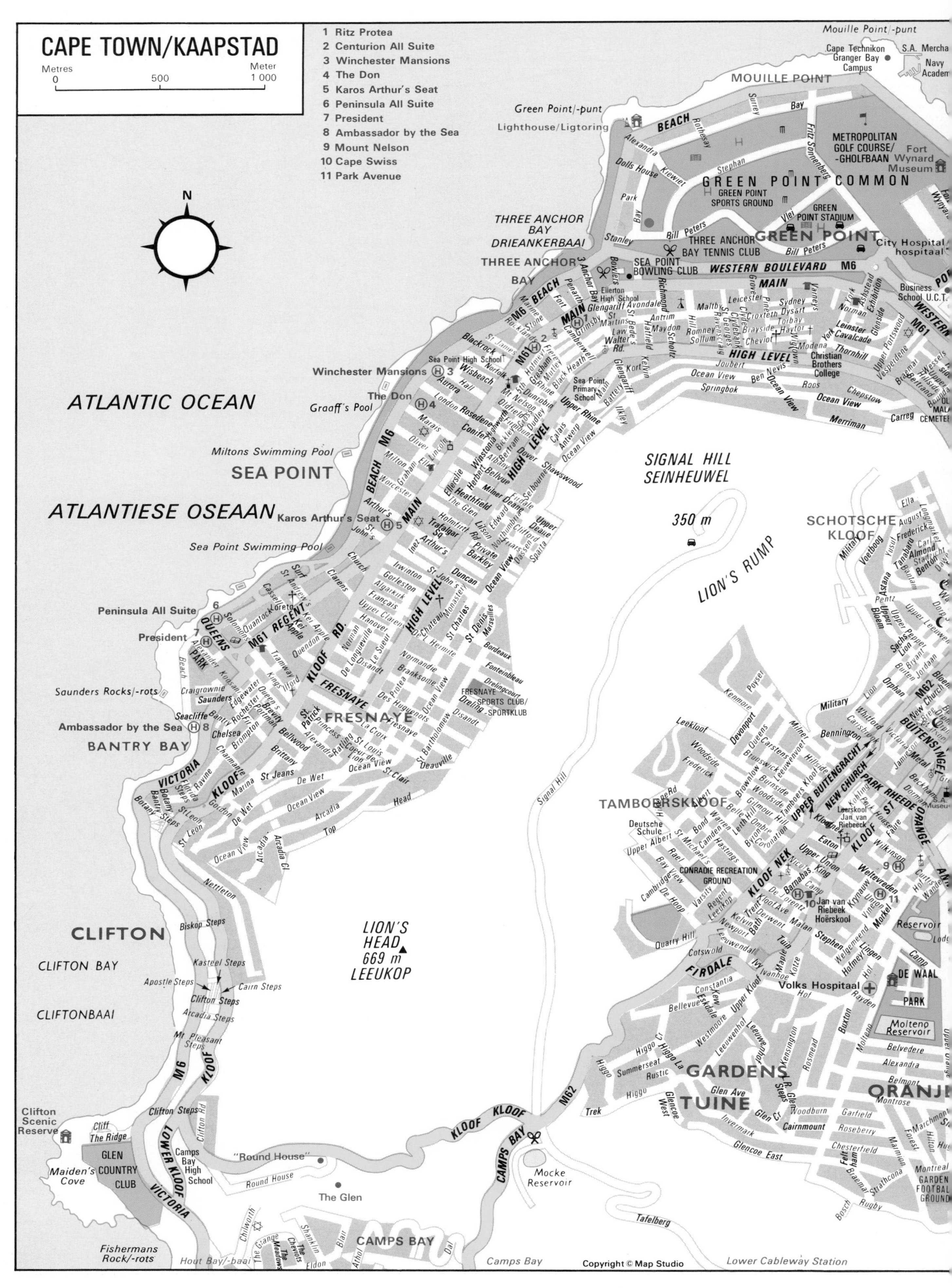

CAPE TOWN/KAAPSTAD

Metres
0   500
Meter
1 000

1 Ritz Protea
2 Centurion All Suite
3 Winchester Mansions
4 The Don
5 Karos Arthur's Seat
6 Peninsula All Suite
7 President
8 Ambassador by the Sea
9 Mount Nelson
10 Cape Swiss
11 Park Avenue

N

ATLANTIC OCEAN

ATLANTIESE OSEAAN

SEA POINT

Winchester Mansions
The Don
Graaff's Pool
Miltons Swimming Pool
Sea Point Swimming Pool
Karos Arthur's Seat

Peninsula All Suite
President

Saunders Rocks/-rots

Ambassador by the Sea
BANTRY BAY

CLIFTON

CLIFTON BAY

CLIFTONBAAI

Clifton Scenic Reserve
Maiden's Cove
GLEN COUNTRY CLUB
Fishermans Rock/-rots

MOUILLE POINT
Mouille Point /-punt

Cape Technikon Granger Bay Campus
S.A. Mercha
Navy Acade

Green Point /-punt
Lighthouse/Ligtoring
BEACH

THREE ANCHOR BAY
DRIEANKERBAAI

THREE ANCHOR BAY

METROPOLITAN GOLF COURSE/-GHOLFBAAN
Fort Wynard Museum

GREEN POINT COMMON
Green Point Sports Ground
GREEN POINT STADIUM

GREEN POINT
City Hospital hospitaal

WESTERN BOULEVARD   M6
MAIN

HIGH LEVEL

Christian Brothers College

SIGNAL HILL
SEINHEUWEL

350 m

LION'S RUMP

SCHOTSCHE KLOOF

HIGH LEVEL

TAMBOERSKLOOF

CONRADIE RECREATION GROUND

Signal Hill

FRESNAYE
Fresnaye Sports Club/ -Sportklub

LION'S HEAD
669 m
LEEUKOP

UPPER BUITENGRACHT
NEW CHURCH

KLOOF NEK

FIRDALE
Volks Hospitaal

Molteno Reservoir

GARDENS TUINE

ORANJE

"Round House"
Camps Bay High School
Round House
The Glen

CAMPS BAY
Hout Bay/-baai

Camps Bay

Mocke Reservoir

Tafelberg

Lower Cableway Station

Copyright © Map Studio

4

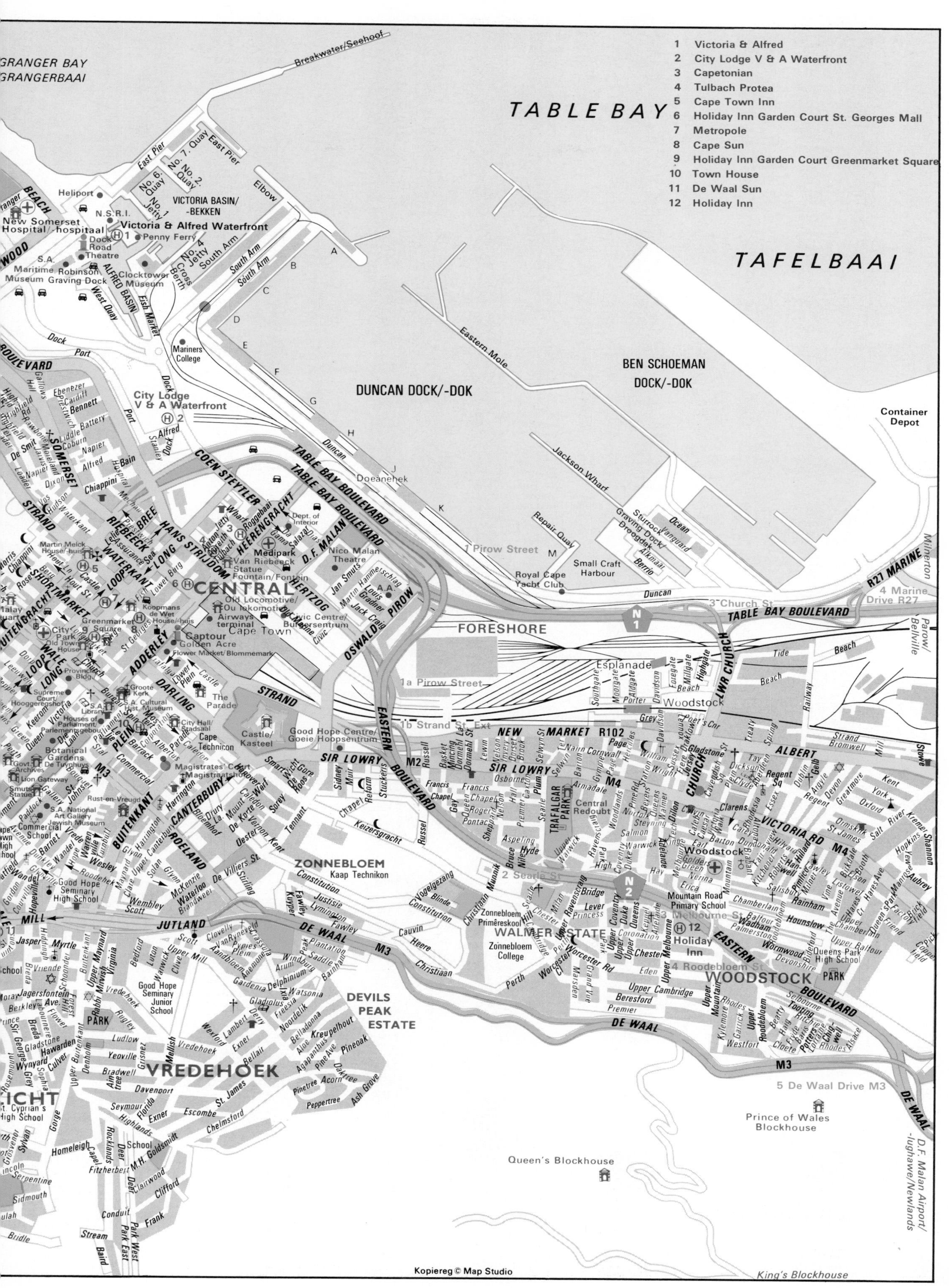

TABLE BAY

TAFELBAAI

1 Victoria & Alfred
2 City Lodge V & A Waterfront
3 Capetonian
4 Tulbach Protea
5 Cape Town Inn
6 Holiday Inn Garden Court St. Georges Mall
7 Metropole
8 Cape Sun
9 Holiday Inn Garden Court Greenmarket Square
10 Town House
11 De Waal Sun
12 Holiday Inn

GRANGER BAY
GRANGERBAAI

Breakwater/Seehoof

DUNCAN DOCK/-DOK

BEN SCHOEMAN
DOCK/-DOK

Container
Depot

FORESHORE

CENTRAL

ZONNEBLOEM

WOODSTOCK

DEVILS
PEAK
ESTATE

VREDEHOEK

Prince of Wales
Blockhouse

Queen's Blockhouse

King's Blockhouse

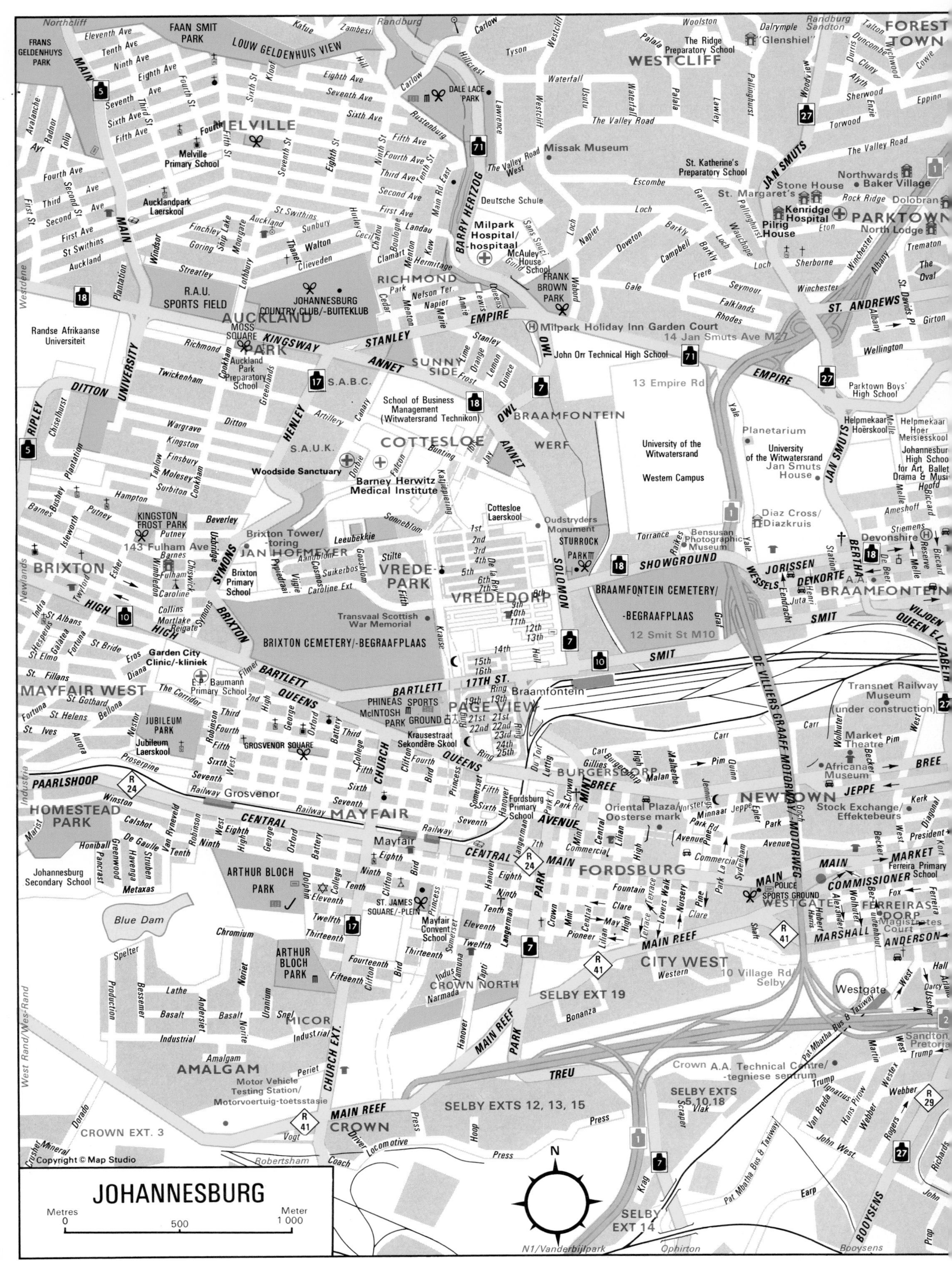

JOHANNESBURG
Metres
0
500
Meter
1 000
Copyright © Map Studio
N
MELVILLE
WESTCLIFF
FOREST TOWN
PARKTOWN
RICHMOND
AUCKLAND PARK
SUNNYSIDE
BRAAMFONTEIN
COTTESLOE
BRIXTON
JAN HOFMEYER
VREDEPARK
VREDEDORP
MAYFAIR WEST
PAGEVIEW
BURGERSDORP
NEWTOWN
FORDSBURG
MAYFAIR
HOMESTEAD PARK
CROWN NORTH
CITY WEST
SELBY EXT 19
MICOR
AMALGAM
CROWN EXT. 3
CROWN
SELBY EXTS 12, 13, 15
SELBY EXTS 5,10,18
SELBY EXT 14
FERREIRASDORP
WESTGATE
Randse Afrikaanse Universiteit
University of the Witwatersrand
Western Campus
R.A.U. SPORTS FIELD
JOHANNESBURG COUNTRY CLUB/-BUITEKLUB
BRIXTON CEMETERY/-BEGRAAFPLAAS
BRAAMFONTEIN CEMETERY/-BEGRAAFPLAAS
Milpark Holiday Inn Garden Court
Milpark Hospital/-hospitaal
Missak Museum
Planetarium
Transnet Railway Museum (under construction)
Market Theatre
Africana Museum
Stock Exchange/Effektebeurs
Oriental Plaza/Oosterse mark
A.A. Technical Centre/-tegniese sentrum
Motor Vehicle Testing Station/Motorvoertuig-toetsstasie
Blue Dam
ARTHUR BLOCH PARK
JUBILEUM PARK
KINGSTON FROST PARK
FRANK BROWN PARK
DALE LACE PARK
FAAN SMIT PARK
FRANS GELDENHUYS PARK
JAN SMUTS
BARRY HERTZOG
EMPIRE
DE VILLIERS GRAAFF MOTORWAY/-MOTORWEG
MAIN REEF
N1/Vanderbijlpark

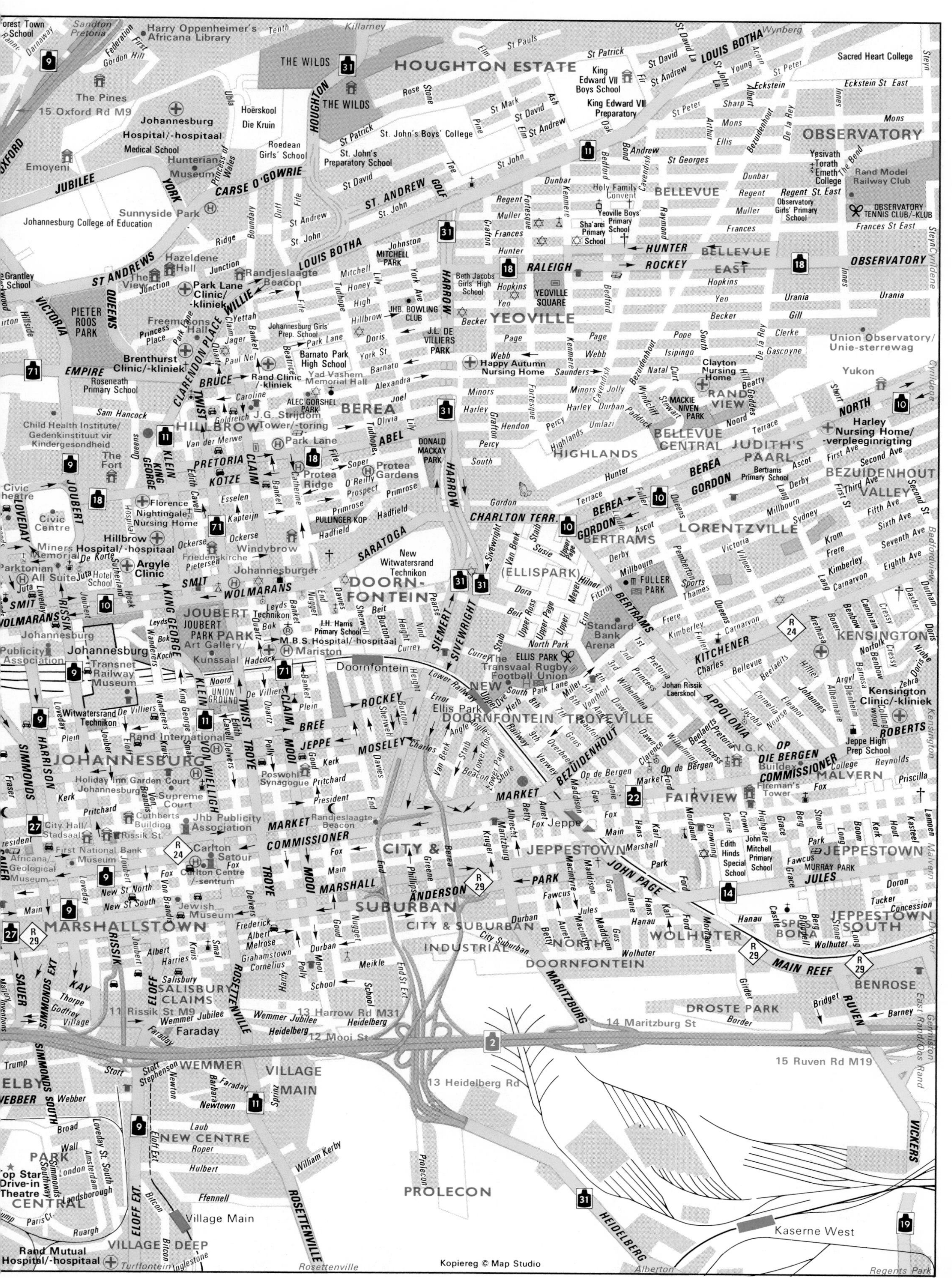

HOUGHTON ESTATE
THE WILDS
Harry Oppenheimer's Africana Library
Sacred Heart College
King Edward VII Boys School
King Edward VII Preparatory
The Pines
15 Oxford Rd M9
Johannesburg Hospital/-hospitaal
Medical School
Hoërskool Die Kruin
Roedean Girls' School
St. John's Boys' College
St. John's Preparatory School
OBSERVATORY
Emoyeni
Hunterian Museum
Sunnyside Park
Johannesburg College of Education
Holy Family Convent
BELLEVUE
Yeshivath Torath Emeth College
Rand Model Railway Club
Observatory Girls' Primary School
OBSERVATORY TENNIS CLUB/-KLUB
Yeoville Boys' Primary School
Sha'arei Primary School
Hazeldene Hall
Randjeslaagte Beacon
Park Lane Clinic/-kliniek
MITCHELL PARK
Beth Jacobs Girls' High School
YEOVILLE SQUARE
YEOVILLE
BELLEVUE EAST
PIETER ROOS PARK
Freemasons Hall
JHB. BOWLING CLUB
J.L. DE VILLIERS PARK
Johannesburg Girls' Prep. School
Barnato Park High School
Yad Vashem Memorial Hall
Happy Autumn Nursing Home
Clayton Nursing Home
Union Observatory/Unie-sterrewag
Yukon
Brenthurst Clinic/-kliniek
Rand Clinic/-kliniek
Roseneath Primary School
ALEC GORSHEL PARK
BEREA
MACKIE NIVEN PARK
RAND VIEW
Harley Nursing Home/-verpleeginrigting
Child Health Institute/Gedenkinstituut vir Kindergesondheid
HILLBROW
J.G. Strijdom Tower/-toring
Park Lane
DONALD MACKAY PARK
HIGHLANDS
BELLEVUE CENTRAL
JUDITH'S PAARL
Bertrams Primary School
BEZUIDENHOUT VALLEY
The Fort
Protea Ridge
Protea Gardens
Civic Theatre
Civic Centre
Florence Nightingale Nursing Home
PULLINGER KOP
Hillbrow Hospital/-hospitaal
Miners Memorial
Argyle Clinic
Johannesburger
New Witwatersrand Technikon
DOORNFONTEIN
(ELLISPARK)
FULLER PARK
LORENTZVILLE
BERTRAMS
JOUBERT PARK
Johannesburg Art Gallery/Kunssaal
Technikon
I.H. Harris Primary School
M.B.S. Hospital/-hospitaal
Mariston
Standard Bank Arena
KENSINGTON
ELLIS PARK
The Transvaal Rugby Football Union
Johannesburg Publicity Association
Transnet Railway Museum
Doornfontein
UNION GROUND
NEW DOORNFONTEIN
TROYEVILLE
Johann Rissik Laerskool
Kensington Clinic/-kliniek
Witwatersrand Technikon
Rand International
JOHANNESBURG
Holiday Inn Garden Court Johannesburg
Poswohl Synagogue
Jeppe High Prep School
OP DIE BERGEN
N.G.K.
MALVERN
Supreme Court
Randjeslaagte Beacon
Fireman's Tower
FAIRVIEW
City Hall/Stadsaal
Cuthberts Building
Jhb Publicity Association
Rissik St.
First National Bank Museum
Carlton Centre/-sentrum
Satour
Africana/Geological Museum
CITY & SUBURBAN
Jeppe
JEPPESTOWN
Edith Hinds Special School
John Mitchell Primary School
MURRAY PARK
Jewish Museum
MARSHALLSTOWN
CITY & SUBURBAN INDUSTRIAL
NORTH DOORNFONTEIN
WOLHUTER
SPES BONA
JEPPESTOWN SOUTH
SALISBURY CLAIMS
11 Rissik St M9
13 Harrow Rd M31
12 Mooi St
14 Maritzburg St
DROSTE PARK
BENROSE
Faraday
15 Ruven Rd M19
WEMMER
VILLAGE MAIN
SELBY
13 Heidelberg Rd
NEW CENTRE
PARK CENTRAL
Top Star Drive-in Theatre
PROLECON
Village Main
Kaserne West
VILLAGE DEEP
Rand Mutual Hospital/-hospitaal
Turffontein
Rosettenville
Alberton
Regents Park
Kopiereg © Map Studio

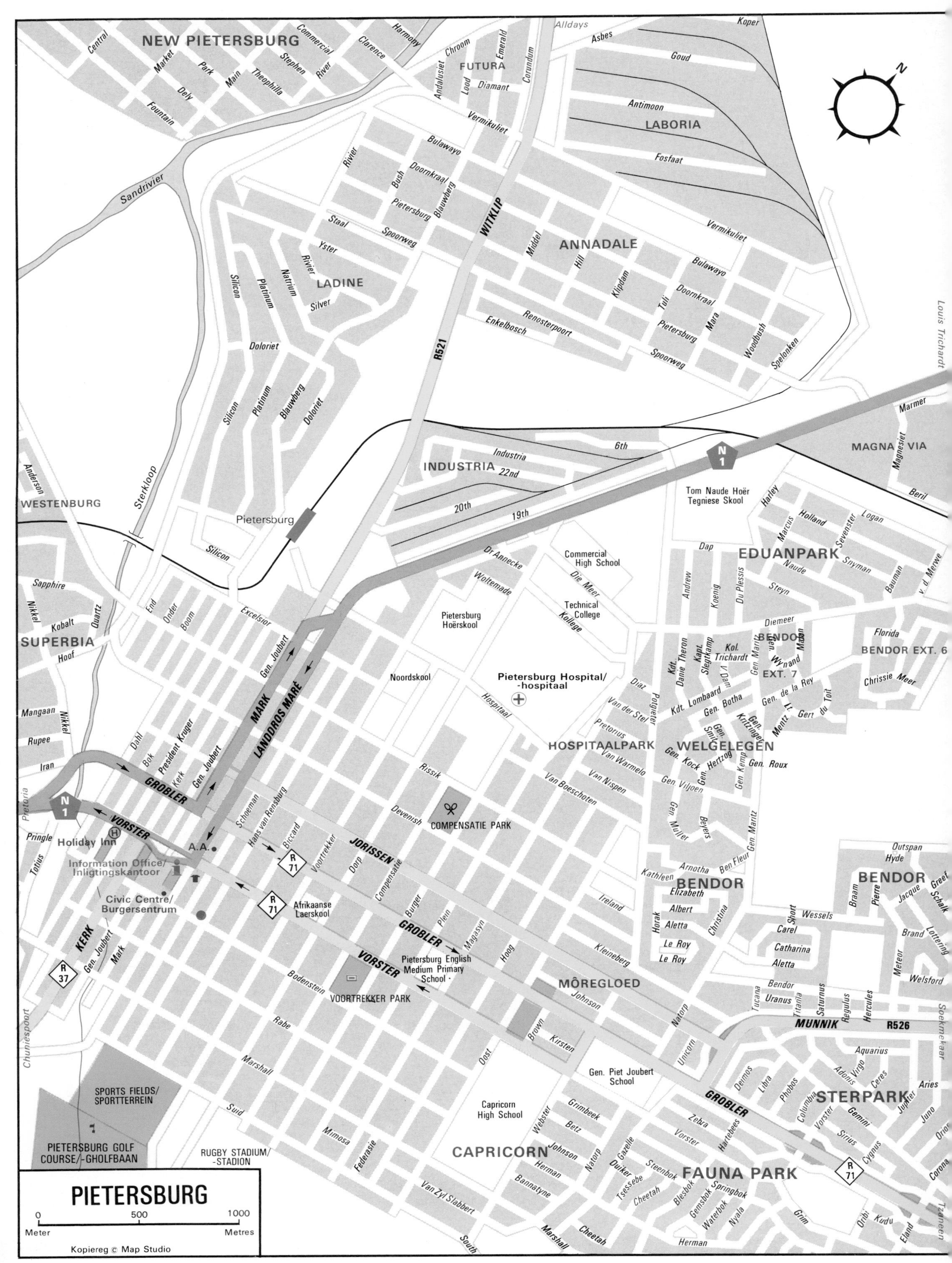
PIETERSBURG
0
500
1000
Meter
Metres
Kopiereg © Map Studio
NEW PIETERSBURG
FUTURA
LABORIA
ANNADALE
LADINE
INDUSTRIA
MAGNA VIA
WESTENBURG
SUPERBIA
EDUANPARK
BENDOR
BENDOR EXT. 7
BENDOR EXT. 6
HOSPITAALPARK
WELGELEGEN
MÔREGLOED
STERPARK
FAUNA PARK
CAPRICORN
Alldays
Louis Trichardt
Pretoria
Chuniespoort
Soekmekaar
Tzaneen
N1
R521
R71
R37
R526
WITKLIP
MARK
LANDDROS MARÉ
GROBLER
VORSTER
JORISSEN
KERK
MUNNIK
Pietersburg
Sandrivier
Sterkloop
Tom Naude Hoër Tegniese Skool
Commercial High School
Technical College
Pietersburg Hoërskool
Noordskool
Pietersburg Hospital/ -hospitaal
COMPENSATIE PARK
Holiday Inn
Information Office/ Inligtingskantoor
Civic Centre/ Burgersentrum
A.A.
Afrikaanse Laerskool
Pietersburg English Medium Primary School
VOORTREKKER PARK
Gen. Piet Joubert School
Capricorn High School
SPORTS FIELDS/ SPORTTERREIN
PIETERSBURG GOLF COURSE/-GHOLFBAAN
RUGBY STADIUM/ -STADION

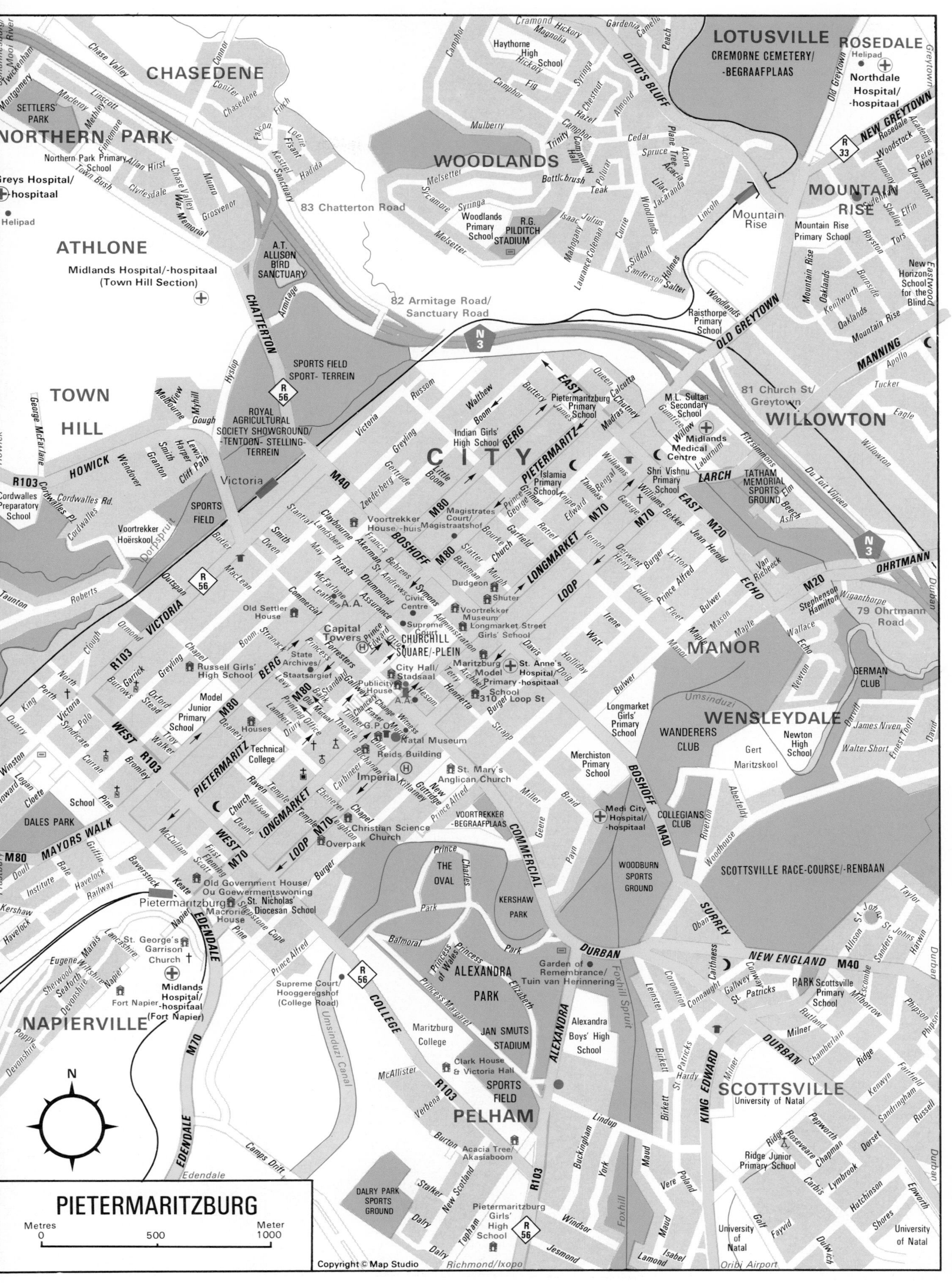
PIETERMARITZBURG
Metres
Meter
0
500
1000
N
Copyright © Map Studio
CHASEDENE
NORTHERN PARK
SETTLERS' PARK
Northern Park Primary School
Greys Hospital/-hospitaal
Helipad
ATHLONE
Midlands Hospital/-hospitaal (Town Hill Section)
TOWN HILL
Cordwalles Preparatory School
Voortrekker Hoërskool
SPORTS FIELD
Victoria
A.T. ALLISON BIRD SANCTUARY
83 Chatterton Road
82 Armitage Road/ Sanctuary Road
SPORTS FIELD SPORT- TERREIN
ROYAL AGRICULTURAL SOCIETY SHOWGROUND/ -TENTOON- STELLING- TERREIN
WOODLANDS
Haythorne High School
Woodlands Primary School
R.G. PILDITCH STADIUM
LOTUSVILLE
CREMORNE CEMETERY/ -BEGRAAFPLAAS
ROSEDALE
Helipad
Northdale Hospital/ -hospitaal
MOUNTAIN RISE
Mountain Rise
Mountain Rise Primary School
New Horizon School for the Blind
Raisthorpe Primary School
81 Church St/ Greytown
WILLOWTON
M.L. Sultan Secondary School
Midlands Medical Centre
Shri Vishnu Primary School
TATHAM MEMORIAL SPORTS GROUND
CITY
Pietermaritzburg Primary School
Indian Girls' High School
Islamia Primary School
Magistrates Court/ Magistraatshof
Voortrekker House/ -huis
Dudgeon
Shuter
Civic Centre
A.A.
Old Settler House
Voortrekker Museum
Longmarket Street Girls' School
Supreme Court
Capital Towers
CHURCHILL SQUARE/-PLEIN
State Archives/ Staatsargief
City Hall/ Stadsaal
Publicity House
Maritzburg Model Primary School
St. Anne's Hospital/ -hospitaal
310 Loop St
Russell Girls' High School
Model Junior Primary School
Houses
Technical College
G.P.O.
Natal Museum
Reids Building
Imperial
St. Mary's Anglican Church
Christian Science Church
Overpark
VOORTREKKER -BEGRAAFPLAAS
DALES PARK
School
Old Government House/ Ou Goewermentswoning
Pietermaritzburg
St. Nicholas' Diocesan School
Macrorie House
St. George's Garrison Church
Midlands Hospital/ -hospitaal (Fort Napier)
Fort Napier
NAPIERVILLE
MANOR
79 Ohrtmann Road
GERMAN CLUB
WENSLEYDALE
WANDERERS CLUB
Gert Maritzskool
Newton High School
Longmarket Girls' Primary School
Merchiston Primary School
Medi City Hospital/ -hospitaal
COLLEGIANS CLUB
WOODBURN SPORTS GROUND
SCOTTSVILLE RACE-COURSE/-RENBAAN
THE OVAL
KERSHAW PARK
ALEXANDRA PARK
Garden of Remembrance/ Tuin van Herinnering
Supreme Court/ Hooggeregshof (College Road)
Maritzburg College
JAN SMUTS STADIUM
Alexandra Boys' High School
Clark House & Victoria Hall
SPORTS FIELD
PELHAM
Acacia Tree/ Akasiaboom
DALRY PARK SPORTS GROUND
Pietermaritzburg Girls' High School
Scottsville Primary School
SCOTTSVILLE
University of Natal
Ridge Junior Primary School
University of Natal
University of Natal
CHATTERTON
HOWICK
VICTORIA
BERG
PIETERMARITZ
LONGMARKET
LOOP
BOSHOFF
EAST
WEST
COMMERCIAL
COLLEGE
ALEXANDRA
DURBAN
SURREY
NEW ENGLAND
KING EDWARD
EDENDALE
MAYORS WALK
OLD GREYTOWN
NEW GREYTOWN
OHRTMANN
MANNING
LARCH
ECHO
OTTO'S BLUFF
R103
R56
R33
N3
M40
M80
M70
M20
Richmond/Ixopo
Oribi Airport

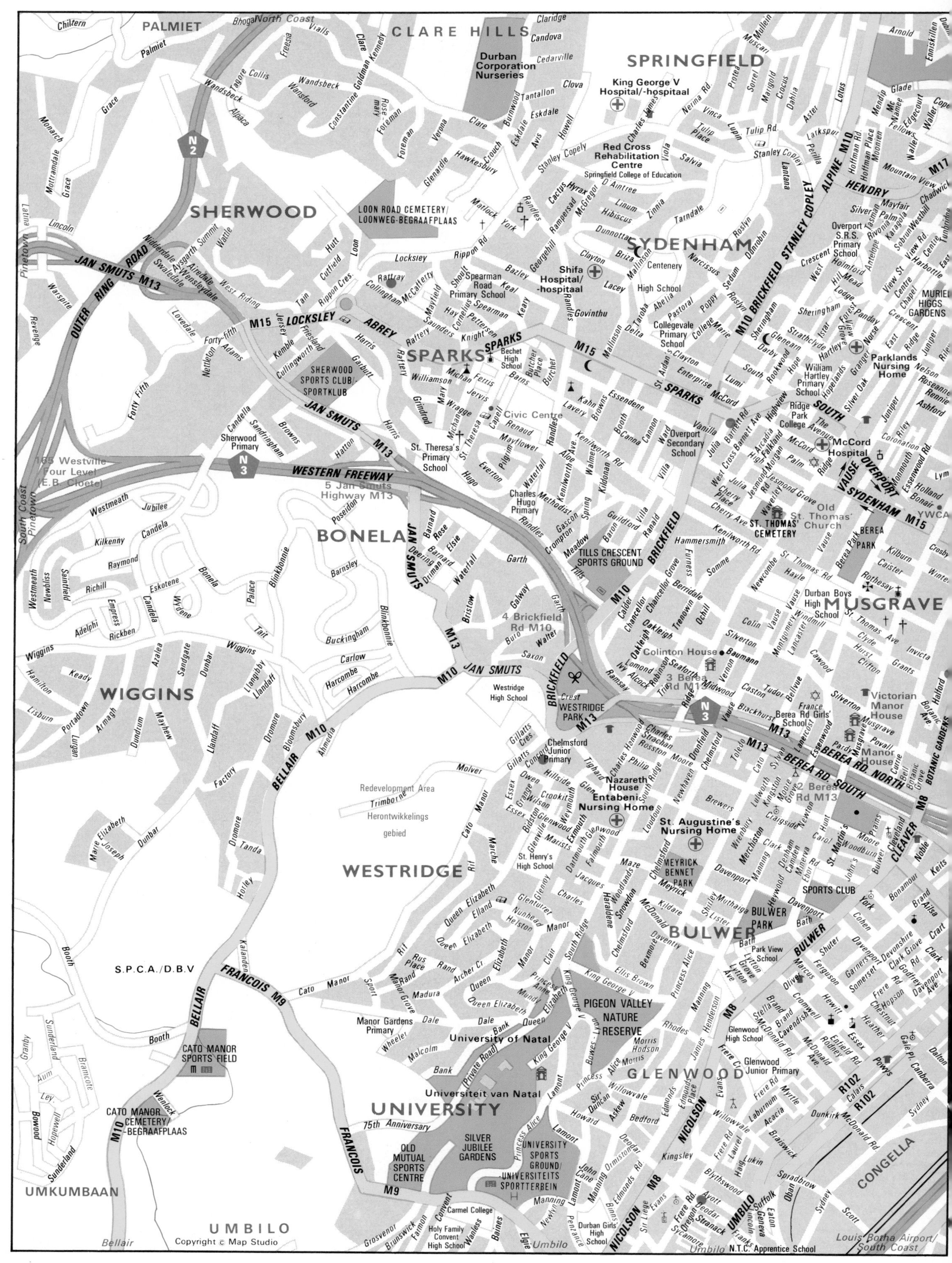

PALMIET
CLARE HILLS
SPRINGFIELD
Durban Corporation Nurseries
King George V Hospital/-hospitaal
Red Cross Rehabilitation Centre
Springfield College of Education
SHERWOOD
LOON ROAD CEMETERY/ LOONWEG-BEGRAAFPLAAS
SYDENHAM
Shifa Hospital/ -hospitaal
Spearman Road Primary School
High School
Collegevale Primary School
JAN SMUTS M13
OUTER RING ROAD
M15 LOCKSLEY
ABREY
SPARKS
Bechet High School
SHERWOOD SPORTS CLUB/ SPORTKLUB
Civic Centre
Overport Secondary School
Parklands Nursing Home
William Hartley Primary School
Ridge Park College
McCord Hospital
Overport S.R.S. Primary School
MURIEL HIGGS GARDENS
Sherwood Primary
165 Westville Four Level (E.B. Cloete)
WESTERN FREEWAY
5 Jan Smuts Highway M13
St. Theresa's Primary School
Charles Hugo Primary
BONELA
TILLS CRESCENT SPORTS GROUND
BRICKFIELD
ST. THOMAS' CEMETERY
St. Thomas' Church
Old
BEREA PARK
YWCA
Durban Boys High School
MUSGRAVE
4 Brickfield Rd M10
Colinton House
3 Berea Rd M13
Victorian Manor House
Berea Rd Girls' School
Musgrave Manor House
WIGGINS
M10 JAN SMUTS
Westridge High School
WESTRIDGE PARK
BEREA RD. NORTH
BEREA RD. SOUTH
BOTANIC GARDENS
Chelmsford Junior Primary
Nazareth House
Entabeni Nursing Home
St. Augustine's Nursing Home
2 Berea Rd M13
Redevelopment Area
Herontwikkelings gebied
WESTRIDGE
St. Henry's High School
MEYRICK BENNET PARK
SPORTS CLUB
BULWER PARK
BULWER
Park View School
S.P.C.A./D.B.V
FRANCOIS M9
BELLAIR
PIGEON VALLEY NATURE RESERVE
Manor Gardens Primary
University of Natal
Universiteit van Natal
CATO MANOR SPORTS FIELD
CATO MANOR CEMETERY/ -BEGRAAFPLAAS
UNIVERSITY
GLENWOOD
Glenwood High School
Glenwood Junior Primary
OLD MUTUAL SPORTS CENTRE
SILVER JUBILEE GARDENS
UNIVERSITY SPORTS GROUND/ UNIVERSITEITS SPORTTERBEIN
CONGELLA
UMKUMBAAN
UMBILO
Carmel College
Holy Family Convent High School
Durban Girls' High School
N.T.C. Apprentice School
Louis Botha Airport/ South Coast
Copyright c Map Studio

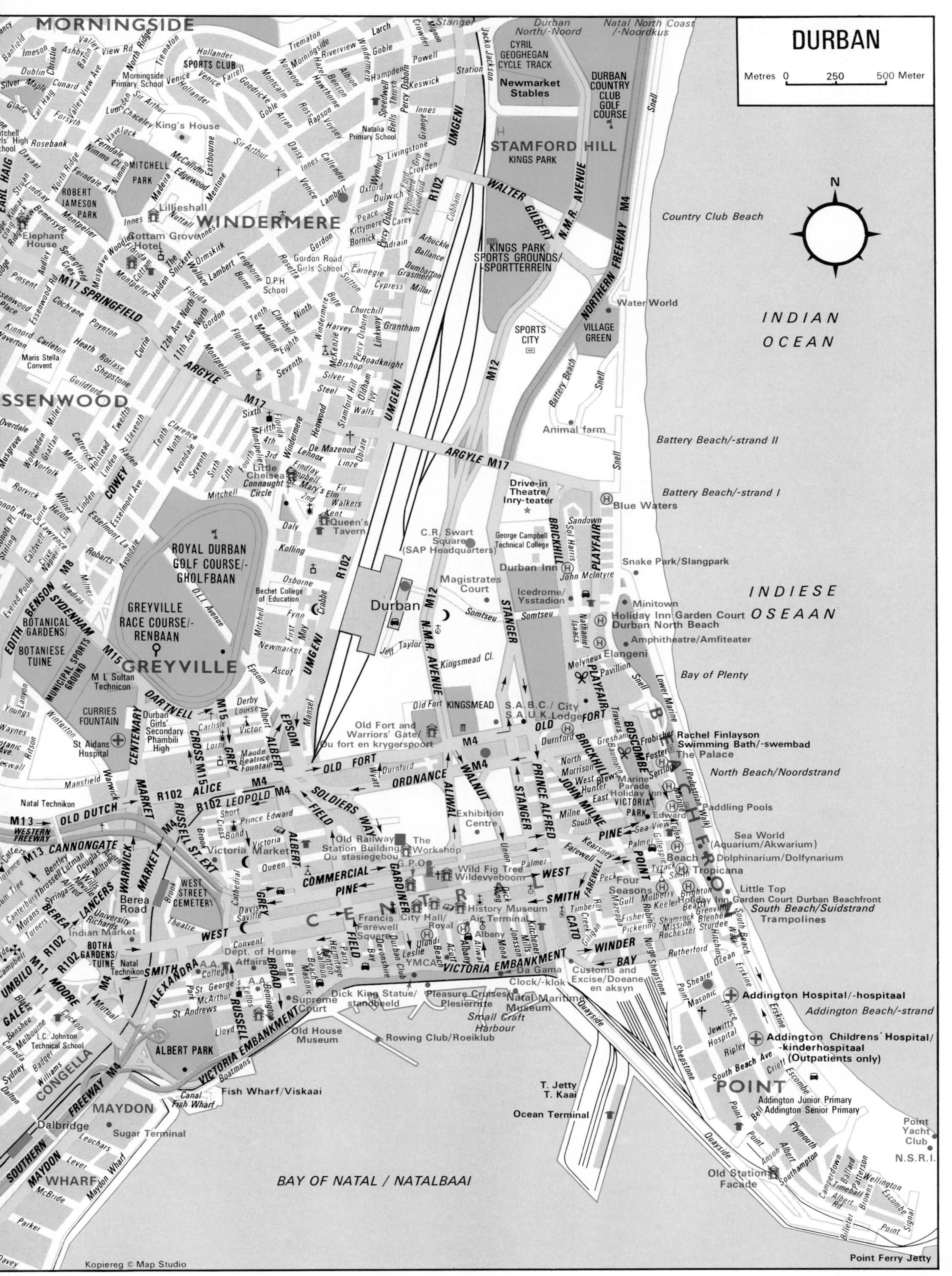
DURBAN
Metres 0 250 500 Meter
N
MORNINGSIDE
WINDERMERE
ESSENWOOD
GREYVILLE
CENTRAL
CONGELLA
MAYDON
POINT
STAMFORD HILL
KINGS PARK
INDIAN OCEAN
INDIESE OSEAAN
BAY OF NATAL / NATALBAAI
Durban North/-Noord
Natal North Coast/-Noordkus
CYRIL GEOGHEGAN CYCLE TRACK
Newmarket Stables
DURBAN COUNTRY CLUB GOLF COURSE
SPORTS CLUB
Morningside Primary School
King's House
Natalia Primary School
MITCHELL PARK
ROBERT JAMESON PARK
Lillieshall
Cottam Grove Hotel
Elephant House
Mitchell Girls' High School
Gordon Road Girls School
D.P.H. School
Maris Stella Convent
KINGS PARK SPORTS GROUNDS/-SPORTTERREIN
Country Club Beach
Water World
VILLAGE GREEN
SPORTS CITY
Animal farm
Battery Beach/-strand II
Battery Beach/-strand I
Drive-in Theatre/Inry-teater
Blue Waters
C.R. Swart Square (SAP Headquarters)
George Campbell Technical College
Snake Park/Slangpark
Durban Inn
Magistrates Court
Icedrome/Ysstadion
Minitown
Holiday Inn Garden Court Durban North Beach
Amphitheatre/Amfiteater
Elangeni
Pavillion
Bay of Plenty
ROYAL DURBAN GOLF COURSE/-GHOLFBAAN
GREYVILLE RACE COURSE/-RENBAAN
Bechet College of Education
Durban
BOTANICAL GARDENS/BOTANIESE TUINE
MUNICIPAL SPORTS GROUND
M L Sultan Technicon
CURRIES FOUNTAIN
St Aidans Hospital
Durban Girls' Secondary
Phambili High
Old Fort and Warriors' Gate/Ou fort en krygerspoort
KINGSMEAD
S.A.B.C./S.A.U.K.
City Lodge
Rachel Finlayson Swimming Bath/-swembad
The Palace
North Beach/Noordstrand
Paddling Pools
Marine Parade Holiday Inn
VICTORIA PARK
Sea World (Aquarium/Akwarium)
Dolphinarium/Dolfynarium
Beach
Tropicana
Little Top
Holiday Inn Garden Court Durban Beachfront
South Beach/Suidstrand
Trampolines
Four Seasons
Exhibition Centre
Old Railway Station Building/Ou stasiegebou
The Workshop
Wild Fig Tree/Wildevyeboom
G.P.O.
Victoria Market
Natal Technikon
WEST STREET CEMETERY
Berea Road
Indian Market
Francis Farewell Square
City Hall/Royal
History Museum
Air Terminal
Albany
YMCA
Dept. of Home Affairs
A.A.
BOTHA GARDENS/TUINE
Natal Technikon
Da Gama Clock/-klok
Customs and Excise/Doeane en aksyn
Dick King Statue/standbeeld
Pleasure Cruises/Plesierritte
Natal Maritime Museum
Small Craft Harbour
Supreme Court
Old House Museum
Rowing Club/Roeiklub
L.C. Johnson Technical School
ALBERT PARK
Fish Wharf/Viskaai
Canal
Fish Wharf
Sugar Terminal
Dalbridge
WHARF
T. Jetty T. Kaai
Ocean Terminal
Addington Hospital/-hospitaal
Addington Beach/-strand
Addington Childrens' Hospital/-kinderhospitaal (Outpatients only)
Addington Junior Primary
Addington Senior Primary
Point Yacht Club
N.S.R.I.
Old Station Facade
Point Ferry Jetty
WESTERN FREEWAY
NORTHERN FREEWAY M4
SOUTHERN FREEWAY M4
VICTORIA EMBANKMENT
M17 SPRINGFIELD
ARGYLE M17
WALTER GILBERT
N.M.R. AVENUE
UMGENI
OLD FORT
ALICE
LEOPOLD
SOLDIERS WAY
ORDNANCE
ALIWAL
WALNUT
STANGER
PRINCE ALFRED
JOHN MILNE
BRICKHILL
PLAYFAIR
BOSCOMBE
PINE
COMMERCIAL
WEST
SMITH
WINDER
BAY
GARDINER
FIELD
BROAD
RUSSELL
ALEXANDRA
MARKET
WARWICK
CENTENARY
DARTNELL
EDITH BENSON
SYDENHAM
OLD DUTCH
CANNONGATE
BEREA
LANCERS
UMBILO
MOORE
GALE
BEACH FRONT

Kopiereg © Map Studio

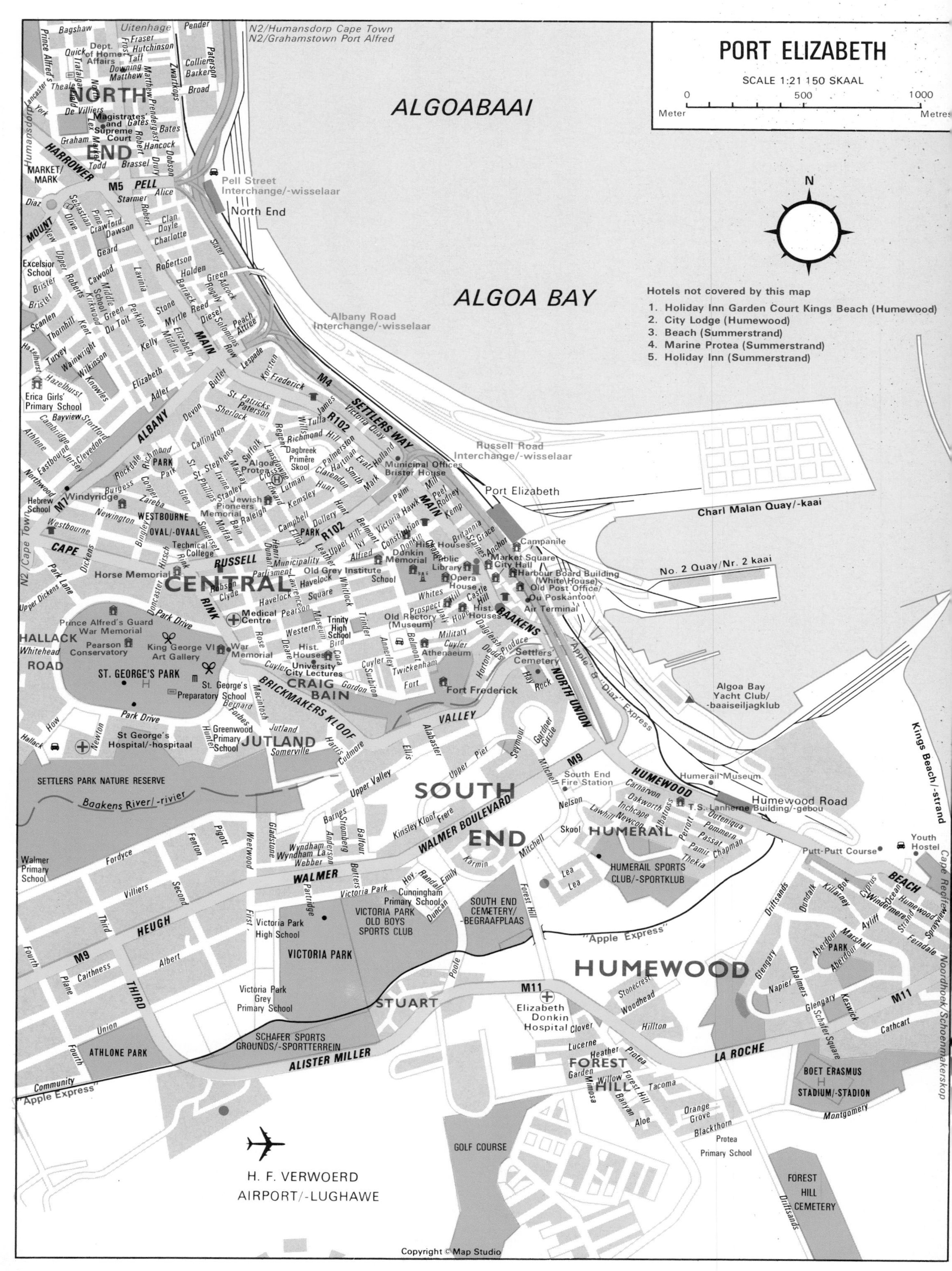

PORT ELIZABETH

SCALE 1:21 150 SKAAL

ALGOABAAI

ALGOA BAY

Hotels not covered by this map
1. Holiday Inn Garden Court Kings Beach (Humewood)
2. City Lodge (Humewood)
3. Beach (Summerstrand)
4. Marine Protea (Summerstrand)
5. Holiday Inn (Summerstrand)

H. F. VERWOERD
AIRPORT/-LUGHAWE

Copyright © Map Studio

12

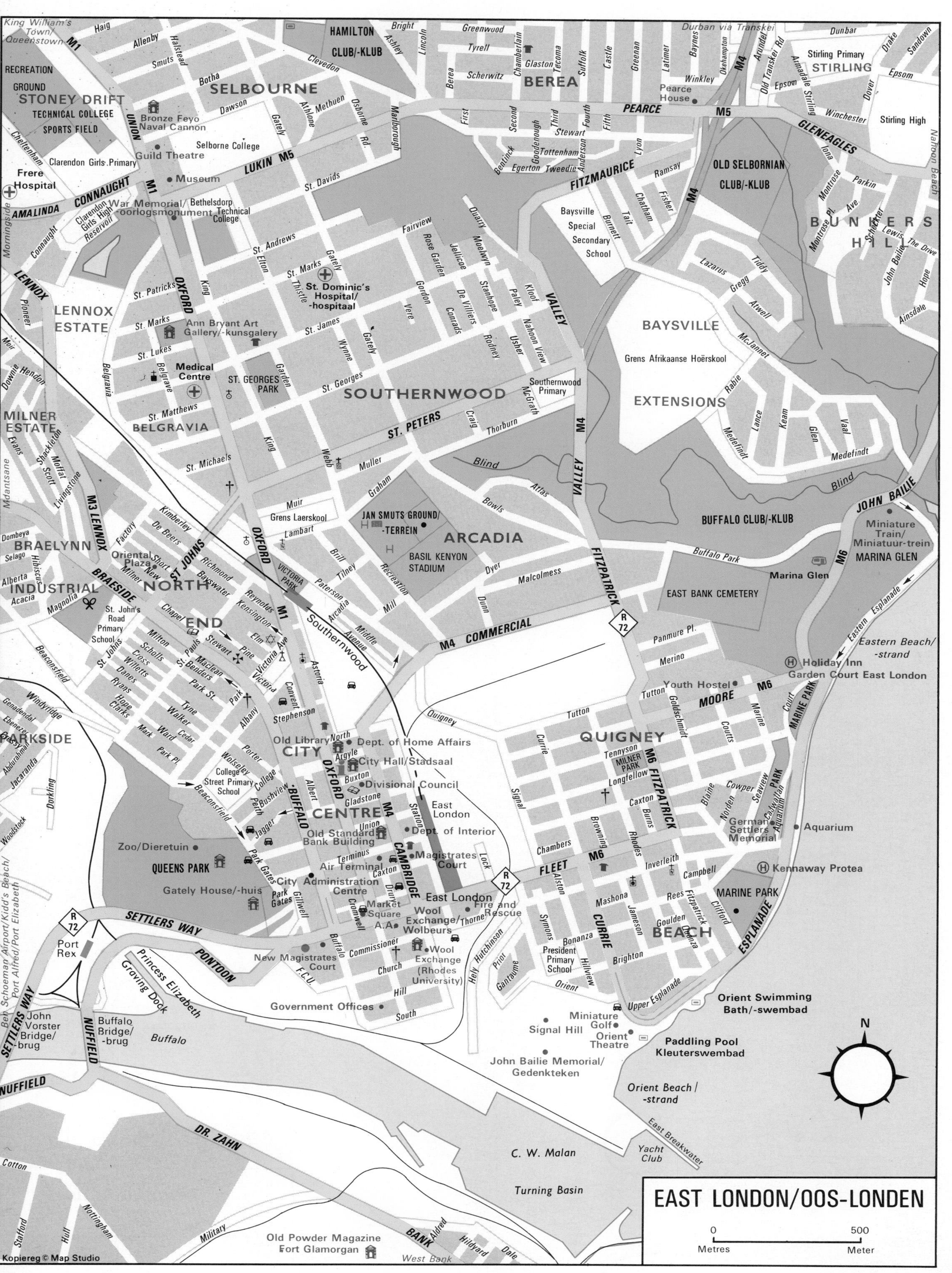

EAST LONDON/OOS-LONDEN
0
500
Metres
Meter
Kopiereg © Map Studio
King William's Town/Queenstown
Haig
Allenby
Smuts
Halstead
Botha
SELBOURNE
Dawson
Athlone
Methuen
Osborne
Rd.
Gately
HAMILTON CLUB/-KLUB
Clevedon
Bright
Ashley
Lincoln
Marlborough
Greenwood
Tyrell
Scherwitz
Berea
Chamberlain
Glaston
Tecoma
Suffolk
Castle
Greenan
Latimer
Baynes
Okehampton
Durban via Transkei
BEREA
Pearce House
Winkley
Arundel
Old Transkei Rd
Dunbar
Stirling Primary
STIRLING
Armadale
Epsom
Old Epsom
Stirling
Drake
Sandown
Dover
Winchester
Stirling High
Nahoon Beach
GLENEAGLES
PEARCE
M5
M4
First
Second
Goodenough
Third
Stewart
Fourth
Fifth
Anderson
Tottenham
Tweedie
Egerton
Bentinck
Lyon
FITZMAURICE
Ramsay
Fisher
Chatham
Tait
Burnett
OLD SELBORNIAN CLUB/-KLUB
Iona
Montrose
Parkin
Montrose Pl.
Ave.
Schelter
Lewis
The Drive
BUNKERS HILL
John Bailie
Hope
Ainsdale
RECREATION GROUND
STONEY DRIFT
TECHNICAL COLLEGE SPORTS FIELD
UNION
Bronze Feyo Naval Cannon
Selborne College
Guild Theatre
Clarendon Girls Primary
Cheltenham
Frere Hospital
LUKIN M5
M1
Museum
St. Davids
CONNAUGHT
AMALINDA
Clarendon Girls High
Reservoir
War Memorial/-oorlogsmonument
Bethelsdorp Technical College
Morningside
Connaught
Quarry
Fairview
Baysville Special Secondary School
Lazarus
Tiddy
Gregg
Atwell
St. Andrews
Elton
St. Marks
Gately
Thistle
St. Dominic's Hospital/-hospitaal
Rose Garden
Jellicoe
Moelwyn
Stanhope
Paley
Kloof
VALLEY
LENNOX
Pioneer
St. Patricks
King
OXFORD
LENNOX ESTATE
St. Marks
Ann Bryant Art Gallery/-kunsgalery
St. James
Gordon
De Villiers
Conrads
Vere
Wynne
Rodney
Usher
Nahoon View
BAYSVILLE
Grens Afrikaanse Hoërskool
McJannet
EXTENSIONS
Rabie
Moir
Downie
Hendon
Belgravia
St. Lukes
Belgrave
Medical Centre
ST. GEORGES PARK
Garden
St. Georges
SOUTHERNWOOD
Southernwood Primary
McGrath
MILNER ESTATE
St. Matthews
BELGRAVIA
ST. PETERS
Craig
Thorburn
Medefindt
Lance
Keam
Glen
Vaal
Evans
Shackleton
Moffat
Scott
Livingstone
St. Michaels
Webb
Muller
Blind
Atlas
Bowls
Mdantsane
M3 LENNOX
Graham
Muir
Grens Laerskool
JAN SMUTS GROUND/-TERREIN
ARCADIA
BASIL KENYON STADIUM
BUFFALO CLUB/-KLUB
JOHN BAILIE
Miniature Train/Miniatuur-trein
MARINA GLEN
M6
Dombeya
Selago
BRAELYNN
Factory
Kimberley
De Beers
Oriental Plaza
Short
New
ST JOHNS
Richmond
Bayswater
Lambart
Brill
Tilney
Recreation
Dyer
Malcolmess
Buffalo Park
Marina Glen
Alberta
Acacia
Hibiscus
INDUSTRIAL
Magnolia
BRAESIDE
Milner
NORTH END
VICTORIA PARK
Paterson
Arcadia
Dunn
FITZPATRICK
EAST BANK CEMETERY
Esplanade
Eastern Esplanade
Eastern Beach/-strand
St. John's Road Primary School
Chapel
Reynolds
Kensington
M1
Southernwood
Avenue
Middle
Mill
M4 COMMERCIAL
R 72
Panmure Pl.
Merino
Holiday Inn Garden Court East London
Beaconsfield
Milton
St. Johns
Scholls
Cross
Willetts
Danes
Ryans
Stewart
St. Pauls
Maclean
Benders
Elm
Pine
Victoria Ave
Victoria
Astoria
Park St.
Park
Tyne
Walker
Cedar
Hope
Clarks
Mark
Ward
Park Pl.
Convent
Stephenson
Tutton
Youth Hostel
MOORE
Goldschmidt
Marine
Court
MARINE PARK
Windyridge
Genadendal
Ebenezer
PARKSIDE
Abdurahman
Jacaranda
Dorking
Woodstock
Wolseley
Porter
College Street Primary School
College
Bushview
Perth
Beaconsfield
Jagger
Albany
Old Library
North
Dept. of Home Affairs
CITY
Argyle
City Hall/Stadsaal
Buxton
Divisional Council
Albert
OXFORD
Gladstone
BUFFALO
CENTRE
M4
Station
East London
Quigney
Tutton
Currie
QUIGNEY
Tennyson
MILNER PARK
M6 FITZPATRICK
Longfellow
Coutts
Signal
Caxton
Burns
Blaine
Cowper
Seaview
Norden
Cathcart
PARK
German Settlers Memorial
Aquarium
Zoo/Dieretuin
Union
Old Standard Bank Building
Dept. of Interior
Terminus
Air Terminal
Caxton
CAMBRIDGE
Magistrates Court
Lock
Chambers
Browning
Rhodes
Inverleith
Campbell
Kennaway Protea
QUEENS PARK
Park Gates
City Administration Centre
Gately House/-huis
Gillwell
Drury
R 72
FLEET
M6
Alston
Mashona
Jameson
Rees
Fitzpatrick
Clifford
MARINE PARK
Ben Schoeman Airport/Kidd's Beach/Port Alfred/Port Elizabeth
SETTLERS WAY
Cromwell
Market Square
A.A.
Wool Exchange/Wolbeurs
East London Fire and Rescue
Thorne
Symons
CURRIE
Goulden
BEACH
Bonanza
ESPLANADE
Port Rex
PONTOON
New Magistrates Court
Buffalo
Commissioner
Church
Wool Exchange (Rhodes University)
Hely Hutchinson
Prior
Gantaume
President Primary School
Hillview
Brighton
Orient
F.C.U.
Hill
Upper Esplanade
Orient Swimming Bath/-swembad
Princess Elizabeth
Graving Dock
Government Offices
South
Miniature Golf
Signal Hill
Orient Theatre
Paddling Pool Kleuterswembad
SETTLERS WAY
John Vorster Bridge/-brug
NUFFIELD
Buffalo Bridge/-brug
Buffalo
John Bailie Memorial/Gedenkteken
N
Orient Beach/-strand
NUFFIELD
DR. ZAHN
East Breakwater
Yacht Club
C. W. Malan
Turning Basin
Cotton
Stafford
Hull
Nottingham
Military
Old Powder Magazine Fort Glamorgan
BANK
Aldred
Hildyard
Dale
West Bank

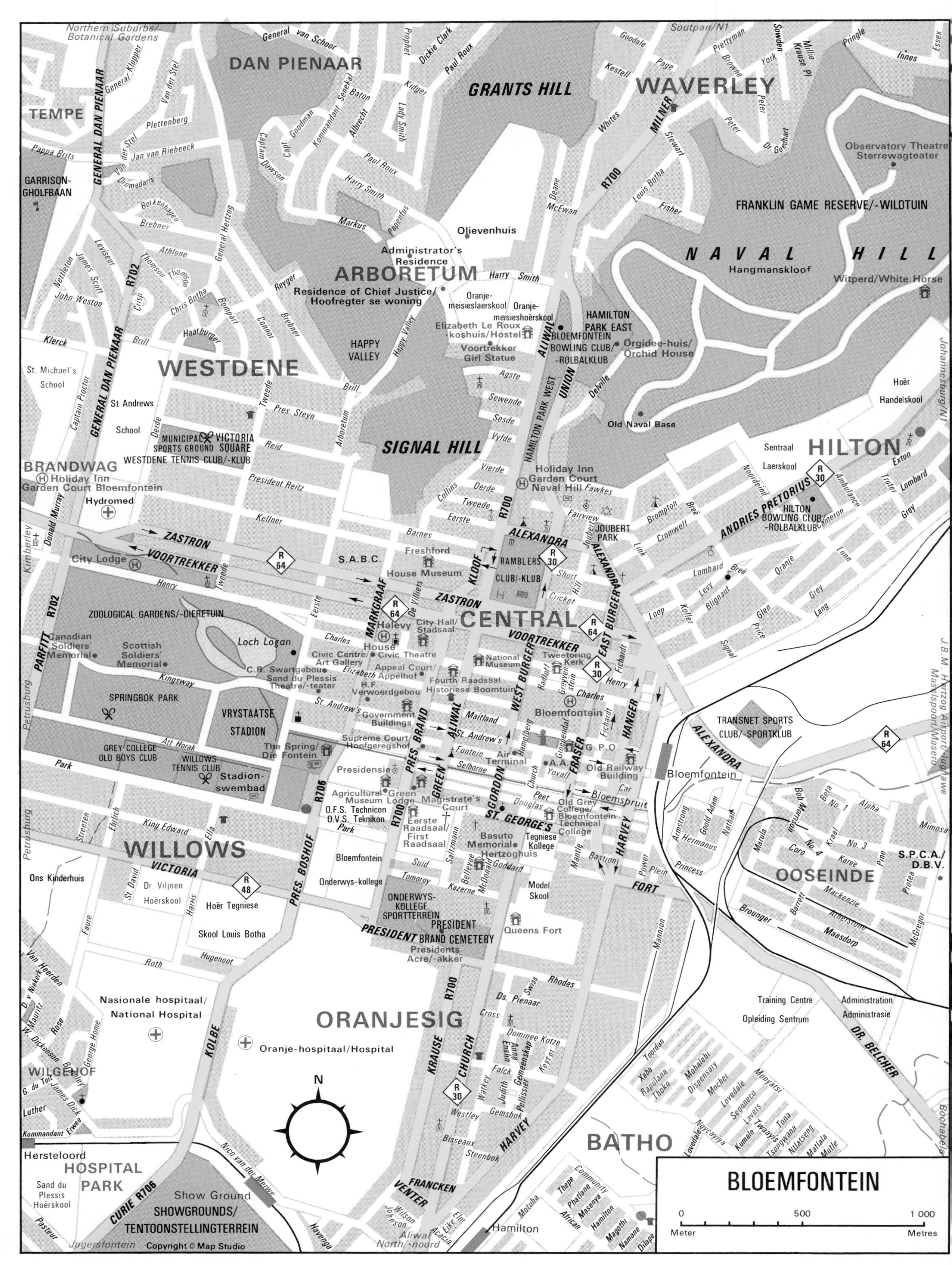
BLOEMFONTEIN
0
500
1 000
Meter
Metres
Northern Suburbs/
Botanical Gardens
DAN PIENAAR
GRANTS HILL
WAVERLEY
TEMPE
GARRISON-
GHOLFBAAN
Observatory Theatre
Sterrewagteater
FRANKLIN GAME RESERVE/-WILDTUIN
NAVAL HILL
Hangmanskloof
Witperd/White Horse
Olievenhuis
Administrator's
Residence
ARBORETUM
Residence of Chief Justice/
Hoofregter se woning
Oranje-
meisieslaerskool
Oranje-
meisieshoërskool
Elizabeth Le Roux
-koshuis/Hostel
Voortrekker
Girl Statue
HAMILTON
PARK EAST
BLOEMFONTEIN
BOWLING CLUB/
-ROLBALKLUB
Orgidee-huis/
Orchid House
HAPPY
VALLEY
WESTDENE
St. Michael's
School
St Andrews
School
MUNICIPAL
SPORTS GROUND
VICTORIA
SQUARE
WESTDENE TENNIS CLUB/-KLUB
SIGNAL HILL
Old Naval Base
Hoër
Handelskool
Sentraal
Laerskool
HILTON
HILTON
BOWLING CLUB
-ROLBALKLUB
BRANDWAG
Holiday Inn
Garden Court Bloemfontein
Hydromed
Holiday Inn
Garden Court
Naval Hill
JOUBERT
PARK
S.A.B.C.
Freshford
House Museum
RAMBLERS
CLUB/-KLUB
City Lodge
ZOOLOGICAL GARDENS/-DIERETUIN
CENTRAL
Canadian
Soldiers'
Memorial
Scottish
Soldiers'
Memorial
Loch Logan
Halevy
House
City Hall/
Stadsaal
Civic Centre/
Art Gallery
Civic Theatre
C.R. Swartgebou
Sand du Plessis
Theatre/-teater
Appeal Court/
Appèlhof
H.F.
Verwoerdgebou
National
Museum
Tweetoring
Kerk
Fourth Raadsaal
Historiese Boomtuin
SPRINGBOK PARK
VRYSTAATSE
STADION
Government
Buildings
Bloemfontein
GREY COLLEGE
OLD BOYS CLUB
WILLOWS
TENNIS CLUB
Stadion-
swembad
The Spring/
Die Fontein
Supreme Court/
Hoofgeregshof
Presidensie
Air
Terminal
A.A.
G.P.O.
Old Railway
Building
TRANSNET SPORTS
CLUB/-SPORTKLUB
Bloemfontein
Agricultural
Museum
Green
Lodge
Magistrate's
Court
O.F.S. Technicon
O.V.S. Teknikon
Old Grey
College/
Bloemfontein
Technical
College
Eerste
Raadsaal/
First
Raadsaal
Basuto
Memorial
Tegniese
Kollege
Hertzoghuis
WILLOWS
Ons Kinderhuis
Dr. Viljoen
Hoërskool
Hoër Tegniese
Skool Louis Botha
Bloemfontein
Onderwys-kollege
ONDERWYS-
KOLLEGE
SPORTTERREIN
PRESIDENT
BRAND CEMETERY
Presidents
Acre/-akker
Model
Skool
Queens Fort
OOSEINDE
S.P.C.A./
D.B.V.
Training Centre
Opleiding Sentrum
Administration
Administrasie
Nasionale hospitaal/
National Hospital
ORANJESIG
Oranje-hospitaal/Hospital
WILGEHOF
BATHO
Hersteloord
HOSPITAL
PARK
Sand du
Plessis
Hoërskool
Show Ground
SHOWGROUNDS/
TENTOONSTELLINGTERREIN
Hamilton
Aliwal
North/-noord
Jagersfontein
Copyright © Map Studio
ZASTRON
VOORTREKKER
ALEXANDRA
ANDRIES PRETORIUS
GENERAL DAN PIENAAR
MILNER
ALIWAL
UNION
HAMILTON PARK WEST
MARKGRAAF
KLOOF
WEST BURGER
EAST BURGER
PRES. BRAND
GREEN
GORDON
FRASER
HANGER
HARVEY
ST. GEORGE'S
VICTORIA
PRES. BOSHOF
PRESIDENT
FORT
KRAUSE
CHURCH
KOLBE
CURIE R706
VENTER
FRANCKEN
DR. BELCHER
PARFITT
R700
R702
R706
R64
R30
R48

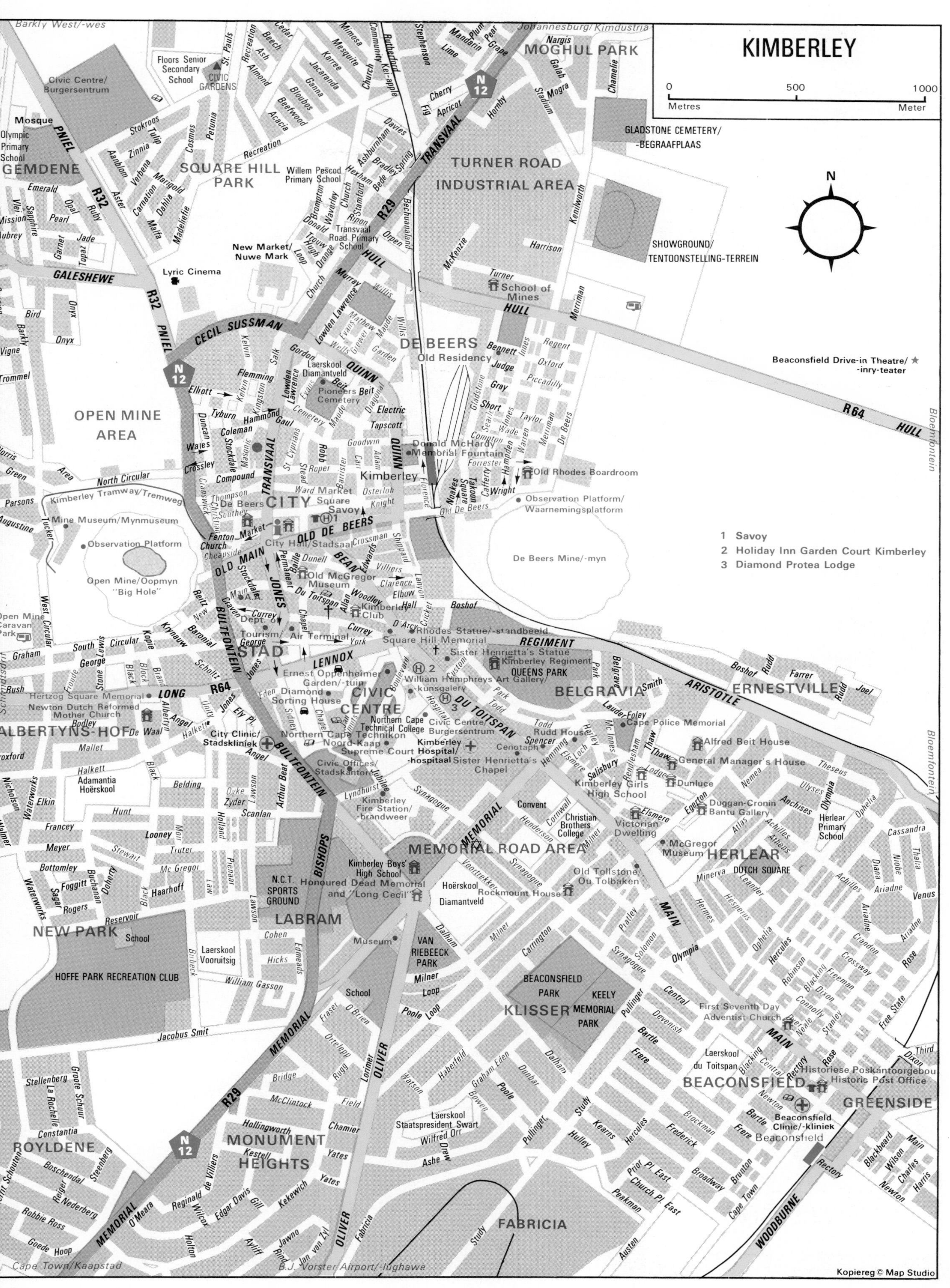

KIMBERLEY

Metres / Meter
0   500   1000

N

1 Savoy
2 Holiday Inn Garden Court Kimberley
3 Diamond Protea Lodge

Kopiereg © Map Studio

15

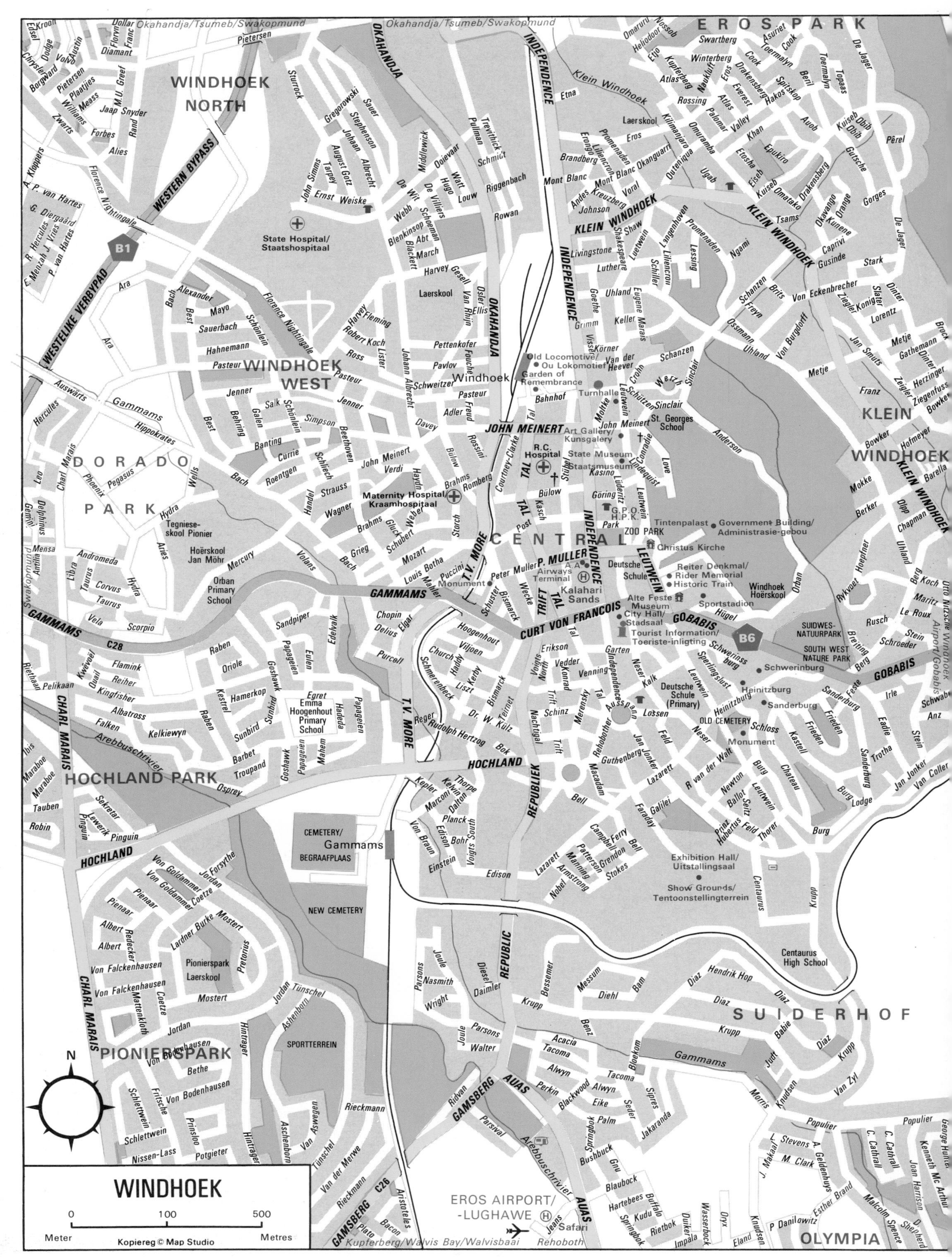

WINDHOEK
0
100
500
Meter
Metres
Kopiereg © Map Studio
Okahandja/Tsumeb/Swakopmund
Kupferberg/Walvis Bay/Walvisbaai
Rehoboth
EROS AIRPORT/
-LUGHAWE
WINDHOEK NORTH
WINDHOEK WEST
DORADO PARK
CENTRAL
KLEIN WINDHOEK
EROS PARK
HOCHLAND PARK
PIONIERSPARK
SUIDERHOF
OLYMPIA
B1
B6
C28
C26
WESTERN BYPASS
WESTELIKE VERBYPAD
OKAHANDJA
INDEPENDENCE
KLEIN WINDHOEK
JOHN MEINERT
GAMMAMS
CURT VON FRANCOIS
GOBABIS
T.V. MORE
HOCHLAND
CHARL MARAIS
REPUBLIEK
REPUBLIC
GAMSBERG
AUAS
LEUTWEIN
TAL
TRIFT
P. MULLER
State Hospital/
Staatshospitaal
Laerskool
Old Locomotive/
Ou Lokomotief
Garden of
Remembrance
Turnhalle
Art Gallery/
Kunsgalery
St. Georges
School
R.C.
Hospital
State Museum
Staatsmuseum
Maternity Hospital/
Kraamhospitaal
G.P.O.
H.P.K.
Tintenpalast
Government Building/
Administrasie-gebou
ZOO PARK
Christus Kirche
Tegniese-
skool Pionier
Hoërskool
Jan Möhr
Orban
Primary
School
Monument
Airways
Terminal
Kalahari
Sands
Deutsche
Schule
Reiter Denkmal/
Rider Memorial
Historic Train
Alte Feste
Museum
City Hall/
Stadsaal
Tourist Information/
Toeriste-inligting
Sportstadion
Windhoek
Hoërskool
SUIDWES-
NATUURPARK
SOUTH WEST
NATURE PARK
Schwerinsburg
Heinitzburg
Sanderburg
Deutsche
Schule
(Primary)
OLD CEMETERY
Monument
Emma
Hoogenhout
Primary
School
CEMETERY/
BEGRAAFPLAAS
Gammams
NEW CEMETERY
Exhibition Hall/
Uitstallingsaal
Show Grounds/
Tentoonstellingterrein
Centaurus
High School
Pionierspark
Laerskool
SPORTTERREIN
Safari
N

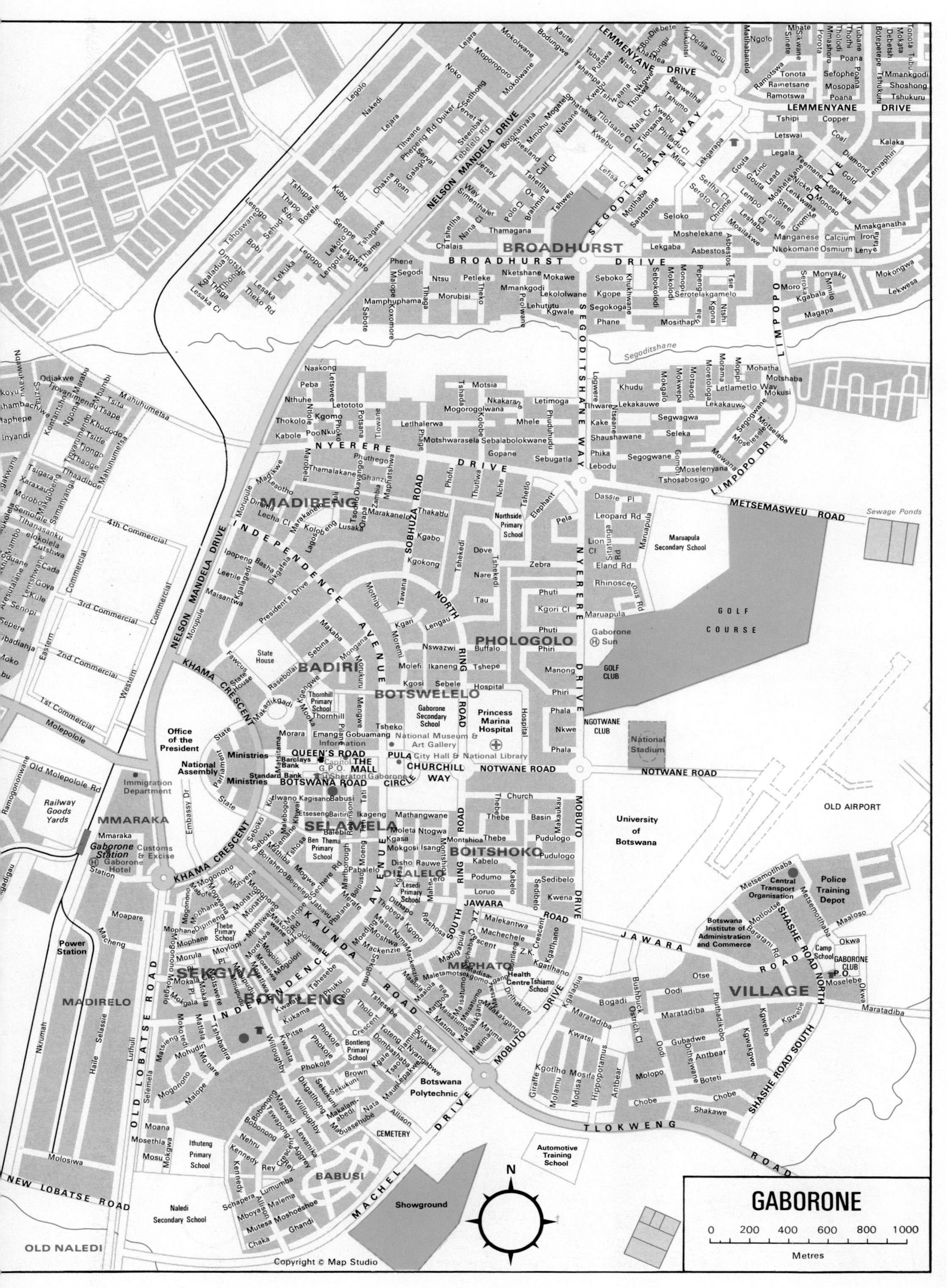

GABORONE
0 200 400 600 800 1000
Metres
BROADHURST
MADIRENG
BADIRI
BOTSWELELO
PHOLOGOLO
SELAMELA
BOITSHOKO
DISALELO
MMARAKA
SEKGWA
BONTLENG
MAPHATO
VILLAGE
BABUSI
MADIRELO
OLD NALEDI
NELSON MANDELA DRIVE
SEGODITSHANE WAY
BROADHURST DRIVE
LEMMENYANE DRIVE
LIMPOPO DRIVE
NYERERE DRIVE
INDEPENDENCE AVENUE
KHAMA CRESCENT
NOTWANE ROAD
MOBUTO DRIVE
KAUNDA ROAD
JAWARA ROAD
SHASHE ROAD NORTH
SHASHE ROAD SOUTH
TLOKWENG ROAD
MACHEL DRIVE
OLD LOBATSE ROAD
NEW LOBATSE ROAD
METSEMASWEU ROAD
SOBHUZA ROAD
NORTH RING ROAD
SOUTH RING ROAD
QUEEN'S ROAD
BOTSWANA ROAD
THE MALL
CHURCHILL WAY
PULA CIRCLE
Office of the President
National Assembly
Ministries
State House
Princess Marina Hospital
University of Botswana
GOLF COURSE
GOLF CLUB
NGOTWANE CLUB
National Stadium
Gaborone Sun
National Museum & Art Gallery
City Hall & National Library
Sheraton Gaborone
G.P.O.
Barclays Bank
Standard Bank
Gaborone Station
Gaborone Hotel
Customs & Excise
Immigration Department
Railway Goods Yards
Power Station
OLD AIRPORT
Police Training Depot
Central Transport Organisation
Botswana Institute of Administration and Commerce
GABORONE CLUB
Botswana Polytechnic
CEMETERY
Showground
Automotive Training School
Naledi Secondary School
Ithuteng Primary School
Bontleng Primary School
Ben Thema Primary School
Lesedi Primary School
Thornhill Primary School
Gaborone Secondary School
Northside Primary School
Maruapula Secondary School
Thebe Primary School
Health Centre
Tshiamo School
Sewage Ponds
Segoditshane
1st Commercial
2nd Commercial
3rd Commercial
4th Commercial
Copyright © Map Studio

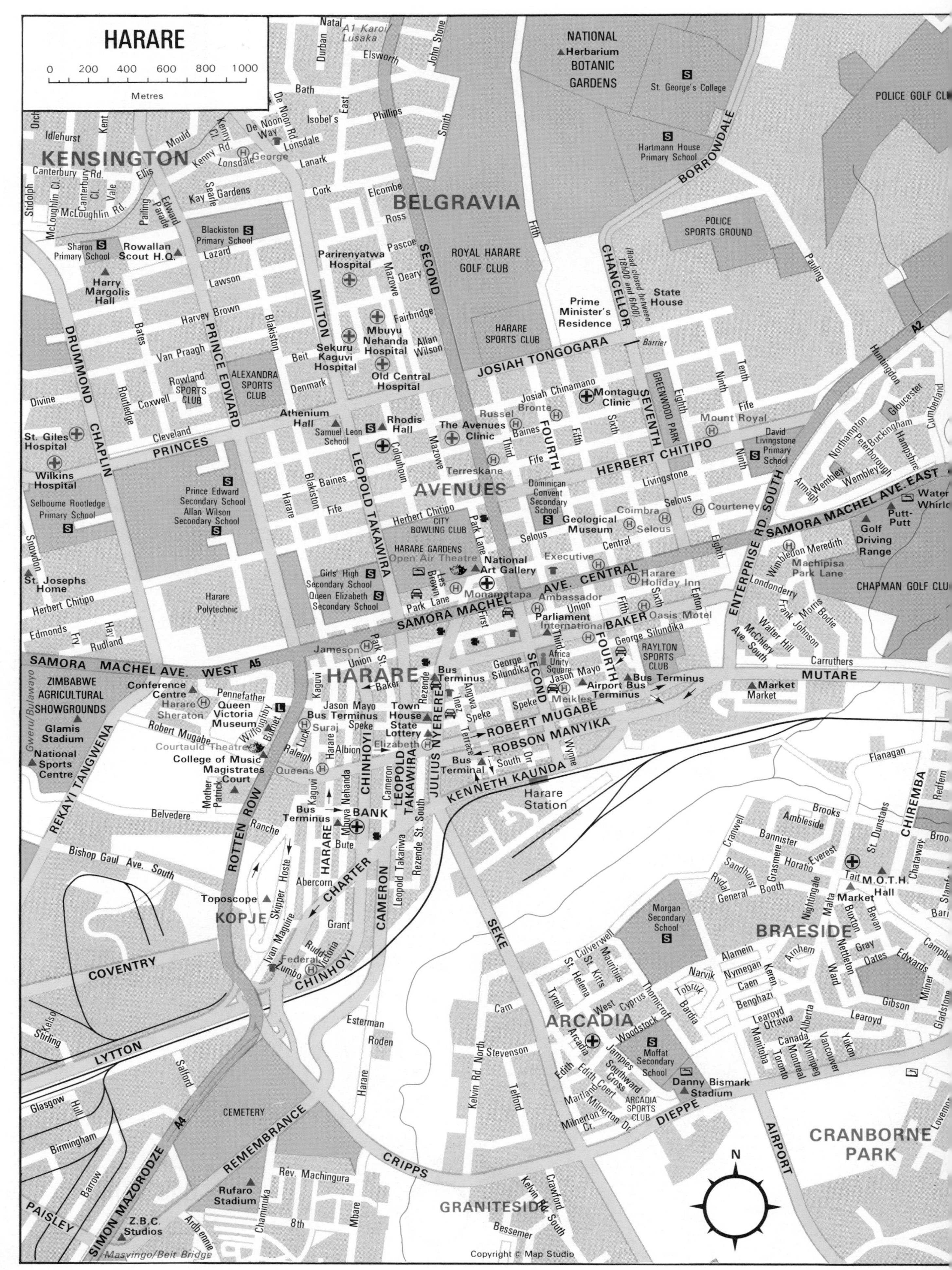

HARARE
0 200 400 600 800 1000
Metres
KENSINGTON
BELGRAVIA
AVENUES
HARARE
KOPJE
ARCADIA
BRAESIDE
CRANBORNE PARK
GRANITESIDE
NATIONAL Herbarium BOTANIC GARDENS
St. George's College
Hartmann House Primary School
POLICE GOLF CLUB
POLICE SPORTS GROUND
ROYAL HARARE GOLF CLUB
HARARE SPORTS CLUB
Prime Minister's Residence
State House
(Road closed between 18h00 and 6h00)
Barrier
Blackiston Primary School
Sharon Primary School
Rowallan Scout H.Q.
Harry Margolis Hall
Parirenyatwa Hospital
Mbuyu Nehanda Hospital
Sekuru Kaguvi Hospital
Old Central Hospital
ALEXANDRA SPORTS CLUB
Rowland SPORTS CLUB
Athenium Hall
Samuel Leon School
Rhodis Hall
The Avenues Clinic
Montagu Clinic
GREENWOOD PARK
David Livingstone Primary School
St. Giles Hospital
Wilkins Hospital
Selbourne Rootledge Primary School
Prince Edward Secondary School
Allan Wilson Secondary School
St. Josephs Home
Harare Polytechnic
Girls' High Secondary School
Queen Elizabeth Secondary School
CITY BOWLING CLUB
HARARE GARDENS
Open Air Theatre
National Art Gallery
Dominican Convent Secondary School
Geological Museum
Executive
Harare Holiday Inn
Monomatapa
Ambassador
Parliament
International
Oasis Motel
Courteney
Coimbra
Selous
Terreskane
Russel
Bronte
Baines
Mount Royal
Water Whirl
Putt-Putt
Golf Driving Range
Machipisa Park Lane
CHAPMAN GOLF CLUB
RAYLTON SPORTS CLUB
Africa Unity Square
Jason Mayo
Meikles
Airport Bus Terminus
Bus Terminus
Market
ZIMBABWE AGRICULTURAL SHOWGROUNDS
Glamis Stadium
National Sports Centre
Conference Centre
Harare Sheraton
Queen Victoria Museum
Courtauld Theatre
College of Music
Magistrates Court
Town House
State Lottery
Jason Mayo Bus Terminus
Suraj
Albion
Elizabeth
Queens
Bus Terminal
BANK
Harare Station
Toposcope
Federal
Zumbo
Morgan Secondary School
Moffat Secondary School
Danny Bismark Stadium
ARCADIA SPORTS CLUB
M.O.T.H. Hall
Market
CEMETERY
Rufaro Stadium
Z.B.C. Studios
A1 Karoi/Lusaka
Gweru/Bulawayo
Masvingo/Beit Bridge
SAMORA MACHEL AVE. WEST A5
SAMORA MACHEL AVE. CENTRAL
SAMORA MACHEL AVE. EAST
JOSIAH TONGOGARA
HERBERT CHITIPO
PRINCES
DRUMMOND CHAPLIN
PRINCE EDWARD
MILTON
LEOPOLD TAKAWIRA
SECOND
FOURTH
SEVENTH
CHANCELLOR
BORROWDALE
ENTERPRISE RD. SOUTH
MUTARE
ROBERT MUGABE
ROBSON MANYIKA
KENNETH KAUNDA
JULIUS NYERERE
CHINHOYI
CAMERON
HARARE
CHARTER
ROTTEN ROW
REKAYI TANGWENA
COVENTRY
LYTTON
SIMON MAZORODZE
REMEMBRANCE
PAISLEY
CRIPPS
SEKE
DIEPPE
AIRPORT
CHIREMBA
BAKER
A2
A4
N
Copyright © Map Studio

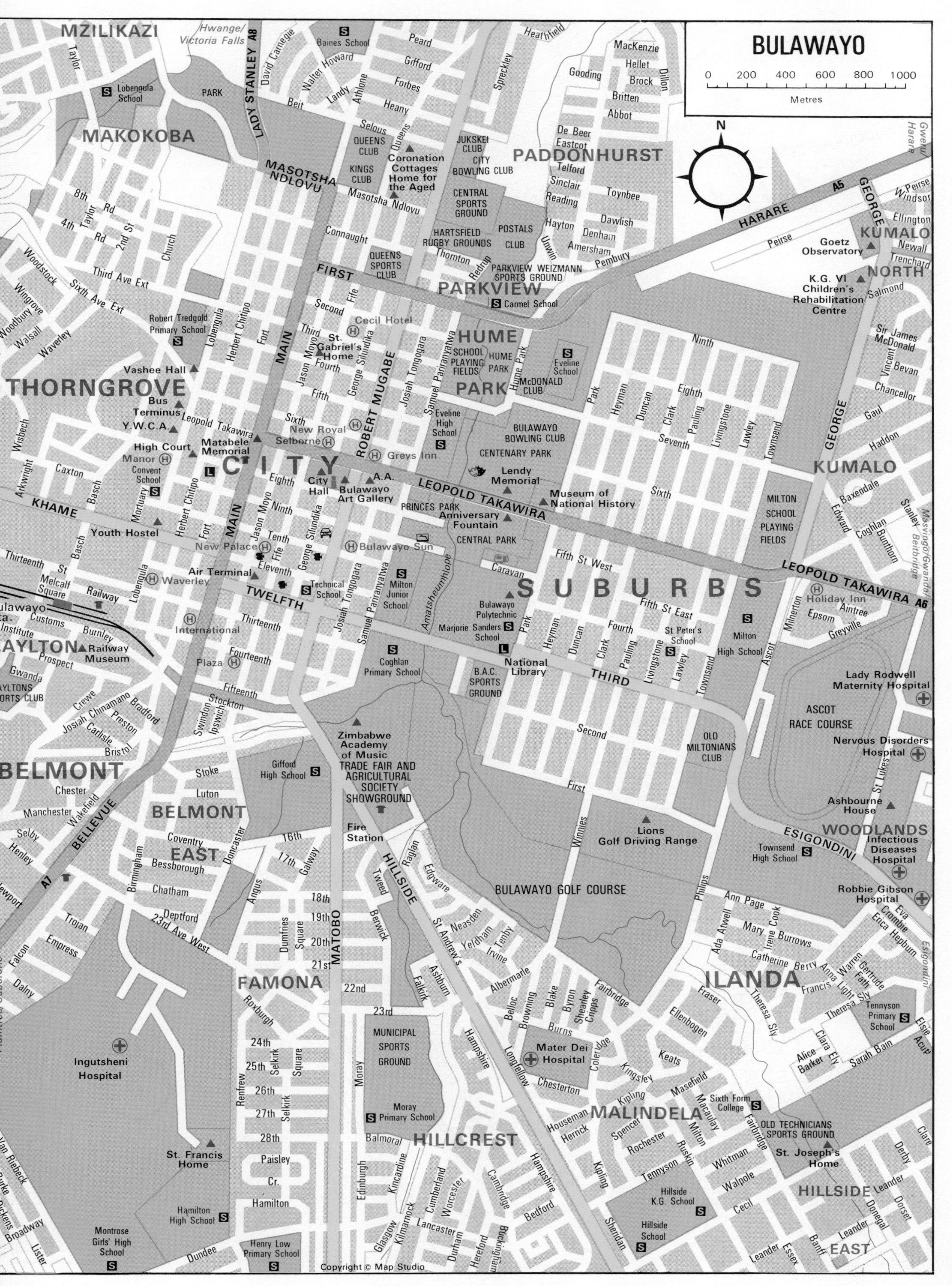
BULAWAYO
0 200 400 600 800 1000
Metres
N
MZILIKAZI
Hwange/ Victoria Falls
A8
LADY STANLEY
MAKOKOBA
Lobengula School
PARK
Baines School
MASOTSHA NDLOVU
QUEENS CLUB
KINGS CLUB
Coronation Cottages Home for the Aged
JUKSKEI CLUB
CITY BOWLING CLUB
CENTRAL SPORTS GROUND
HARTSFIELD RUGBY GROUNDS
POSTALS CLUB
QUEENS SPORTS CLUB
PARKVIEW WEIZMANN SPORTS GROUND
PADDONHURST
PARKVIEW
Carmel School
Gwenu/ Harare
A5
HARARE
GEORGE
KUMALO
Goetz Observatory
NORTH
K.G. VI Children's Rehabilitation Centre
FIRST
THORNGROVE
Robert Tredgold Primary School
Vashee Hall
Bus Terminus
Y.W.C.A.
High Court
Manor
Convent School
Matabele Memorial
CITY
Cecil Hotel
St. Gabriel's Home
HUME PARK
SCHOOL PLAYING FIELDS
Eveline School
McDONALD CLUB
Eveline High School
New Royal
Selborne
Greys Inn
BULAWAYO BOWLING CLUB
CENTENARY PARK
Lendy Memorial
Museum of National History
City Hall
Bulawayo Art Gallery
A.A.
PRINCES PARK
Anniversary Fountain
CENTRAL PARK
LEOPOLD TAKAWIRA
KHAME
MAIN
ROBERT MUGABE
Youth Hostel
New Palace
Bulawayo Sun
Air Terminal
Waverley
Technical School
Milton Junior School
Caravan
SUBURBS
MILTON SCHOOL PLAYING FIELDS
Holiday Inn
A6
Masvingo/Gwanda/ Beitbridge
Metcalf Square
Bulawayo Sta.
Customs
Institute
RAYLTON
Railway Museum
RAYLTONS SPORTS CLUB
TWELFTH
International
Plaza
Bulawayo Polytechnic
Marjorie Sanders School
National Library
Coghlan Primary School
B.A.C. SPORTS GROUND
St Peter's School
Milton High School
THIRD
Lady Rodwell Maternity Hospital
ASCOT RACE COURSE
Nervous Disorders Hospital
OLD MILTONIANS CLUB
BELMONT
Gifford High School
Zimbabwe Academy of Music
TRADE FAIR AND AGRICULTURAL SOCIETY SHOWGROUND
Fire Station
Lions Golf Driving Range
Ashbourne House
WOODLANDS
ESIGONDINI
Townsend High School
Infectious Diseases Hospital
BELMONT EAST
BELLEVUE
A7
BULAWAYO GOLF COURSE
Robbie Gibson Hospital
HILLSIDE
MATOBO
FAMONA
ILANDA
Tennyson Primary School
Ingutsheni Hospital
MUNICIPAL SPORTS GROUND
Mater Dei Hospital
MALINDELA
Sixth Form College
OLD TECHNICIANS SPORTS GROUND
Moray Primary School
HILLCREST
St. Joseph's Home
St. Francis Home
HILLSIDE EAST
Hillside K.G. School
Hillside School
Hamilton High School
Montrose Girls' High School
Henry Low Primary School
Copyright © Map Studio

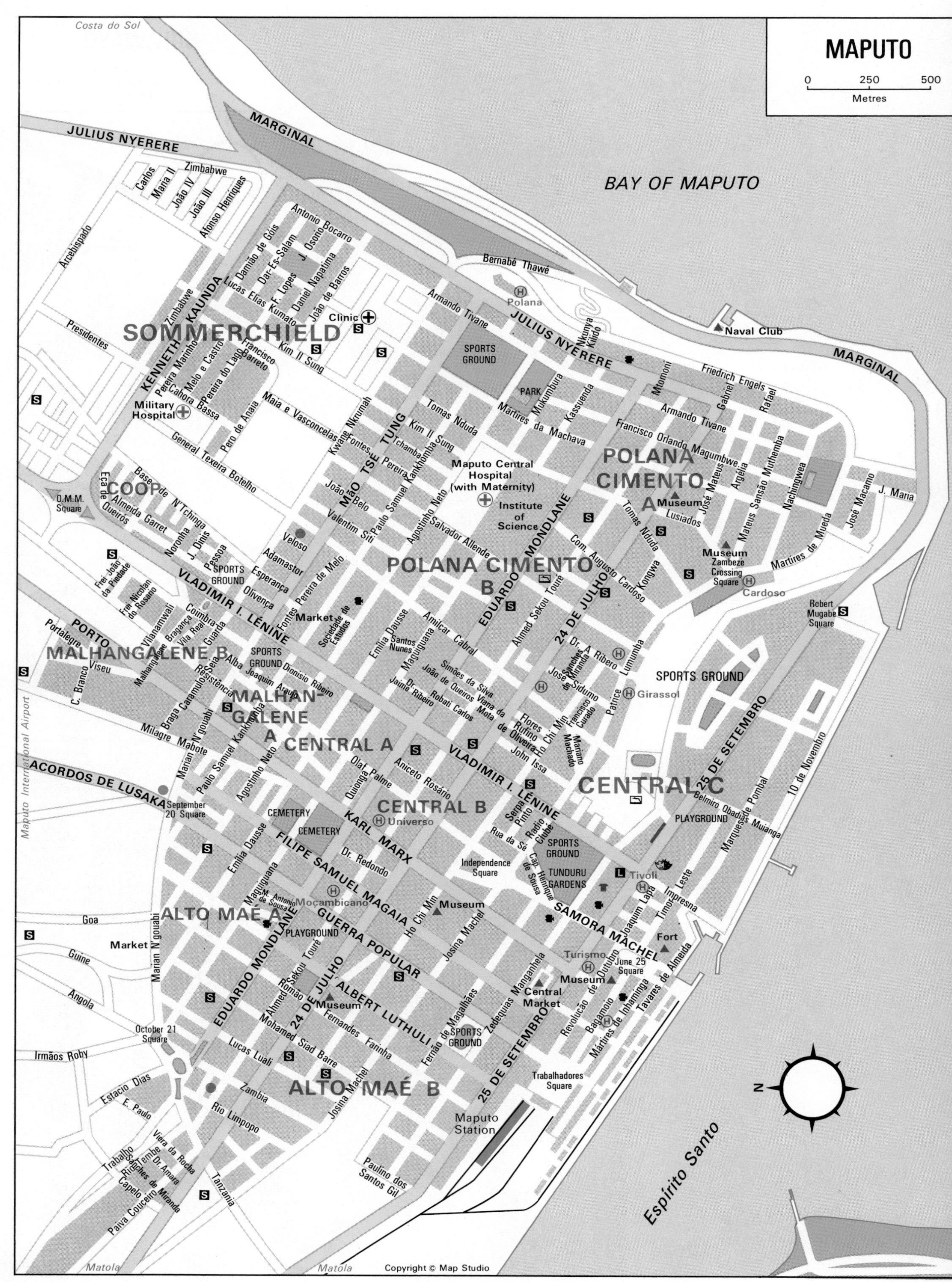

MAPUTO

0   250   500
Metres

Costa do Sol

BAY OF MAPUTO

Espírito Santo

SOMMERCHIELD

POLANA CIMENTO A

POLANA CIMENTO B

CENTRAL C

CENTRAL A

CENTRAL B

MALHANGALENE B

MALHAN-GALENE A

PORTO

COOP

ALTO MAÉ A

ALTO MAÉ B

Maputo International Airport

Matola   *Matola*   Copyright © Map Studio

20

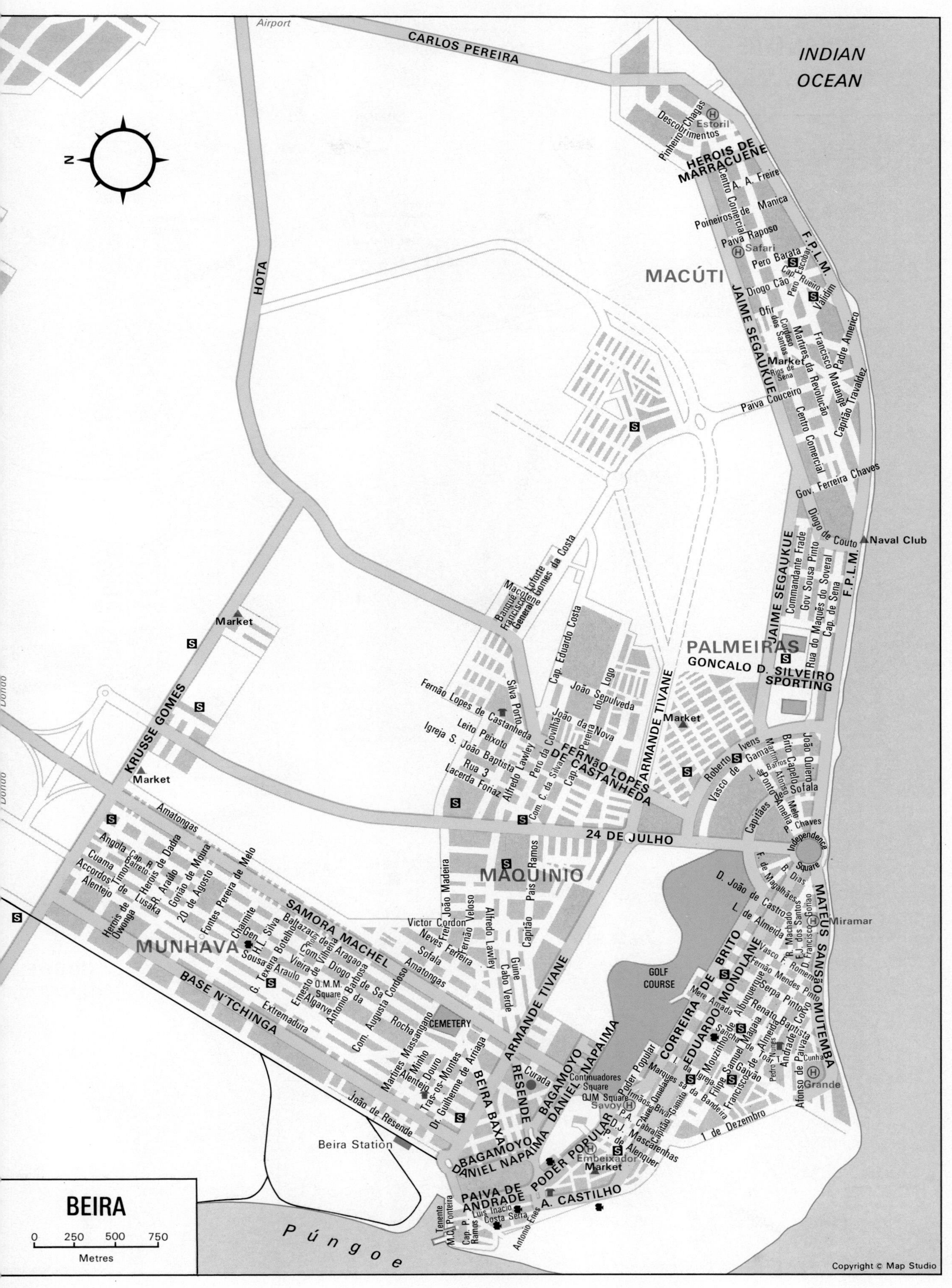

BEIRA
0 250 500 750
Metres
INDIAN OCEAN
MACÚTI
PALMEIRAS
MAQUINIO
MUNHAVA
Púngoe
Airport
CARLOS PEREIRA
HOTA
KRUSSE GOMES
HEROIS DE MARRACUENE
JAIME SEGAUKUE
F.P.L.M.
ARMANDE TIVANE
FERNÃO LOPES DE CASTANHEDA
24 DE JULHO
SAMORA MACHEL
BASE N'TCHINGA
GONCALO D. SILVEIRO
SPORTING
Independence Square
Naval Club
GOLF COURSE
CEMETERY
Beira Station
Market
Estoril
Safari
Miramar
Grande
Savoy
Embeixador
MATEUS SANSÃO MUTEMBA
CORREIRA DE BRITO
EDUARDO MONDLANE
PODER POPULAR
DANIEL NAPAIMA
BAGAMOYO
RESENDE
BEIRA BAXA
PAIVA DE ANDRADE
A. CASTILHO
Amatongas
Copyright © Map Studio

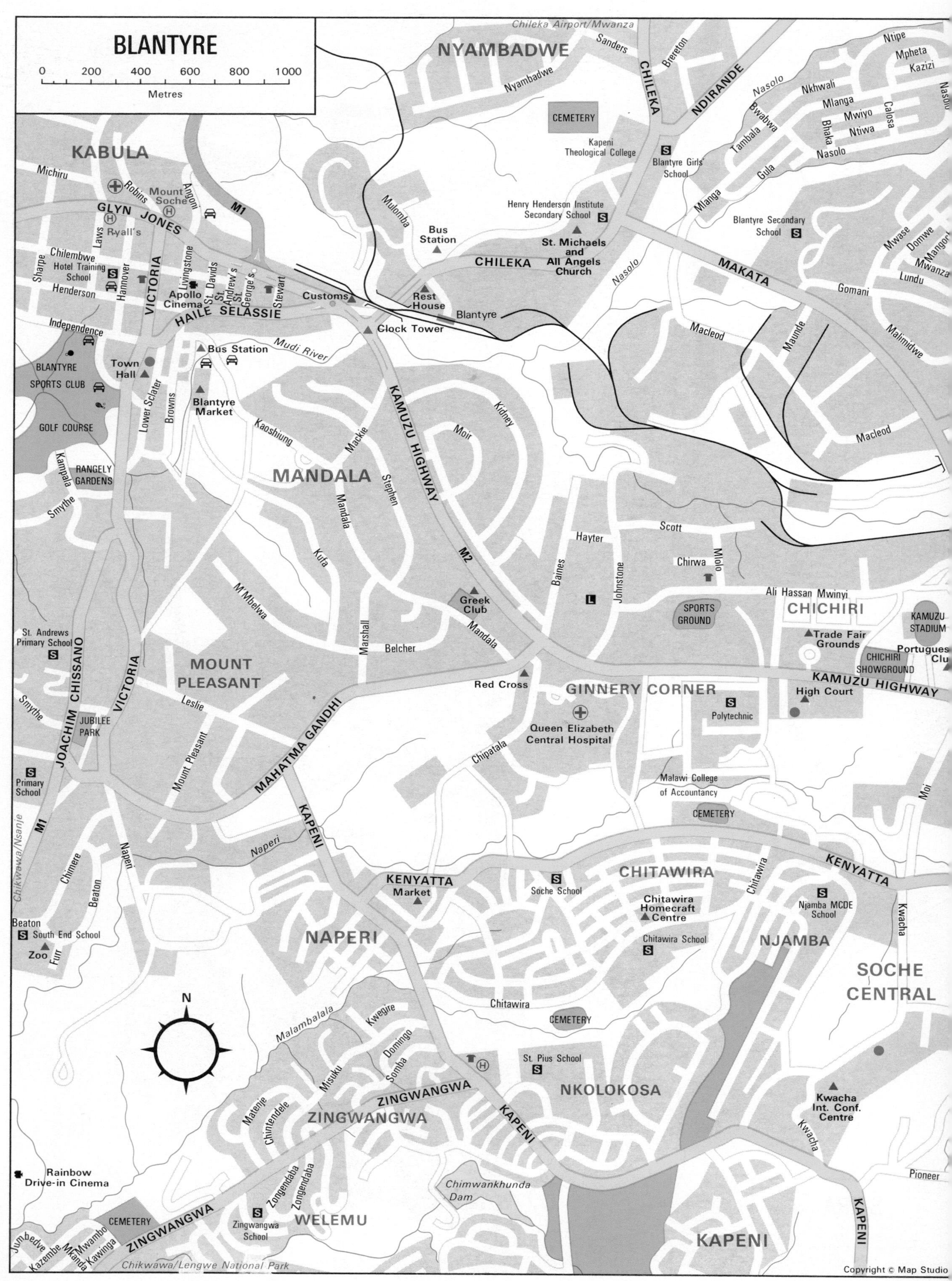

BLANTYRE

0 200 400 600 800 1000
Metres

NYAMBADWE

Chileka Airport/Mwanza

Sanders

Ntipe
Mpheta
Kazizi

Brereton
CHILEKA

Nyambadwe

NDIRANDE

Nasolo

Nkhwali
Bwabwa
Mlanga
Mwiyo
Ntiwa

CEMETERY

Kapeni
Theological College

Tambala
Gula

Calosa
Nasolo

Bhaka

Blantyre Girls'
School

Mlanga

KABULA

Michiru

Mulomba

Henry Henderson Institute
Secondary School S

Gula

Blantyre Secondary
School S

Mwase
Domwe
Mwanza
Mangoni

Robins
Mount
Soche

M1

Angoni

Bus
Station

CHILEKA

St. Michaels
and
All Angels
Church

MAKATA

Lundu
Gomani

Malimidwe

GLYN
JONES

H
Ryall's

VICTORIA

Laws

Livingstone

Chilembwe
Hotel Training
School

Sharpe

Hanover

St Davids St
St Andrew's St
George's

Macleod

Henderson

Apollo
Cinema

HAILE SELASSIE

Stewart

Customs

Rest
House

Blantyre

Clock Tower

Macleod

Independence

Town
Hall

Lower Sclater

Browns

Mudi River

KAMUZU HIGHWAY

Kidney

BLANTYRE
SPORTS CLUB

Bus Station

Kaoshiung

Moir

Scott

GOLF COURSE

Blantyre
Market

Mackie

Stephen

Mandala

Hayter

Johnstone

Chirwa

Miolo

CHICHIRI

KAMUZU
STADIUM

Kampala

RANGELY
GARDENS

MANDALA

Mandala

Baines

Ali Hassan Mwinyi

Smythe

Kufa

L

St. Andrews
Primary School S

M Mbelwa

SPORTS
GROUND

Trade Fair
Grounds

CHICHIRI
SHOWGROUND

Portugues
Clu

JOACHIM CHISSANO

VICTORIA

MOUNT
PLEASANT

Marshall

Belcher

Greek
Club

Mandala

GINNERY CORNER

High Court

KAMUZU HIGHWAY

Smythe

Leslie

Red Cross

Polytechnic

S

JUBILEE
PARK

Mount Pleasant

MAHATMA GANDHI

Chipatala

Queen Elizabeth
Central Hospital

Primary School S

Naperi

KAPENI

Malawi College
of Accountancy

CEMETERY

KENYATTA

Chikwawa/Nsanje M1

Beaton
S South End School

Chimere

Beaton

Naperi

KENYATTA
Market

Soche School S

CHITAWIRA

Chitawira

Njamba MCDE
School S

Chitawira
Homecraft
Centre

Kwacha

Zoo

Furr

NAPERI

Chitawira School S

NJAMBA

Malambalala

Kwegire

SOCHE
CENTRAL

N

Misuku

Domingo
Somha

Chitawira

CEMETERY

St. Pius School

Materje

Chuntendele

ZINGWANGWA

H

NKOLOKOSA

Kwacha
Int. Conf.
Centre

Rainbow
Drive-in Cinema

Zongendaba

WELEMU

Chimwankhunda
Dam

KAPENI

Pioneer

CEMETERY

ZINGWANGWA

Zingwangwa
School S

Jumbedve
Kazembe
Mkanda
Mwambo
Kawinga

KAPENI

Chikwawa/Lengwe National Park

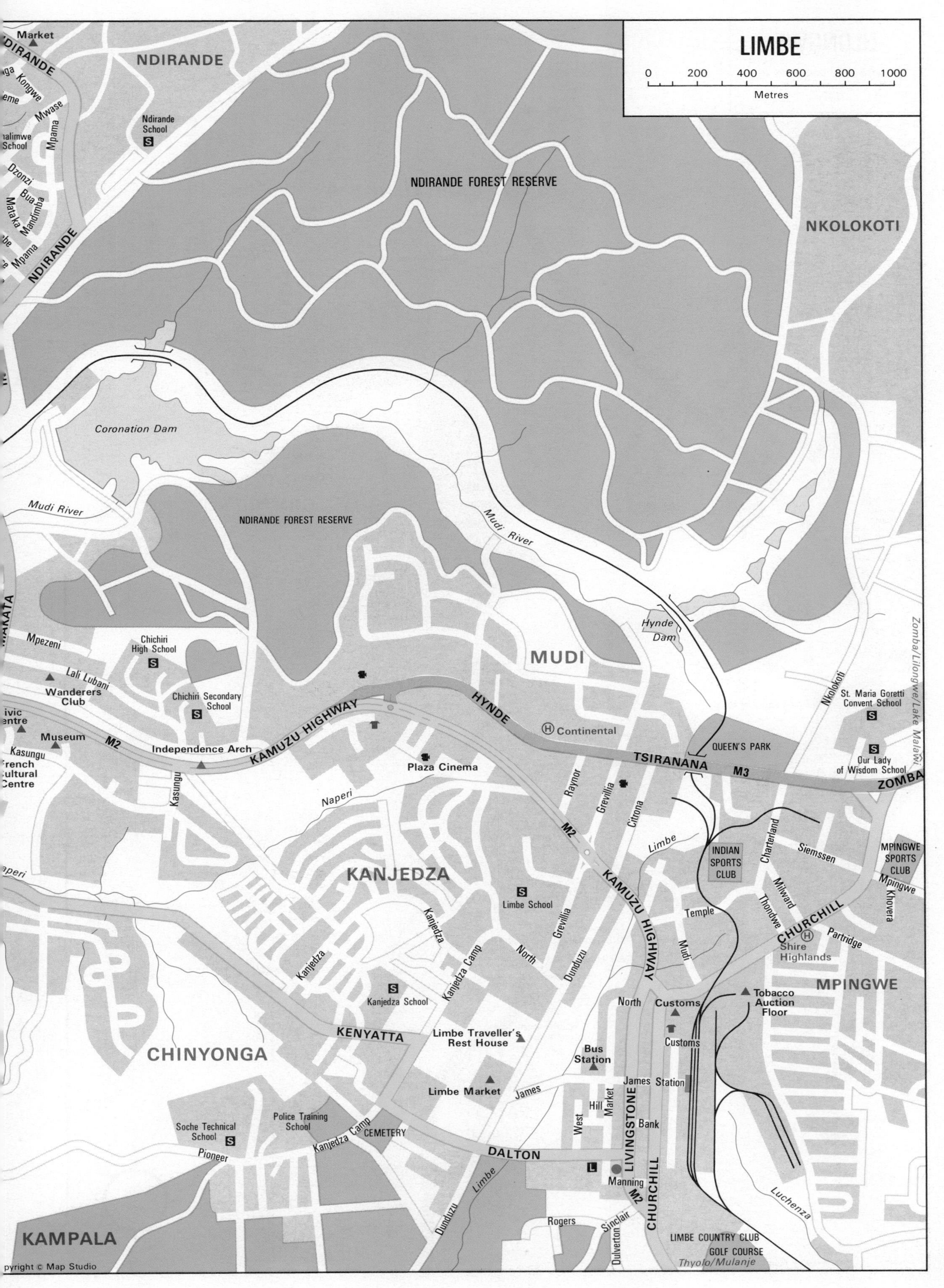

LIMBE

0 200 400 600 800 1000
Metres

NDIRANDE

NKOLOKOTI

NDIRANDE FOREST RESERVE

Market

Ndirande School

NDIRANDE

Mwase
Mpama
Kongwe
Dzonzi
Bua
Mataka
Mandimba

Coronation Dam

Mudi River

NDIRANDE FOREST RESERVE

Mudi River

Hynde Dam

MUDI

Zomba/Lilongwe/Lake Malawi

Mpezeni

Chichiri High School

Lali Lubani
Wanderers Club

Chichiri Secondary School

Nkolokoti
St. Maria Goretti Convent School

Civic Centre

Museum

Kasungu

French Cultural Centre

M2

Independence Arch

Kasungu

HYNDE

Continental

Queen's Park

Our Lady of Wisdom School

TSIRANANA

M3

ZOMBA

Naperi

Plaza Cinema

Raynor

Grevillia

Citrona

Limbe

INDIAN SPORTS CLUB

Charterland

Siemssen

MPINGWE SPORTS CLUB

Naperi

KANJEDZA

Kanjedza

Kanjedza

Kanjedza Camp

North

Grevillia

Dunduzu

KAMUZU HIGHWAY

Limbe School

Mudi

Temple

Milward
Thondwe

Mpingwe

Khovera

CHURCHILL

Shire Highlands

Partridge

MPINGWE

Kanjedza School

KENYATTA

Limbe Traveller's Rest House

North

Customs

Customs

Tobacco Auction Floor

CHINYONGA

Limbe Market

James

Bus Station

James Station

Soche Technical School

Police Training School

Kanjedza Camp

CEMETERY

West
Hill
Market

Bank

Pioneer

DALTON

LIVINGSTONE

Manning

KAMPALA

Dunduzu

Limbe

Rogers

Sinclair

Dulverton

CHURCHILL

M2

LIMBE COUNTRY CLUB GOLF COURSE
Thyolo/Mulanje

Luchenza

pyright © Map Studio

23

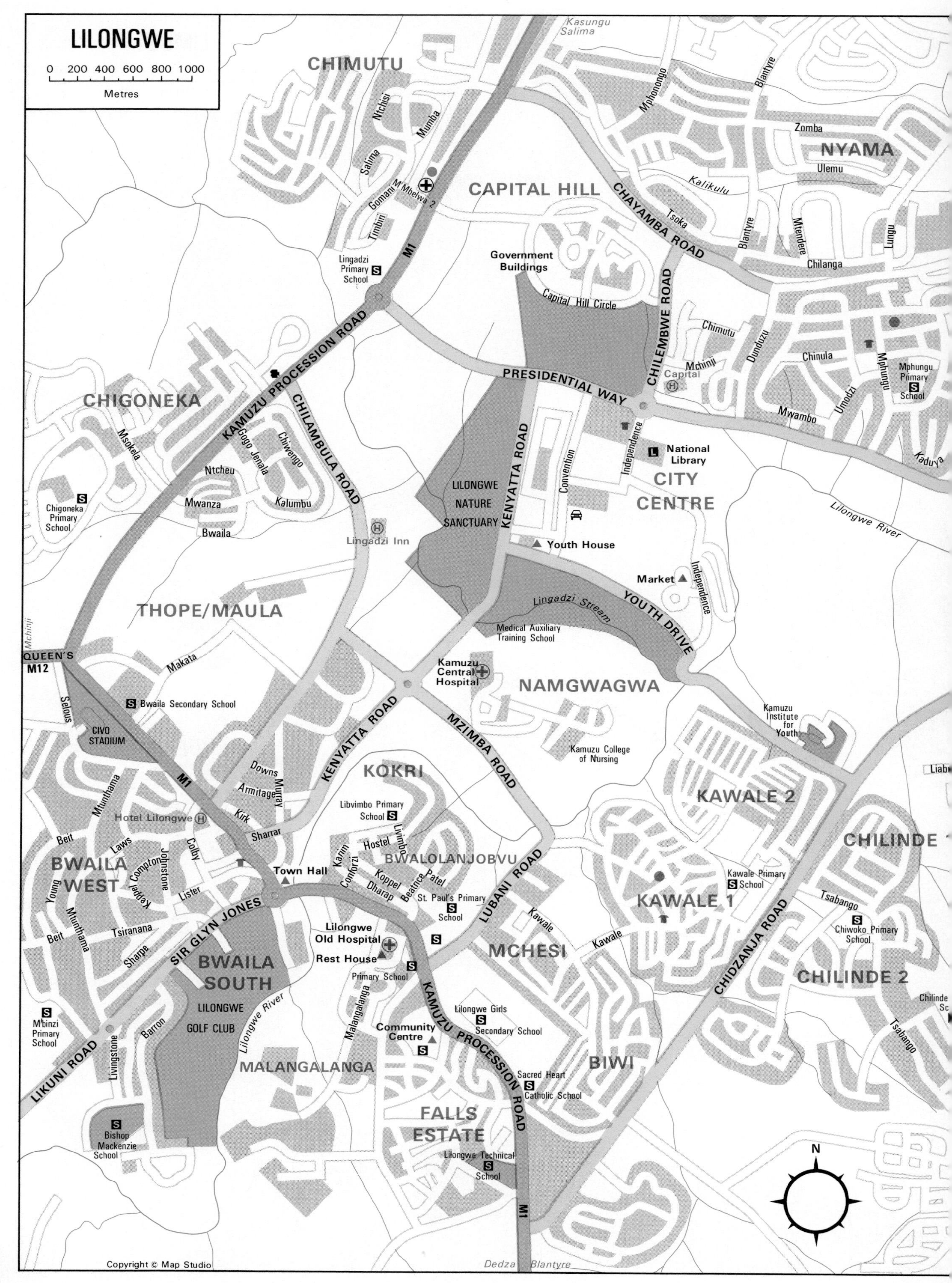

LILONGWE

0 200 400 600 800 1000
Metres

CHIMUTU

CAPITAL HILL

CHAYAMBA ROAD

NYAMA

Zomba
Ulemu

Kasungu
Salima

Mphorongo
Blantyre

Kalikulu
Tsoka

Blantyre
Mfendere
Chilanga

Ntchisi
Salima
Mumba
M'Mbelwa 2

CHILEMBWE ROAD

Chimutu

Gomani
Timbini
M1

Government
Buildings

Capital Hill Circle

Dunduzu
Chinula

Mphungu
Primary
School

Lingadzi Primary
School

PRESIDENTIAL WAY

Mchinji
Capital

Mwambo
Umodzi

Kaduya

CHIGONEKA

KAMUZU PROCESSION ROAD

CHILAMBULA ROAD

Msokela

Gogo Jenala
Chiwengo

Ntcheu

Mwanza

Kalumbu

Bwaila

Lingadzi Inn

KENYATTA ROAD

LILONGWE
NATURE
SANCTUARY

Convention

Independence

National
Library

CITY
CENTRE

Lilongwe River

Chigoneka
Primary
School

THOPE/MAULA

Youth House

Market
Independence

YOUTH DRIVE

Lingadzi Stream

Medical Auxiliary
Training School

NAMGWAGWA

Kamuzu
Institute
for Youth

Mchinji
QUEEN'S
M12

Selous

Makata

Bwaila Secondary School

CIVO
STADIUM

M1

Downs
Murray
Armitage

Kirk

Sharrar

KENYATTA ROAD

Kamuzu
Central
Hospital

MZIMBA ROAD

KOKRI

Libvimbo Primary
School

Kamuzu College
of Nursing

KAWALE 2

Liabw

CHILINDE 1

Mtunthama
Beit
Laws
Young
Keppel
Compton
Johnstone
Jardine
Lister
Bert
Mtunthama
Tsiranana
Sharpe

Hotel Lilongwe

Colby

BWAILA
WEST

Town Hall

Karim
Conforzi
Koppel
Dharap

Hostel
Livimbo

Beatrice Patel

BWALOLANJOBVU

St. Paul's Primary
School

LUBANI ROAD

Kawale

Kawale

MCHESI

Kawale Primary
School

KAWALE 1

Tsabango

Chiwoko Primary
School

CHILINDE 2

CHIDZANJA ROAD

Tsabango

Lilongwe
Old Hospital

Rest House

Primary School

Lilongwe Girls
Secondary School

Chilinde
Sc

SIR GLYN JONES

BWAILA
SOUTH

LILONGWE
GOLF CLUB

Lilongwe River

KAMUZU PROCESSION ROAD

Malangalanga

Community
Centre

Sacred Heart
Catholic School

BIWI

M'binzi
Primary
School

LIKUNI ROAD

Livingstone

Barron

MALANGALANGA

FALLS
ESTATE

Lilongwe Technical
School

M1

Bishop
Mackenzie
School

N

Copyright © Map Studio

Dedza   Blantyre

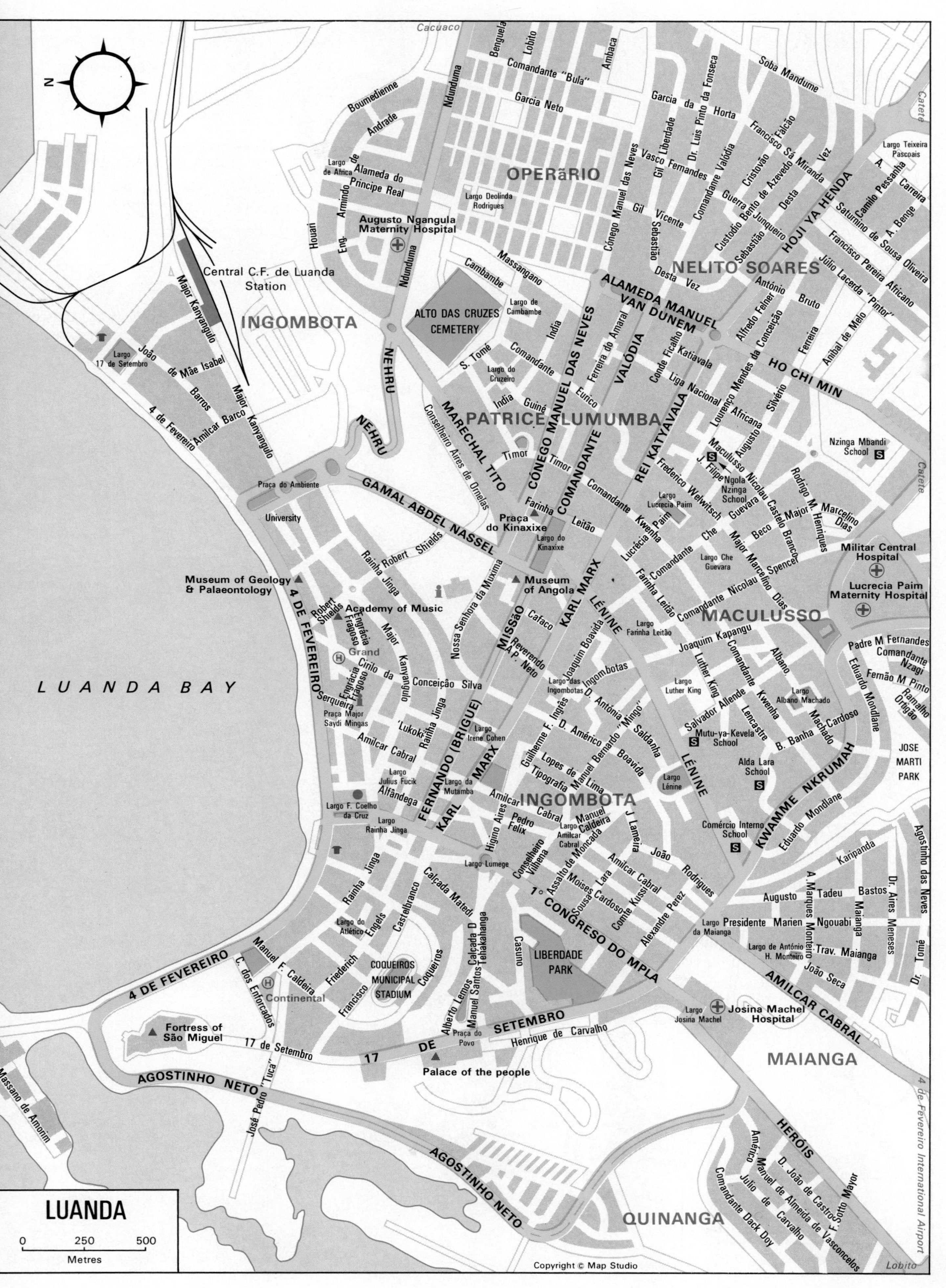
LUANDA
0
250
500
Metres
Copyright © Map Studio
LUANDA BAY
OPERáRIO
INGOMBOTA
NELITO SOARES
PATRICE LUMUMBA
MACULUSSO
INGOMBOTA
MAIANGA
QUINANGA
JOSE MARTI PARK
Central C.F. de Luanda Station
Augusto Ngangula Maternity Hospital
ALTO DAS CRUZES CEMETERY
Museum of Geology & Palaeontology
Academy of Music
Museum of Angola
Praça do Kinaxixe
University
Praça do Ambiente
Grand
Continental
Fortress of São Miguel
Palace of the people
COQUEIROS MUNICIPAL STADIUM
LIBERDADE PARK
Josina Machel Hospital
Militar Central Hospital
Lucrecia Paim Maternity Hospital
Nzinga Mbandi School
Ngola Nzinga School
Mutu-ya-Kevela School
Alda Lara School
Comércio Interno School
Cacuaco
Catete
4 de Fevereiro International Airport
Lobito
GAMAL ABDEL NASSEL
NEHRU
MARECHAL TITO
CÓNEGO MANUEL DAS NEVES
COMANDANTE VALÓDIA
REI KATYAVALA
ALAMEDA MANUEL VAN DUNEM
HO CHI MIN
HOJI YA HENDA
KARL MARX
FERNANDO (BRIGUE)
MISSÃO
LÉNINE
KWAMME NKRUMAH
4 DE FEVEREIRO
AGOSTINHO NETO
17 DE SETEMBRO
1° CONGRESO DO MPLA
AMILCAR CABRAL
HERÓIS

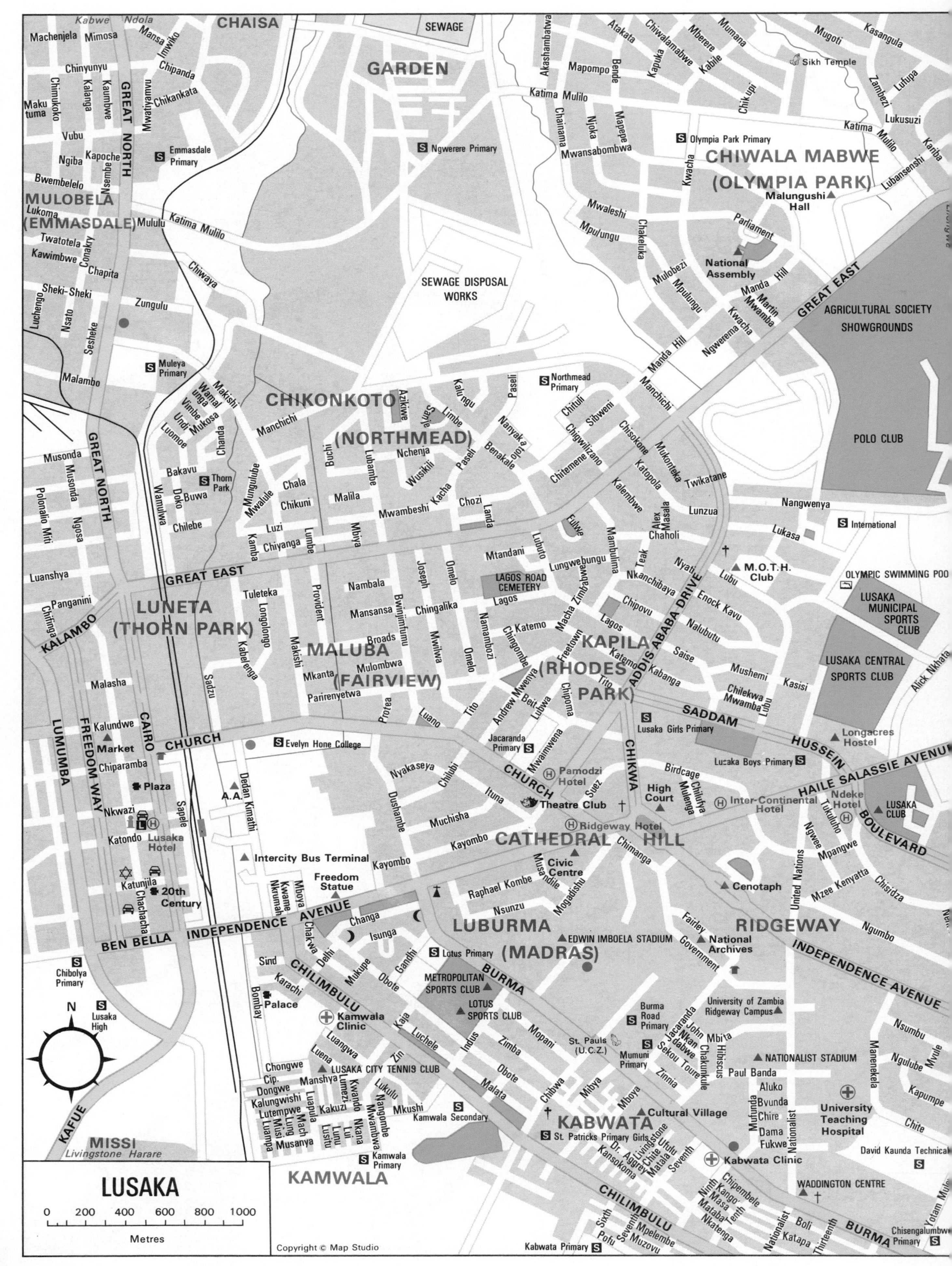

LUSAKA
0 200 400 600 800 1000
Metres
Copyright © Map Studio
CHAISA
GARDEN
SEWAGE
SEWAGE DISPOSAL WORKS
Kabwe
Ndola
Machenjela
Mimosa
Mansa
Imwiko
Chinyunyu
Chipanda
Chimukoko
Kalanga
Kaumbwe
GREAT NORTH
Mwatiyamu
Chikankata
Maku tuma
Vubu
Ngiba
Kapoche
Nsembe
Emmasdale Primary
Bwembelelo
MULOBELA
(EMMASDALE)
Lukoma
Mululu
Katima Mulilo
Twatotela
Conakry
Kawimbwe
Chapita
Chiwaya
Sheki-Sheki
Zungulu
Luchengo
Nsato
Sesheke
Muleya Primary
Malambo
Ngwerere Primary
Akashambatwa
Atakata
Chiwalamabwe
Mberere
Mumana
Mugoti
Kasangula
Sikh Temple
Mapompo
Bende
Kapuka
Kabile
Chikupi
Zambezi
Lufupa
Katima Mulilo
Chainama
Njoka
Mapepe
Lukusuzi
Olympia Park Primary
Katima Mulilo
Kariba
Mwansabombwa
CHIWALA MABWE
(OLYMPIA PARK)
Lubansenshi
Kwacha
Malungushi Hall
Mwaleshi
Mpulungu
Chakeluka
Parliament
National Assembly
Mulobezi
Mpulungu
Manda Hill
Martin Mwamba
Kwacha
Ngwerema
GREAT EAST
AGRICULTURAL SOCIETY SHOWGROUNDS
POLO CLUB
Manda Hill
Manchichi
Northmead Primary
Paseli
Chituli
Sibweni
CHIKONKOTO
(NORTHMEAD)
Azikiwe
Sanje
Kalungu
Limbe
Nanyaka
Benakale
Chigwilizano
Chisokone
Chitemene
Mukonteka
Twikatane
Katopola
Kalembwe
Makishi
Wamal unga
Vimbe
Undi
Mukosa
Luomoe
Chanda
Manchichi
Musonda
Bakavu
Thorn Park
Doko
Buwa
Chilebe
Wamulwa
GREAT NORTH
Musonda
Polonalio
Miti
Ngosa
Mungulube
Mwalule
Chala
Chikuni
Luzi
Chiyanga
Kamba
Lumbe
Buchi
Lubambe
Malila
Mbiya
Nchenja
Wusikili
Kacha
Mwambeshi
Chozi
Landa
Fulwe
Alex Masala
Chaholi
Lunzua
Nangwenya
International
Lukasa
Mtandani
Lubuto
Lungwebungu
Mambulima
Teak
Nyati
Lubu
M.O.T.H. Club
OLYMPIC SWIMMING POO
LUSAKA MUNICIPAL SPORTS CLUB
Luanshya
GREAT EAST
Tuleteka
Nambala
Joseph
Omelo
LAGOS ROAD CEMETERY
Lagos
Zimbabwe
Nkanchibaya
Enock Kavu
Chipovu
Panganini
Chifinga
KALAMBO
LUNETA
(THORN PARK)
Longolongo
Kabelenga
Provident
Makishi
Mansansa
Bwinjimfumu
Chingalika
Mwilwa
Namambozi
Katemo
Chingombe
Macha
Freetown
Lagos
KAPILA
(RHODES PARK)
ADDIS ABABA DRIVE
Nalubutu
Saise
LUSAKA CENTRAL SPORTS CLUB
Alick Nkhata
MALUBA
(FAIRVIEW)
Broads
Mulombwa
Mkanta
Parirenyetwa
Omelo
Katemo
Kabanga
Tito
Mushemi
Chilekwa Mwamba
Kasisi
Lubu
Malasha
Sadzu
Protea
Luano
Tito
Andrew Mwenya
Beit
Lubwa
Chiponda
SADDAM HUSSEIN
Lusaka Girls Primary
Longacres Hostel
LUMUMBA
FREEDOM WAY
Kalundwe
Market
CAIRO
CHURCH
Evelyn Hone College
Jacaranda Primary
Mwaimwena
Lusaka Boys Primary
HAILE SALASSIE AVENUE
Chiparamba
Plaza
A.A.
Dedan Kimathi
Nyakaseya
Chilubi
Iluna
CHURCH
Pamodzi Hotel
Suez
CHIKWA
Birdcage
High Court
Chilufya Mulenga
Inter-Continental Hotel
Ndeke Hotel
Tukuluho
LUSAKA CLUB
BOULEVARD
Nkwazi
Lusaka Hotel
Sapele
Katondo
Dushambe
Muchisha
Theatre Club
Ridgeway Hotel
CATHEDRAL HILL
Kayombo
Chimanga
Ngwee
Mpangwe
Intercity Bus Terminal
Kayombo
Musandile
Civic Centre
Cenotaph
United Nations
Mzee Kenyatta
Chisidza
Katunjila
20th Century
Chachacha
Mboya
Kwame Nkrumah
Freedom Statue
Raphael Kombe
Nsunzu
Mogadishu
BEN BELLA
INDEPENDENCE AVENUE
Changa
Isunga
Chakwa
Delhi
LUBURMA
(MADRAS)
EDWIN IMBOELA STADIUM
Fairley
National Archives
Government
RIDGEWAY
Ngumbo
INDEPENDENCE AVENUE
Chibolya Primary
Sind
CHILIMBULU
Karachi
Mukupe
Gandhi
Obote
Lotus Primary
METROPOLITAN SPORTS CLUB
BURMA
Bombay
Palace
Kamwala Clinic
LOTUS SPORTS CLUB
Kaja
Luchele
Indus
Zimba
Mopani
Burma Road Primary
Jacaranda
Nkan dabwe
John Mbita
Chakunkule
Sekou Toure
University of Zambia Ridgeway Campus
Nsumbu
N
Lusaka High
Luangwa
Luena
Zin
St. Pauls (U.C.Z.)
Mumuni Primary
Zinnia
Hibiscus
NATIONALIST STADIUM
Paul Banda
Aluko
Bvunda
Chire
Dama
Fukwe
Mufunda
Nationalist
Manenekela
Ngulube
Mvule
Kapumpe
Chongwe
Cip.
Dongwe
Kalungwishi
Lutempwe
Luampa
Misi
Lung
Mach
Manshya
Lumezi
Kwando
Luapula
Kakuzi
Lui
Lusitu
Nkana
Mwambwa
Nangombe
Lukulu
Musanya
LUSAKA CITY TENNIS CLUB
Mkushi
Kamwala Secondary
Obote
Malata
Chibwa
Mbiya
Mboya
Cultural Village
University Teaching Hospital
Chite
KABWATA
St. Patricks Primary Girls
Ufulu
Livingstone
Chite
Matala
Seventh
Kansokoma
Dr. Aggrey
Kabwata Clinic
David Kaunda Technical
KAFUE
MISSI
Livingstone
Harare
KAMWALA
Kamwala Primary
CHILIMBULU
Chipembele
Kango
Ninth
Masa
Tenth
Mataba
Nkatenga
Sixth
Pofu
Seventh
Mpelembe
Muzovu
Kabwata Primary
Nationalist
Boli
Katapa
Thirteenth
BURMA
WADDINGTON CENTRE
Chisengalumbwe Primary
Yotam M

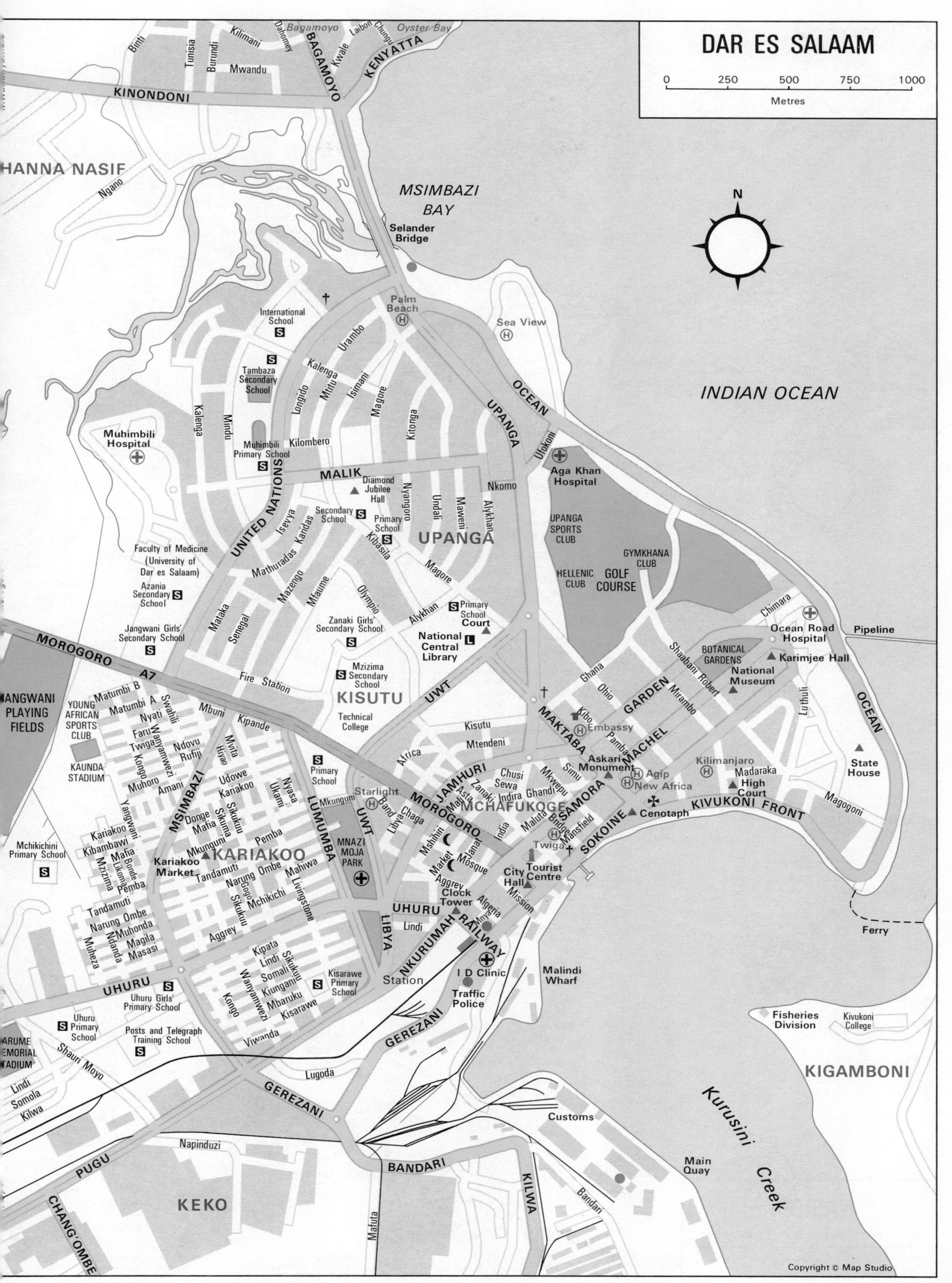
DAR ES SALAAM
0
250
500
750
1000
Metres
N
INDIAN OCEAN
MSIMBAZI BAY
Selander Bridge
KINONDONI
BAGAMOYO
KENYATTA
HANNA NASIF
UNITED NATIONS
MALIK
UPANGA
OCEAN
Muhimbili Hospital
Aga Khan Hospital
UPANGA SPORTS CLUB
GYMKHANA CLUB
HELLENIC CLUB
GOLF COURSE
National Central Library
Court
Ocean Road Hospital
Pipeline
BOTANICAL GARDENS
Karimjee Hall
National Museum
State House
KISUTU
MORO GORO A7
JANGWANI PLAYING FIELDS
YOUNG AFRICAN SPORTS CLUB
KAUNDA STADIUM
KARIAKOO
Kariakoo Market
MCHAFUKOGE
MNAZI MOJA PARK
Askari Monument
Cenotaph
KIVUKONI FRONT
High Court
City Hall
Tourist Centre
Clock Tower
Station
I D Clinic
Traffic Police
Malindi Wharf
Ferry
Fisheries Division
Kivukoni College
KIGAMBONI
Kurusini Creek
Customs
Main Quay
GEREZANI
BANDARI
KILWA
PUGU
CHANG'OMBE
KEKO

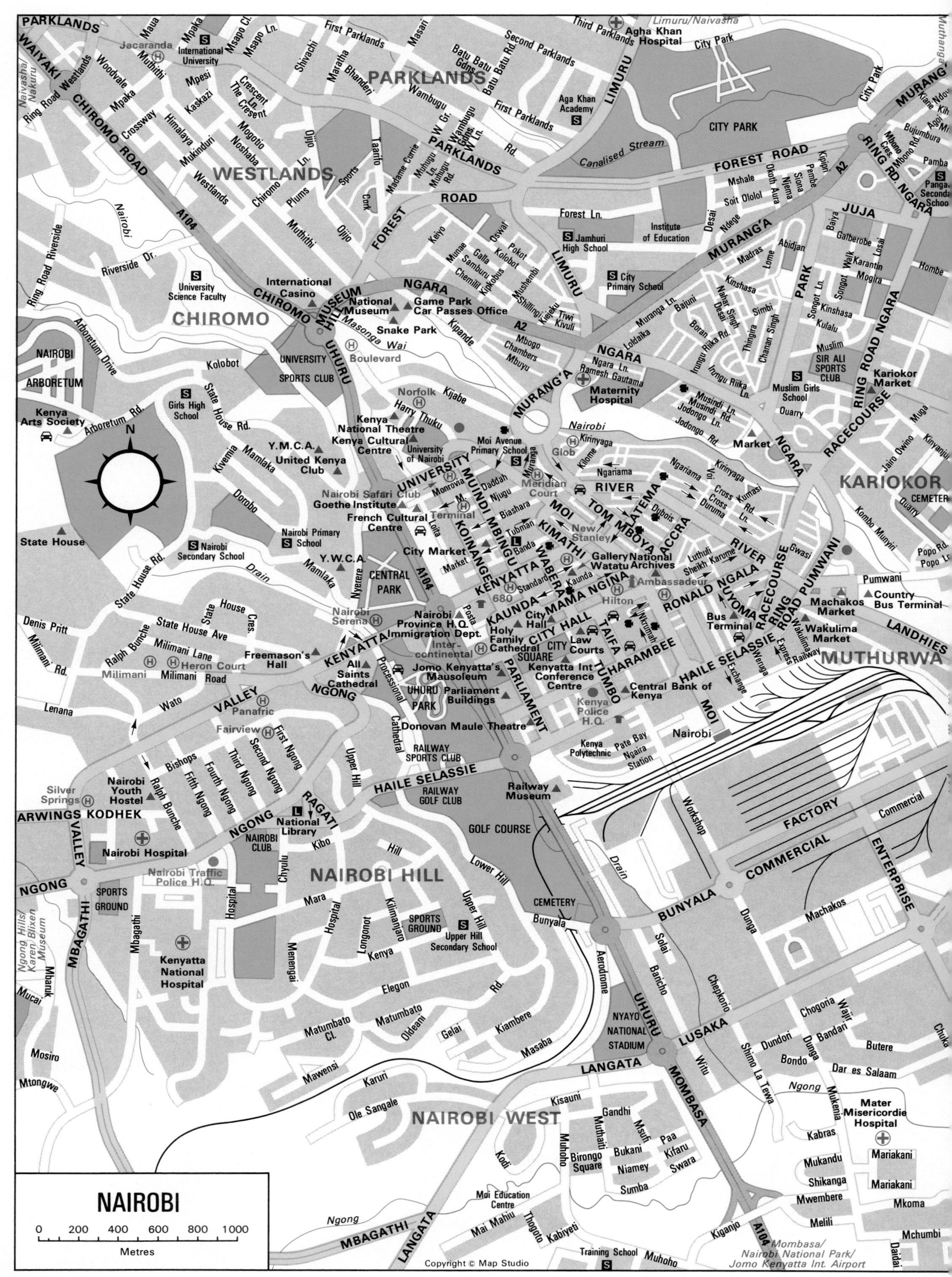

PARKLANDS
WESTLANDS
CHIROMO
KARIOKOR
MUTHURWA
NAIROBI HILL
NAIROBI WEST
CITY PARK
CHIROMO ROAD
WAIYAKI
Ring Road Westlands
Woodvale
Mpaka
Crossway
Himalaya
Mukinduri
Noshaba
Mogotio
Kaskazi
Mpesi
Muthithi
Jacaranda
International University
Msapo Cl.
Msapo Ln.
Shivachi
First Parklands
Masari
Maratha
Bhanderi
Batu Batu Gdns.
Batu Batu Rd.
Second Parklands
Third Parklands
Agha Khan Hospital
Limuru/Naivasha
City Park
Wambugu
Aga Khan Academy
First Parklands
LIMURU
Canalised Stream
FOREST ROAD
Crescent Ln.
The Cresent
Ojijo
Sports
Taarifa
Madame Curie
Muhugu Ln.
Muhugu Rd.
W Gr.
Wambugu Gdns.
W Ln.
PARKLANDS
Rd.
ROAD
FOREST
Forest Ln.
Institute of Education
Jamhuri High School
Mshale
Soit Ololol
Okoth Aura
Njema
Siona
Pembe
Kipipiri
Desai
Ndege
MURANG'A
RING RD. NGARA
JUJA
A2
A104
Nairobi
Riverside Dr.
Ring Road Riverside
University Science Faculty
International Casino
MUSEUM HILL
NGARA
National Museum
Game Park Car Passes Office
Snake Park
Masonga Wai
Boulevard
UHURU
Keiyo
Munae
Galla
Samburu
Chemilil
Kipkobus
Kolobot
Oswal
Pokot
Mushembi
Shillingi
Kiajuku
Tiwi
Kivuli
Kipande
Mbogo
Chambers
Mbuyu
City Primary School
Madras
Lome
Abidjan
Kinshasa
Muranga Ln.
Loldaika
Bajuni
Boran
Desai
Nahar Singh
Thingira
Simbi
Chanan Singh
Irungu Riika Rd.
Irungu Riika Ln.
PARK
Songot Ln.
Songot
Walk
Kinshasa
Kulalu
Muslim
Baiya
Galberobe
Losai
Karantin
Mogira
Hombe
RING ROAD NGARA
SIR ALI SPORTS CLUB
Kariokor Market
Muslim Girls School
Quarry
RACECOURSE
NGARA
Kiane
Ndovu
Kihi
Bujumbura
Mboo Cres.
Mbono Rd.
Angi
Pamba
City Park
MURANG'A
Muthaiga
NAIROBI ARBORETUM
Arboretum Drive
Kolobot
UNIVERSITY SPORTS CLUB
Kenya Arts Society
Arboretum Rd.
Girls High School
State House Rd.
N
Kivemia
Mamlaka
Dorobo
Norfolk
Kijabe
Harry Thuku
Kenya National Theatre
Kenya Cultural Centre
University of Nairobi
Y.M.C.A.
United Kenya Club
NGARA
Ngara Ln.
Ramesh Gautama
Maternity Hospital
Musindi Ln.
Musindi Rd.
Jodongo Ln.
Jodongo Rd.
Market
MURANG'A
Nairobi
Kirinyaga
Moi Avenue Primary School
Muranga
Glob
Kilome
Meridian Court
Ngariama
RIVER
Kirinyaga
Voi
Cross
Duruma
Kumasi
Rd.
Ln.
Jairo Owino
Muga
Kinyanjui
Kombo Munyiri
Quarry
CEMETERY
Popo Rd.
Popo Ln.
UNIVERSITY
Monrovia
Daddah
Njugu
Biashara
Nairobi Safari Club
Goethe Institute
French Cultural Centre
M. Terminal
Loita
MUINDI MBINGU
KOINANGE
MOI
KIMATHI
Tubman
Banda
New Stanley
TOM MBOYA
LATEMA
Dubois
ACCRA
RIVER
Luthuli
Sheikh Karume
Gwasi
PUMWANI
State House
Nairobi Primary School
Nairobi Secondary School
Y.W.C.A.
CENTRAL PARK
Nyerere
City Market
Market
A104
KENYATTA
WABERA
Standard
680
Gallery Watatu
National Archives
Kaunda
MAMA NGINA
Ambassadeur
Hilton
RONALD NGALA
RACECOURSE
UYOMA
RING ROAD PUMWANI
Pumwani
Country Bus Terminal
Machakos Market
Drain
State House Rd.
Mamlaka
State House Cres.
Denis Pritt
State House Ave
Ralph Bunche
Milimani Lane
Milimani Rd.
Heron Court
Milimani
Milimani Road
Nairobi Serena
Freemason's Hall
KENYATTA
All Saints Cathedral
Nairobi Province H.Q.
Immigration Dept.
Posta
Inter-continental
KAUNDA
City Hall
CITY HALL
Holy Family Cathedral
CITY SQUARE
Law Courts
TAIFA
Nkrumah
Bus Terminal
Wakulima
Wakulima Market
LANDHIES
Express
Railway
HAILE SELASSIE
Weruga
Exchange
HARAMBEE
TUMBO
Kenyatta Int Conference Centre
Central Bank of Kenya
MOI
Jomo Kenyatta's Mausoleum
PARLIAMENT
Parliament Buildings
UHURU PARK
Processional
NGONG
Lenana
Wato
VALLEY
Panafric
Kenya Police H.Q.
Fairview
First Ngong
Second Ngong
Third Ngong
Fourth Ngong
Fifth Ngong
Bishops
Ralph Bunche
Upper Hill
Cathedral
Donovan Maule Theatre
RAILWAY SPORTS CLUB
Kenya Polytechnic
Pate Bay
Ngaira
Station
Nairobi
Silver Springs
Nairobi Youth Hostel
HAILE SELASSIE
RAILWAY GOLF CLUB
Railway Museum
ARWINGS KODHEK
RAGATI
NGONG
National Library
NAIROBI CLUB
Kibo
Nairobi Hospital
Hill
GOLF COURSE
Workshop
FACTORY
Commercial
COMMERCIAL
ENTERPRISE
Drain
Lower Hill
Nairobi Traffic Police H.Q.
NGONG
MBAGATHI
SPORTS GROUND
Hospital
Chyulu
Mara
Hospital
Kilimanjaro
Longonot
SPORTS GROUND
Upper Hill
Upper Hill Secondary School
CEMETERY
Bunyala
BUNYALA
Dunga
Machakos
Ngong Hills/Karen Blixen Museum
Mbagathi
Kenyatta National Hospital
Menengai
Kenya
Mbaruk
Mucai
Elegon
Rd.
Aerodrome
Solai
Baricho
Chepkorio
Mosiro
Matumbato Cl.
Matumbato
Oldeani
Gelai
Kiambere
NYAYO NATIONAL STADIUM
UHURU
LUSAKA
Chogoria
Wajir
Bandari
Dundori
Dunga
Butere
Chuka
Bondo
Dar es Salaam
Mtongwe
Mawensi
Masaba
LANGATA
Karuri
Witu
Shimo La Tewa
MOMBASA
Ngong
Mukenia
Mater Misericordie Hospital
Ole Sangale
Kisauni
Gandhi
Muthaiti
Msufi
Paa
Kifaru
Swara
Muhoho
Birongo Square
Bukani
Niamey
Kodi
Sumba
Kabras
Mariakani
Mukandu
Shikanga
Mariakani
Mwembere
Mkoma
Melili
Mchumbi
Daidai
Moi Education Centre
Ngong
Mai Mahiu
Thogoto
Kabiyeti
Kiganjo
A104
MBAGATHI
LANGATA
Training School
Muhoho
Mombasa/Nairobi National Park/Jomo Kenyatta Int. Airport
Copyright © Map Studio
NAIROBI
0 200 400 600 800 1000
Metres

AREA MAPS
GEBIEDSKAARTE

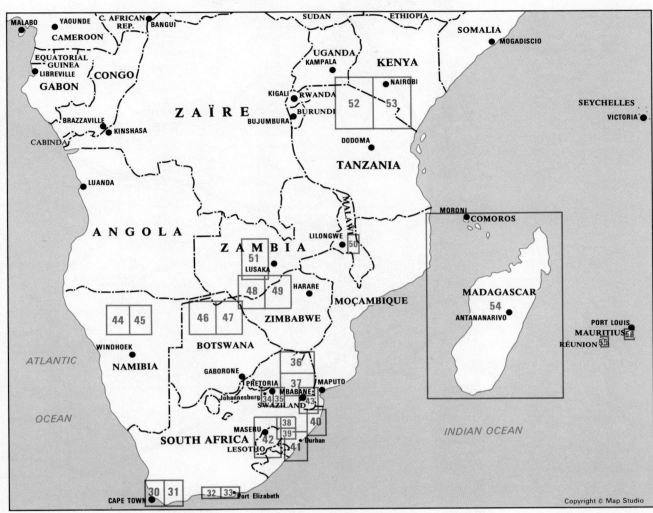

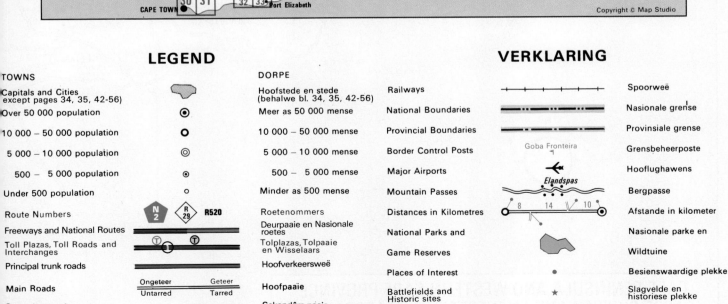

LEGEND | DORPE

TOWNS

Capitals and Cities (except pages 34, 35, 42-56) | Hoofstede en stede (behalwe bl. 34, 35, 42-56)

Over 50 000 population | Meer as 50 000 mense

10 000 – 50 000 population | 10 000 – 50 000 mense

5 000 – 10 000 population | 5 000 – 10 000 mense

500 – 5 000 population | 500 – 5 000 mense

Under 500 population | Minder as 500 mense

Route Numbers | Roetenommers

Freeways and National Routes | Deurpaaie en Nasionale roetes

Toll Plazas, Toll Roads and Interchanges | Tolplazas, Tolpaaie en Wisselaars

Principal trunk roads | Hoofverkeersweë

Main Roads | Hoofpaaie
Ongeteer / Geteer
Untarred / Tarred

Secondary roads | Sekondêre paaie

Roads under construction | Paaie in aanbou

VERKLARING

Railways | Spoorweë

National Boundaries | Nasionale grense

Provincial Boundaries | Provinsiale grense

Border Control Posts | Grensbeheerposte
Goba Fronteira

Major Airports | Hooflughawens

Mountain Passes | Bergpasse
Elandspas

Distances in Kilometres | Afstande in kilometer
8   14   10

National Parks and | Nasionale parke en

Game Reserves | Wildtuine

Places of Interest | Besienswaardige plekke

Battlefields and Historic sites | Slagvelde en historiese plekke

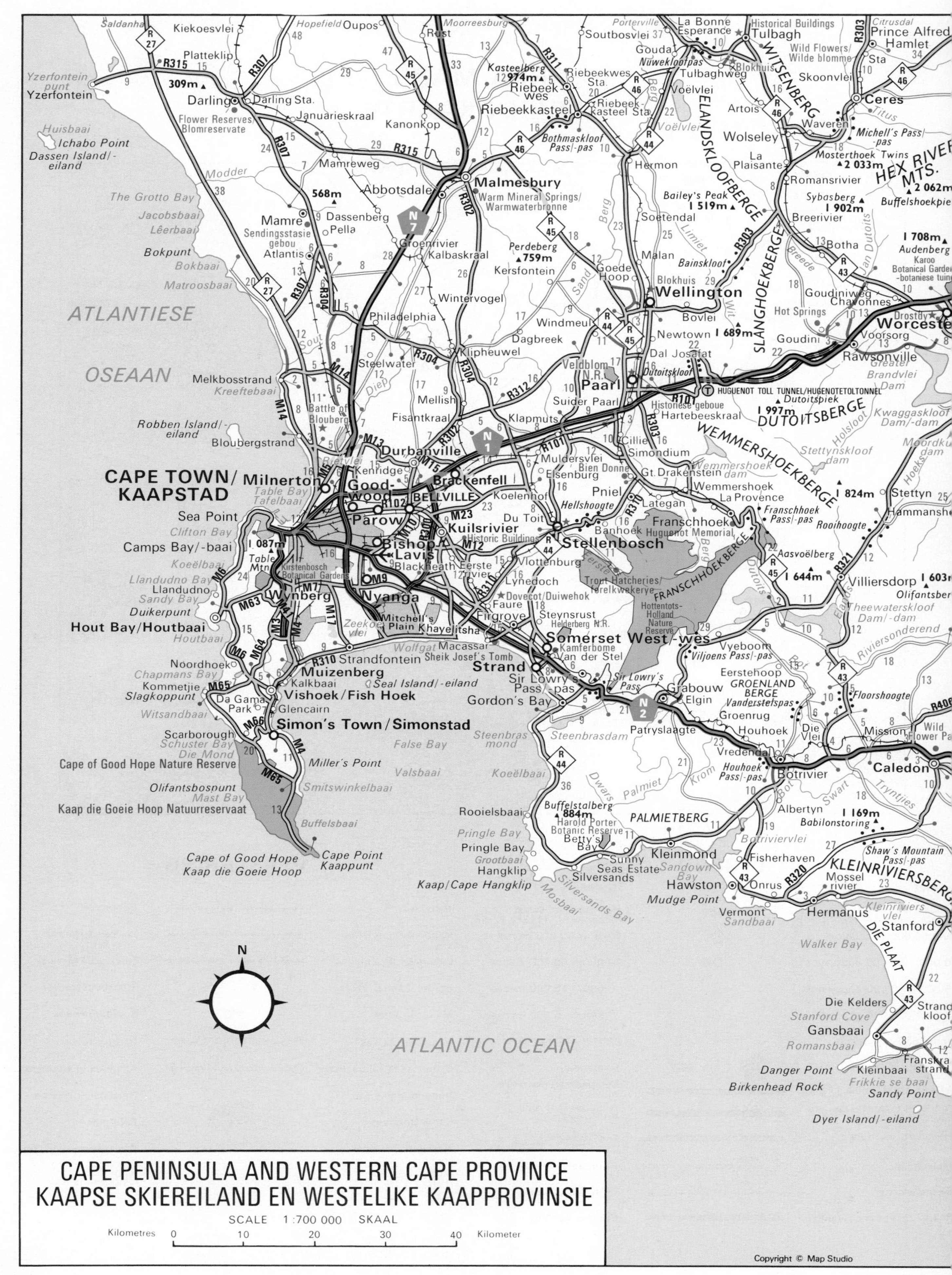

CAPE PENINSULA AND WESTERN CAPE PROVINCE
KAAPSE SKIEREILAND EN WESTELIKE KAAPPROVINSIE

SCALE   1 : 700 000   SKAAL

Kilometres   0   10   20   30   40   Kilometer

Copyright © Map Studio

30

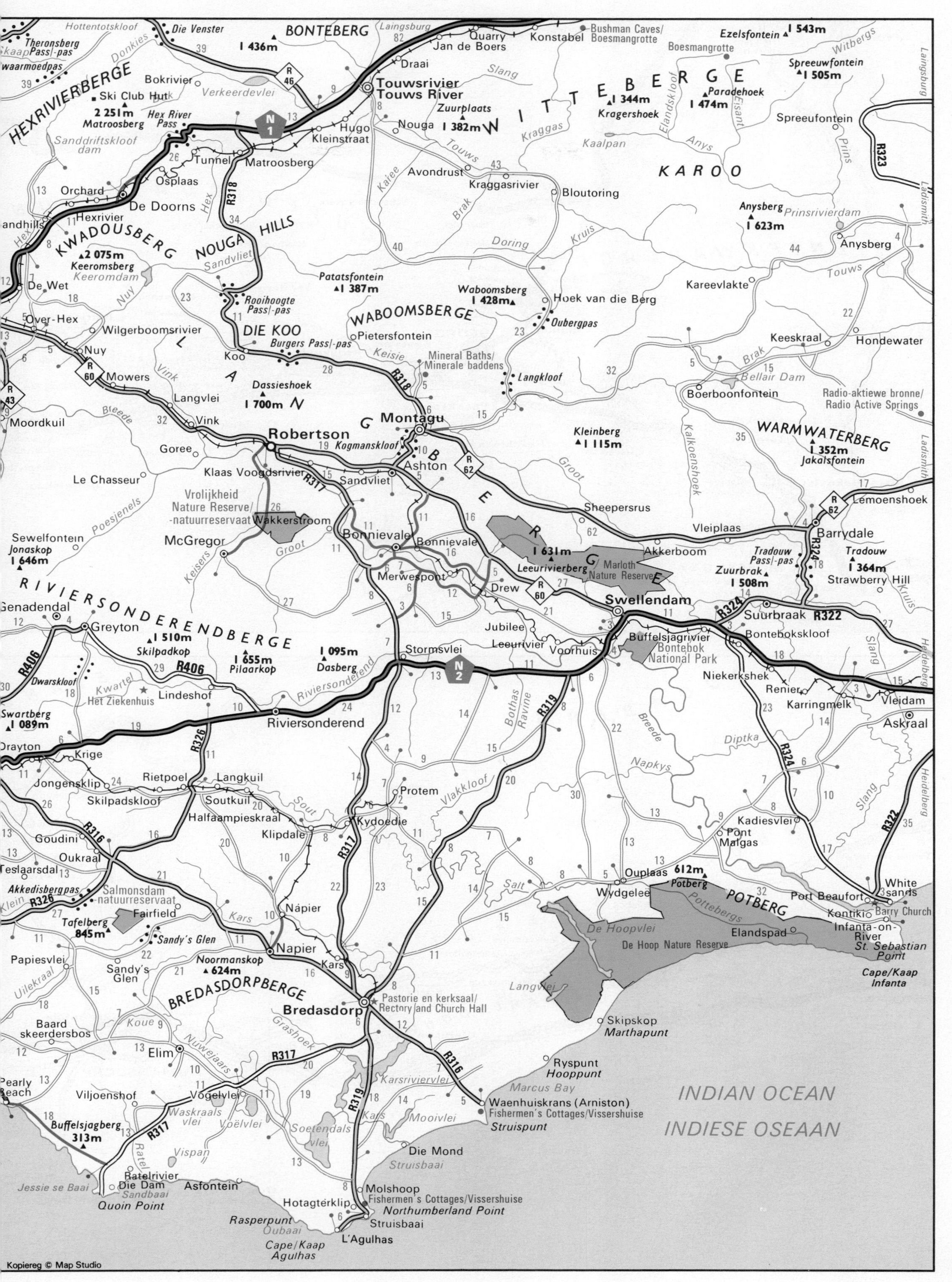
HEXRIVIERBERGE
BONTEBERG
WITTEBERGE
KAROO
KWADOUSBERG
NOUGA HILLS
WABOOMSBERGE
DIE KOO
LANGEBERGE
RIVIERSONDERENDBERGE
BREDASDORPBERGE
POTBERG
WARMWATERBERG
Touwsrivier
Touws River
Robertson
Montagu
Ashton
Bonnievale
McGregor
Swellendam
Barrydale
Greyton
Riviersonderend
Napier
Bredasdorp
Elim
Suurbraak
De Doorns
Hexrivier
Worcester
Matroosberg
Kleinstraat
Hugo
Nouga
Avondrust
Kraggasrivier
Bloutoring
Koo
Nuy
Mowers
Langvlei
Vink
Moordkuil
Goree
Le Chasseur
Klaas Voogdsrivier
Sandvliet
Wakkerstroom
Merwespont
Drew
Jubilee
Leeurivier
Voorhuis
Buffelsjagrivier
Bontebok National Park
Stormsvlei
Lindeshof
Het Ziekenhuis
Krige
Rietpoel
Langkuil
Soutkuil
Skilpadskloof
Jongensklip
Halfaampieskraal
Klipdale
Kydoedie
Protem
Goudini
Oukraal
Salmonsdam natuurreservaat
Fairfield
Sandy's Glen
Papiesvlei
Baard skeerdersbos
Viljoenshof
Vogelvlei
Ratelrivier
Die Dam
Asfontein
Hotagterklip
Molshoop
Struisbaai
L'Agulhas
Cape/Kaap Agulhas
Quoin Point
Rasperpunt
Die Mond
Waenhuiskrans (Arniston)
Fishermen's Cottages/Vissershuise
Struispunt
Ryspunt
Hooppunt
Skipskop
Marthapunt
De Hoop Nature Reserve
De Hoopvlei
Elandspad
Infanta-on-River
St. Sebastian Point
Cape/Kaap Infanta
Kontiki
Barry Church
Port Beaufort
Witsands
Wydgeleë
Ouplaas
612m Potberg
Pont Malgas
Kadiesvlei
Karringmelk
Vleidam
Askraal
Renier
Niekerkshek
Bontebokskloof
Strawberry Hill
Tradouw Pass/-pas
Zuurbrak 1 508m
Tradouw 1 364m
Lemoenshoek
Vleiplaas
Akkerboom
Marloth Nature Reserve
Leeurivierberg 1 631m
Sheepersrus
Kleinberg 1 115m
Jakalsfontein 1 352m
Boerboonfontein
Radio-aktiewe bronne/Radio Active Springs
Bellair Dam
Keeskraal
Hondewater
Kareevlakte
Anysberg
Anysberg 1 623m
Prinsrivierdam
Spreeufontein
Spreeuwfontein 1 505m
Paradehoek 1 474m
Kragershoek 1 344m
Ezelsfontein 1 543m
Boesmangrotte
Bushman Caves/Boesmangrotte
Konstabel
Jan de Boers
Quarry
Draai
Zuurplaats 1 382m
Hoek van die Berg
Oubergpas
Langkloof
Waboomsberg 1 428m
Patatsfontein 1 387m
Pietersfontein
Mineral Baths/Minerale baddens
Burgers Pass/-pas
Dassieshoek 1 700m
Rooihoogte Pass/-pas
Kogmanskloof
Keeromsberg 2 075m
Keeromdam
De Wet
Over-Hex
Wilgerboomsrivier
Orchard
Osplaas
Tunnel
Hex River Pass
Ski Club Hut
Matroosberg 2 251m
Bokrivier
Verkeerdevlei
Sanddriftskloof dam
Die Venster
Theronsberg Pass/-pas
Hottentotskloof
Vrolijkheid Nature Reserve/-natuurreservaat
Sewelfontein
Jonaskop 1 646m
Genadendal
Skilpadkop 1 510m
Pilaarkop 1 655m
Dasberg 1 095m
Dwarskloof
Swartberg 1 089m
Drayton
Akkedisbergpas
Tafelberg 845m
Noormanskop 624m
Buffelsjagberg 313m
Pearly Beach
Jessie se Baai
Sandbaai
Oubaai
Northumberland Point
Pastorie en kerksaal/Rectory and Church Hall
Marcus Bay
Mooivlei
Soetendalsvlei
Waskraals vlei
Voëlvlei
Vispan
Karsriviervlei
Langvlei
Struisbaai
INDIAN OCEAN
INDIESE OSEAAN

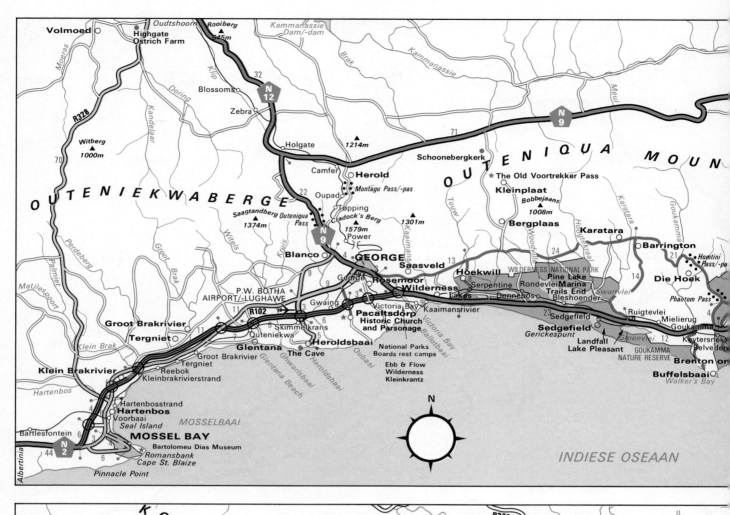

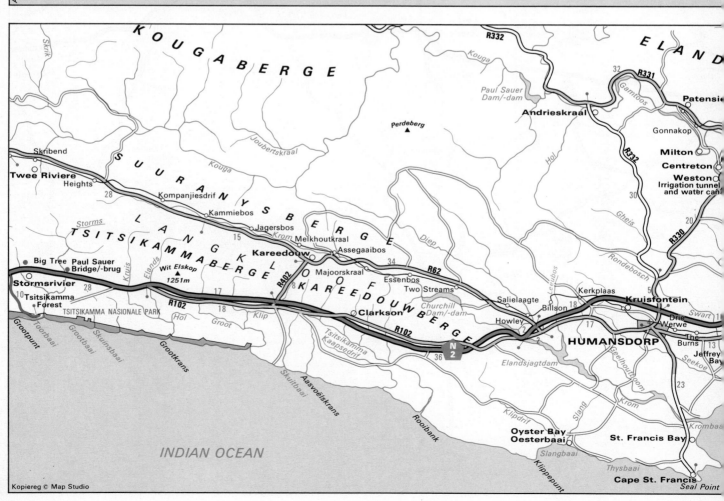

Kopiereg © Map Studio

Volmoed
Oudtshoorn
Highgate Ostrich Farm
Rooiberg 645m
Kammanassie Dam/-dam
Moeras
Brak
Kammanassie
Klip
32
Blossoms
N 12
Doring
Meul
R328
Zebra
Kandelaar
N 9
Witberg 1000m
71
Holgate
1214m
70
Schoonebergkerk
OUTENIQUA MOUN
Camfer
Herold
The Old Voortrekker Pass
OUTENIEKWABERGE
Montagu Pass/-pas
Kleinplaat
22
Oupad
Topping
Bobbejaans 1008m
Saagtandberg 1374m
Outeniqua Pass
Cradock's Berg 1579m
1301m
Touw
Karatara
Goukamma
Perdeberg
Groot
Witels
Kruis
N 9
Power
Kaaimans
Bergplaas
Hoogtekraal
Woodville
Karatara
Barrington
Palmiet
Brak
Blanco
4
GEORGE
Saasveld
13
24
21
Homtini Pass/-pas
Matjiespoort
9
George
Rosemoor
Hoekwill
WILDERNESS NATIONAL PARK
Die Hoek
P.W. BOTHA AIRPORT/-LUGHAWE
9
Wilderness
8
Serpentine
Rondevlei
Pine Lake Marina
Trails End
14
11
R102
Gwaing
Lakes
Dennebos
Swartvlei
Phantom Pass
3
Victoria Bay
Kaaimansrivier
Bleshoender
Groot Brakrivier
Skimmelkrans
Pacaltsdorp
Historic Church and Parsonage
Victoria Bay
23
Sedgefield
Ruigtevlei
Mielierug
Goukamma
11
Outeniekwa
Ballotbaai
Sedgefield
Gerickespunt
Tergniet
7
5
Heroldsbaai
Landfall
Groenvlei
12
Keytersnek
Belvedere
Klein Brak
Glentana
The Cave
National Parks Boards rest camps
Lake Pleasant
GOUKAMMA NATURE RESERVE
Groot Brakrivier
Tergniet
Glentana Beach
Gwarisbaai
Heroldsbaai
Oubaai
Brenton on
Klein Brakrivier
Reebok
Ebb & Flow
Wilderness
Kleinkrantz
Buffelsbaai
Kleinbrakrivierstrand
Walker's Bay
Hartenbos
Hartenbosstrand
N
Hartenbos
Voorbaai
Seal Island
MOSSELBAAI
Bartlesfontein
MOSSEL BAY
N 2
44
Bartolomeu Dias Museum
Romansbank
Cape St. Blaize
INDIESE OSEAAN
Albertinia
Pinnacle Point
KOUGABERGE
R332
ELAND
Skrik
Kouga
32
R331
Paul Sauer Dam/-dam
Gamtoos
Patensie
Andrieskraal
Perdeberg
Gonnakop
Joubertskraal
R332
Milton
Skribend
Kouga
Hol
Centreton
Twee Riviere
SUURANYSBERGE
Weston
Heights
Irrigation tunnel and water canal
28
Kompanjiesdrif
30
Storms
Kammiebos
Gheis
LANGKLOOF
20
Jagersbos
15
Krom
Melkhoutkraal
Diep
R330
TSITSIKAMMABERGE
Assegaaibos
Kareedouw
Rondebosch
Big Tree
Paul Sauer Bridge/-brug
Kruis
Elands
Wit Elskop 1251m
34
R62
Majoorskraal
R402
Stormsrivier
KAREEDOUWBERGE
Essenbos
Two Streams
Leeubos
Kerkplaas
5
28
Kruisfontein
Tsitsikamma Forest
17
Salielaagte
Churchill Dam/-dam
Billson
18
Swart
10
Drie Werwe
TSITSIKAMMA NASIONALE PARK
R102
18
Clarkson
Hol
Groot
Klip
Howley
17
Grootpunt
Toorbaai
R102
2
HUMANSDORP
The Burns
13
Grootbaai
Skuinsbaai
Tsitsikamma Kaapsedrif
N 2
Jeffrey's Bay
36
Elandsjagtdam
Seekoe
Grootkrans
Geelhoutboom
Skuitbaai
Aasvoëlskrans
23
Krom
Klipdrif
Slang
Rooibank
Krombaai
Oyster Bay
Oesterbaai
St. Francis Bay
Slangbaai
INDIAN OCEAN
Klippepunt
Thysbaai
Cape St. Francis
Seal Point

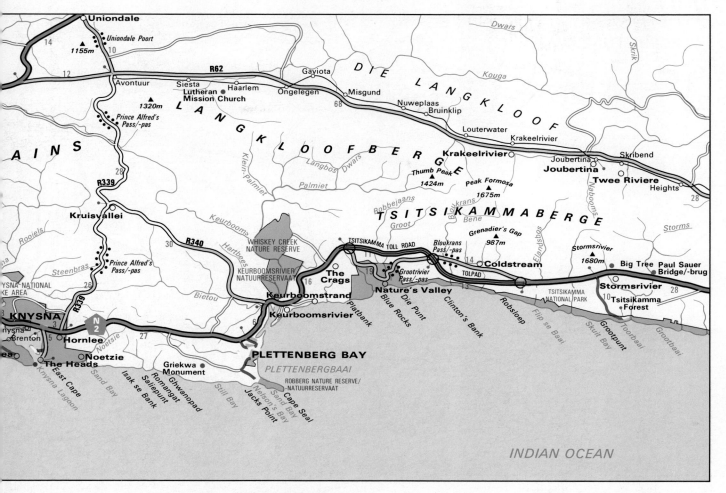

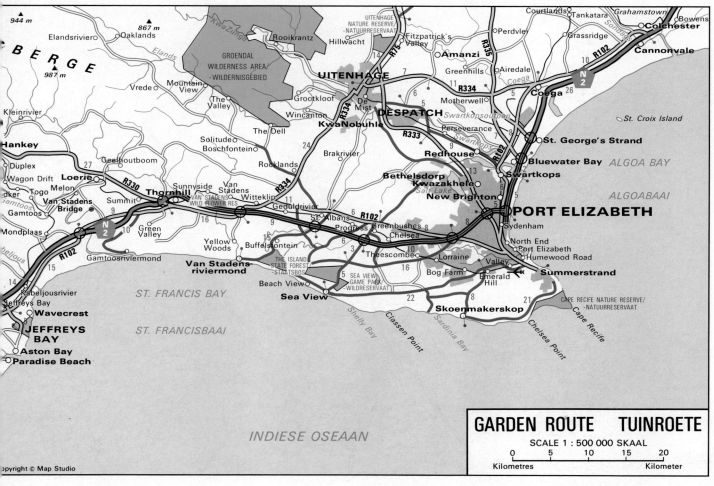

GARDEN ROUTE   TUINROETE

SCALE 1 : 500 000 SKAAL

Kilometres 0 5 10 15 20 Kilometer

Copyright © Map Studio

33

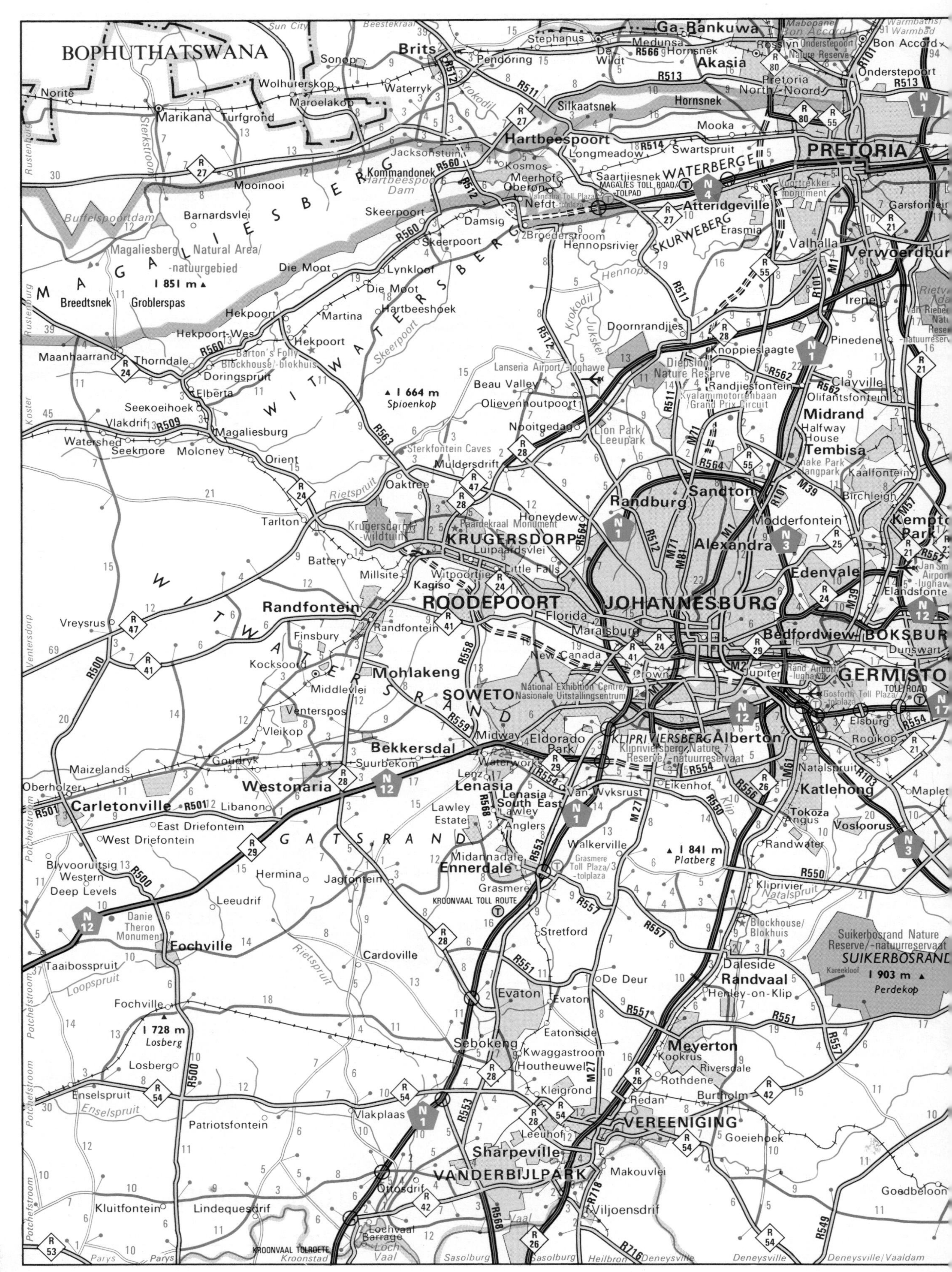
BOPHUTHATSWANA
Sun City
Beestekraal
Brits
Ga-Rankuwa
Mabopane
Bon Accord
Warmbaths/Warmbad
Stephanus
Medunsa
De Wildt
Hornsnek
Akasia
Rosslyn
Onderstepoort Nature Reserve
Onderstepoort
Sonop
Pendoring
Wolhuterskop
Waterryk
Maroelakop
Norite
Marikana
Turfgrond
Krokodil
Silkaatsnek
Hornsnek
Pretoria North/-Noord
Mooka
Hartbeespoort
Longmeadow
Swartspruit
PRETORIA
Jacksonstuin
Kommandonek
Hartbeespoort Dam
Kosmos
Meerhof
Oberon
Nefdt
Saartjiesnek
WATERBERGE
MAGALIES TOLL ROAD/-TOLPAD
Voortrekker-monument
Mooinooi
MAGALIESBERG
Buffelspoortdam
Barnardsvlei
Skeerpoort
Damsig
Broederstroom
Atteridgeville
Erasmia
SKURWEBERG
Garsfontein
Valhalla
Verwoerdburg
Magaliesberg Natural Area/-natuurgebied
Hennopsrivier
Hennops
1 851 m
Die Moot
Lynkloof
Breedtsnek
Grobler spas
Hartbeeshoek
Martina
Hekpoort
Hekpoort-Wes
Irene
Doornrandjies
Jukskei
Maanhaarrand
Thorndale
Barton's Folly Blockhouse/-blokhuis
Doringspruit
Elberta
Lanseria Airport/-lughawe
Beau Valley
Diepsloot Nature Reserve
Knoppieslaagte
Pinedene
Randjiesfontein
Kyalamimotorrenbaan/Grand Prix Circuit
Clayville
Olifantsfontein
1 664 m Spioenkop
Olievenhoutpoort
Seekoeihoek
Vlakdrif
Magaliesburg
WITWATERSBERG
Nooitgedag
Lion Park/Leeupark
Midrand
Halfway House
Tembisa
Watershed
Seekmore
Moloney
Orient
Sterkfontein Caves
Muldersdrift
Snake Park/Slangpark
Kaalfontein
Rietspruit
Oaktree
Sandton
Birchleigh
Randburg
Modderfontein
Kempton Park
Tarlton
Krugersdorp-wildtuin
Paardekraal Monument
Honeydew
KRUGERSDORP
Luipaardsvlei
Alexandra
Battery
Millsite
Witpoortjie
Little Falls
Kagiso
Edenvale
Jan Smuts Airport/-lughawe
Elandsfontein
Randfontein
ROODEPOORT
JOHANNESBURG
Florida
Vreysrus
Finsbury
Randfontein
Maraisburg
Bedfordview
BOKSBURG
Dunswart
WITWATERSRAND
Kocksoord
Middlevlei
Mohlakeng
New Canada
Crown
Jupiter
Rand Airport/-lughawe
GERMISTON
SOWETO
National Exhibition Centre/Nasionale Uitstallingsentrum
Gosforth Toll Plaza/-tolplaza
Venterspos
Vleikop
Midway
Eldorado Park
KLIPRIVIERSBERG
Alberton
Elsburg
Rooikop
Maizelands
Goudryk
Bekkersdal
Suurbekom
Waterworks
Klipriviersberg Nature Reserve/-natuurreservaat
Oberholzer
Westonaria
Lenz
Lenasia
Eikenhof
Natalspruit
Katlehong
Maple
Carletonville
Libanon
Lawley Estate
Lenasia South East
Lawley
Van Wyksrust
Klip
Tokoza
Angus
Vosloorus
East Driefontein
West Driefontein
GATSRAND
Anglers
Walkerville
Grasmere Toll Plaza/-tolplaza
1 841 m Platberg
Randwater
Blyvooruitsig
Western Deep Levels
Hermina
Jagfontein
Midannadale
Ennerdale
Grasmere
Kliprivier
Natalspruit
KROONVAAL TOLL ROUTE
Leeudrif
Danie Theron Monument
Blockhouse/Blokhuis
Suikerbosrand Nature Reserve/-natuurreservaat
SUIKERBOSRAND
Fochville
Stretford
Taaibosspruit
Cardoville
Rietspruit
Daleside
Randvaal
Kareekloof
1 903 m Perdekop
Loopspruit
Evaton
De Deur
Henley-on-Klip
Fochville
Evaton
1 728 m Losberg
Eatonside
Meyerton
Sebokeng
Kookrus
Losberg
Kwaggastroom
Houtheuwel
Riversdale
Rothdene
Enselspruit
Kleigrond
Burtholm
Redan
Vlakplaas
VEREENIGING
Patriotsfontein
Leeuhof
Goeiehoek
Sharpeville
VANDERBIJLPARK
Makouvlei
Ottosdrif
Viljoensdrif
Goedbeloon
Kluitfontein
Lindequesdrif
Lochvaal Barrage
Loch Vaal
Vaal
KROONVAAL TOLROETE
Parys
Kroonstad
Sasolburg
Heilbron
Deneysville
Deneysville/Vaaldam
Potchefstroom
Rustenburg
Koster
Ventersdorp

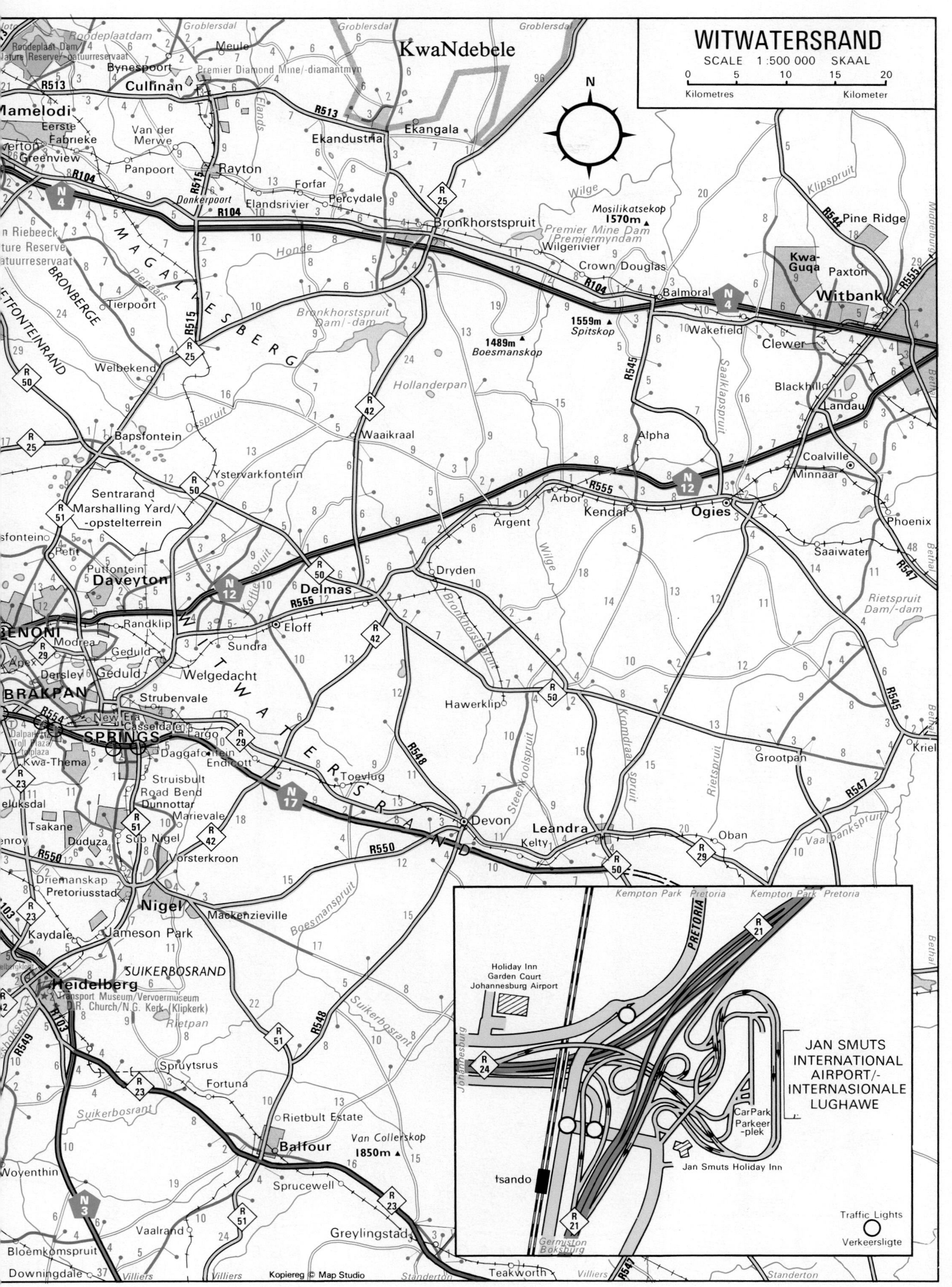

WITWATERSRAND
SCALE 1:500 000 SKAAL
0 5 10 15 20
Kilometres
Kilometer
N
KwaNdebele
Groblersdal
Roodeplaatdam
Roodeplaat Dam/ Nature Reserve/-natuurreservaat
Meule
Premier Diamond Mine/-diamantmyn
Bynespoort
Cullinan
R513
Mamelodi
Eerste Fabrieke
Van der Merwe
Ekandustria
Ekangala
Greenview
Panpoort
Rayton
R104
R515
Donkerpoort
Elandsrivier
Forfar
Percydale
R25
Bronkhorstspruit
Premier Mine Dam /Premiermyndam
Mosilikatsekop 1570m
Wilgerivier
Crown Douglas
Balmoral
N4
Wilge
Klipspruit
R544
Pine Ridge
Kwa-Guqa
Paxton
Witbank
R555
Elands
Honde
Pienaars
MAGALIESBERG
BRONBERGE
Tierpoort
Bronkhorstspruit Dam/-dam
1559m Spitskop
Wakefield
Clewer
1489m Boesmanskop
Hollanderpan
R545
Saalklapspruit
Blackhill
Landau
Welbekend
R50
R42
Waaikraal
Alpha
Bapsfontein
Osspruit
Coalville
Minnaar
Ystervarkfontein
R555
N12
Arbor
Kendal
Ogies
Sentrarand Marshalling Yard/-opstelterrein
R51
Argent
Phoenix
Petit
Saaiwater
R547
Puttontein
Daveyton
Dryden
Delmas
Wilge
Rietspruit Dam/-dam
Koffiespruit
Bronkhorstspruit
Randklip
BENONI
Eloff
Modrea
Sundra
R29
Apex
Geduld
Dersley
Geduld
Welgedacht
BRAKPAN
Strubenvale
WITWATERSRAND
Hawerklip
R554
New Era
Casseldale
Largo
SPRINGS
Daggafontein
Endicott
Kwa-Thema
R548
Steenkoolspruit
Kromdraaispruit
Rietspruit
Grootpan
Kriel
Struisbult
Road Bend
Toevlug
N17
Dunnottar
Marievale
R23
Tsakane
Devon
Leandra
Oban
Duduza
Sub Nigel
Kelty
Vaalbankspruit
R550
Vorsterkroon
Driemanskap
Pretoriusstad
Nigel
Mackenzieville
Boesmanspruit
Kaydale
Jameson Park
SUIKERBOSRAND
Heidelberg
Transport Museum/Vervoermuseum
D.R. Church/N.G. Kerk (Klipkerk)
Rietpan
Suikerbosrant
R103
R549
Spruytsrus
Fortuna
Suikerbosrant
Rietbult Estate
Van Collerskop 1850m
Balfour
Woyenthin
N3
Sprucewell
Vaalrand
Greylingstad
Bloemkomspruit
Downingdale
Teakworth
Villiers
Standerton
Bethal
Middelburg
Kopiereg © Map Studio
Kempton Park
Pretoria
PRETORIA
R21
R24
Holiday Inn Garden Court Johannesburg Airport
Johannesburg
JAN SMUTS INTERNATIONAL AIRPORT/-INTERNASIONALE LUGHAWE
CarPark Parkeer-plek
Jan Smuts Holiday Inn
Isando
Germiston Boksburg
Traffic Lights
Verkeersligte

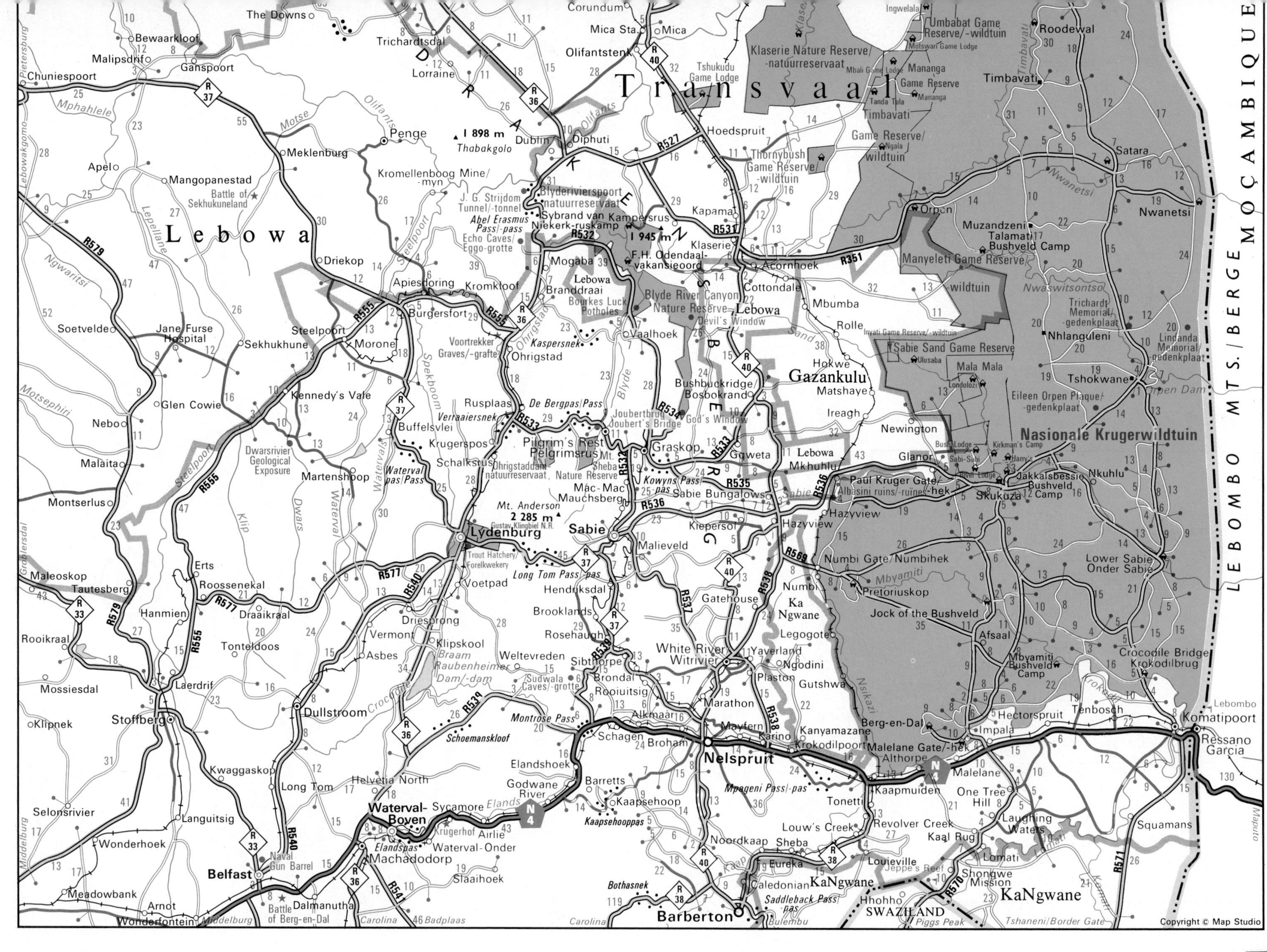

Transvaal
Lebowa
Gazankulu
KaNgwane
SWAZILAND
MOÇAMBIQUE
LEBOMBO MTS./BERGE
Nasionale Krugerwildtuin
Pietersburg
Lebowakgomo
Groblersdal
Middelburg
Belfast
Dullstroom
Waterval-Boven
Machadodorp
Lydenburg
Steelpoort
Burgersfort
Ohrigstad
Pilgrim's Rest
Graskop
Sabie
Hazyview
White River
Nelspruit
Barberton
Carolina
Badplaas
Hoedspruit
Klaserie
Acornhoek
Orpen
Satara
Skukuza
Lower Sabie
Malelane
Komatipoort
Crocodile Bridge
Ressano Garcia
Maputo

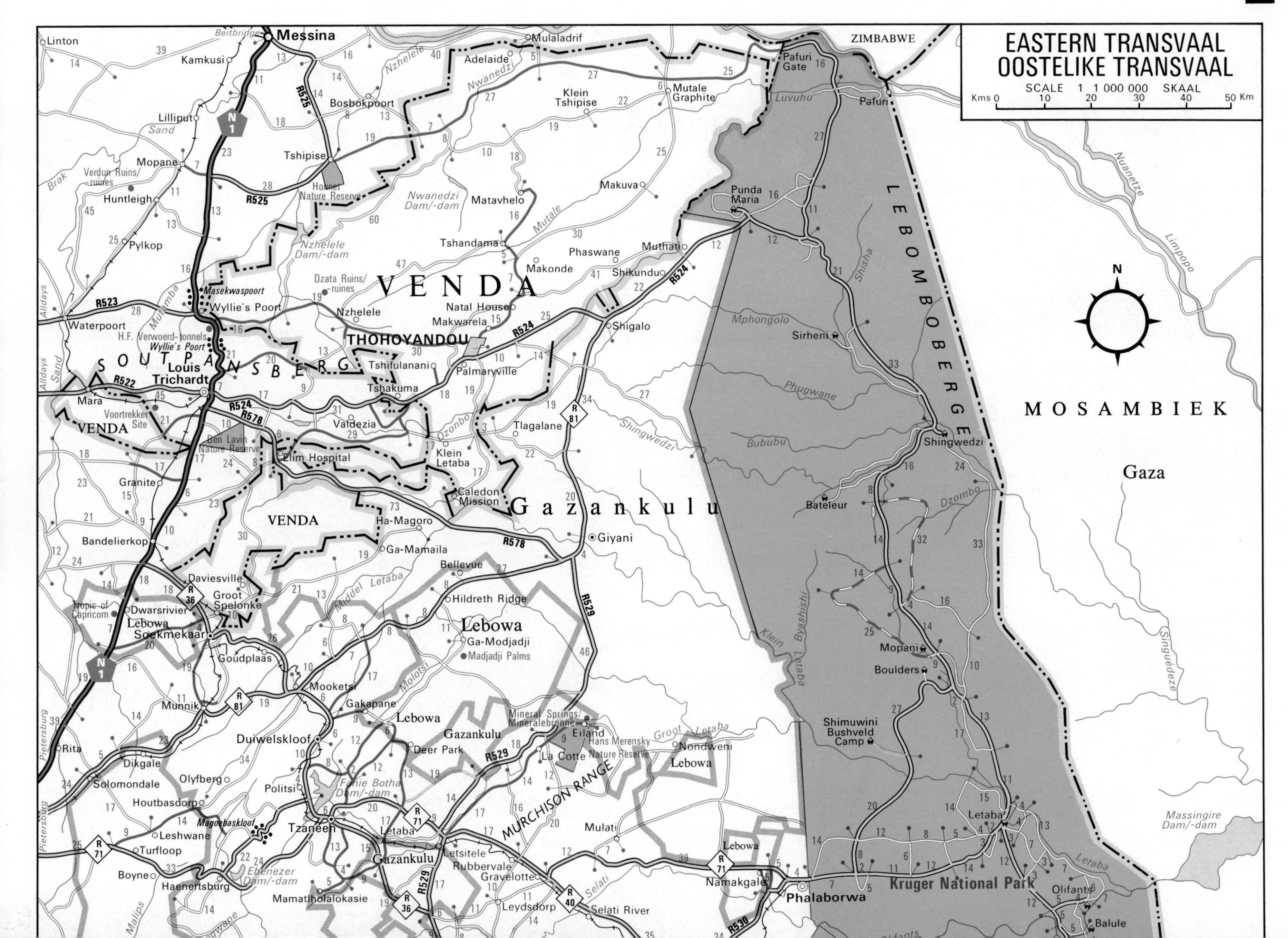

EASTERN TRANSVAAL
OOSTELIKE TRANSVAAL
SCALE 1 1 000 000 SKAAL
Kms 0 10 20 30 40 50 Km
N
ZIMBABWE
MOSAMBIEK
Gaza
VENDA
Gazankulu
Lebowa
LEBOMBOBERGE
SOUTPANSBERG
MURCHISON RANGE
Kruger National Park
Messina
Linton
Kamkusi
Beitbridge
Lilliput
Mopane
Verdun Ruins/-ruines
Huntleigh
Pylkop
Tshipise
Honnet Nature Reserve
Bosbokpoort
Adelaide
Mulaladrif
Klein Tshipise
Mutale Graphite
Pafuri Gate
Pafuri
Matavhelo
Makuva
Nwanedzi Dam/-dam
Nzhelele Dam/-dam
Tshandama
Punda Maria
Phaswane
Muthati
Makonde
Shikundu
Dzata Ruins/-ruines
Masekwaspoort
Wyllie's Poort
Waterpoort
H.F. Verwoerd-tonnels
Nzhelele
Natal House
Makwarela
THOHOYANDOU
Shigalo
Sirheni
Tshifulanani
Palmaryville
Tshakuma
Louis Trichardt
Mara
Voortrekker Site
Ben Lavin Nature Reserve
Valdezia
Tlagalane
Elim Hospital
Klein Letaba
Caledon Mission
Shingwedzi
Granite
Bandelierkop
Ha-Magoro
Ga-Mamaila
Giyani
Bateleur
Bellevue
Daviesville
Groot Spelonke
Tropic of Capricorn
Dwarsrivier
Lebowa
Soekmekaar
Hildreth Ridge
Ga-Modjadji
Madjadji Palms
Goudplaas
Mooketsi
Gakapane
Mopani
Boulders
Munnik
Duiwelskloof
Mineral Springs/ Mineralebronne
Eiland
Hans Merensky Nature Reserve
Nondweni
Deer Park
La Cotte
Shimuwini Bushveld Camp
Rita
Dikgale
Solomondale
Olyfberg
Houtbasdorp
Politsi
Fanie Botha Dam/-dam
Magoebaskloof
Leshwane
Turfloop
Tzaneen
Letaba
Mulati
Boyne
Haenertsburg
Ebenezer Dam/-dam
Letsitele
Rubbervale
Gravelotte
Namakgale
Phalaborwa
Mamatholalokasie
Leydsdorp
Selati River
Olifants
Balule
Massingire Dam/-dam
Pietersburg
Alldays
Limpopo
Nuanetze
Singuédeze
Luvuhu
Mutale
Nwanedzi
Nzhelele
Mutamba
Sand
Brak
Shisha
Mphongolo
Phugwane
Bububu
Shingwedzi
Dzombo
Klein Letaba
Byashishi
Middel Letaba
Molotsi
Groot Letaba
Selati
Malips
N1
R523
R525
R522
R524
R578
R529
R530
R36
R81
R71
R40

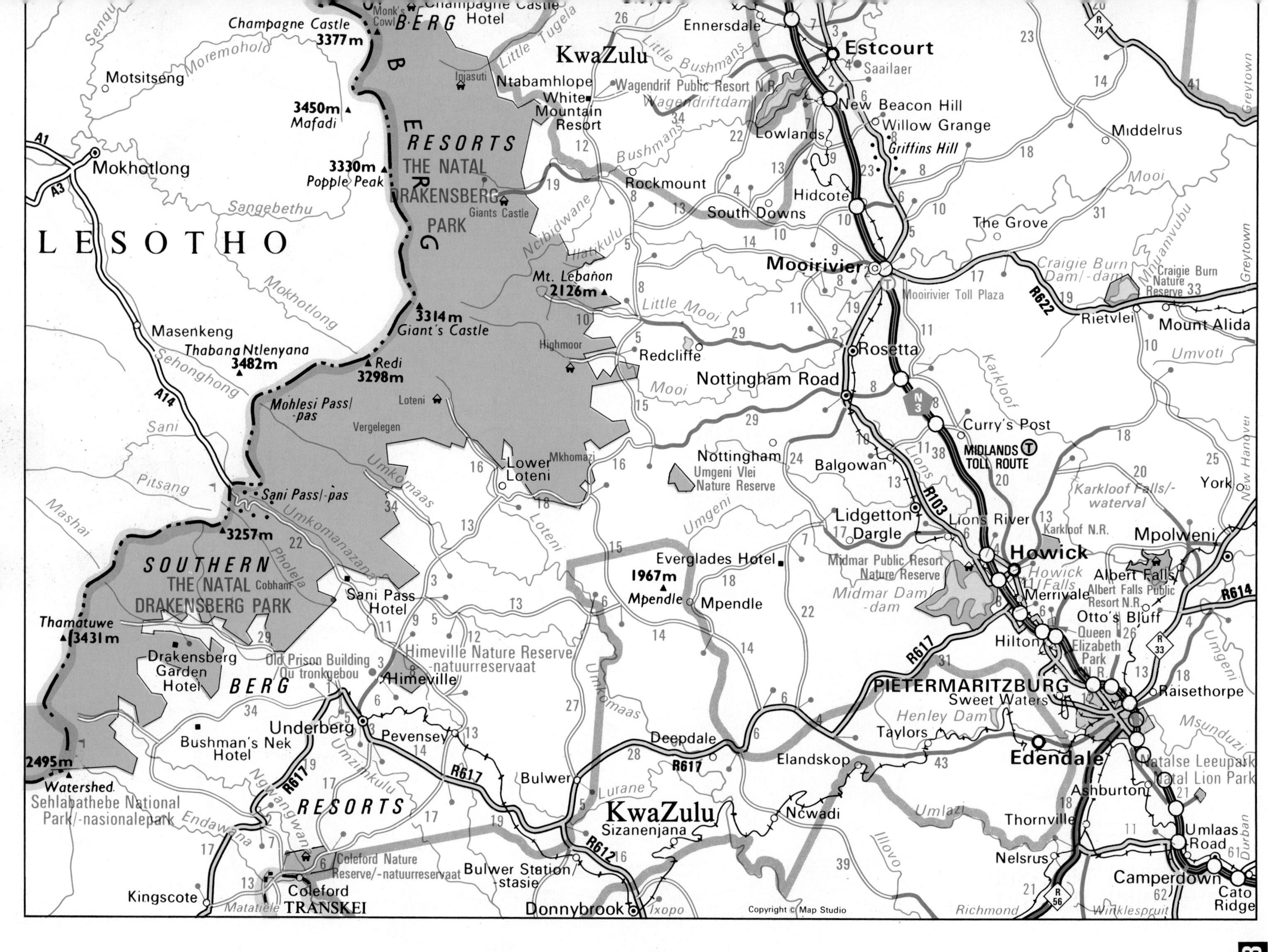
Champagne Castle 3377m
Monk's Cowl
BERG
Champagne Castle Hotel
KwaZulu
Ennersdale
Estcourt
Saailaer
Motsitseng
Moremoholo
Senqu
Little Tugela
Little Bushmans
Injasuti
Ntabamhlope
White Mountain Resort
Wagendrif Public Resort N.R.
Wagendriftdam
New Beacon Hill
Willow Grange
Griffins Hill
Middelrus
3450m Mafadi
3330m Popple Peak
RESORTS
THE NATAL DRAKENSBERG PARK
Giants Castle
Mokhotlong
A1
A3
Sangebethu
LESOTHO
Bushmans
Rockmount
Lowlands
Hidcote
South Downs
The Grove
Mooi
Mnuamvubu
Ncibidwane
Hlatikulu
Mooirivier
Mooirivier Toll Plaza
Craigie Burn Dam/-dam
Craigie Burn Nature Reserve
R622
Rietvlei
Mount Alida
Umvoti
Greytown
Mokhotlong
Mt. Lebanon 2126m
3314m Giant's Castle
Little Mooi
Masenkeng
Thabana Ntlenyana 3482m
Sehonghong
Highmoor
Redi 3298m
Redcliffe
Rosetta
Nottingham Road
N3
Karkloof
Curry's Post
MIDLANDS TOLL ROUTE
A14
Mohlesi Pass/-pas
Loteni
Vergelegen
Sani
Pitsang
Mashai
Sani Pass/-pas
Umkomaas
Mkhomazi
Lower Loteni
Nottingham
Umgeni Vlei Nature Reserve
Balgowan
Lions
R103
Karkloof Falls/-waterval
York
New Hanover
3257m
Umkomanazana
Pholela
Loteni
Umgeni
Lidgetton
Dargle
Lions River
Karkloof N.R.
Mpolweni
SOUTHERN
THE NATAL DRAKENSBERG PARK
Cobham
Sani Pass Hotel
Everglades Hotel
1967m Mpendle
Mpendle
Midmar Public Resort Nature Reserve
Midmar Dam/-dam
Howick
Howick Falls
Albert Falls
Albert Falls Public Resort N.R.
Merrivale
Otto's Bluff
R614
Thamatuwe 3431m
Drakensberg Garden Hotel
Old Prison Building/Ou tronkgebou
Himeville Nature Reserve/-natuurreservaat
Himeville
Hilton
Queen Elizabeth Park N.R.
R33
Umgeni
R617
PIETERMARITZBURG
Sweet Waters
Raisethorpe
BERG
Underberg
Pevensey
Bushman's Nek Hotel
Umzimkulu
Henley Dam
Taylors
Deepdale
Elandskop
Edendale
Msunduzi
2495m Watershed
Sehlabathebe National Park/-nasionalepark
Endawana
Ngwangwana
RESORTS
Bulwer
Lurane
KwaZulu
Sizanenjana
Ncwadi
Umlazi
Illovo
Natalse Leeupark
Natal Lion Park
Ashburton
Thornville
Umlaas Road
Durban
Coleford Nature Reserve/-natuurreservaat
Bulwer Station/-stasie
R612
Nelsrus
Camperdown
Cato Ridge
Kingscote
Coleford
Matatiele
TRANSKEI
Donnybrook
Ixopo
Copyright © Map Studio
Richmond
R56
Winklespruit
R74

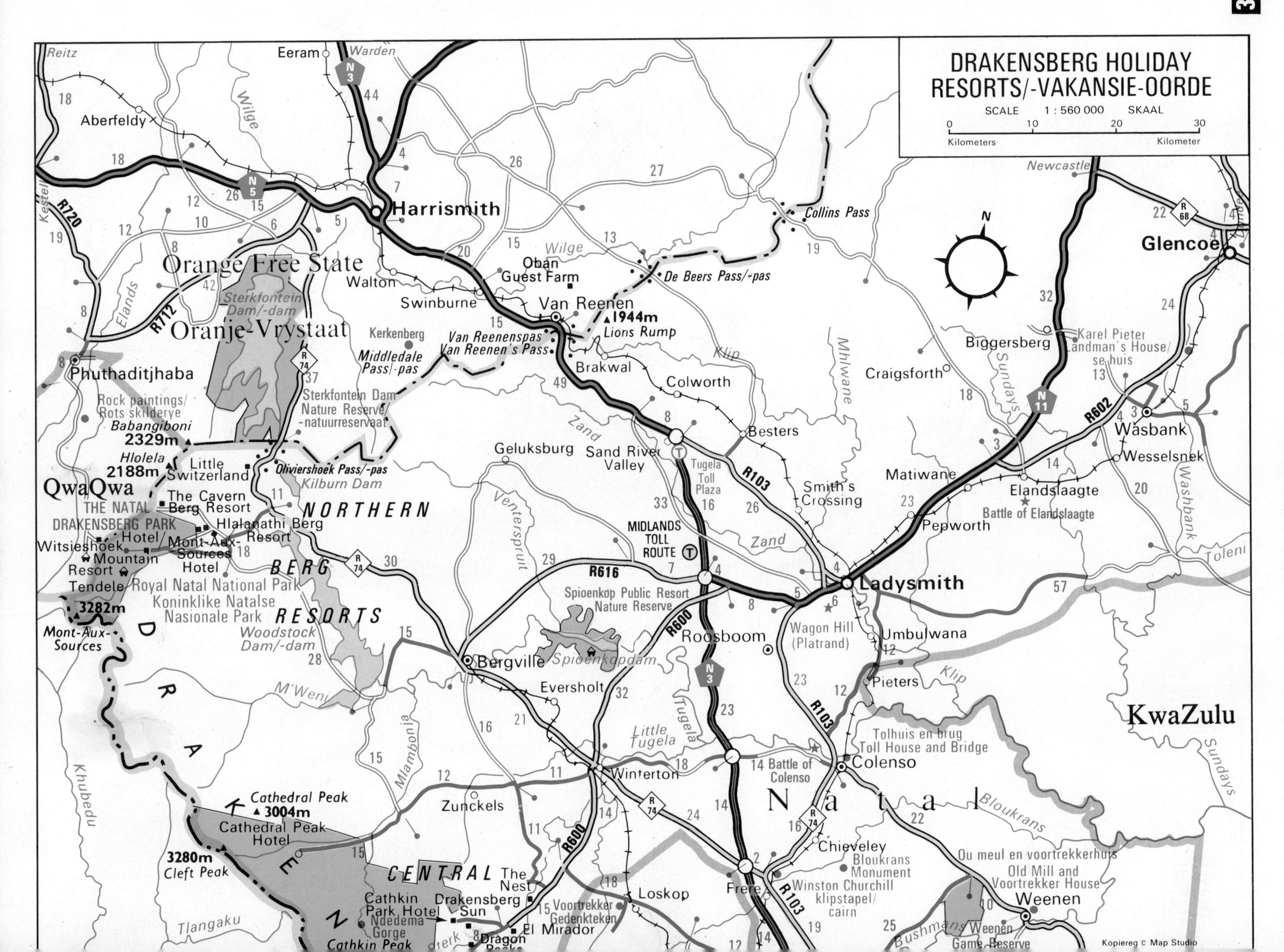

DRAKENSBERG HOLIDAY
RESORTS/-VAKANSIE-OORDE

SCALE 1 : 560 000 SKAAL

Kilometers

0 10 20 30

Kilometer

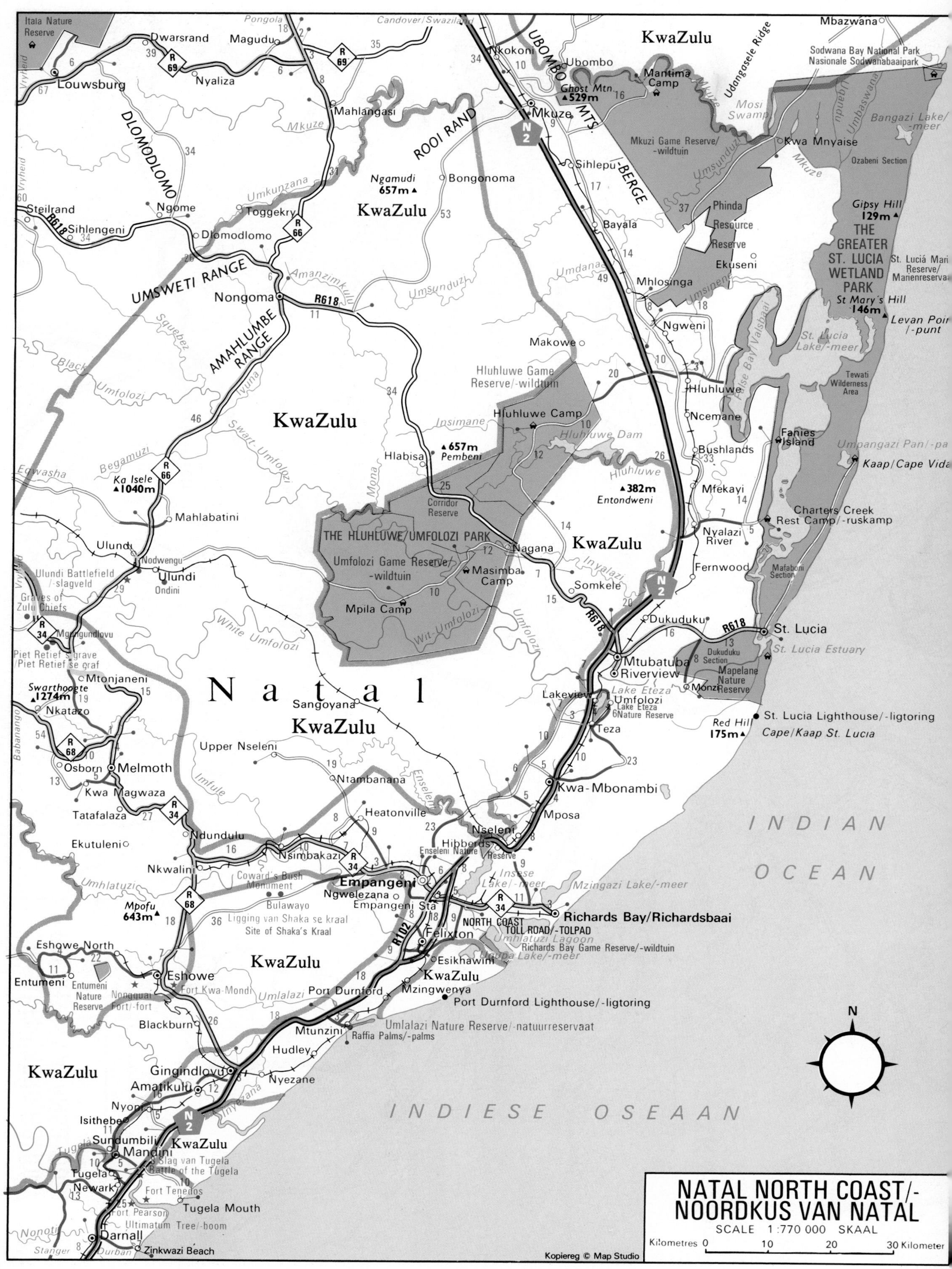

NATAL NORTH COAST/-
NOORDKUS VAN NATAL
SCALE 1:770 000 SKAAL
Kilometres 0   10   20   30 Kilometer

40

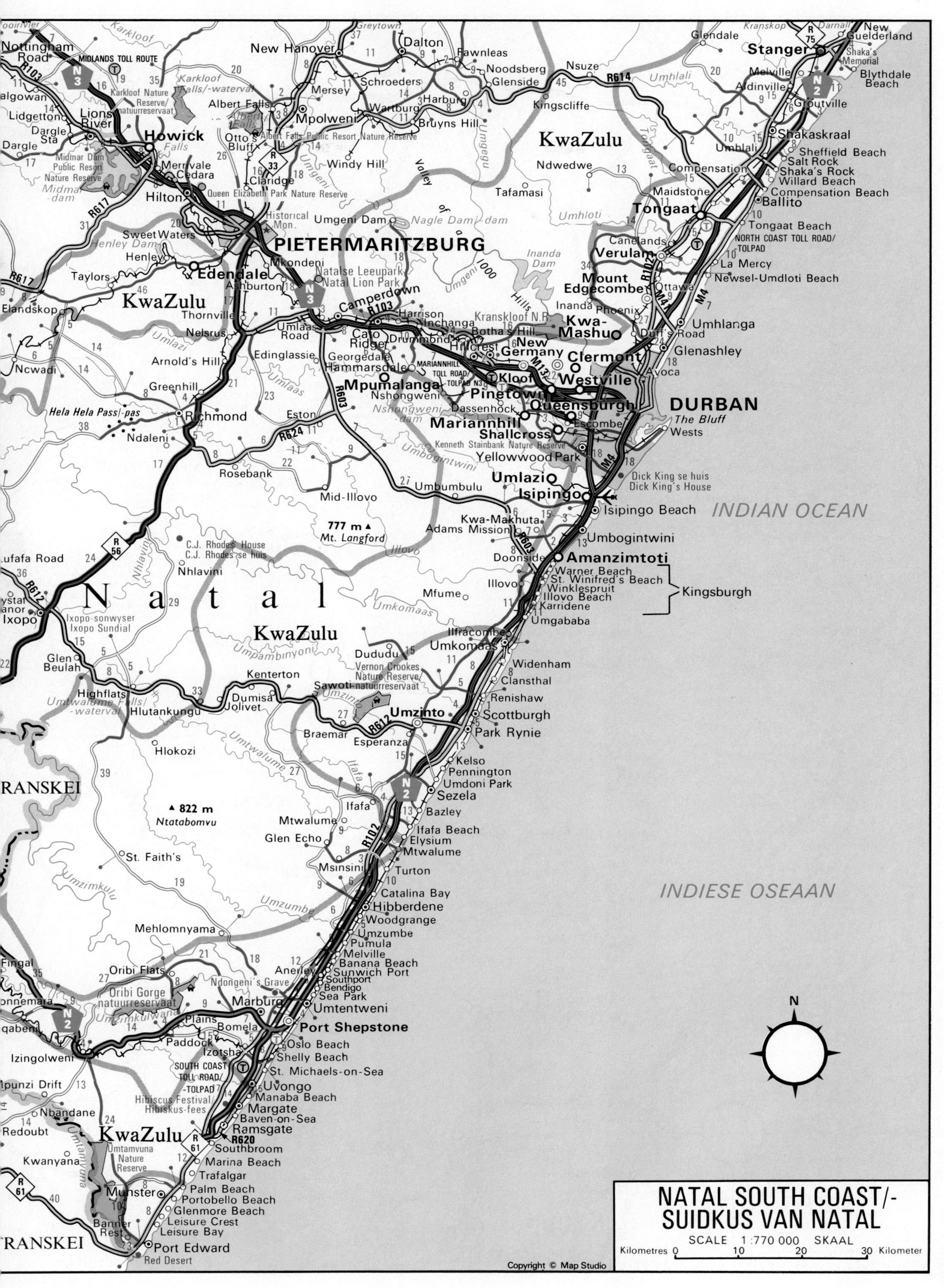

NATAL SOUTH COAST/-
SUIDKUS VAN NATAL

SCALE 1:770 000 SKAAL

Kilometres 0   10   20   30 Kilometer

Copyright © Map Studio

41

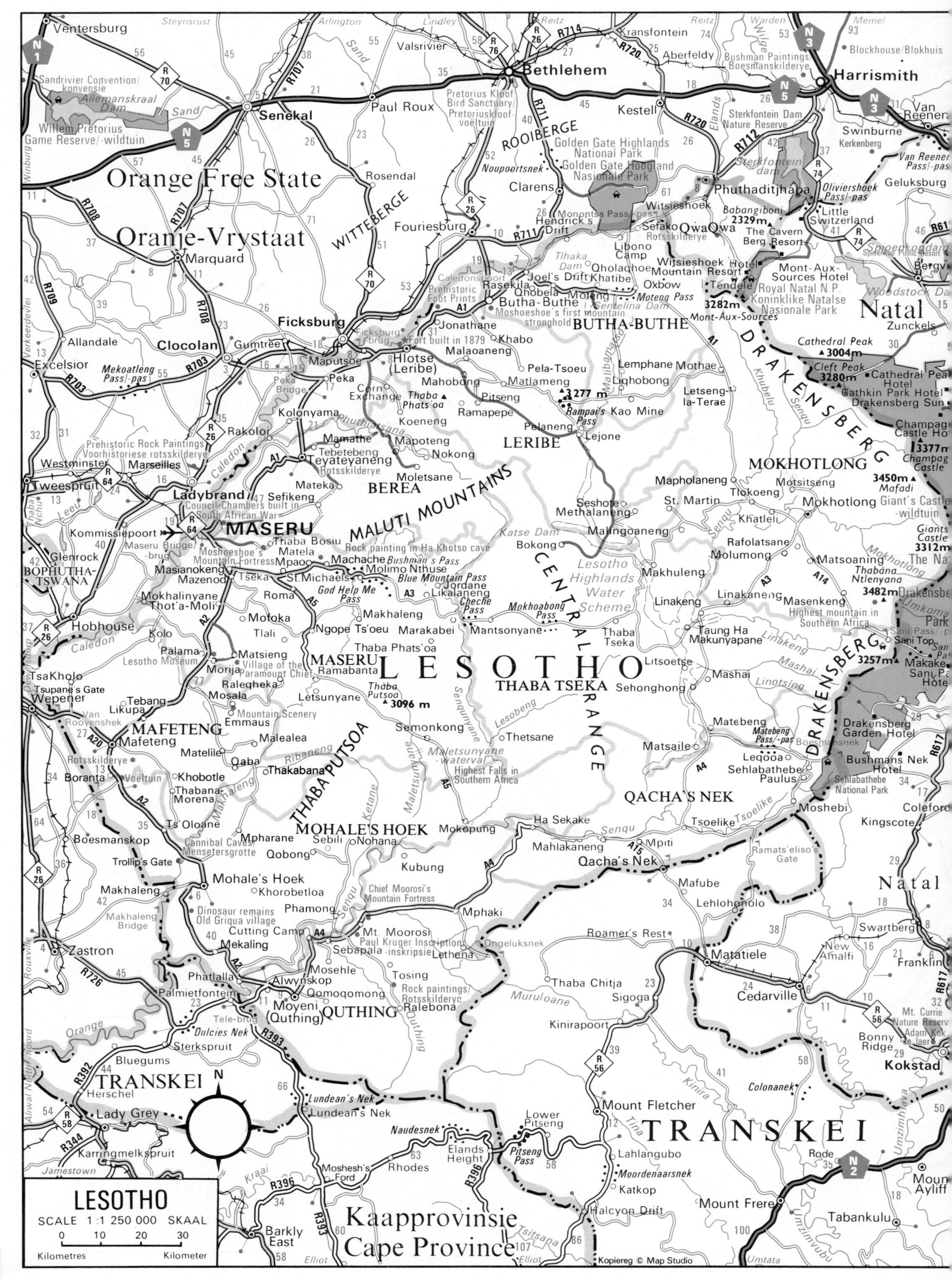

LESOTHO
SCALE 1:1 250 000 SKAAL
0 10 20 30
Kilometres Kilometer
Kopiereg © Map Studio
Orange Free State
Oranje-Vrystaat
Natal
TRANSKEI
Kaapprovinsie
Cape Province
BOPHUTHA-TSWANA
QwaQwa
L E S O T H O
MALUTI MOUNTAINS
CENTRAL RANGE
DRAKENSBERG
THABA PUTSOA
WITTEBERGE
ROOIBERGE
MASERU
BUTHA-BUTHE
LERIBE
BEREA
MAFETENG
MOHALE'S HOEK
QUTHING
QACHA'S NEK
THABA TSEKA
MOKHOTLONG
Ventersburg
Bethlehem
Harrismith
Senekal
Paul Roux
Kestell
Clarens
Fouriesburg
Rosendal
Marquard
Ficksburg
Clocolan
Excelsior
Allandale
Ladybrand
Tweespruit
Westminster
Marseilles
Hobhouse
Wepener
Zastron
Sterkspruit
Lady Grey
Herschel
Barkly East
Rhodes
Matatiele
Cedarville
Kokstad
Mount Fletcher
Mount Frere
Phuthaditjhaba
Maputsoe
Hlotse (Leribe)
Teyateyaneng
Mokhotlong
Mafeteng
Mohale's Hoek
Moyeni (Quthing)
Qacha's Nek
Semonkong
Thaba Tseka
Katse Dam
Lesotho Highlands Water Scheme
Golden Gate Highlands National Park
Royal Natal N.P.
Sehlabathebe National Park
Sani Pass
Thabana Ntlenyana 3482m
Highest mountain in Southern Africa
Maletsunyane waterval
Highest Falls in Southern Africa
Mount-Aux-Sources 3282m
Cathedral Peak 3004m
Giants Castle 3312m
Thaba Putsoa 3096 m

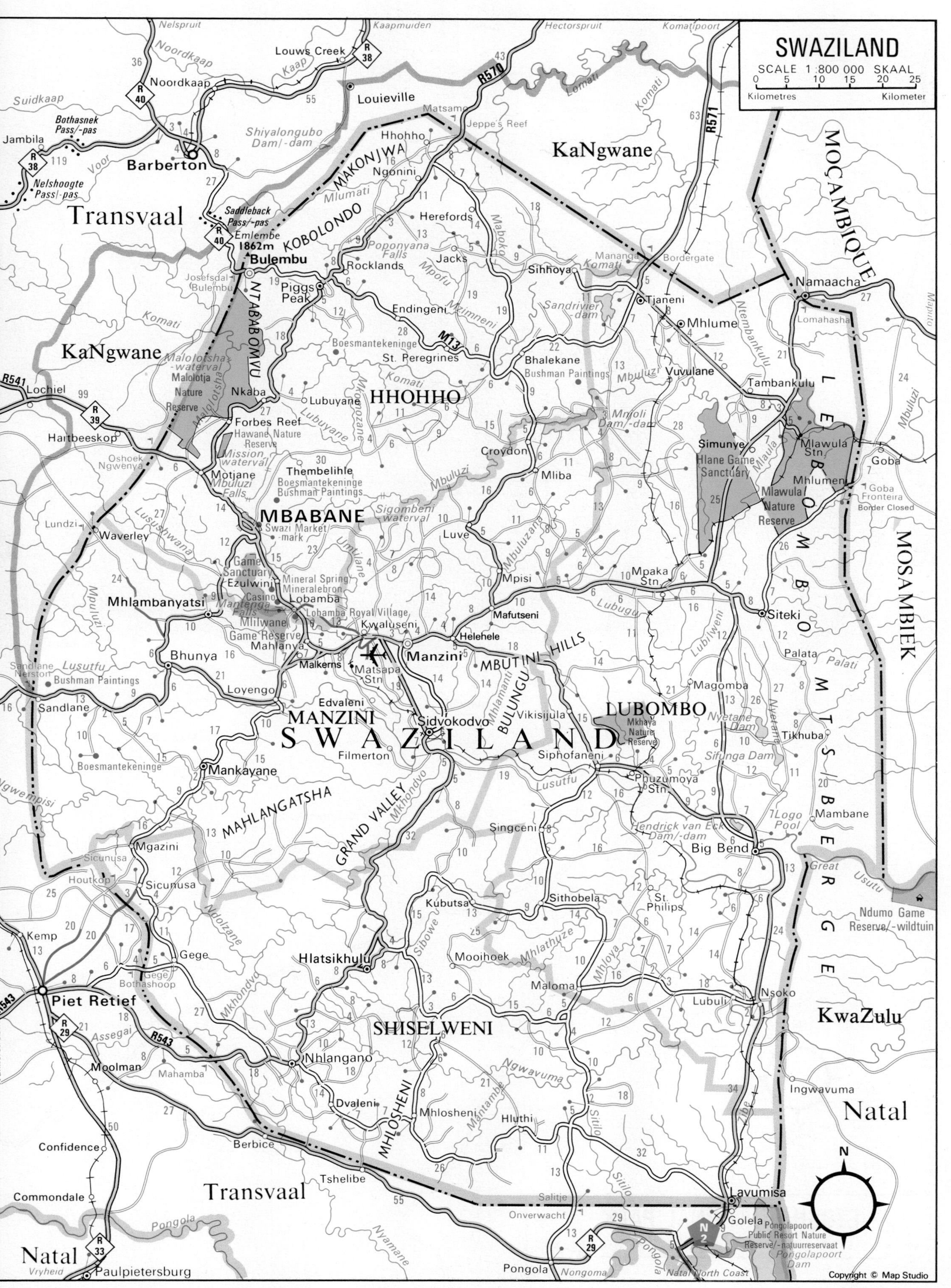

SWAZILAND

SCALE 1 : 800 000 SKAAL

0   5   10   15   20   25
Kilometres   Kilometer

43

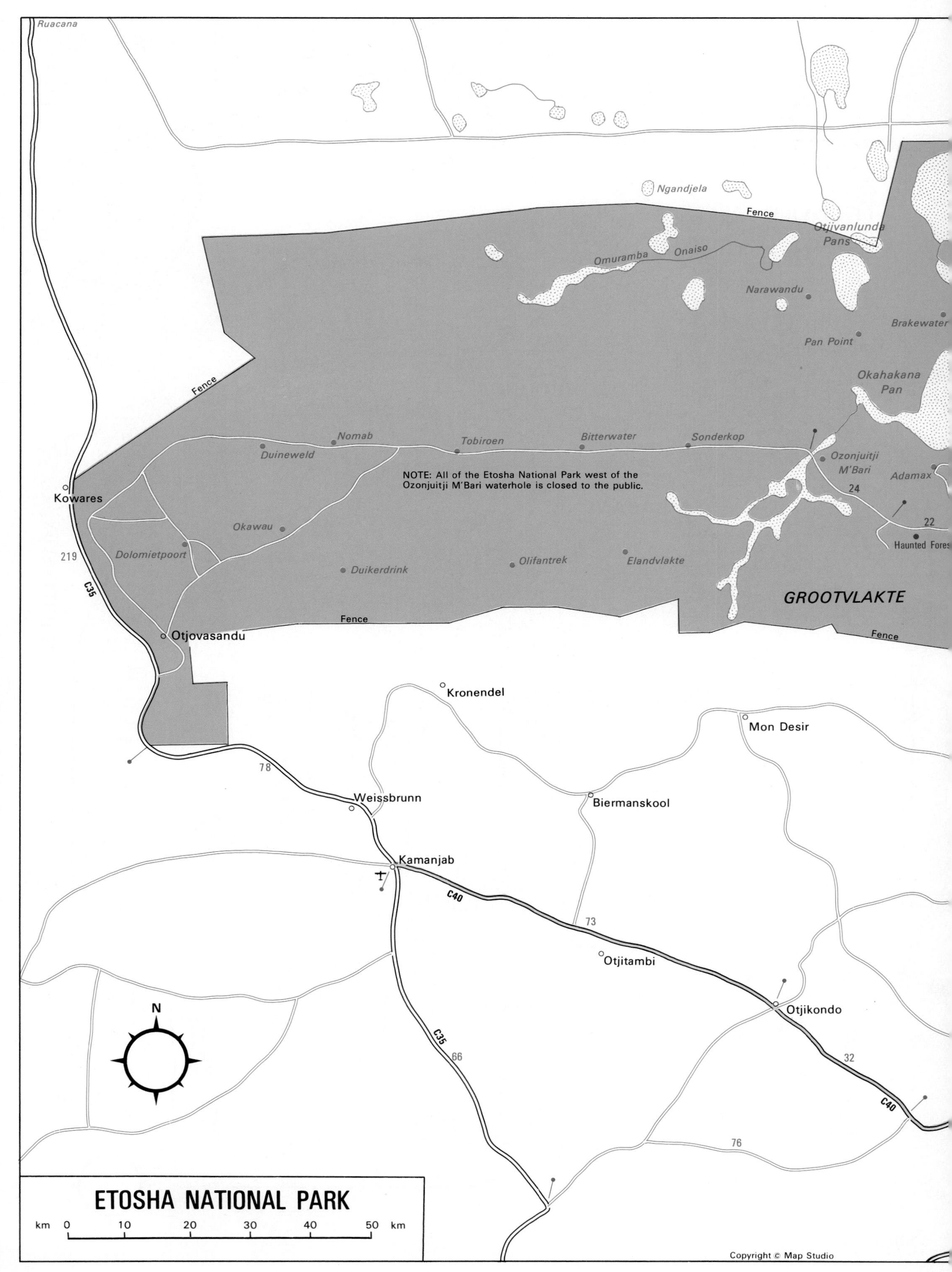

Ruacana

Ngandjela

Fence

Otjivanlunda
Pans

Omuramba Onaiso

Narawandu

Brakewater

Pan Point

Fence

Okahakana
Pan

Duineweld   Nomab   Tobiroen   Bitterwater   Sonderkop

Ozonjuitji
M'Bari

Kowares

NOTE: All of the Etosha National Park west of the
Ozonjuitji M'Bari waterhole is closed to the public.

24

Adamax

219

Okawau

22

C35

Dolomietpoort

Duikerdrink   Olifantrek   Elandvlakte

Haunted Fores

GROOTVLAKTE

Fence

Otjovasandu

Fence

Fence

Kronendel

Mon Desir

78

Weissbrunn

Biermanskool

Kamanjab

C40

73

C35

Otjitambi

Otjikondo

66

32

N

C40

76

ETOSHA NATIONAL PARK

km 0   10   20   30   40   50 km

44

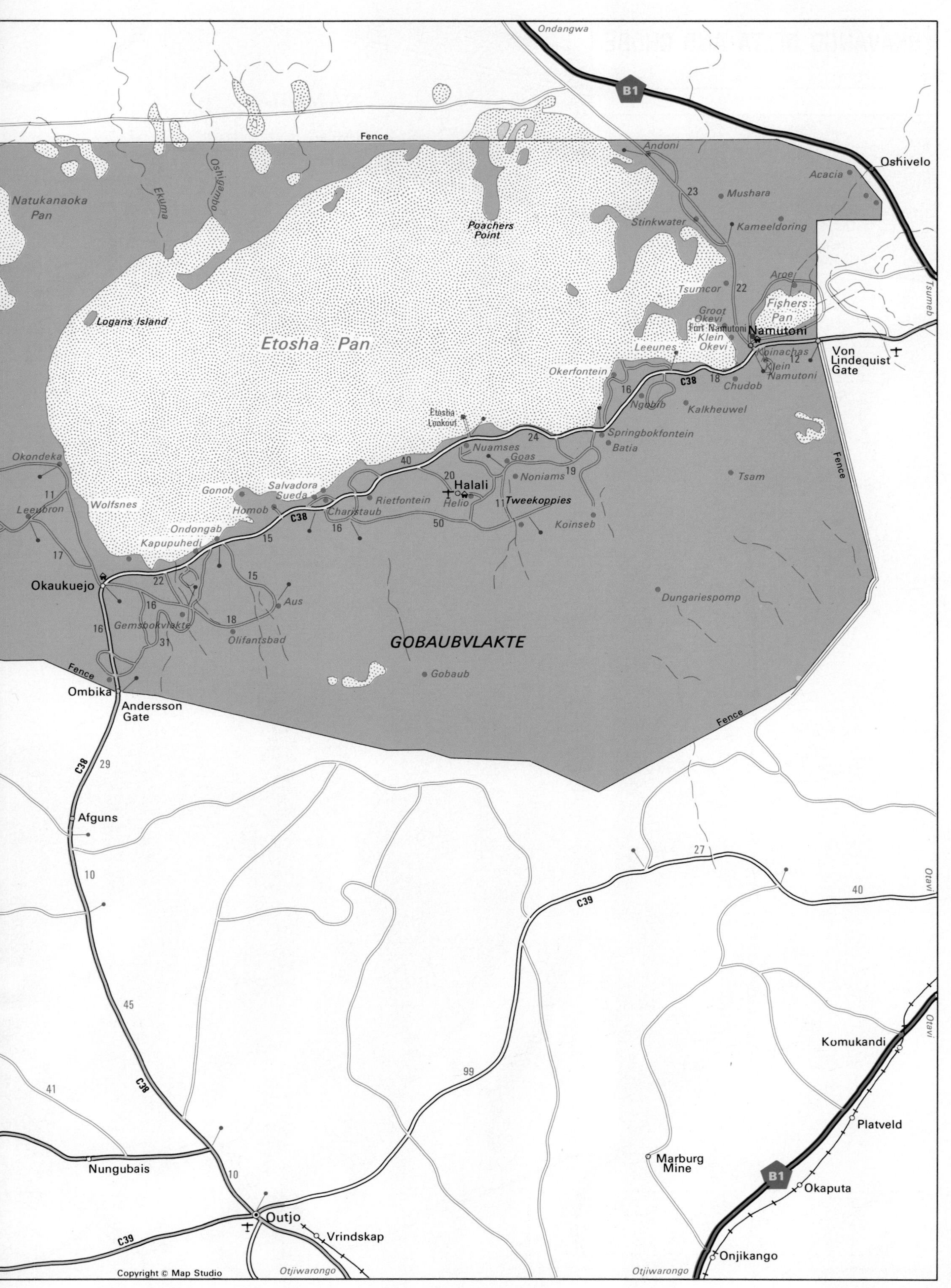

Ondangwa

B1

Oshivelo

Andoni
Acacia

Natukanaoka
Pan

Ekuma

Oshigambo

23   Mushara

Stinkwater   Kameeldoring

Poachers
Point

Tsumeb

Aroe
22   Fishers
Tsumcor   Pan

Groot
Okevi   Fort Namutoni   **Namutoni**
Logans Island   Klein
Okevi
Leeunes   Koinachas   Von
Lindequist
Etosha   Pan   Okerfontein   12   Klein   Gate
C38   Namutoni
18   Chudob
16   Ngobib   Kalkheuwel

Okondeka   Etosha
Lookouf   24   Springbokfontein   Batia
Fence
40   Nuamses   Goas   Tsam
11   Salvadora   Rietfontein   20   Noniams   19
Leeubron   Wolfsnes   Gonob   Sueda   Halali
Homob   Helio   11
C38   Charitstaub   50   Tweekoppies   Koinseb
Ondongab   15   16
17   Kapupuhedi
15
22   Aus   Dungariespomp
Okaukuejo   16
18
16   Gemsbokvlakte   Olifantsbad   **GOBAUBVLAKTE**
31
Fence
Ombika   Gobaub
Andersson
Gate

C38   29

Afguns

10   27
C39   40

Otavi
45
Komukandi   Otavi

41   **C38**
99
Platveld

Nungubais   Marburg   **B1**
10   Mine   Okaputa
Outjo
C39   Vrindskap   Onjikango
Copyright © Map Studio   Otjiwarongo   Otjiwarongo   **45**

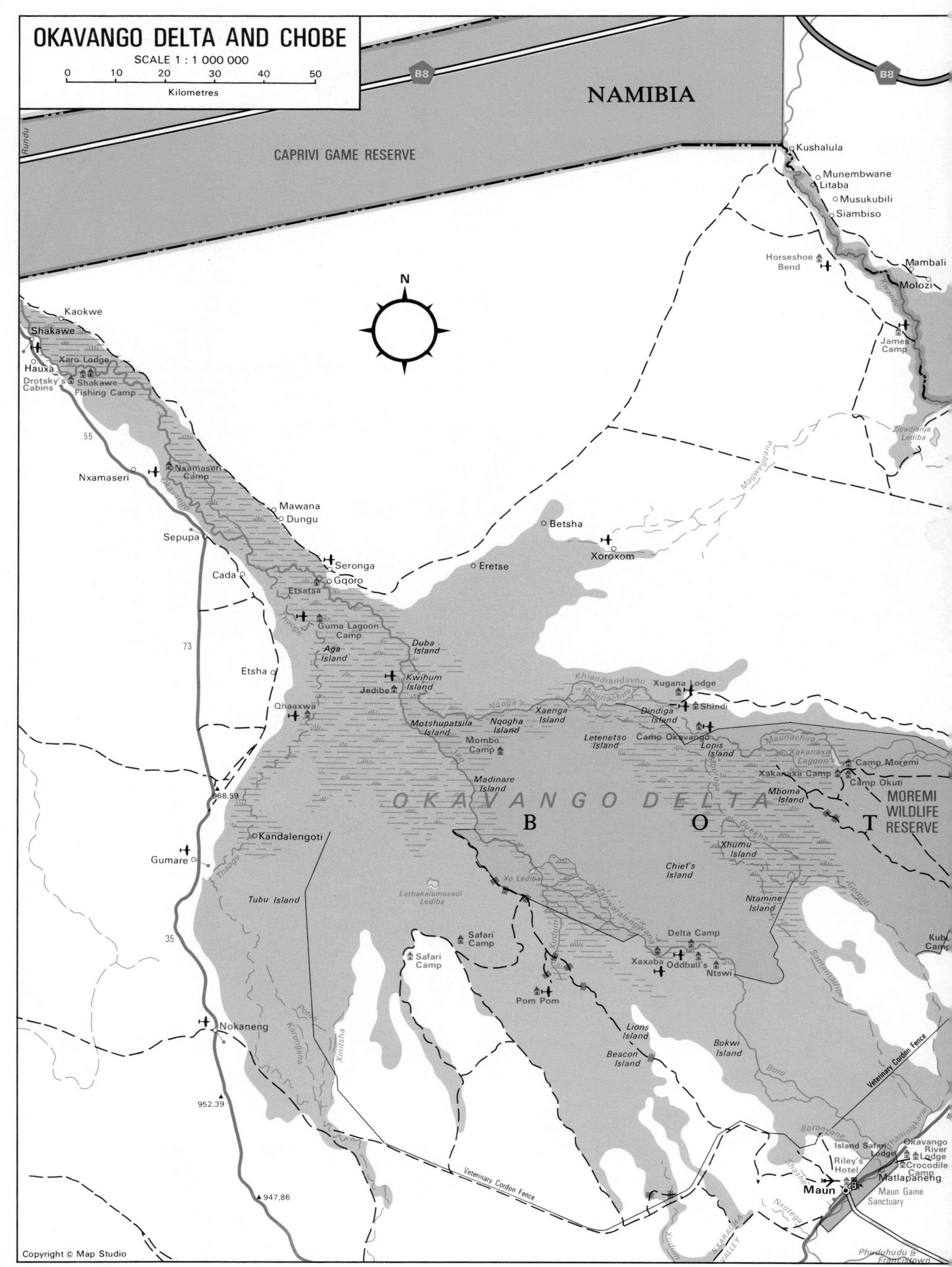

OKAVANGO DELTA AND CHOBE

SCALE 1 : 1 000 000

0   10   20   30   40   50
Kilometres

NAMIBIA

CAPRIVI GAME RESERVE

B8

N

Kushalula

Munembwane
Litaba
Musukubili
Siambiso

Horseshoe
Bend

Mambali
Molozi

James
Camp

Zibadianja
Lediba

Kaokwe
Shakawe
Xaro Lodge
Hauxa
Drotsky's
Cabins
Shakawe
Fishing Camp

55

Nxamaseri
Camp

Nxamaseri

Mawana
Dungu

Betsha

Xoroxom

Sepupa

Cada

Seronga
Gqoro
Etsatsa

Eretse

73

Guma Lagoon
Camp

Aga
Island

Duba
Island

Khiandiandvhu

Xugana Lodge
Shindi

Etsha

Kwihum
Island

Jedibe

Xaenga
Island

Dindiga
Island

Camp Okavango

Maunachira

Maunachira

Xakanaxa
Lagoon

Camp Moremi

Qhaaxwa

Ngoga

Ngogha
Island

Letenetso
Island

Lopis
Island

Camp Okuti

Motshupatsila
Island

Mombo
Camp

Xakanaxa Camp

Mboma
Island

MOREMI
WILDLIFE
RESERVE

968,59

O K A V A N G O   D E L T A

B   O   T

Madinare
Island

Xhumu
Island

Kandalengoti

Xo Lediba

Chief's
Island

Ntamine
Island

Kuba
Camp

Gumare

Tubu Island

Lethakalamasadi
Lediba

Delta Camp

35

Safari
Camp

Xaxaba   Oddball's
Ntswi

Safari
Camp

Pom Pom

Nokaneng

Lions
Island

Beacon
Island

Bokwi
Island

Veterinary Cordon Fence

952.39

Veterinary Cordon Fence

Island Safari
Lodge
Okavango
River
Lodge
Riley's
Hotel
Crocodile
Camp
Matlapaneng

Maun

Maun Game
Sanctuary

▲ 947,86

Phuduhudu &
Francistown

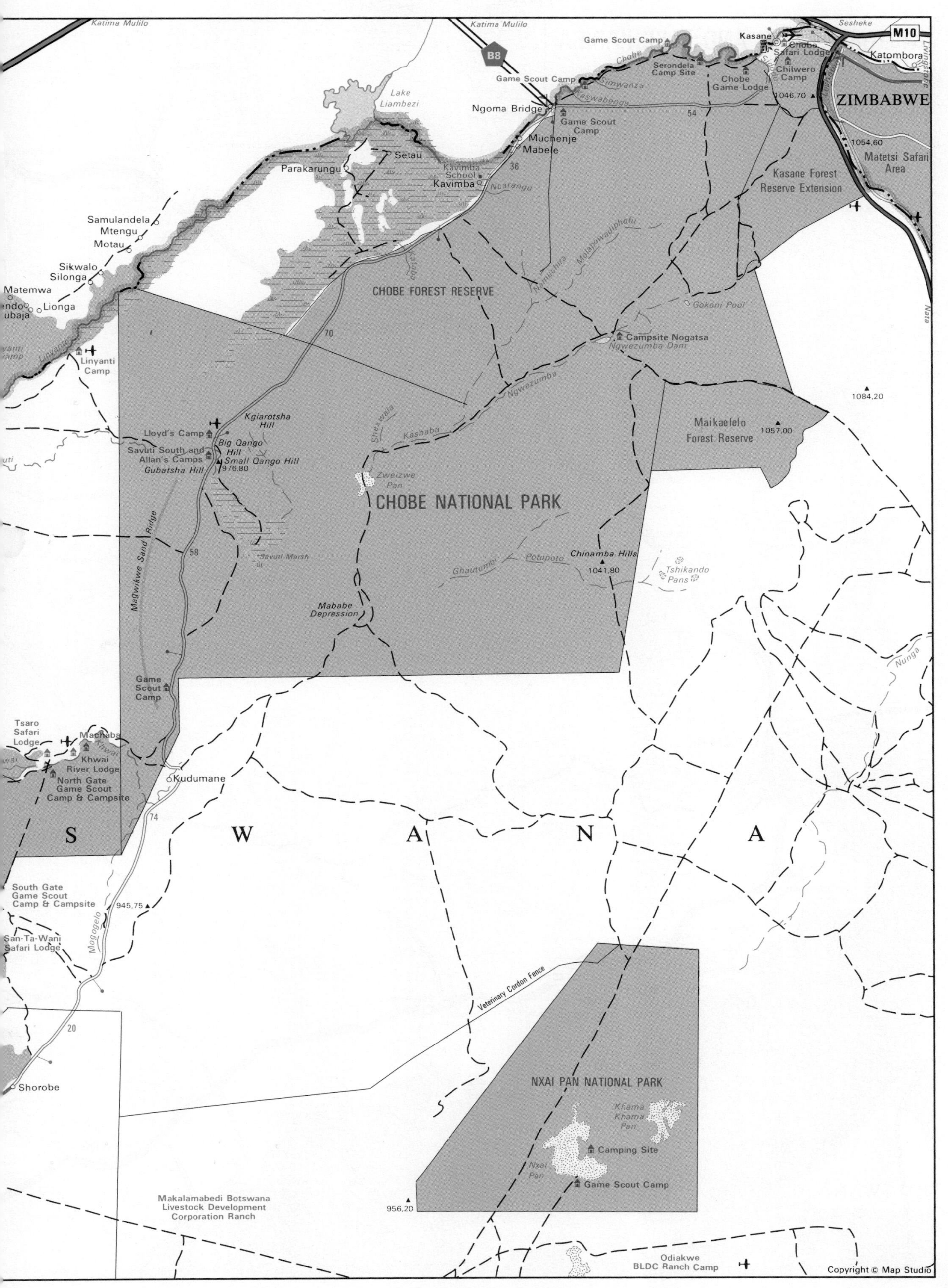

Katima Mulilo

Katima Mulilo

Seshake

B8

M10

Game Scout Camp

Kasane

Katombora

Game Scout Camp

Chobe

Serondela Camp Site

Chobe Safari Lodge

Chobe Game Lodge

Chilwero Camp

Lake Liambezi

Game Scout Camp

Simwanza

Kaswabenga

ZIMBABWE

Ngoma Bridge

1046.70

54

1054.60

Muchenje

Mabele

Matetsi Safari Area

Parakarungu

Setau

Kavimba School

36

Kavimba

Ncarangu

Kasane Forest Reserve Extension

Samulandela
Mtengu
Motau

Molapowadiphofu

Sikwalo
Silonga

CHOBE FOREST RESERVE

Namuchira

Matemwa

ndo
ubaja

Lionga

70

Gokoni Pool

Campsite Nogatsa

Ngwezumba Dam

1084.20

Linyanti

Linyanti
Camp

Ngwezumba

Maikaelelo
Forest Reserve

1057.00

Kgiarotsha
Hill

Lloyd's Camp

Sekwala

Kashaba

Savuti South and
Allan's Camps

Big Qango
Hill

Small Qango Hill

976.80

Zweizwe
Pan

Gubatsha Hill

CHOBE NATIONAL PARK

58

Magwikwe Sand Ridge

Savuti Marsh

Ghautumbi

Potopoto

Chinamba Hills

1041.80

Tshikando
Pans

Mababe
Depression

Nunga

Game
Scout
Camp

Tsaro
Safari
Lodge

Machaba

Khwai

Khwai
River Lodge

S   W   A   N   A

Kudumane

North Gate
Game Scout
Camp & Campsite

S

74

South Gate
Game Scout
Camp & Campsite

945.75

Mogogelo

San-Ta-Wani
Safari Lodge

20

Veterinary Cordon Fence

NXAI PAN NATIONAL PARK

Shorobe

Khama
Khama
Pan

Camping Site

Nxai
Pan

Game Scout Camp

Makalamabedi Botswana
Livestock Development
Corporation Ranch

956.20

Odiakwe
BLDC Ranch Camp

Copyright © Map Studio

47

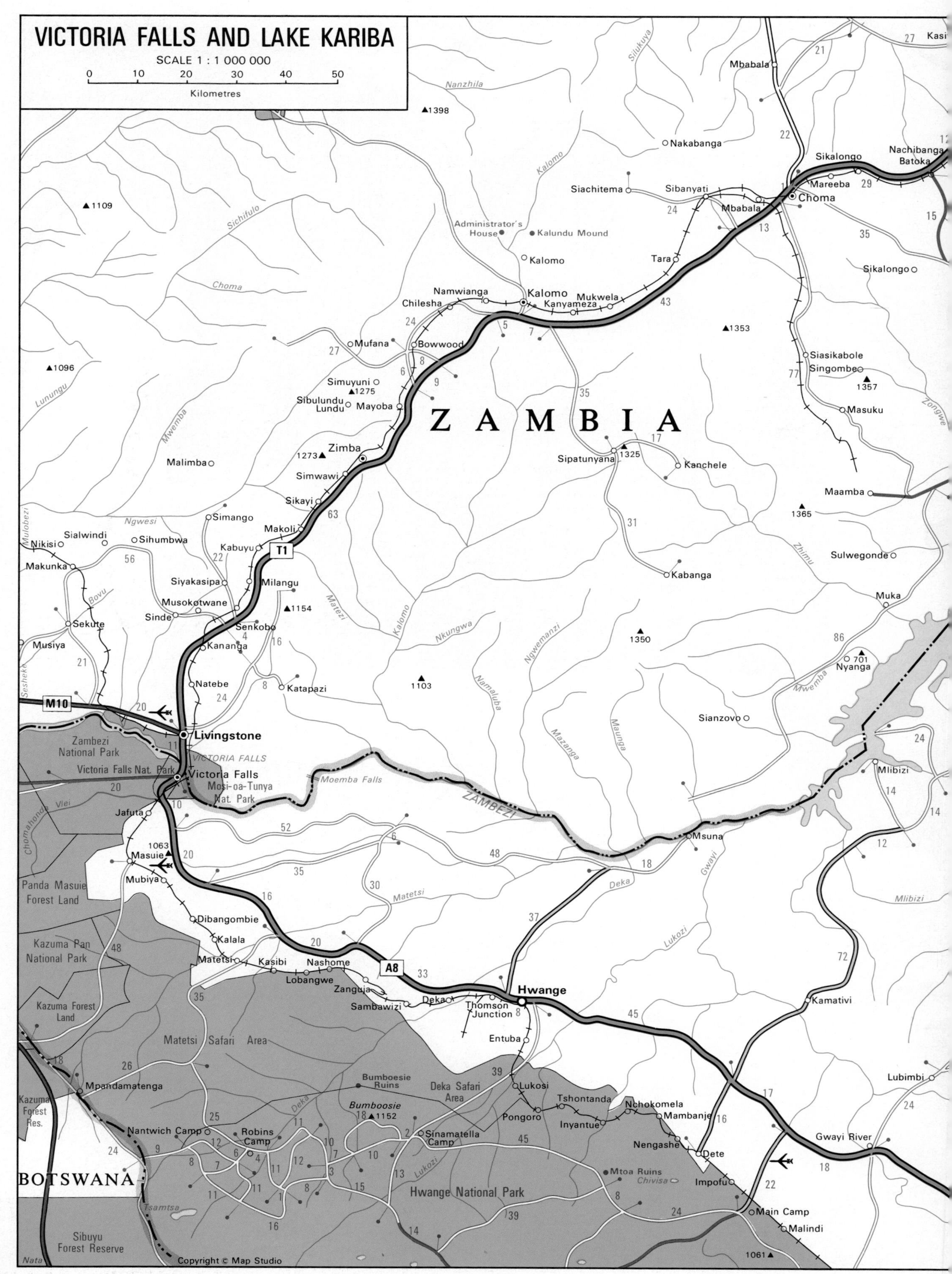

VICTORIA FALLS AND LAKE KARIBA

SCALE 1 : 1 000 000

0 10 20 30 40 50
Kilometres

ZAMBIA

BOTSWANA

48

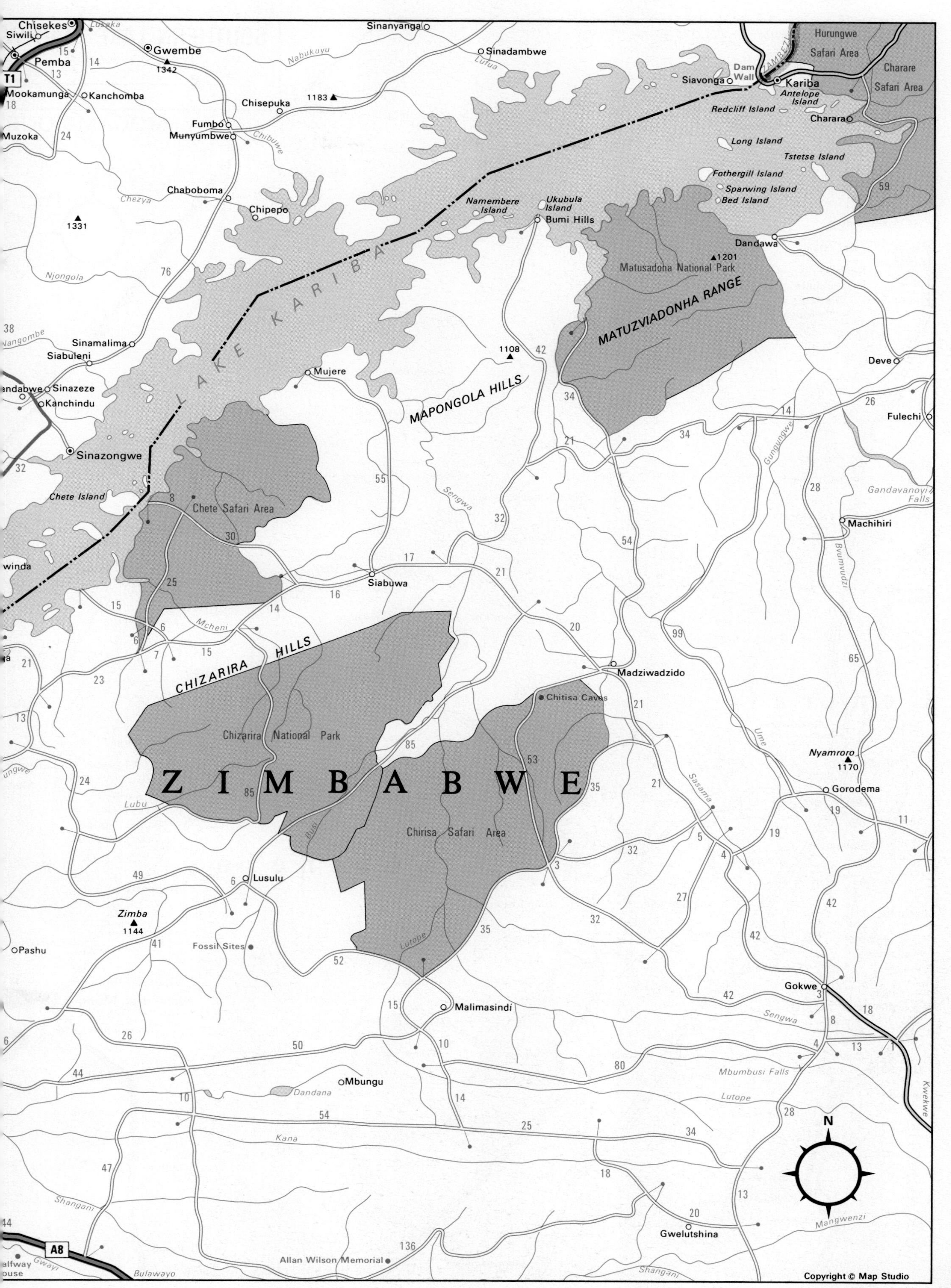

ZIMBABWE
LAKE KARIBA
Kariba
Siavonga
Dam Wall
Hurungwe Safari Area
Charare Safari Area
Antelope Island
Redcliff Island
Chararа
Long Island
Tstetse Island
Fothergill Island
Sparwing Island
Bed Island
Namembere Island
Ukubula Island
Bumi Hills
Dandawa
Matusadona National Park
MATUZVIADONHA RANGE
Deve
Fulechi
MAPONGOLA HILLS
Mujere
Sinanyanga
Sinadambwe
Chisekes
Siwili
Gwembe
Pemba
Mookamunga
Kanchomba
Chisepuka
Fumbo
Munyumbwe
Muzoka
Chaboboma
Chipepo
Sinamalima
Siabuleni
Sinazeze
Kanchindu
Sinazongwe
Chete Island
Chete Safari Area
Siabuwa
CHIZARIRA HILLS
Chizarira National Park
Chirisa Safari Area
Madziwadzido
Chitisa Caves
Machihiri
Nyamroro
Gorodema
Lusulu
Zimba
Pashu
Fossil Sites
Malimasindi
Gokwe
Mbungu
Gwelutshina
Allan Wilson Memorial
Mbumbusi Falls
Gandavanoyi Falls
Copyright © Map Studio

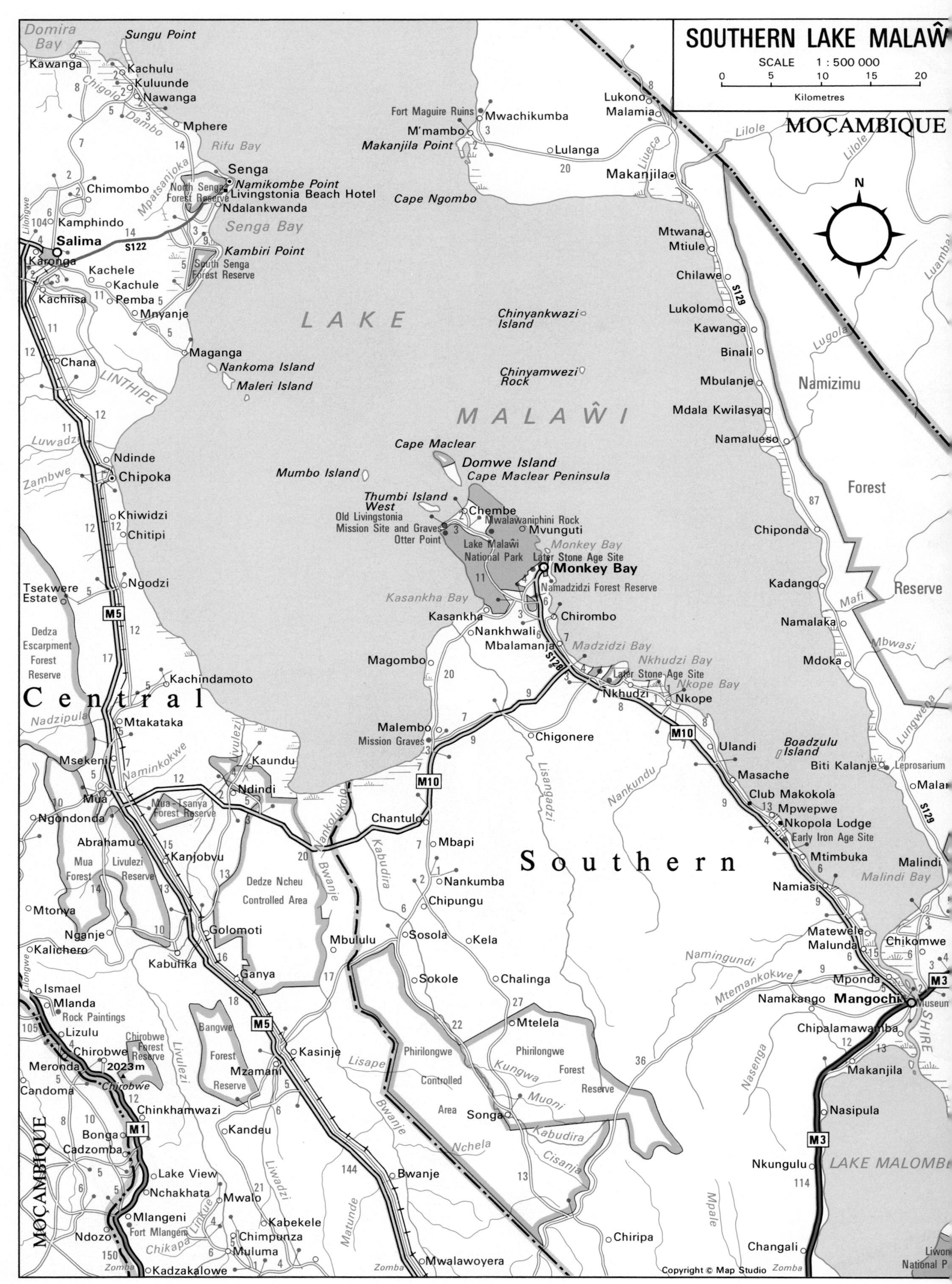
SOUTHERN LAKE MALAŴI
SCALE 1 : 500 000
0 5 10 15 20
Kilometres
MOÇAMBIQUE
N
LAKE MALAŴI
Central
Southern
Salima
Monkey Bay
Mangochi
Senga
Senga Bay
Kambiri Point
Namikombe Point
Livingstonia Beach Hotel
Sungu Point
Domira Bay
Rifu Bay
Cape Ngombo
Makanjila Point
Fort Maguire Ruins
Mwachikumba
Lulanga
Makanjila
Lukono
Malamia
Chinyankwazi Island
Chinyamwezi Rock
Nankoma Island
Maleri Island
Cape Maclear
Domwe Island
Cape Maclear Peninsula
Mumbo Island
Thumbi Island West
Old Livingstonia Mission Site and Graves
Otter Point
Chembe
Mwalawaniphini Rock
Mvunguti
Lake Malaŵi National Park
Monkey Bay
Later Stone Age Site
Namadzidzi Forest Reserve
Kasankha Bay
Kasankha
Chirombo
Nankhwali
Mbalamanja
Madzidzi Bay
Nkhudzi Bay
Nkhudzi
Nkope
Nkope Bay
Chigonere
Ulandi
Boadzulu Island
Biti Kalanje
Leprosarium
Masache
Club Makokola
Mpwepwe
Nkopola Lodge
Early Iron Age Site
Mtimbuka
Malindi
Malindi Bay
Namiasi
Matewele
Malunda
Chikomwe
Mponda
Namakango
Museum
Chipalamawamba
Makanjila
Nasipula
Nkungulu
LAKE MALOMBE
Changali
Chiripa
Magombo
Malembo
Mission Graves
Chantulo
Mbapi
Nankumba
Chipungu
Sosola
Kela
Mbululu
Sokole
Chalinga
Mtelela
Phirilongwe Forest Reserve
Phirilongwe Controlled Area
Songa
Bwanje
Mwalawoyera
Mtwana
Mtiule
Chilawe
Lukolomo
Kawanga
Binali
Mbulanje
Mdala Kwilasya
Namalueso
Chiponda
Kadango
Namalaka
Mdoka
Namizimu Forest Reserve
Kawanga
Kachulu
Kuluunde
Nawanga
Mphere
Chimombo
Kamphindo
North Senga Forest Reserve
Ndalankwanda
South Senga Forest Reserve
Karonga
Kachele
Kachule
Kachiisa
Pemba
Mnyanje
Maganga
Chana
LINTHIPE
Luwadzi
Zambwe
Ndinde
Chipoka
Khiwidzi
Chitipi
Ngodzi
Tsekwere Estate
Dedza Escarpment Forest Reserve
Kachindamoto
Nadzipula
Mtakataka
Msekeni
Naminkokwe
Kaundu
Ndindi
Mua
Mua-Tsanya Forest Reserve
Ngondonda
Abrahamu
Kanjobvu
Mua Livulezi Forest Reserve
Dedze Ncheu Controlled Area
Mtonya
Nganje
Golomoti
Kalichero
Kabulika
Ganya
Ismael
Mlanda
Rock Paintings
Lizulu
Chirobwe
Chirobwe Forest Reserve
2023m
Meronda
Candoma
Bangwe Forest Reserve
Mzamani
Kasinje
Chinkhamwazi
Kandeu
Bonga
Cadzomba
Lake View
Nchakhata
Mwalo
Mlangeni
Fort Mlangeni
Ndozo
Kabekele
Chimpunza
Muluma
Kadzakalowe
Zomba
M1
M3
M5
M10
S122
S128
S129
Lilole
Liueca
Lugola
Mafi
Mbwasi
Lungwena
Namingundi
Mtemankokwe
Nasenga
Mpale
Lisangadzi
Nankundu
Kabudira
Nankulukolo
Bwanje
Livulezi
Lisape
Kungwa
Muoni
Nchela
Cisanja
Liwadzi
Matunde
Linkue
Chikapa
Chigolo Dambo
Mpatsanjoka
SHIRE
Liwonde National Park
Copyright © Map Studio

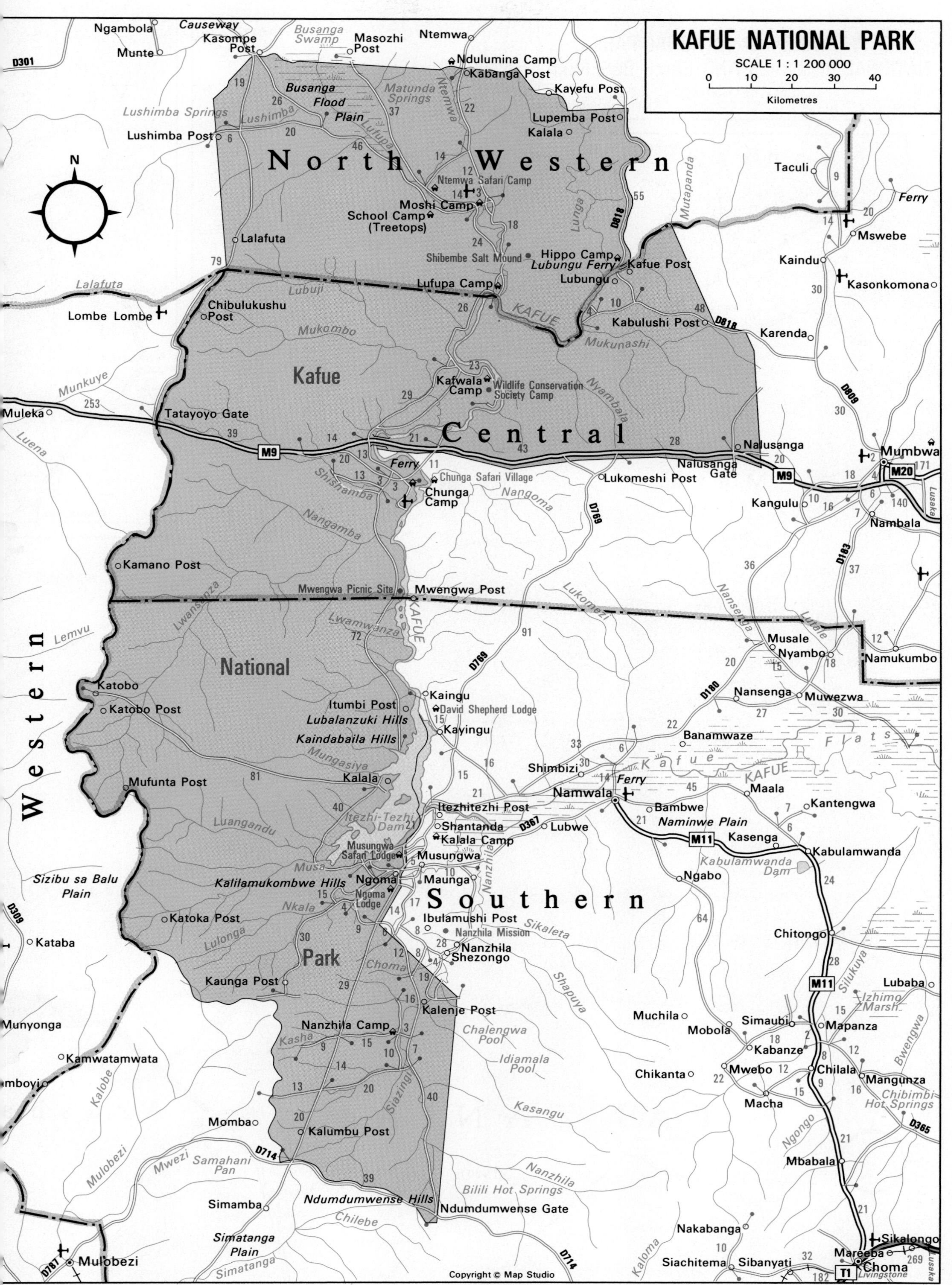

KAFUE NATIONAL PARK

SCALE 1 : 1 200 000

0 10 20 30 40

Kilometres

Copyright © Map Studio

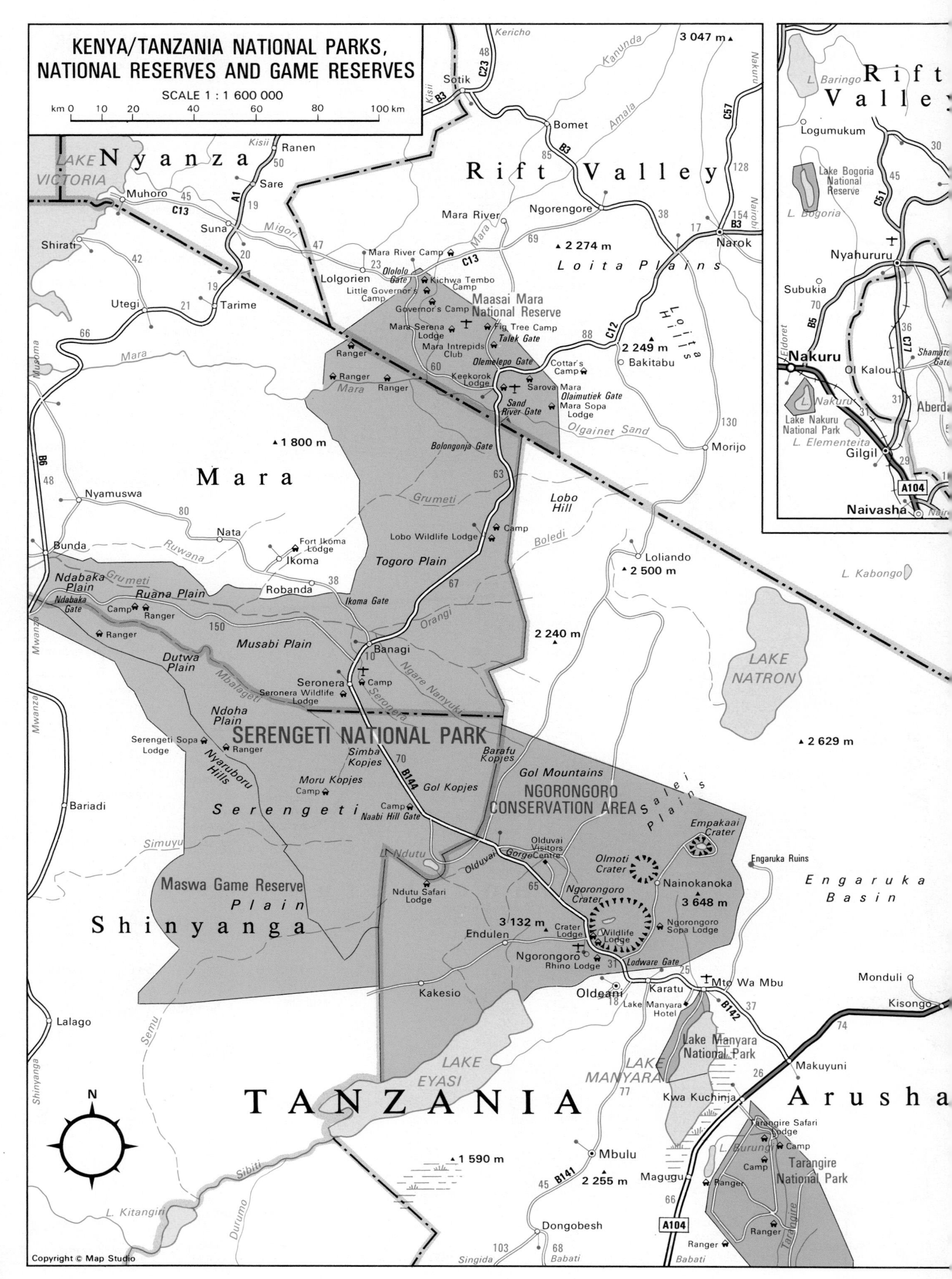

KENYA/TANZANIA NATIONAL PARKS, NATIONAL RESERVES AND GAME RESERVES

SCALE 1 : 1 600 000

km 0   10   20   40   60   80   100 km

Rift Valley

L. Baringo

Logumukum

Lake Bogoria
National Reserve

L. Bogoria

Nyahururu

Subukia

C51

Shamata Gate

Nakuru

Ol Kalou

Aberd

Lake Nakuru
National Park

L. Nakuru

L. Elementeita

Gilgil

A104

Naivasha

Kericho

Kanunda

3 047 m

Sotik   C23   48

Bomet   B3   85

Amala   C57

Nakuru   Nairobi

N y a n z a   Kisii   Ranen

LAKE
VICTORIA   Muhoro   45   A1   Sare   50

C13   Suna   19

Mara River   Ngorengore   38   17   B3   Narok   154

Shirati   42   20   Migori   47   Mara   69   **Loita Plains**

Utegi   21   19   Tarime   23   Mara River Camp   C13   88   C12   2 274 m

Lolgorien   Olololo   Kichwa Tembo   **L o i t a**

Little Governor's   Camp   **Maasai Mara**   2 249 m   Bakitabu   **H i l l s**

Mara   66   Governor's Camp   **National Reserve**

Mara Serena   Fig Tree Camp   Talek Gate

Lodge   Mara Intrepids

Club   Olemelepo Gate   Cottar's

B6   48   Ranger   60   Keekorok   Camp

Nyamuswa   Ranger   Lodge   Sarova Mara   Olaimutiek Gate

M a r a   Ranger   Sand   Mara Sopa   130   Morijo

1 800 m   River Gate   Lodge   Olgainet Sand

80   Mara   63   **Lobo**

Ruwana   Bolongonja Gate   **Hill**

Nata   Grumeti   Boledi

Fort Ikoma   Lobo Wildlife Lodge   Camp   2 500 m

Bunda   Lodge   Loliando   L. Kabongo

Ikoma   38   **Togoro Plain**

Ndabaka   Grumeti   Robanda   Ikoma Gate   67

Plain   **Ruana Plain**   Orangi

Ndabaka   Camp   Ranger   150   Banagi   10   2 240 m   **LAKE**

Gate   **Musabi Plain**   Ngare Nanyuki   **NATRON**

Ranger   Seronera   Camp   2 629 m

Dutwa   Seronera Wildlife   Seronera

Plain   Lodge

Mbalageti   **Ndoha**   Camp   **SERENGETI NATIONAL PARK**   Barafu

Serengeti Sopa   **Plain**   Simba   Kopjes

Lodge   Ranger   Kopjes   70   **Gol Mountains**   Empakaai

Nyaruboru   Moru Kopjes   B144   Gol Kopjes   **NGORONGORO**   Crater

Hills   Camp   **CONSERVATION AREA**   Salei

S e r e n g e t i   Camp   Olduvai   Plains

Simuyu   Naabi Hill Gate   Visitors   Engaruka Ruins

L. Ndutu   Centre   Olmoti

Olduvai   Crater   Nainokanoka   **E n g a r u k a**

Maswa Game Reserve   Gorge   65   Ngorongoro   **B a s i n**

Bariadi   **P l a i n**   Ndutu Safari   Crater   3 648 m

Lodge   Ngorongoro Sopa Lodge

S h i n y a n g a   3 132 m   Crater   Wildlife

Endulen   Lodge   Lodge   Monduli

Ngorongoro   Lodware Gate   25

Rhino Lodge   31   Kisongo

Kakesio   18   Lake Manyara   Makuyuni

Oldeani   Karatu   Hotel   B142   37

Mto Wa Mbu   74

Lalago   **LAKE**   **LAKE**   **Lake Manyara**

EYASI   **MANYARA**   **National Park**

Semu   Kwa Kuchinja   **A r u s h a**

T A N Z A N I A   77

Shinyanga   Tarangire Safari

L. Burungi   Lodge   Camp

N   1 590 m   Mbulu   **Tarangire**

National Park

Sibiti   Magugu   Ranger

L. Kitangiri   45   B141   2 255 m

Durumo   2 255 m   66

103   68   Dongobesh   A104   Ranger

Singida   Babati   Babati   Tarangire

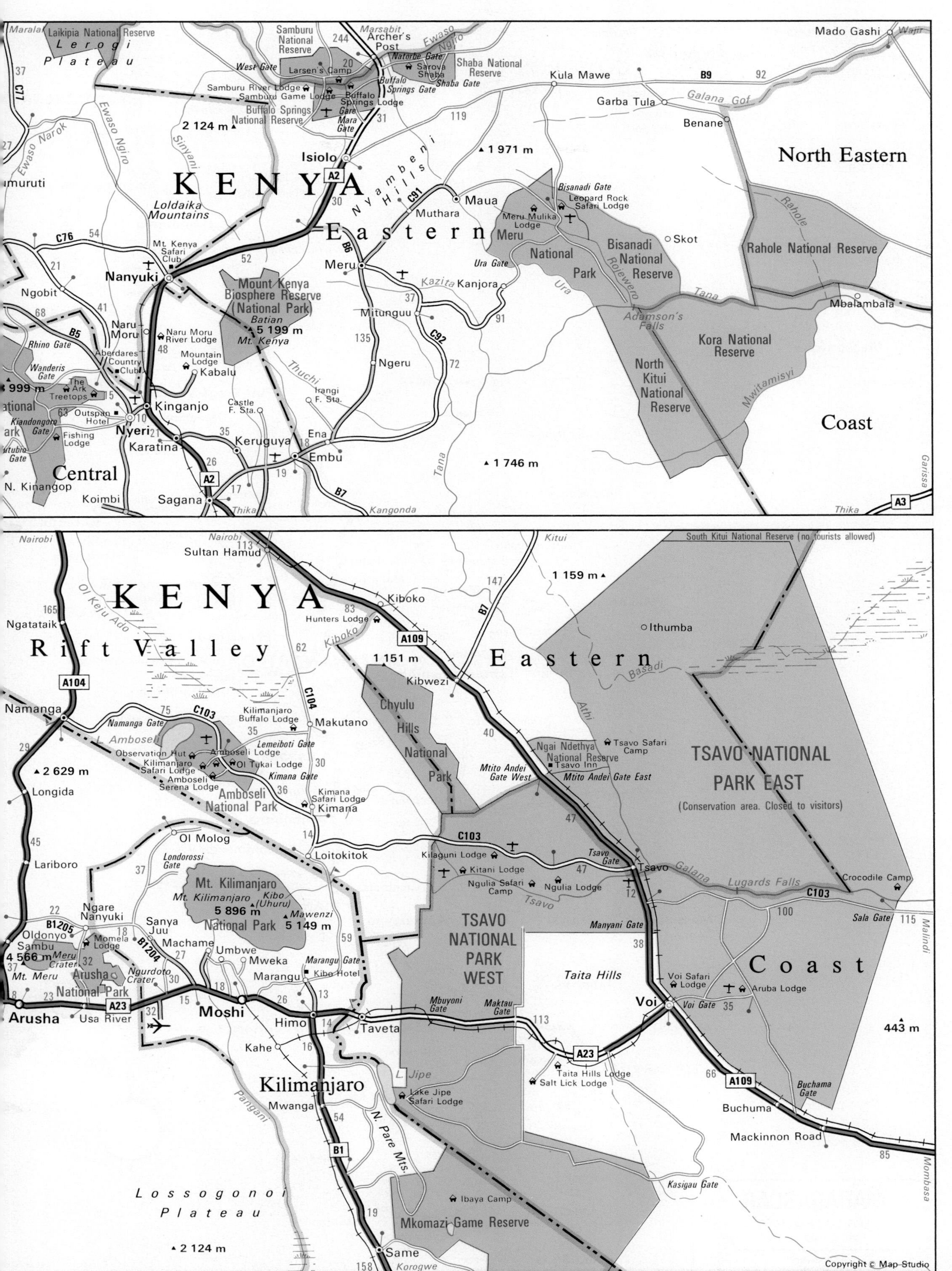

Top map:

KENYA

Eastern

North Eastern

Coast

Central

Maralal · Laikipia National Reserve · *Lerogi Plateau* · 37 · C17 · West Gate · Sambu River Lodge · Sambu Game Lodge · Buffalo Springs National Reserve · 2 124 m · Sambu National Reserve · 244 · Archer's Post · *Marsabit* · *Ewaso Ngiro* · Natorbe Gate · Sarova Shaba · Shaba National Reserve · Shaba Gate · Buffalo Springs Gate · Buffalo Springs Lodge · Mara Gate · 20 · 31 · 119 · Kula Mawe · B9 · 92 · Garba Tula · Galana Gof · Benane · Mado Gashi · Wajir

Imuruti · 27 · *Ewaso Narok* · *Ewaso Ngiro* · Isiolo · A2 · Loldaika Mountains · 1971 m · Nyambeni Hills · C91 · Muthara · Maua · Meru · Bisanadi Gate · Leopard Rock Safari Lodge · Meru. Mulika Lodge · Skot · Bisanadi National Reserve · Rahole National Reserve · Rahole

C76 · 54 · Mt Kenya Safari Club · Nanyuki · 30 · 52 · B6 · Meru · Ura Gate · National Park · Kazita · Kanjora · Ura · Mbalambala · Tana · Adamson's Falls · Kora National Reserve

Ngobit · 21 · 68 · B5 · 41 · Naru Moru · Naru Moru River Lodge · 48 · Mountain Lodge · Mount Kenya Biosphere Reserve (National Park) · *Batian* · 5 199 m · Mt Kenya · Mitunguu · 37 · C92 · 91 · 135 · Rolewero · North Kitui National Reserve

Rhino Gate · Wanderis Gate · Aberdares Country Club · Kabalu · Ngeru · 72 · 999 m · The Ark Treetops · 5 · Kiandongoro Gate · 63 · Outspan Hotel · 10 · Kinganjo · Irangi F. Sta. · Castle F. Sta. · Fishing Lodge · Nyeri · 21 · Karatina · 35 · Keruguya · Ena · Embu · 18 · 1746 m · Coast

N. Kinangop · Koimbi · Sagana · A2 · 26 · 19 · 17 · Thika · Kangonda · Tana · B7 · Thika · A3

Bottom map:

KENYA

Rift Valley

Eastern

Coast

Kilimanjaro

Nairobi · Nairobi · 113 · Sultan Hamud · Kitui · South Kitui National Reserve (no tourists allowed) · 147 · 1 159 m · Kiboko · 83 · Hunters Lodge · A109 · Ithumba · B7

Ngatataik · 165 · Ol Keju Ado · 62 · Kiboko · 1 151 m · Kibwezi · Chyulu Hills National Park · 40 · Basadi · Athi · Tsavo National Park East (Conservation area. Closed to visitors)

A104 · Namanga · Namanga Gate · 75 · C103 · Kilimanjaro Buffalo Lodge · C104 · Makutano · Lemeboti Gate · 30 · Ngai Ndethya National Reserve · Tsavo Safari Camp · Tsavo Inn · Mtito Andei Gate West · Mtito Andei Gate East

29 · L Amboseli · 2 629 m · Observation Hut · Kilimanjaro Safari Lodge · Amboseli Serena Lodge · Ol Tukai Lodge · Kimana Gate · 36 · Kimana Safari Lodge · Kimana · 47

Longida · Amboseli National Park · 14 · Loitokitok · C103 · Kilaguni Lodge · Tsavo Gate · 47 · Tsavo · Galana · Lugards Falls · Crocodile Camp · C103

45 · Lariboro · Ol Molog · Kitani Lodge · Ngulia Safari Camp · Ngulia Lodge · 12 · 100 · Sala Gate · 115 · Malindi

Ngare Nanyuki · 22 · Londorossi Gate · 37 · Mt. Kilimanjaro · Kibo (Uhuru) · 5 896 m · Mt. Kilimanjaro National Park · Mawenzi · 5 149 m · 59 · Tsavo National Park West · Manyani Gate · 38 · Voi Safari Lodge · Aruba Lodge · Coast

B1205 · Oldonyo Sambu · 18 · Sanya Juu · Momela Lodge · Machame · 27 · Umbwe · Mweka · Marangu Gate · Kibo Hotel · Taita Hills · 443 m

4 566 m · Meru Crater · 32 · B1204 · Ngurdoto Crater · 30 · Marangu · 13 · Voi · Voi Safari Lodge · Voi Gate · 35

37 · Mt. Meru · Arusha National Park · A23 · 15 · Moshi · 26 · Himo · 14 · Taveta · Mbuyoni Gate · Maktau Gate · 113 · A23 · A109 · 66

8 · 23 · Arusha · Usa River · 32 · Kahe · 16 · Tsavo National Park West · Taita Hills Lodge · Salt Lick Lodge · Buchama Gate

Kilimanjaro · L Jipe · Lake Jipe Safari Lodge · Mwanga · 54 · N. Pare Mts. · Kasigau Gate · Buchuma · Mackinnon Road · 85 · Mombasa

Lossogonoi Plateau · 2 124 m · B1 · Ibaya Camp · Mkomazi Game Reserve · Same · 158 · Korogwe · 19 · *Pangani*

53

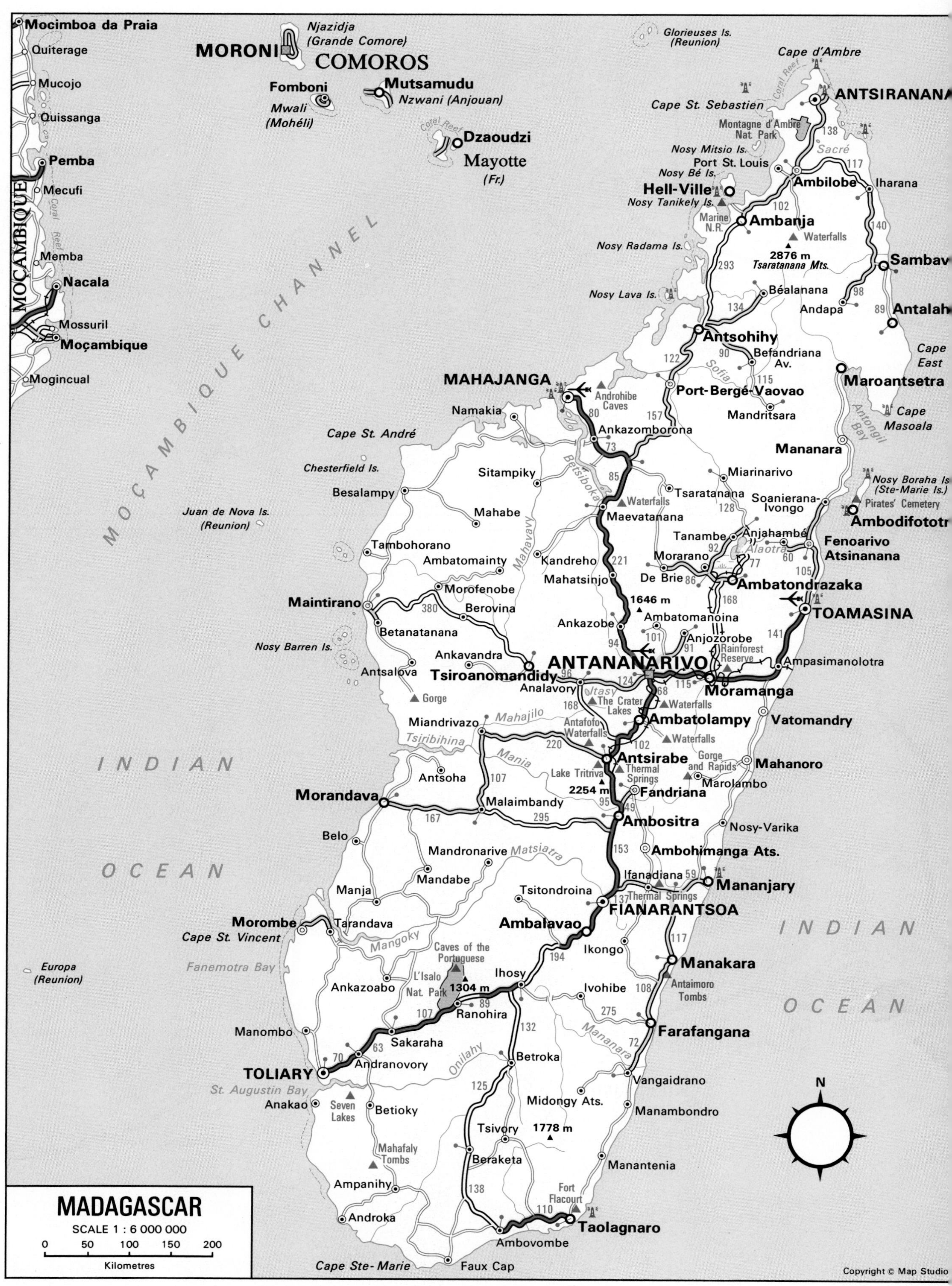

MADAGASCAR

SCALE 1 : 6 000 000

0   50   100   150   200

Kilometres

54

Copyright © Map Studio

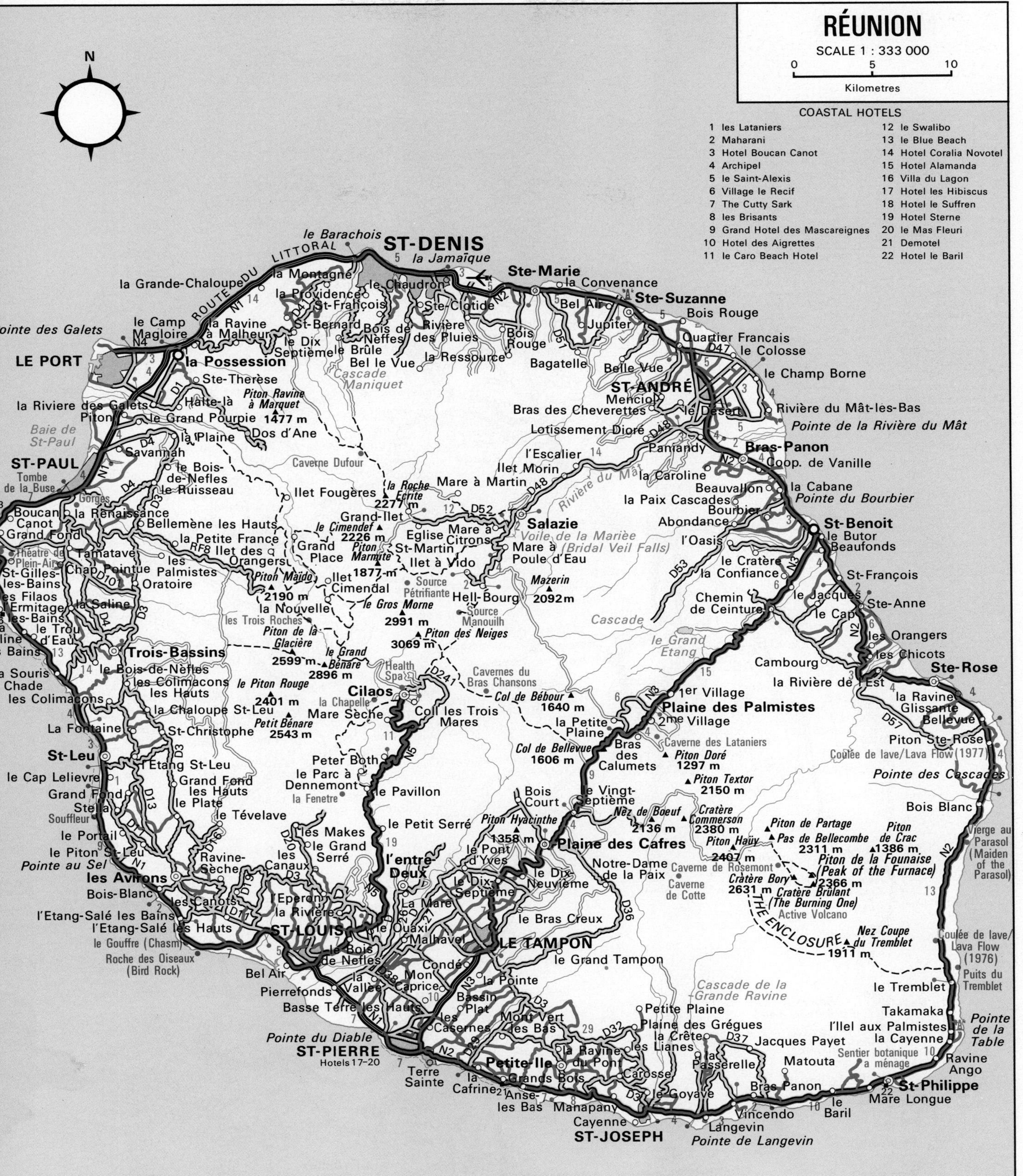

RÉUNION

SCALE 1 : 333 000

0   5   10

Kilometres

COASTAL HOTELS

1	les Lataniers	12	le Swalibo
2	Maharani	13	le Blue Beach
3	Hotel Boucan Canot	14	Hotel Coralia Novotel
4	Archipel	15	Hotel Alamanda
5	le Saint-Alexis	16	Villa du Lagon
6	Village le Recif	17	Hotel les Hibiscus
7	The Cutty Sark	18	Hotel le Suffren
8	les Brisants	19	Hotel Sterne
9	Grand Hotel des Mascareignes	20	le Mas Fleuri
10	Hotel des Aigrettes	21	Demotel
11	le Caro Beach Hotel	22	Hotel le Baril

N

le Barachois
ST-DENIS
la Jamaïque
la Grande-Chaloupe DU LITTORAL
la Montagne
la Providence
St-François
Ste-Marie
la Convenance
le Chaudron
Ste-Clotide
Bel Air
Ste-Suzanne
Bois Rouge
la Ravine à Malheur
St-Bernard Bois de Neffes Rivière des Pluies
Jupiter
Quartier Francais
le Colosse
le Camp Magloire
Septième le Brûle
Bois Rouge
Belle Vue
le Champ Borne
Pointe des Galets
LE PORT
la Possession
Ste-Thérèse
Bel le Vue
la Ressource
Bagatelle
ST-ANDRÉ
Menciol
Rivière du Mât-les-Bas
Piton Ravine à Marquet
Cascade Maniquet
Bras des Cheverettes
le Desert
Pointe de la Rivière du Mât
la Rivière des Galets
Halte-là
le Grand Pourpie 1477 m
Dos d'Ane
Lotissement Dioré
Paniandy
Bras-Panon
Coop. de Vanille
Baie de St-Paul
Savannah
la Plaine
l'Escalier
Ilet Morin
la Caroline
la Cabane
Pointe du Bourbier
ST-PAUL
Tombe de la Buse
le Bois-de-Nefles
le Ruisseau
Ilet Fougères
la Roche Ecrite 2277 m
Mare à Martin
la Paix Cascades
Beauvallon
Bourbier
St-Benoit
le Butor
Gorges
Boucan Canot
la Renaissance
Bellemène les Hauts
la Petite France
Grand-Ilet
D52
Mare à Citrons
Salazie
Abondance
l'Oasis
Beaufonds
le Cratère
Théâtre de Plein-Air
Grand Fond
Chap. Pointue
les Palmistes
RF8 Ilet des Orangers
le Cimendef 2226 m
Eglise St-Martin
Ilet à Vido
Voile de la Mariée (Bridal Veil Falls)
la Confiance
St-François
St-Gilles-les-Bains
les Filaos
la Saline
Oratoire
Piton Maïdo
Ilet Cimendal
1877 m
Mazerin
2092 m
Cascade
Chemin de Ceinture
le Jacques
Ste-Anne
les Bains
Ermitage
la Nouvelle
2190 m
Source Pétrifiante
Hell-Bourg
le Gros Morne
Source Manouilh
le Grand Etang
le Cap
la Saline d'Eau
les Bains
les Trois Roches
Piton de la Glacière
2991 m
Piton des Neiges
3069 m
les Orangers
Trois-Bassins
le Bois-de-Nefles
les Colimacons les Hauts
le Grand Bénare 2896 m
le Piton Rouge
2599 m
Cavernes du Bras Chansons
Cambourg
la Rivière de l'Est
les Chicots
Ste-Rose
la Souris Chade
les Colimacons
la Chaloupe St-Leu
les Hauts
2401 m
la Chapelle
Mare Sèche
Col de Bébour
1640 m
15
1er Village
Plaine des Palmistes
2me Village
la Ravine Glissante
Bellevue
Piton Ste-Rose
La Fontaine
St-Christophe
Petit Bénare 2543 m
Coll les Trois Mares
la Petite Plaine
Caverne des Lataniers
Coulée de lave/Lava Flow (1977)
St-Leu
le Cap Lelievre
Etang St-Leu
Grand Fond les Hauts
le Plate
Peter Both
le Parc à Dennemont
la Fenetre
le Pavillon
Col de Bellevue 1606 m
Bras des Calumets
Piton Doré 1297 m
Piton Textor 2150 m
Nez de Boeuf 2136 m
Pointe des Cascades
Bois Blanc
Grand Fond Stella
Souffleur
le Portail
le Piton St-Leu
les Makes
le Grand Serré
le Petit Serré
Piton Hyacinthe
1358 m
le Pont d'Yves
Vingt-Septième
Bois Court
Cratère Commerson 2380 m
Piton Haüy
2407 m
Piton de Partage 2311 m
Pas de Bellecombe
Piton de Crac
1386 m
Vierge au Parasol (Maiden of the Parasol)
Pointe au Sel
les Avirons
Bois-Blanc
Ravine-Sèche
les Canaux
l'entre Deux
Plaine des Cafres
Notre-Dame de la Paix
Caverne de Rosemont
Caverne de Cotte
Piton de la Founaise (Peak of the Furnace)
Cratère Bory 2366 m
Cratère Brûlant (The Burning One)
2631 m
Active Volcano
13
l'Etang-Salé les Bains
les Canots
Eperon
la Rivière
le Dix-Septième
le Neuvième
Nez Coupe du Tremblet
1911 m
Coulée de lave/Lava Flow (1976)
l'Etang-Salé les Hauts
le Gouffre (Chasm)
Roche des Oiseaux (Bird Rock)
ST-LOUIS
Bois de Nefles
Ouaxi
Malhavel
La Mare
le Bras Creux
THE ENCLOSURE
Puits du Tremblet
Bel Air
LE TAMPON
le Grand Tampon
le Tremblet
Pierrefonds
la Vallée
Mont Caprice
la Pointe
Basse Terre les Hauts
Bassin Plat
Mont Vert les Bas
Cascade de la Grande Ravine
Takamaka
Pointe de la Table
Pointe du Diable
ST-PIERRE
Hotels 17-20
les Casernes
Petite Plaine
Plaine des Grégues
la Crête
les Lianes
Jacques Payet
Matouta
l'Ilel aux Palmistes
la Cayenne
Sentier botanique à ménage
Ravine Ango
Terre Sainte
la Cafrine
Petite-Ile
Grands Bois
Carosse
la Passerelle
Bras Panon
St-Philippe
Anse les Bas
Manapany
Cayenne
les Goyave
Vincendo
le Baril
Mâre Longue
ST-JOSEPH
Langevin
Pointe de Langevin

INDIAN OCEAN

Copyright © Map Studio

55

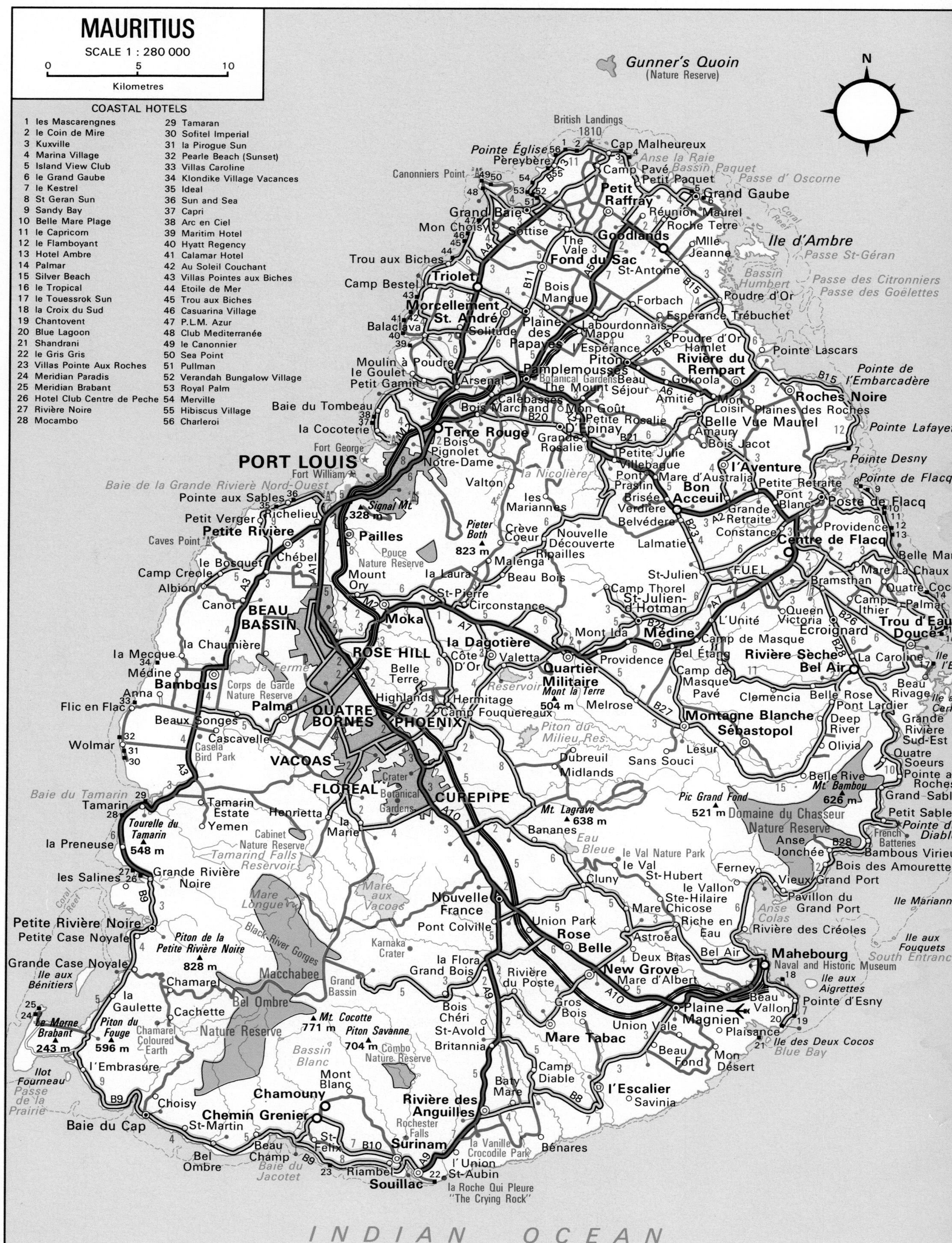

MAURITIUS

SCALE 1 : 280 000

0   5   10

Kilometres

COASTAL HOTELS

1 les Mascarengnes	29 Tamaran
2 le Coin de Mire	30 Sofitel Imperial
3 Kuxville	31 la Pirogue Sun
4 Marina Village	32 Pearle Beach (Sunset)
5 Island View Club	33 Villas Caroline
6 le Grand Gaube	34 Klondike Village Vacances
7 le Kestrel	35 Ideal
8 St Geran Sun	36 Sun and Sea
9 Sandy Bay	37 Capri
10 Belle Mare Plage	38 Arc en Ciel
11 le Capricorn	39 Maritim Hotel
12 le Flamboyant	40 Hyatt Regency
13 Hotel Ambre	41 Calamar Hotel
14 Palmar	42 Au Soleil Couchant
15 Silver Beach	43 Villas Pointes aux Biches
16 le Tropical	44 Etoile de Mer
17 le Touessrok Sun	45 Trou aux Biches
18 la Croix du Sud	46 Casuarina Village
19 Chantovent	47 P.L.M. Azur
20 Blue Lagoon	48 Club Mediterranée
21 Shandrani	49 le Canonnier
22 le Gris Gris	50 Sea Point
23 Villas Pointe Aux Roches	51 Pullman
24 Meridian Paradis	52 Verandah Bungalow Village
25 Meridian Brabant	53 Royal Palm
26 Hotel Club Centre de Peche	54 Merville
27 Rivière Noire	55 Hibiscus Village
28 Mocambo	56 Charleroi

N

INDIAN OCEAN

56

Copyright © Map Studio

MAIN MAP SECTION
HOOFKAARTGEDEELTE

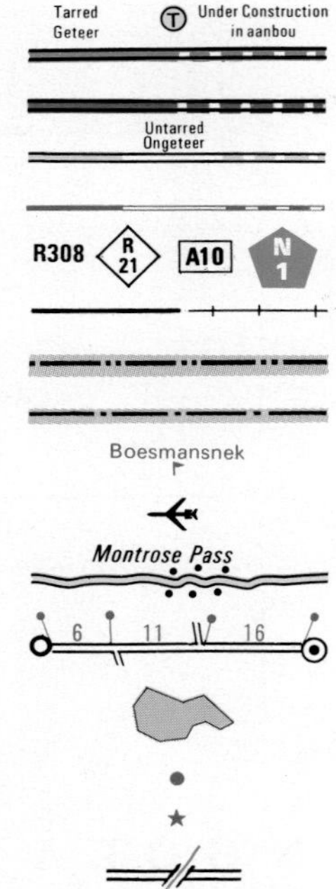

LEGEND

VERKLARING

LEGEND	VERKLARING
Toll Routes Freeways and National routes	Tolroetes Deurpaaie en Nasionale roetes
Principal Trunk Roads	Hoofverkeersweë
Main Roads	Hoofpaaie
Secondary Roads	Sekondêre paaie
Route numbers	Roetenommers
Railways	Spoorweë
National Boundaries	Nasionale grense
Provincial Boundaries	Provinsiale grense
Border Control Posts	Grensbeheerposte
Major Airports	Hooflughawens
Mountain Passes	Bergpasse
Distances in Kilometres	Afstande in kilometer
National Parks and Nature Reserves	Nasionale parke en Natuurreservate
Places of Interest	Besienswaardige plekke
Battlefields and Historic Sites	Slagvelde en Historiese plekke
Ferries	Ponte

1 : 1 500 000

Kilometres 0 10 20 30 40 50 Kilometer

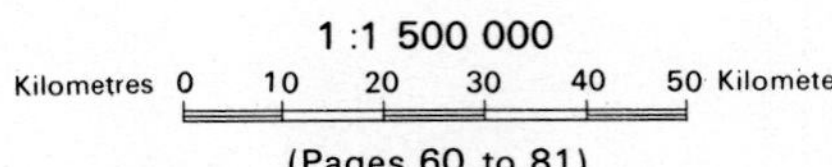

(Pages 60 to 81)

1 : 3 000 000

Kilometres 0 50 100 Kilometer

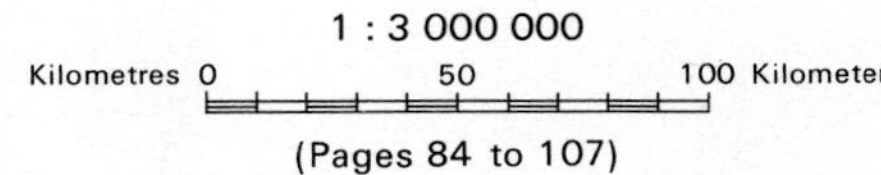

(Pages 84 to 107)

KARTENHAUPTTEIL
SECTION DE LA CARTE PRINCIPALE

LEGENDE

LEGENDE

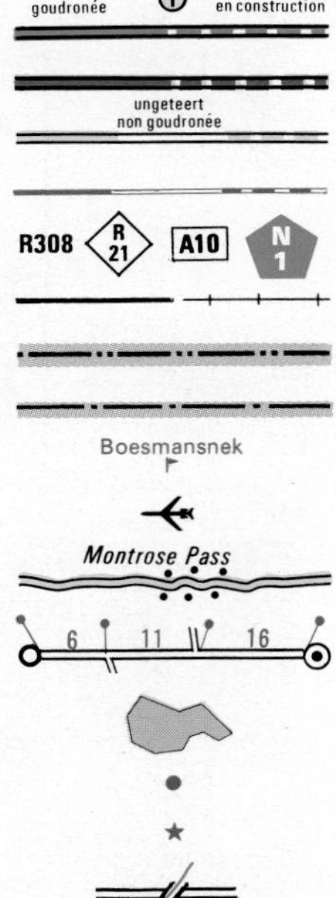

LEGENDE	LEGENDE
Toll-strassen Autobahnen und Nationalrouten	Routes à péage Autoroutes et Routes nationales
Hauptstrassen	Routes de grande circulation
Bundesstrassen	Routes principales
Nebenstrassen	Routes secondaires
Routenummern	Numéros des routes
Eisenbahnen	Chemins de fer
Landesgrenzen	Frontières nationales
Provinzgrenzen	Frontières provinciales
Grenzposten	Postes frontières
Flughäfen	Aéroportés principals
Bergpässe	Cols de montagnes
Entfernungen in Kilometer	Distances en kilometres
National Parks und Naturschutzgebiete	Parcs nationals et Réserves naturals
Besonders sehenswerte Objekte	Lieux d'interet
Schlachtfelder und historische Plätze	Champs de bataille et localités d'histoires
Fähren	Bacs

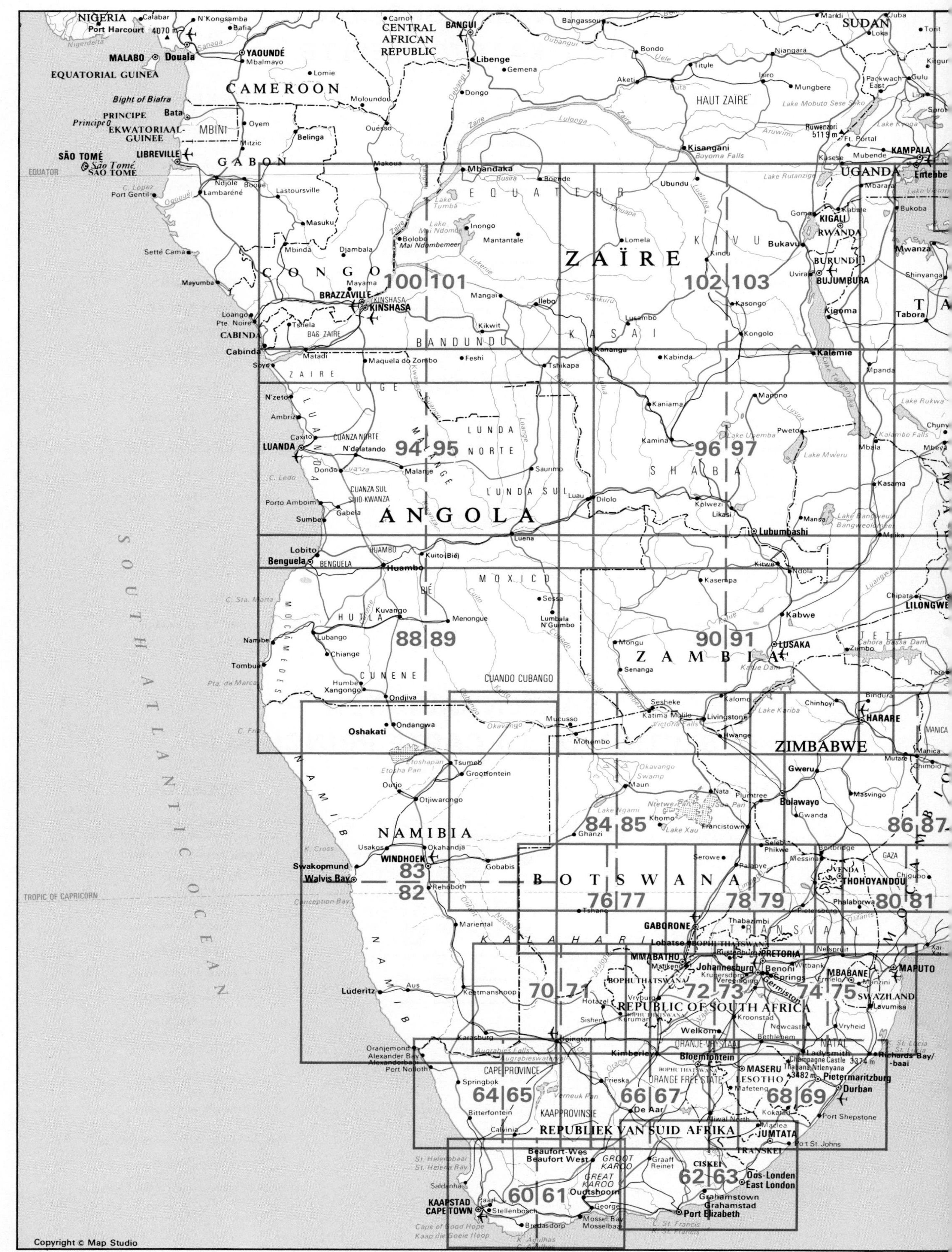

Copyright © Map Studio

NIGERIA
Port Harcourt
Calabar
N'Kongsamba
Bafia
4070 m
Nigerdelta
Sanaga
MALABO
Douala
YAOUNDÉ
Mbalmayo
EQUATORIAL GUINEA
Lomie
CAMEROON
Bight of Biafra
PRINCIPE
Principe
Bata
EKWATORIAAL-GUINEE
MBINI
Oyem
Mitzic
Belinga
Moloundou
Ouésso
SÃO TOMÉ
São Tomé
SAO TOME
LIBREVILLE
GABON
EQUATOR
Makoua
Ndjole
Booué
Lambaréné
Port Gentil
C. Lopez
Ogooué
Lastoursville
Masuku
Setté Cama
Mbinda
Djambala
Mayumba
CONGO
Mayama
BRAZZAVILLE
KINSHASA
Loango
Pte. Noire
CABINDA
Cabinda
Tshela
BAS ZAIRE
Matadi
Soyo
ZAIRE
Carnot
CENTRAL AFRICAN REPUBLIC
BANGUI
Libenge
Gemena
Dongo
Ubangi
Bangassou
Oubangui
Bondo
Uele
Titule
Niangara
Aketi
Buta
Isiro
Mungbere
HAUT ZAIRE
Lake Mobuto Sese Seko
Zaire
Lulonga
Aruwimi
Kisangani
Boyoma Falls
Mbandaka
Busira
Boende
EQUATEUR
Lake Tumba
Lake Mai Ndombe
Bolobo
Mai Ndombemeer
Inongo
Mantantale
Lukenie
ZAÏRE
Ubundu
Lomela
Tshuapa
Lualaba
KIVU
Kindu
Bukavu
Mangai
Ilebo
Sankuru
Kikwit
BANDUNDU
KASAI
Lusambo
Kasongo
Kongolo
Kananga
Kabinda
Tshikapa
Maquela do Zombo
Feshi
UIGE
N'zeto
Ambriz
Caxito
LUANDA
CUANZA NORTE
N'dalatando
Malanje
LUNDA NORTE
Dondo
C. Ledo
Saurimo
CUANZA SUL
SUID-KWANZA
Porto Amboim
Gabela
Sumbe
ANGOLA
LUNDA SUL
Luau
Dilolo
Luena
Kaniama
Kamina
Lake Upemba
Pweto
Lake Mweru
SHABA
Kolwezi
Likasi
Lubumbashi
Lobito
Benguela
BENGUELA
HUAMBO
Huambo
Kuito (Bié)
BIÉ
MOXICO
Sessa
Lumbala N'Guimbo
C. Sta. Marta
Kuvango
Menongue
HUILA
Namibe
Lubango
Chiange
MOÇÂMEDES
Tombua
Pta. da Marca
Humbe
Xangongo
CUNENE
Ondjiva
CUANDO CUBANGO
C. Frio
Oshakati
Ondangwa
Okavango
Mucusso
Mohembo
Etoshapan
Etosha Pan
Tsumeb
Grootfontein
Outjo
Otjiwarongo
NAMIBIA
K. Cross
Usakos
Okahandja
WINDHOEK
Swakopmund
Walvis Bay
Rehoboth
Gobabis
Conception Bay
TROPIC OF CAPRICORN
Mariental
Lüderitz
Aus
Keetmanshoop
NAMIB
KALAHARI
SOUTH ATLANTIC OCEAN
Oranjemond
Alexander Bay
Alexanderbaai
Port Nolloth
Karasburg
Augrabies Falls
Upington
CAPE PROVINCE
Springbok
Verneuk Pan
Bitterfontein
KAAPPROVINSIE
Calvinia
REPUBLIEK VAN SUID AFRIKA
St. Helenabaai
St. Helena Bay
Saldanha
KAAPSTAD
CAPE TOWN
Paarl
Stellenbosch
Bredasdorp
Cape of Good Hope
Kaap die Goeie Hoop
K. Agulhas
C. Agulhas
Beaufort-Wes
Beaufort West
GROOT KAROO
GREAT KAROO
Oudtshoorn
George
Mossel Bay
Mosselbaai
Graaff Reinet
CISKEI
Oos-Londen
East London
Grahamstown
Grahamstad
Port Elizabeth
C. St. Francis
K. St. Francis
Aliwal North
De Aar
Frieska
Kimberley
Bloemfontein
ORANGE FREE STATE
ORANJE-VRYSTAAT
MASERU
LESOTHO
Mafeteng
Thabana Ntlenyana
3482 m
Champagne Castle
3374 m
Ladysmith
NATAL
Pietermaritzburg
Durban
Port Shepstone
Kokstad
Maclea
UMTATA
TRANSKEI
Port St. Johns
Richards Bay/-baai
K. St. Lucia
C. St. Lucia
Welkom
Kroonstad
Bethlehem
Newcastle
Vryheid
REPUBLIC OF SOUTH AFRICA
Vryburg
Kuruman
Sishen
Hotazel
BOPHUTHATSWANA
MMABATHO
Mafikeng
Johannesburg
Krugersdorp
Vereeniging
Germiston
Springs
Benoni
PRETORIA
Rustenburg
Witbank
Ermelo
MBABANE
SWAZILAND
Lavumisa
Manzini
MAPUTO
Nelspruit
Xai-Xai
GABORONE
Lobatse
Thabazimbi
TRANSVAAL
Tshane
BOTSWANA
Ghanzi
Lake Ngami
Maun
Okavango Swamp
Nata
Ntetwe Pan
Sua Pan
Khomo
Lake Xau
Francistown
Plumtree
Bulawayo
Gwanda
Serowe
Palapye
Selebi Phikwe
Messina
Beitbridge
VENDA
THOHOYANDOU
GAZA
Chigubo
Pietersburg
Phalaborwa
Olifants
Limpopo
ZIMBABWE
Gweru
Masvingo
Mutare
Chimoio
Manica
MANICA
HARARE
Chinhoyi
Bindura
Lake Kariba
Livingstone
Victoria Falls
Katima Mulilo
Sesheke
Kalomo
Hwange
Mongu
Senanga
ZAMBIA
LUSAKA
Kafue Dam
Zumbo
Cahora Bassa Dam
TETE
Kabwe
Kasempa
Kitwe
Ndola
Chipata
LILONGWE
Mansa
Lake Bangweulu
Bangweolomeer
Mpika
Kasama
Mbala
Kalambo Falls
Mbeya
Chuny
Lake Rukwa
Mpanda
Kalemie
Lake Tanganyika
Kigoma
Tabora
Uvira
BUJUMBURA
BURUNDI
Goma
KIGALI
RWANDA
Kabale
Bukoba
Mwanza
Shinyanga
Lake Victoria
Mbarara
UGANDA
Entebbe
KAMPALA
Kasese
Mubende
Lake Rutanzige
Ruwenzori
5119 m
Ft. Portal
Lake Kyoga
Lira
Gulu
Pachwach East
Kitgum
Torit
Juba
Maridi
SUDAN
Loka
Lake Albert
100
101
102
103
94
95
96
97
88
89
90
91
86
87
84
85
83
82
76
77
78
79
80
81
70
71
72
73
74
75
64
65
66
67
68
69
62
63
60
61

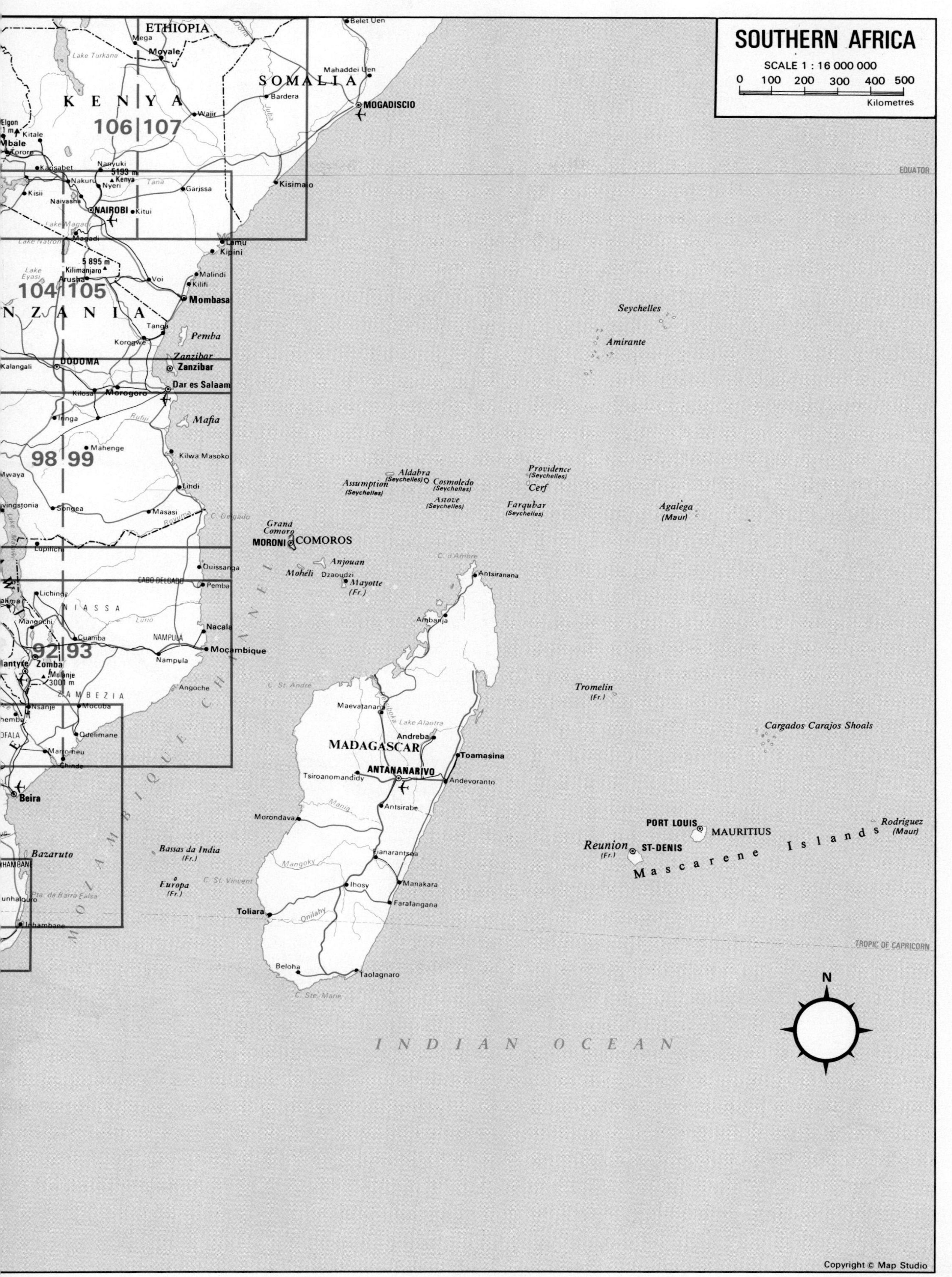

SOUTHERN AFRICA

SCALE 1 : 16 000 000

0   100   200   300   400   500
Kilometres

ETHIOPIA

SOMALIA

Mega
Moyale
Lake Turkana
Mahaddei Uen
Belet Uen

KENYA
106|107

Bardera
Juba
MOGADISCIO

Elgon
Kitale
Kapsabet
Mbale
Tororo
Nanyuki
5 199 m
Nakuru
Nyeri
Kenya 5 193 m
Tana
Garissa
Kisimaio
Kisii
Naivasha
NAIROBI
Kitui
Lake Magadi
Lamu
Kipini
Lake Natron
Magadi

104|105
Kilimanjaro 5 895 m
Arusha
Lake Eyasi
Voi
Malindi
Kilifi
Mombasa

NZANIA
Tanga
Pemba
Korogwe

Kalangali
Zanzibar
DODOMA
Zanzibar
Kilosa
Morogoro
Dar es Salaam

Tunga
Rufiji
Mafia

98|99
Mahenge
Kilwa Masoko

Mwaya
Lindi
vingstonia
Songea
Masasi
C. Delgado

Lake Malawi
Lupichi
Quissanga
MORONI COMOROS
Grand Comoro
Anjouan
C. d'Ambre
Antsiranana

Lichinga
Pemba
Mohéli
Dzaoudzi
Mayotte
(Fr.)

N I A S S A
Lurio
NAMPULA
Nacala

Mangochi
Cuamba
Mocambique
Ambanja

92|93
Nampula

antyre
Zomba
Angoche

Mulanje
3000 m
Z A M B E Z I A

Nsanje
Mocuba
C. St. André

OFALA
Quelimane
Maevatanana
Lake Alaotra
Andreba

Marromeu
Chinde
MADAGASCAR
Toamasina

Beira
ANTANANARIVO
Andevoranto

Tsiroanomandidy

Bazaruto
Morondava
Antsirabe

HAMBAN
Bassas da India (Fr.)
Fianarantsoa

Pta. da Barra Falsa
Europa (Fr.)
C. St. Vincent
Ihosy
Manakara

Mangoky
Farafangana

nhaloure
Toliara
Onilahy

Inhambane

Beloha
Taolagnaro

C. Ste. Marie

Seychelles

Amirante

Providence
(Seychelles)

Aldabra
(Seychelles)
Cosmoledo
(Seychelles)
Cerf

Assumption
(Seychelles)
Astove
(Seychelles)
Farquhar
(Seychelles)

Agalega
(Maur.)

Tromelin
(Fr.)

Cargados Carajos Shoals

PORT LOUIS
Rodriguez
(Maur.)

Reunion
(Fr.)
ST-DENIS
MAURITIUS

M a s c a r e n e   I s l a n d s

EQUATOR

TROPIC OF CAPRICORN

I N D I A N   O C E A N

MOZAMBIQUE CHANNEL

N

59

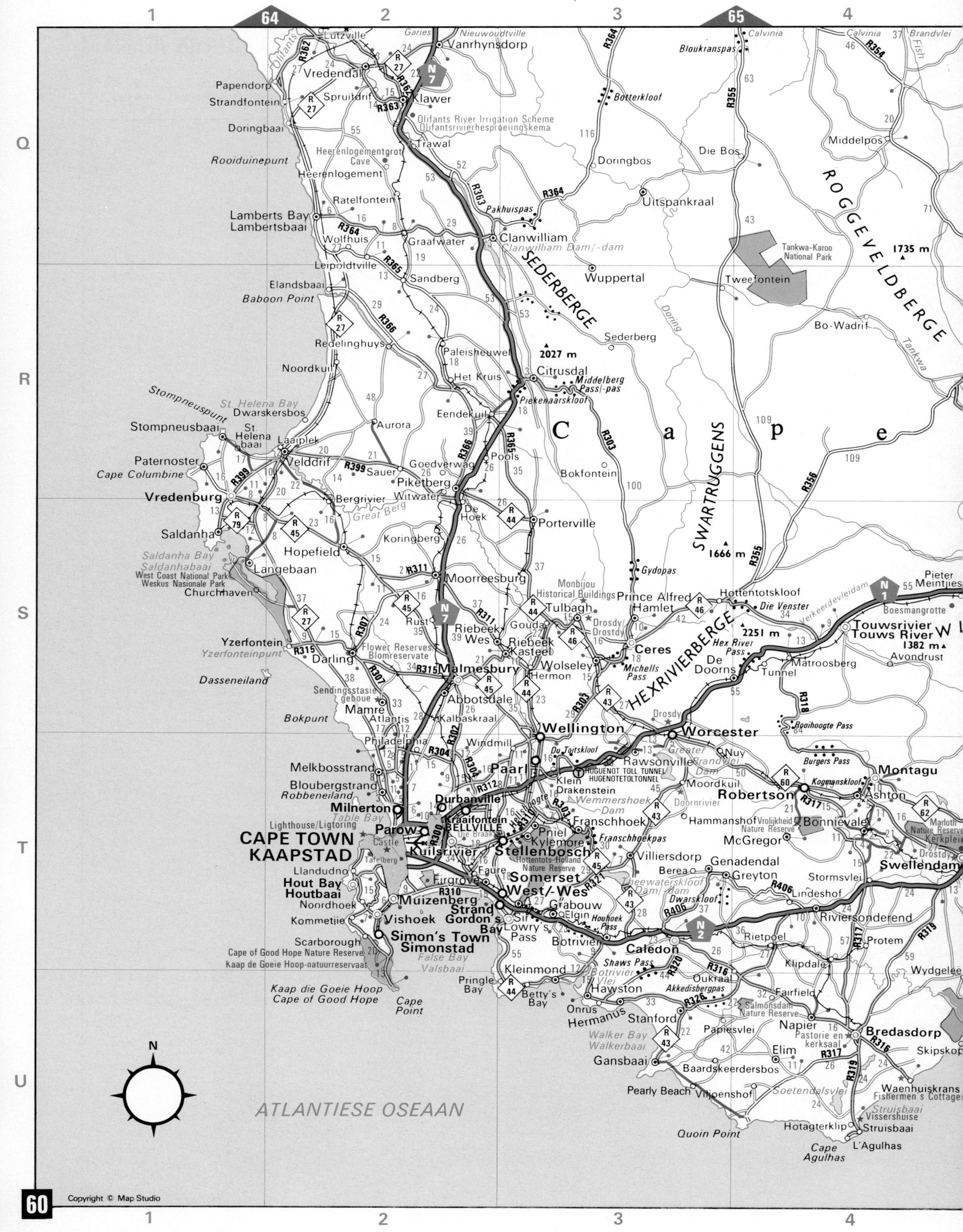

1
2
3
4
64
65
Q
R
S
T
U
Lutzville
Garies
Nieuwoudtville
Vanrhynsdorp
Calvinia
Brandvlei
Vredendal
Papendorp
Strandfontein
Spruitdrif
Klawer
Bloukranspas
Botterkloof
Olifants River Irrigation Scheme
Olifantsrivierbesproeiingskema
Doringbaai
Trawal
Heerenlogementgrot Cave
Heerenlogement
Rooiduinepunt
Doringbos
Die Bos
Middelpos
Uitspankraal
Pakhuispas
Ratelfontein
Lamberts Bay
Lambertsbaai
Wolfhuis
Graafwater
Clanwilliam
Clanwilliam Dam/-dam
Leipoldtville
Sandberg
Elandsbaai
Baboon Point
Wuppertal
Tankwa-Karoo National Park
Tweefontein
1735 m
ROGGEVELDBERGE
SEDERBERGE
Doring
Bo-Wadrif
Tankwa
Sederberg
Redelinghuys
Paleisheuwel
2027 m
Noordkuil
Citrusdal
Middelberg Pass/-pas
Het Kruis
Piekenaarskloof
Stompneuspunt
St. Helena Bay
Dwarskersbos
Stompneusbaai
St. Helena baai
Laaiplek
Aurora
Eendekuil
C a p e
SWARTRUGGENS
Paternoster
Cape Columbine
Velddrif
Sauer
Goedverwag
Pools
Bokfontein
Piketberg
Vredenburg
Bergrivier
Witwater
Great Berg
De Hoek
Porterville
Saldanha
Hopefield
Koringberg
1666 m
Saldanha Bay
Saldanhabaai
Langebaan
West Coast National Park
Weskus Nasionale Park
Moorreesburg
Gydopas
Churchhaven
Monbijou Historical Buildings
Prince Alfred Hamlet
Hottentotskloof
Die Venster
Pieter Meintjies
Verkeerdevleidam
Boesmangrotte
Tulbagh
Drosdy/Drostdy
Rust
Gouda
Riebeek Wes
Riebeek Kasteel
2251 m
Touwsrivier
Touws River
1382 m
Yzerfontein
Yzerfonteinpunt
Darling
Flower Reserves/Blomreservate
Ceres
Hex River Pass
De Doorns
Matroosberg
Avondrust
Malmesbury
Michells Pass
Wolseley
Hermon
Tunnel
HEXRIVIERBERGE
Dasseneiland
Sendingsstasie gebou
Mamre
Atlantis
Abbotsdale
Kalbaskraal
Bokpunt
Drosdy
Rooihoogte Pass
Wellington
Worcester
Philadelphia
Windmill
Du Toitskloof
Rawsonville
Greater Brandvlei Dam
Nuy
Burgers Pass
Melkbosstrand
Paarl
HUGUENOT TOLL TUNNEL
HUGENOTETOLTONNEL
Montagu
Moordkuil
Kogmanskloof
Bloubergstrand
Robbeneiland
Klein Drakenstein
Robertson
Ashton
Milnerton
Table Bay
Durbanville
Wemmershoek Dam
Doornrivier
Lighthouse/Ligtoring
Kraaifontein
Helshoogte
Franschhoek
Hammanshof
Vrolijkheid Nature Reserve
Bonnievale
Marloth Nature Reserve
Parow
BELLVILLE
Die Braak
Pniel
Kylemore
Franschhoekpas
McGregor
Kerkplein
CAPE TOWN
KAAPSTAD
Castle
Tafelberg
Kuilsrivier
Stellenbosch
Hottentots-Holland Nature Reserve
Villiersdorp
Genadendal
Drostdy
Swellendam
Llandudno
Faure
Berea
Greyton
Stormsvlei
Hout Bay
Houtbaai
Firgrove
Somerset West/-Wes
Theewaterskloof Dam/-dam
Lindeshof
Noordhoek
Muizenberg
Strand
Grabouw
Dwarskloof
Kommetjie
Vishoek
Gordon's Bay
Sir Lowry's Pass
Elgin
Houhoek Pass
Riviersonderend
Scarborough
Simon's Town
Simonstad
Botrivier
Caledon
Rietpoel
Protem
Cape of Good Hope Nature Reserve
Kaap de Goeie Hoop-natuurreservaat
False Bay
Valsbaai
Shaws Pass
Klipdale
Wydgelee
Kleinmond
Botrivier Vlei
Oukraal
Kaap die Goeie Hoop
Cape of Good Hope
Pringle Bay
Hawston
Akkedisbergpas
Fairfield
Cape Point
Betty's Bay
Onrus
Hermanus
Stanford
Salmonsdam Nature Reserve
Napier
Pastorie en kerksaal
Bredasdorp
Walker Bay
Walkerbaai
Papiesvlei
Skipskop
Elim
Gansbaai
Baardskeerdersbos
Waenhuiskrans
Fishermen's Cottages
Pearly Beach
Viljoenshof
Soetendalsvlei
Struisbaai
Vissershuise
Hotagterklip
Quoin Point
Cape Agulhas
L'Agulhas
N
ATLANTIESE OSEAAN
WI

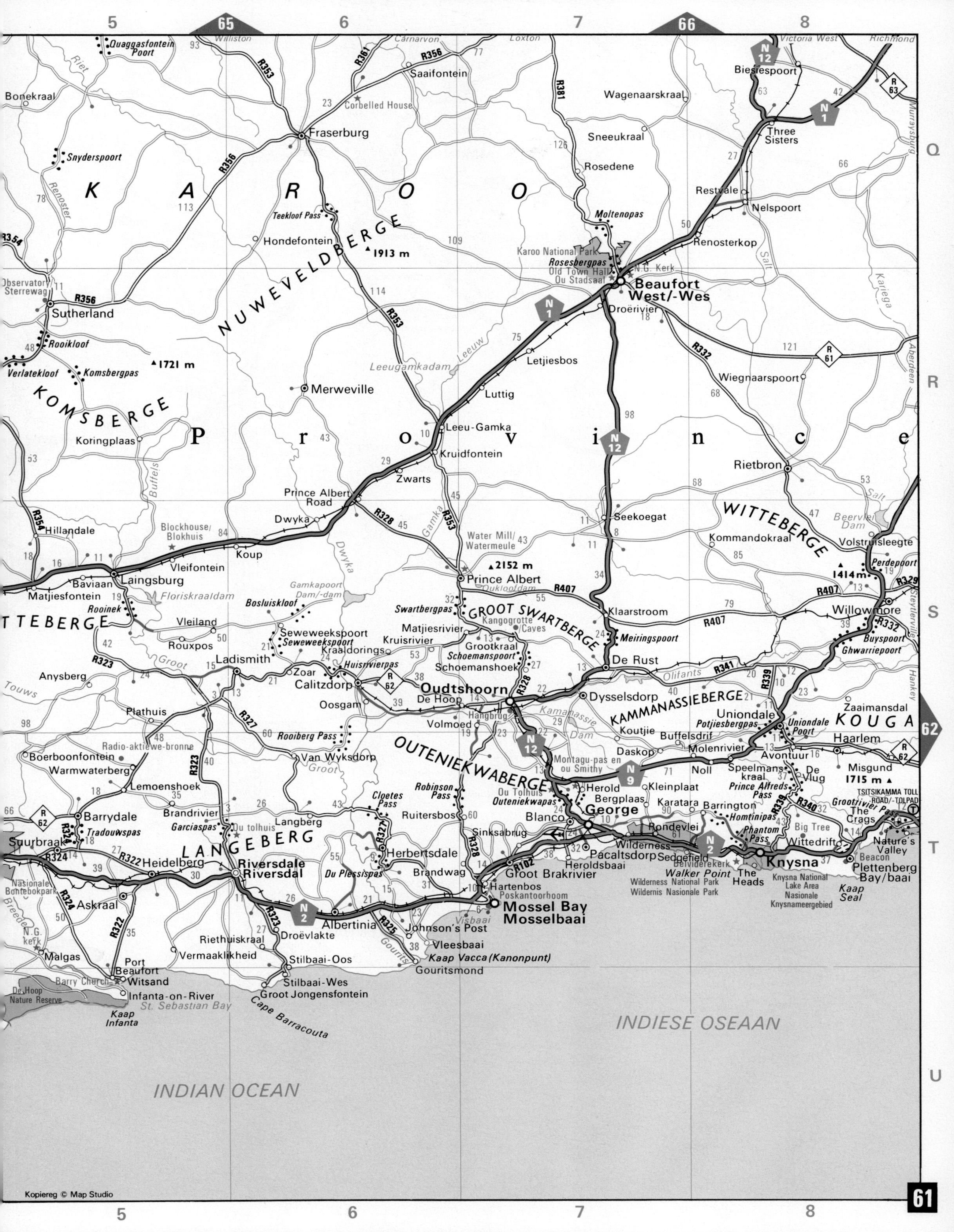

5
65
6
7
66
8
Quaggasfontein Poort
Williston
Carnarvon
Loxton
Victoria West
Richmond
Saaifontein
Corbelled House
Biesiespoort
Bonekraal
Wagenaarskraal
Fraserburg
Sneeukraal
Three Sisters
Snyderspoort
Rosedene
K A R O O
Restvale
Nelspoort
Teekloof Pass
Molteno pas
Hondefontein
NUWEVELDBERGE
1913 m
Karoo National Park
Rosesbergpas
Old Town Hall
Ou Stadsaal
N.G. Kerk
Renosterkop
Beaufort West/-Wes
Observatory Sterrewag
Sutherland
Droërivier
Rooikloof
Verlatekloof
Komsbergpas
1721 m
Letjiesbos
Leeugamkadam
Wiegnaarspoort
KOMSBERGE
Merweville
Luttig
Leeu-Gamka
Koringplaas
P r o v i n c e
Kruidfontein
Rietbron
Zwarts
Prince Albert Road
Seekoegat
WITTEBERGE
Hillandale
Dwyka
Blockhouse/ Blokhuis
Water Mill/ Watermeule
Kommandokraal
Volstruisleegte
Koup
Vleifontein
2152 m
Perdepoort
1414 m
Laingsburg
Prince Albert
Baviaan
Matjiesfontein
Gamkapoort Dam/-dam
Floriskraaldam
Oukloofdam
Bosluiskloof
Rooinek
Swartbergpas
GROOT SWARTBERGE
Klaarstroom
Willowmore
TTEBERGE
Vleiland
Seweweekspoort
Matjiesrivier
Kangogrotte/Caves
Rouxpos
Kruisrivier
Grootkraal
Meiringspoort
Buyspoort
Ghwarriepoort
Kraaldorings
Schoemanspoort
Schoemanshoek
Ladismith
Huisrivierpas
De Rust
Anysberg
Zoar
Calitzdorp
Oudtshoorn
Olifants
Dysselsdorp
KAMMANASSIEBERGE
Touws
Oosgam
De Hoop
Uniondale
Zaaimansdal
Plathuis
Volmoed
Hangbrug
Kamanassie Dam
Koutjie
Potjiesbergpas
Uniondale Poort
KOUGA
Radio-aktiewe-bronne
Rooiberg Pass
Buffelsdrif
Molenrivier
Haarlem
Boerboonfontein
Van Wyksdorp
OUTENIEKWABERGE
Daskop
Avontuur
Warmwaterberg
Groot
Montagu-pas en ou Smithy
Noll
Speelmanskraal
De Vlug
Misgund
1715 m
Lemoenshoek
Robinson Pass
Ou Tolhuis
Outeniekwapas
Herold
Kleinplaat
Prince Alfreds Pass
TSITSIKAMMA TOLL ROAD/-TOLPAD
Cloetes Pass
Bergplaas
Karatara
Barrington
Grootrivier Pass
Barrydale
Brandrivier
Ruitersbos
Blanco
George
Homtinipas
The Crags
Garciaspas
Ou tolhuis
Langberg
Sinksabrug
Rondevlei
Big Tree
Tradouwspas
LANGEBERG
Wilderness
Phantom Pass
Wittedrift
Nature's Valley
Suurbraak
Herbertsdale
Pacaltsdorp
Sedgefield
Beacon
Heidelberg
Riversdale Riversdal
Du Plessispas
Brandwag
Groot Brakrivier
Heroldsbaai
Belvidere kerk
Knysna
Plettenberg Bay/baai
Nasionale Bontebokpark
Hartenbos
Walker Point
The Heads
Wilderness National Park
Wildernis Nasionale Park
Knysna National Lake Area
Knysna Nasionale Knysnameergebied
Kaap Seal
Poskantoorboom
Askraal
Mosselbaai Mosselbaai
Mossel Bay
Albertinia
Visbaai
Johnson's Post
Breede
N.G. kerk
Droëvlakte
Riethuiskraal
Vleesbaai
Malgas
Vermaaklikheid
Gourits
Kaap Vacca (Kanonpunt)
Port Beaufort
Stilbaai-Oos
Gouritsmond
Barry Church
Witsand
Stilbaai-Wes
De Hoop Nature Reserve
Infanta-on-River
Groot Jongensfontein
St. Sebastian Bay
Kaap Infanta
Cape Barracouta
INDIESE OSEAAN
INDIAN OCEAN
Q
R
S
T
U
62
Kopiereg © Map Studio
61
5
6
7
8

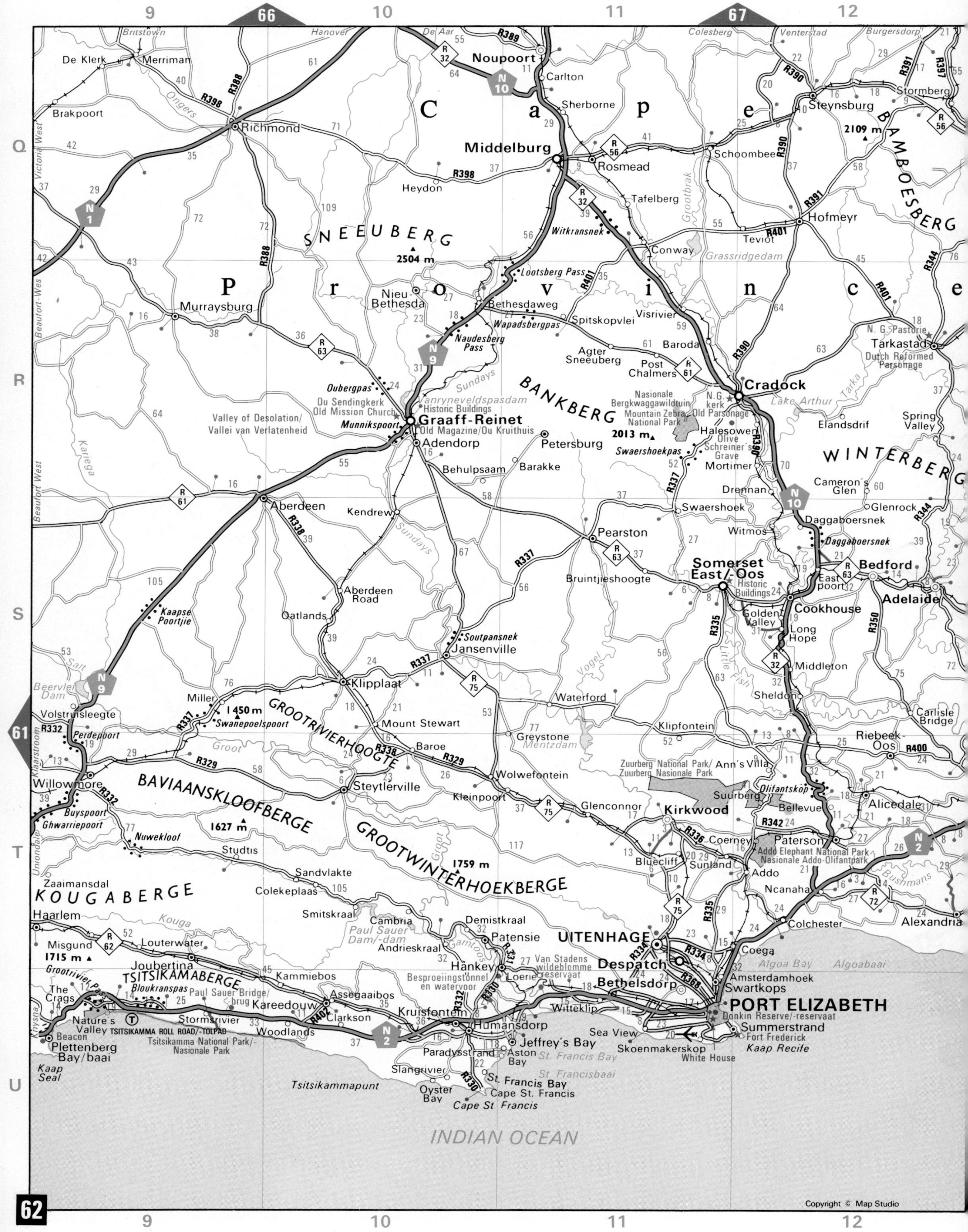

9
66
10
11
67
12
Q
R
S
T
U
61
Cape Province
Britstown
Hanover
De Aar
Noupoort
Colesberg
Venterstad
Burgersdorp
De Klerk
Merriman
Carlton
Sherborne
Steynsburg
Stormberg
Brakpoort
Richmond
Middelburg
Rosmead
Schoombee
Heydon
Tafelberg
Hofmeyr
Teviot
Conway
Grassridgedam
BAMBOESBERG
SNEEUBERG
2504 m
2109 m
Witkransnek
Lootsberg Pass
Nieu-Bethesda
Bethesdaweg
Wapadsbergpas
Spitskopvlei
Visrivier
Murraysburg
Naudesberg Pass
Agter Sneeuberg
Baroda
Post Chalmers
Tarkastad
N. G. Pastorie
Dutch Reformed Parsonage
Oubergpas
Ou Sendingkerk
Old Mission Church
Vanryneveldspasdam
Historic Buildings
Graaff-Reinet
Old Magazine/Ou Kruithuis
Valley of Desolation/
Vallei van Verlatenheid
Munnikspoort
Adendorp
Petersburg
BANKBERG
Cradock
N.G. kerk
Old Parsonage
Lake Arthur
Nasionale Bergkwaggawildtuin
Mountain Zebra National Park
2013 m
Halesowen
Olive Schreiner's Grave
Swaershoekpas
Mortimer
Elandsdrif
Spring Valley
WINTERBERG
Behulpsaam
Barakke
Cameron's Glen
Drennan
Aberdeen
Kendrew
Swaershoek
Glenrock
Daggaboersnek
Witmos
Pearston
Sundays
Somerset East/-Oos
Historic Buildings
Bedford
East poort
Adelaide
Bruintjieshoogte
Aberdeen Road
Cookhouse
Golden Valley
Long Hope
Oatlands
Kaapse Poortjie
Soutpansnek
Jansenville
Middleton
Klipplaat
Sheldon
Waterford
Beervlei Dam
Miller
1450 m
Swanepoelspoort
GROOTRIVIERHOOGTE
Mount Stewart
Volstruisleegte
Perdepoort
Greystone
Mentzdam
Klipfontein
Carlisle Bridge
Riebeek-Oos
Baroe
Willowmore
BAVIAANSKLOOFBERGE
Steytlerville
Wolwefontein
Zuurberg National Park/
Zuurberg Nasionale Park
Ann's Villa
Olifantskop
Suurberg
Bellevue
Alicedale
Buyspoort
Ghwarriepoort
1627 m
Kleinpoort
Glenconnor
Kirkwood
Nuwekloof
Studtis
GROOTWINTERHOEKBERGE
1759 m
Coerney
Paterson
Addo Elephant National Park
Nasionale Addo-Olifantpark
Bluecliff
Sunland
Addo
Zaaimansdal
KOUGABERGE
Sandvlakte
Colekeplaas
Ncanaha
Bushmans
Haarlem
Kouga
Smitskraal
Cambria
Paul Sauer Dam/-dam
Demistkraal
Colchester
Alexandria
Misgund
1715 m
Louterwater
Patensie
Andrieskraal
UITENHAGE
Despatch
Coega
Algoa Bay
Algoabaai
Joubertina
Grootrivierpas
TSITSIKAMABERGE
Bloukranspas
Kammiebos
Hankey
Van Stadens wildeblomme reservaat
Loerie
Besproeiingstonnel en watervoor
Bethelsdorp
Amsterdamhoek
Swartkops
The Crags
Paul Sauer Bridge/-brug
Kareedouw
Assegaaibos
PORT ELIZABETH
Donkin Reserve/-reservaat
Nature's Valley
Stormsrivier
Clarkson
Kruisfontein
Humansdorp
Witteklip
Summerstrand
Fort Frederick
Kaap Recife
Beacon
TSITSIKAMMA ROLL ROAD/-TOLPAD
Woodlands
Sea View
Plettenberg Bay/baai
Tsitsikamma National Park/-Nasionale Park
Jeffrey's Bay
Skoenmakerskop
White House
Paradysstrand
Aston Bay
St. Francis Bay
St. Francisbaai
Kaap Seal
Slangrivier
Tsitsikammapunt
Oyster Bay
St. Francis Bay
Cape St. Francis
Cape St Francis
INDIAN OCEAN
Copyright © Map Studio

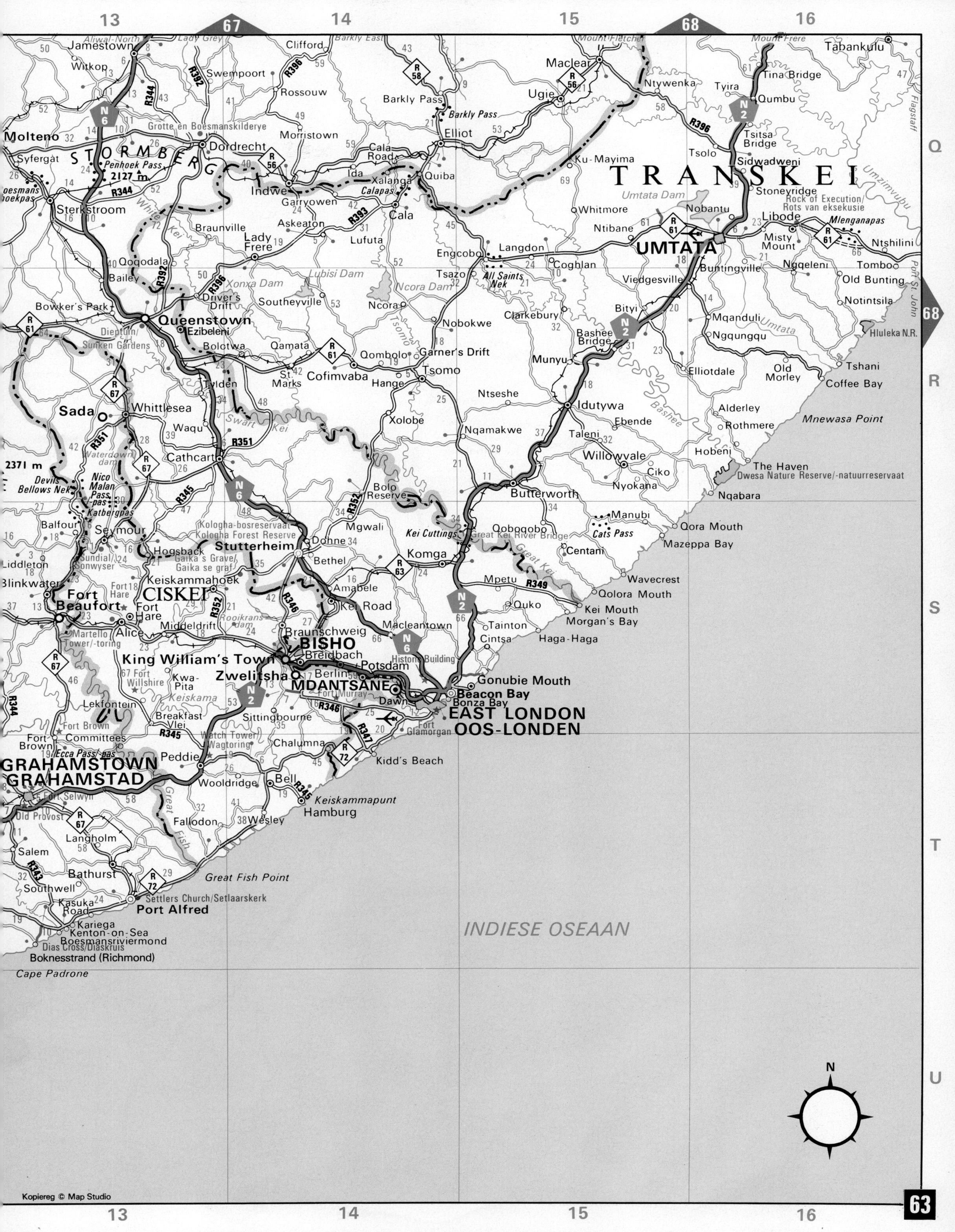

13
67
14
15
68
16
Aliwal-North
Jamestown
Lady Grey
Clifford
Barkly East
Mount Fletcher
Mount Frere
Tabankulu
Witkop
Swempoort
R 58
Maclear
R 56
Ntywenka
Tyira
Tina Bridge
Qumbu
Rossouw
Barkly Pass
Ugie
Barkly Pass
Flagstaff
Grotte en Boesmanskilderye
Elliot
R396
Tsitsa Bridge
Molteno
Morristown
Dordrecht
Cala Road
Tsolo
Sidwadweni
Q
Syfergat
STORMBERG
Penhoek Pass
2127 m
Ida
Ku-Mayima
TRANSKEI
Umzimvubu
Xalanga
Quiba
Calapas
Stoneyridge
Rock of Execution/ Rots van eksekusie
Umtata Dam
Indwe
Garryowen
Cala
Whitmore
Nobantu
Libode
Sterkstroom
White Kei
Braunville
Askeaton
Ntibane
R 61
Mlenganapas
Lady Frere
Lufuta
Langdon
UMTATA
Misty Mount
R 61
Ntshilini
Engcobo
Coghlan
Buntingville
Nqgeleni
Tombo
Qoqodala
Baile
Lubisi Dam
Tsazo
All Saints Nek
Viedgesville
Old Bunting
Port St. John
Xonxa Dam
Driver's Drift
Southeyville
Ncora Dam
Ncora
Notintsila
Bowker's Park
Bityi
Clarkebury
N 2
Mqanduli
Umtata
68
Queenstown
Ezibeleni
Nobokwe
Bashee Bridge
Ngqungqu
Hluleka N.R.
R 61
Dieptun/ Sunken Gardens
Bolotwa
Qamata
R 61
Garner's Drift
Munyu
Tsomo
St. Marks
Cofimvaba
Qombolo
Tsomo
Hange
Elliotdale
Old Morley
Tshani
R
Coffee Bay
R 67
Tylden
Ntseshe
Sada
Whittlesea
Idutywa
Alderley
Swart Kei
Xolobe
Bashee
Mnewasa Point
Waqu
Ebende
Rothmere
Nqamakwe
Taleni
Waterdown dam
R351
R351
Willowvale
Hobeni
2371 m
Cathcart
R 67
The Haven
Ciko
Dwesa Nature Reserve/-natuurreservaat
Devils Bellows Nek
Nico Malan Pass/-pas
Katbergpas
R345
N 6
Bolo Reserve
Butterworth
Nyokana
Nqabara
Kologha-bosreservaat Kologha Forest Reserve
R352
Manubi
Balfour
Mgwali
Qobogobo
Qora Mouth
Seymour
Kei Cuttings
Great Kei River Bridge
Cats Pass
Mazeppa Bay
Stutterheim
Dohne
Centani
Liddleton
Sundial/ Sonwyser
Hogsback
Gaika's Grave/ Gaika se graf
Bethel
Komga
R 63
Great Kei
Blinkwater
Keiskammahoek
Wavecrest
Fort Beaufort
Fort Hare
CISKEI
R352
Amabele
Mpetu
R349
Qolora Mouth
N 2
Kei Road
R346
Quko
Kei Mouth
Alice
Fort Hare
Rooikrans dam
Macleantown
Morgan's Bay
S
Martello Tower/-toring
Middeldrift
Braunschweig
Tainton
BISHO
Cintsa
Haga-Haga
R 67
King William's Town
Breidbach
N 6
Historic Building
Potsdam
Fort Willshire
Kwa-Pita
Zwelitsha
Berlin
Gonubie Mouth
MDANTSANE
Beacon Bay
Keiskama
N 2
Fort Murray
Dawn
Bonza Bay
R344
Lekfontein
R346
EAST LONDON
OOS-LONDEN
Breakfast Vlei
Sittingbourne
Fort Brown
Committees
R345
Watch Tower/ Wagtoring
R347
Fort Glamorgan
Fort Brown
Chalumna
R 72
Ecca Pass/-pas
Peddie
Kidd's Beach
GRAHAMSTOWN
GRAHAMSTAD
Bell
Wooldridge
R345
Fort Selwyn
Great Fish
Keiskammapunt
Hamburg
Old Provost
R 67
Fallodon
Wesley
Langholm
Salem
T
R343
Bathurst
R 72
Great Fish Point
Southwell
Kasuka Road
Settlers Church/Setlaarskerk
Port Alfred
Kariega
Kenton-on-Sea
Boesmansriviermond
Dias Cross/Diaskruis
Boknesstrand (Richmond)
Cape Padrone
INDIESE OSEAAN
N
U
13
14
15
16

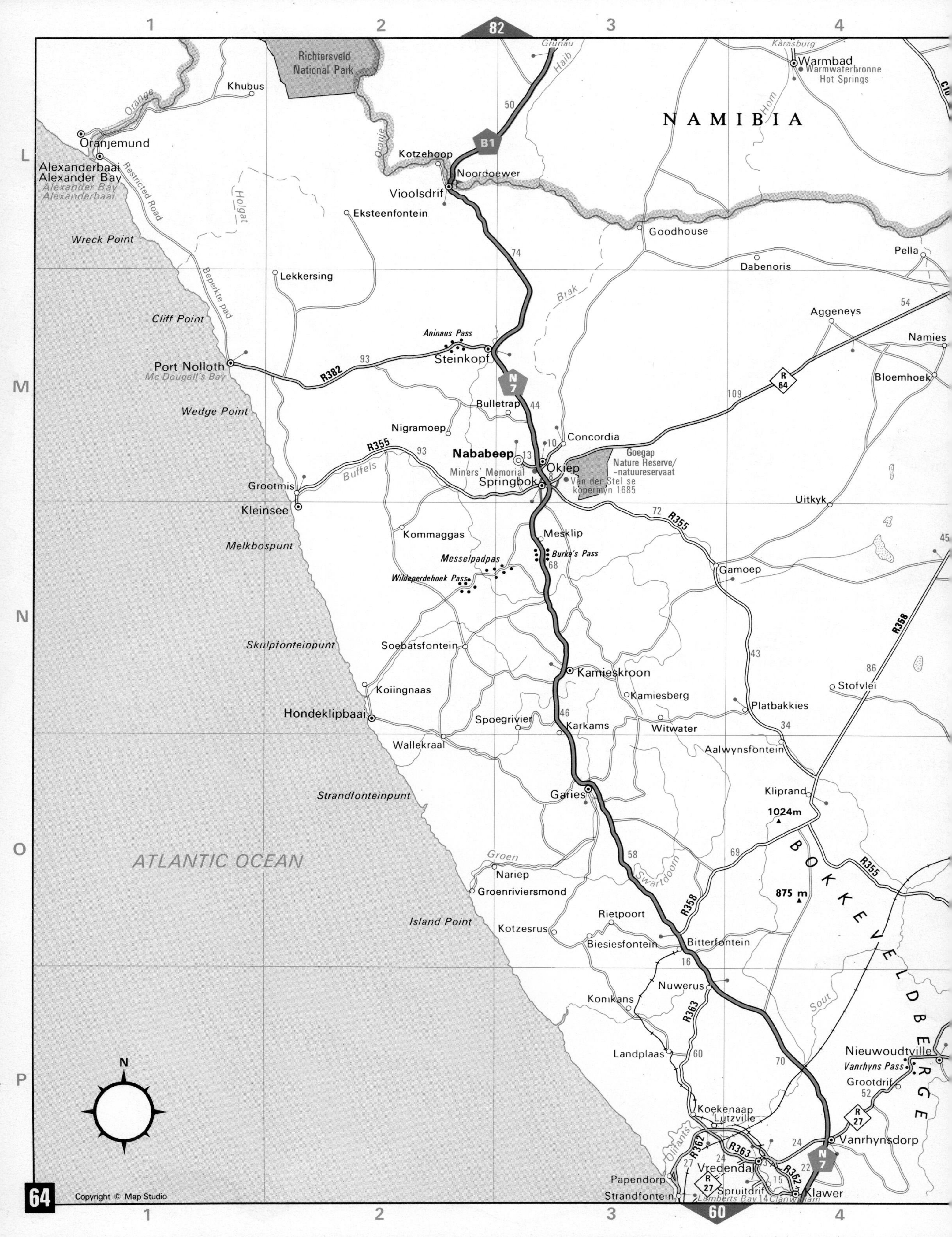
Richtersveld National Park
Khubus
Oranjemund
Alexanderbaai
Alexander Bay
Restricted Road
Holgat
Wreck Point
Lekkersing
Beperkte pad
Cliff Point
Port Nolloth
Mc Dougall's Bay
Wedge Point
Grootmis
Kleinsee
Melkbospunt
Skulpfonteinpunt
Koiingnaas
Hondeklipbaai
Wallekraal
Strandfonteinpunt
ATLANTIC OCEAN
Island Point
NAMIBIA
Warmbad
Warmwaterbronne
Hot Springs
Kotzehoop
Noordoewer
Vioolsdrif
Eksteenfontein
Goodhouse
Dabenoris
Pella
Aggeneys
Namies
Bloemhoek
Aninaus Pass
Steinkopf
Bulletrap
Nigramoep
Concordia
Nababeep
Miners' Memorial
Okiep
Springbok
Goegap Nature Reserve/ -natuureservaat
Van der Stel se kopermyn 1685
Uitkyk
Kommaggas
Mesklip
Burke's Pass
Messelpadpas
Wildeperdehoek Pass
Gamoep
Soebatsfontein
Kamieskroon
Kamiesberg
Stofvlei
Platbakkies
Spoegrivier
Karkams
Witwater
Aalwynsfontein
Kliprand
Garies
1024m
BOKKEVELDBERGE
875 m
Nariep
Groenriviersmond
Kotzesrus
Rietpoort
Biesiesfontein
Bitterfontein
Nuwerus
Konikans
Landplaas
Nieuwoudtville
Vanrhyns Pass
Grootdrif
Koekenaap
Lutzville
Vanrhynsdorp
Vredendal
Papendorp
Strandfontein
Spruitdrif
Klawer
Lamberts Bay
Clanwilliam
Karasburg
Grünau
R382
R355
R358
R363
R362
R27
R64
N7
B1
82
60

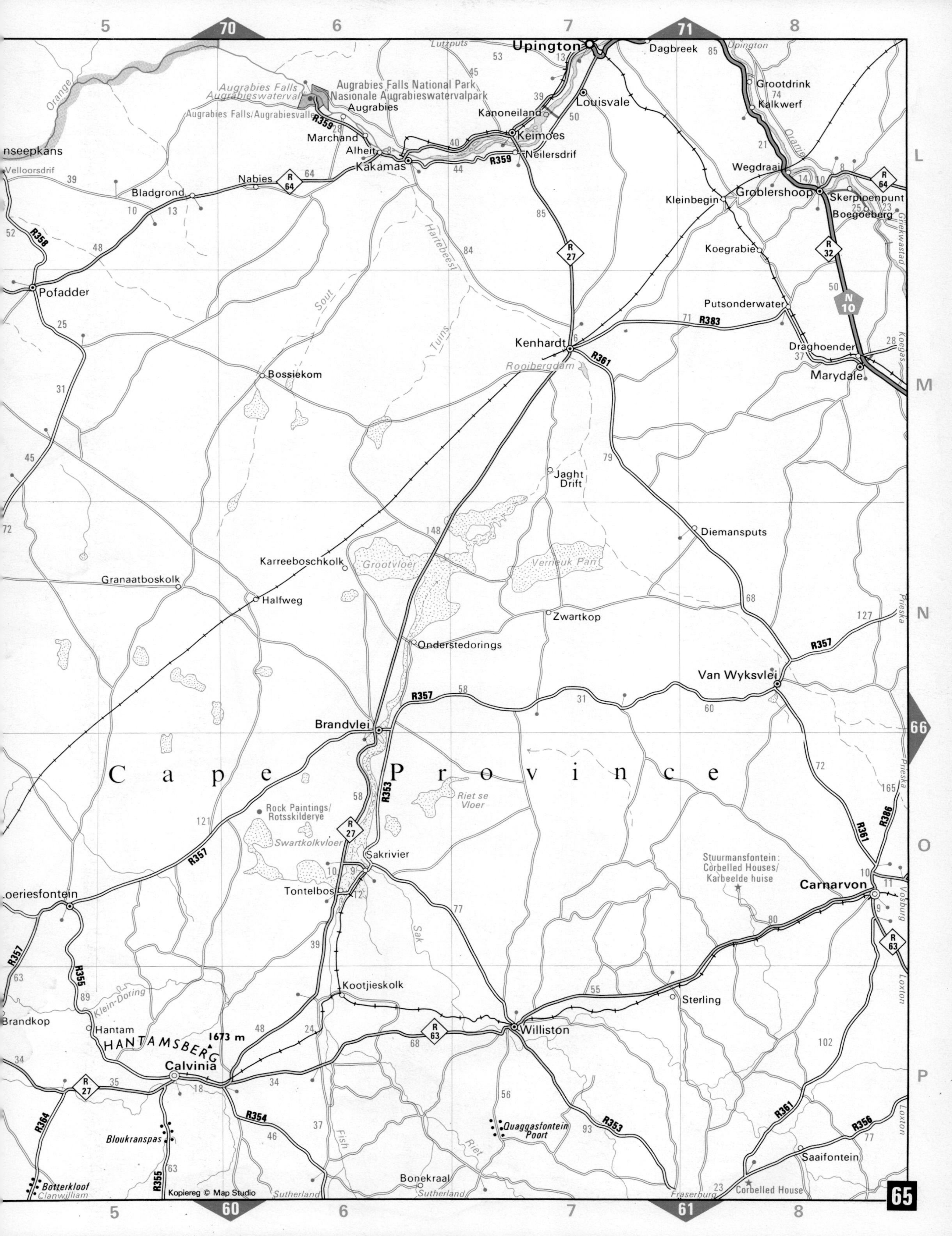

Upington
Dagbreek
Grootdrink
Kalkwerf
Augrabies Falls National Park
Nasionale Augrabieswatervalpark
Augrabies Falls
Augrabieswaterval
Augrabies
Kanoneiland
Louisvale
Keimoes
Neilersdrif
Marchand
Alheit
Kakamas
Onseepkans
Velloorsdrif
Nabies
Bladgrond
Wegdraai
Groblershoop
Skerpioenpunt
Boegoeberg
Kleinbegin
Koegrabie
Pofadder
Putsonderwater
Kenhardt
Draghoender
Marydale
Rooibergdam
Bossiekom
Jaght Drift
Diemansputs
Karreeboschkolk
Grootvloer
Verneuk Pan
Granaatboskolk
Halfweg
Zwartkop
Onderstedorings
Van Wyksvlei
Brandvlei
Cape Province
Riet se Vloer
Rock Paintings/ Rotsskilderye
Swartkolkvloer
Sakrivier
Tontelbos
Stuurmansfontein: Corbelled Houses/ Karbeelde huise
Carnarvon
Loeriesfontein
Kootjieskolk
Sterling
Williston
Brandkop
Hantam
HANTAMSBERG
1673 m
Calvinia
Bloukranspas
Quaggasfontein Poort
Bonekraal
Saaifontein
Botterkloof
Clanwilliam
Sutherland
Fraserburg
Corbelled House
Kopiereg © Map Studio

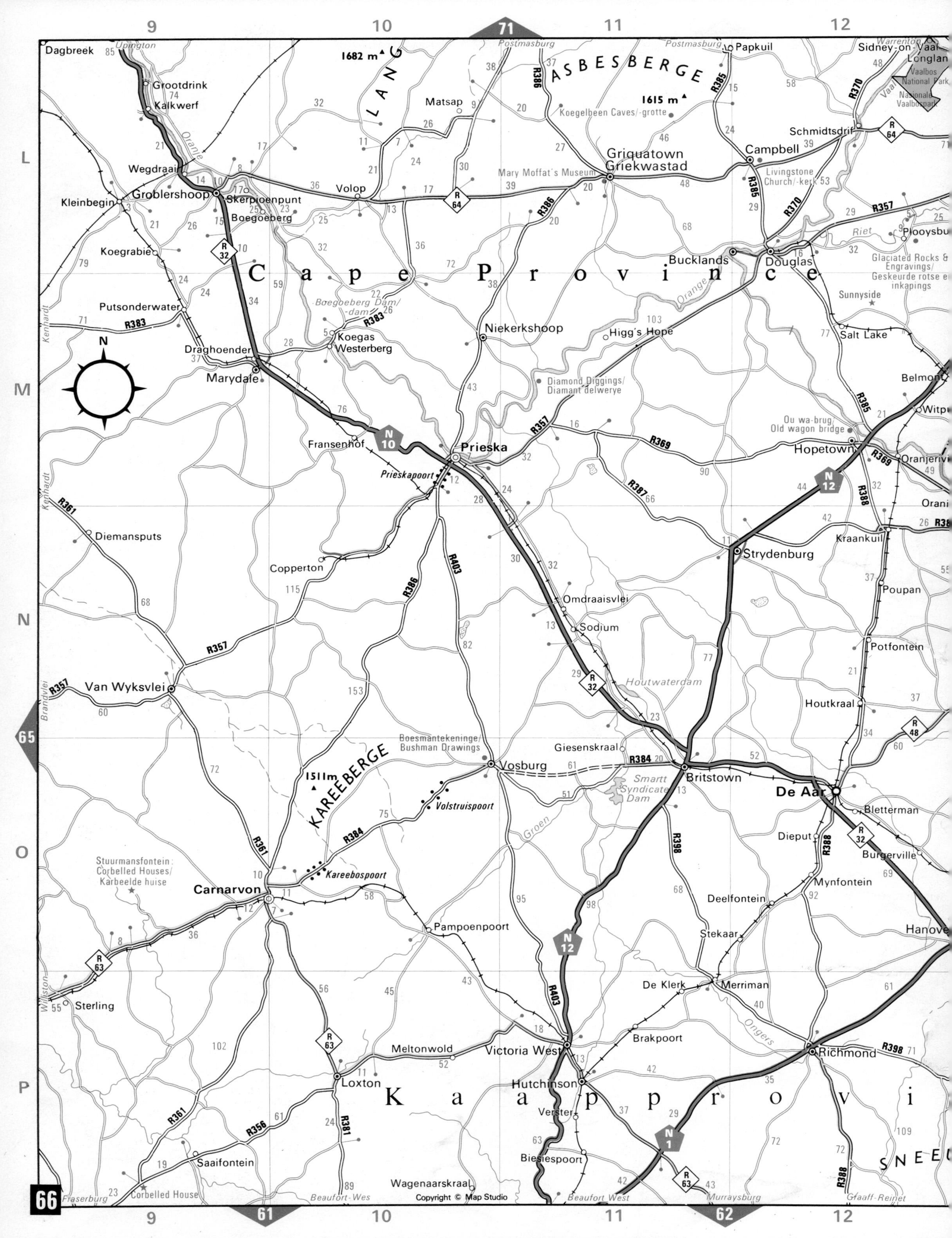

Cape Province
Kapprovi
ASBESBERGE
LANG
KAREEBERGE
SNEEU
Dagbreek
Upington
Grootdrink
Kalkwerf
Oranje
Wegdraai
Kleinbegin
Groblershoop
Skerpioenpunt
Boegoeberg
Koegrabie
Putsonderwater
Draghoender
Marydale
Kenhardt
Volop
Matsap
Boegoeberg Dam/-dam
Koegas
Westerberg
Niekerkshoop
Higg's Hope
Diamond Diggings/Diamant delwerye
Fransenhof
Prieska
Prieskapoort
Postmasburg
Papkuil
Sidney-on-Vaal
Longlands
Vaalbos National Park
Nasionale Vaalbospark
Warrenton
Vaal
Koegelbeen Caves/-grotte
Griquatown
Griekwastad
Mary Moffat's Museum
Campbell
Schmidtsdrif
Livingstone Church/-kerk
Bucklands
Douglas
Riet
Plooysburg
Glaciated Rocks & Engravings/
Geskeurde rotse en inkapings
Sunnyside
Salt Lake
Belmont
Witputs
Ou wa-brug/
Old wagon bridge
Hopetown
Oranjerivier
Orange
Kraankuil
Poupan
Potfontein
Houtkraal
Strydenburg
Omdraaisvlei
Sodium
Houtwaterdam
Diemansputs
Copperton
Van Wyksvlei
Brandvlei
Boesmantekeninge/
Bushman Drawings
Vosburg
Giesenskraal
Britstown
Smartt Syndicate Dam
De Aar
Bletterman
Dieput
Burgerville
Mynfontein
Deelfontein
Stekaar
Hanover
Merriman
De Klerk
Ongers
Richmond
Brakpoort
Volstruispoort
Kareebospoort
Groen
Stuurmansfontein:
Corbelled Houses/
Karbeelde huise
Carnarvon
Pampoenpoort
Sterling
Williston
Meltonwold
Victoria West
Hutchinson
Verster
Biesiespoort
Loxton
Saaifontein
Wagenaarskraal
Fraserburg
Corbelled House
Beaufort-Wes
Beaufort West
Murraysburg
Graaff-Reinet
1682 m
1615 m
1511m
N 10
N 12
N 1
R 32
R 64
R 63
R 48
R383
R386
R385
R370
R357
R369
R387
R388
R361
R403
R384
R398
R356
R381
L
M
N
O
P
9
10
11
12
71
65
61
62
Copyright © Map Studio

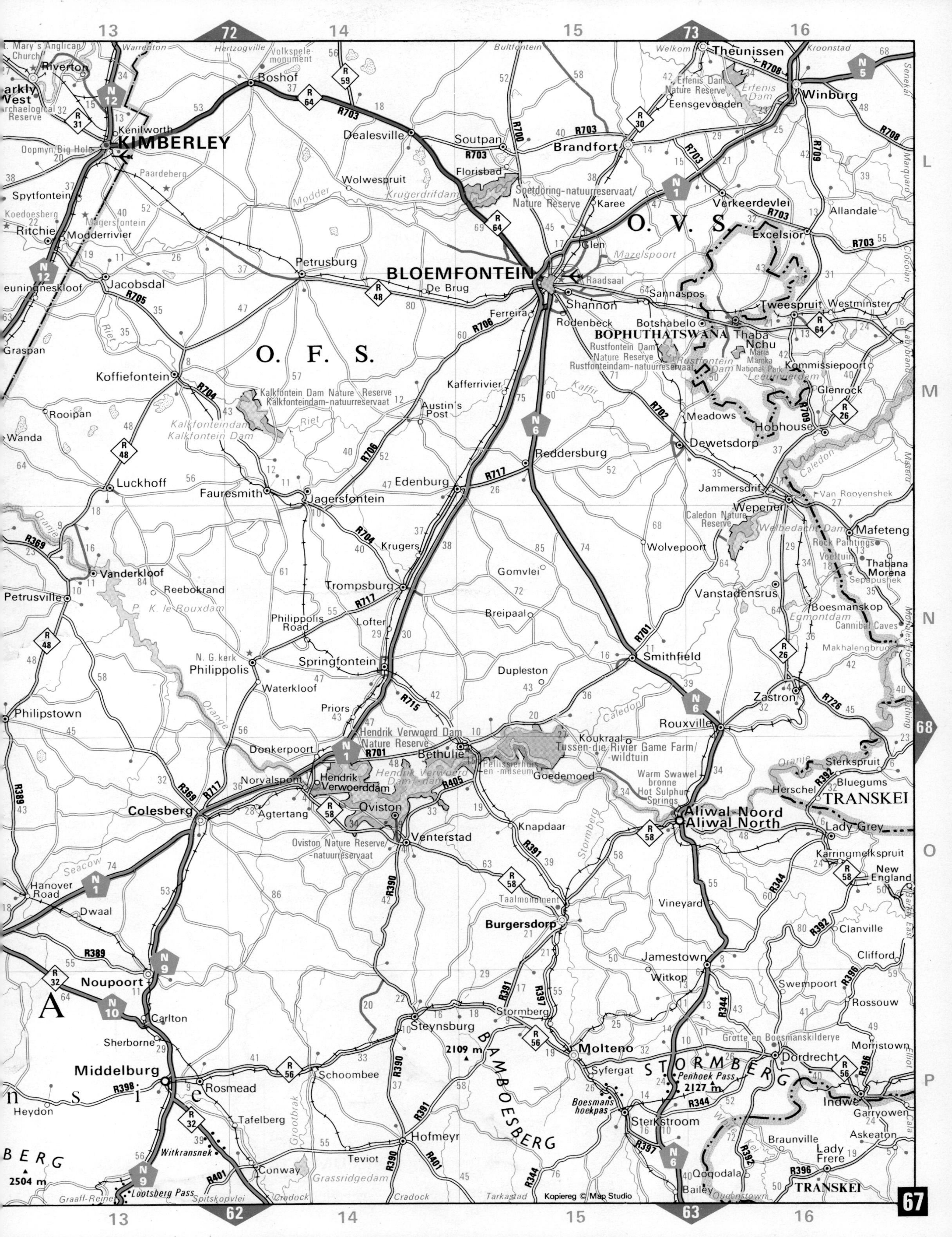

13
72
14
15
73
16
KIMBERLEY
Riverton
Warrenton
Hertzogville
Volkspele-monument
Boshof
Dealesville
Soutpan
Florisbad
Bultfontein
Brandfort
Welkom
Theunissen
Kroonstad
Winburg
Erfenis Dam Nature Reserve
Eensgevonden
Senekal
Kenilworth
Oopmyn/Big Hole
Paardeberg
Wolwespruit
Modder
Krugerdrifdam
Soetdoring-natuurreservaat/ Nature Reserve
Karee
Verkeerdevlei
Allandale
Marquard
Spytfontein
Koedoesberg
Magersfontein
Ritchie
Modderrivier
Petrusburg
BLOEMFONTEIN
Glen
Mazelspoort
Raadsaal
O. V. S.
Excelsior
Clocolan
Jacobsdal
De Brug
Sannaspos
Shannon
Tweespruit
Westminster
Ferreira
Rodenbeck
Botshabelo
Thaba Nchu
BOPHUTHATSWANA
Rustfontein Dam Nature Reserve
Rustfonteindam-natuurreservaat
Maria Moroka National Park
Leeuwkopdam
Kommissiepoort
Glenrock
Graspan
O. F. S.
Koffiefontein
Kalkfontein Dam Nature Reserve
Kalkfonteindam-natuurreservaat
Kafferrivier
Austin's Post
Kaffir
Rooipan
Kalkfonteindam
Kalkfontein Dam
Riet
Meadows
Hobhouse
Wanda
Dewetsdorp
Reddersburg
Edenburg
Luckhoff
Fauresmith
Jagersfontein
Jammersdrif
Van Rooyenshek
Wepener
Caledon
Caledon Nature Reserve
Welbedacht Dam
Mafeteng
Krugers
Wolvepoort
Rock Paintings
Voeltuin
Thabana Morena
Sepapushek
Oranje
Vanderkloof
Reebokrand
Gomvlei
Trompsburg
Vanstadensrus
Petrusville
P. K. le Rouxdam
Boesmanskop
Egmontdam
Cannibal Caves
Breipaal
Philippolis Road
Lofter
Mohaleshoek
Makhalengbrug
Smithfield
N. G. kerk
Philippolis
Springfontein
Dupleston
Waterkloof
Zastron
Quthing
Priors
Philipstown
Orange
Rouxville
Hendrik Verwoerd Dam Nature Reserve
Bethulie
Koukraal
Tussen-die-Rivier Game Farm/ -wildtuin
Donkerpoort
Pellissierhuis en -museum
Goedemoed
Sterkspruit
Norvalspont
Hendrik Verwoerddam
Hendrik Verwoerd Dam
Warm Swawel bronne
Hot Sulphur Springs
Bluegums
Herschel
TRANSKEI
Colesberg
Agtertang
Oviston
Aliwal-Noord
Aliwal North
Lady Grey
Venterstad
Oviston Nature Reserve/ -natuurreservaat
Knapdaar
Stormberg
Karringmelkspruit
Seacow
New England
Hanover Road
Taalmonument
Vineyard
Barkly East
Dwaal
Burgersdorp
Clanville
Jamestown
Clifford
Witkop
Swempoort
Noupoort
Rossouw
A
Carlton
Steynsburg
Sherborne
2109 m
BAMBOESBERG
Molteno
Grotte en Boesmanskilderye
Morristown
Dordrecht
Middelburg
Rosmead
Schoombee
Syfergat
STORMBERG
Penhoek Pass
2127 m
Elliot
Indwe
Heydon
Boesmans hoekpas
Garryowen
Tafelberg
Sterkstroom
Cala
Braunville
Askeaton
White Kei
BERG
2504 m
Witkransnek
Teviot
Hofmeyr
Lady Frere
Conway
Grassridgedam
Qoqodala
Grootbrak
Graaff-Reinet
Lootsberg Pass
Spitskopvlei
Cradock
Tarkastad
Kopiereg © Map Studio
Bailey
Queenstown
L
M
N
O
P
62
63
68

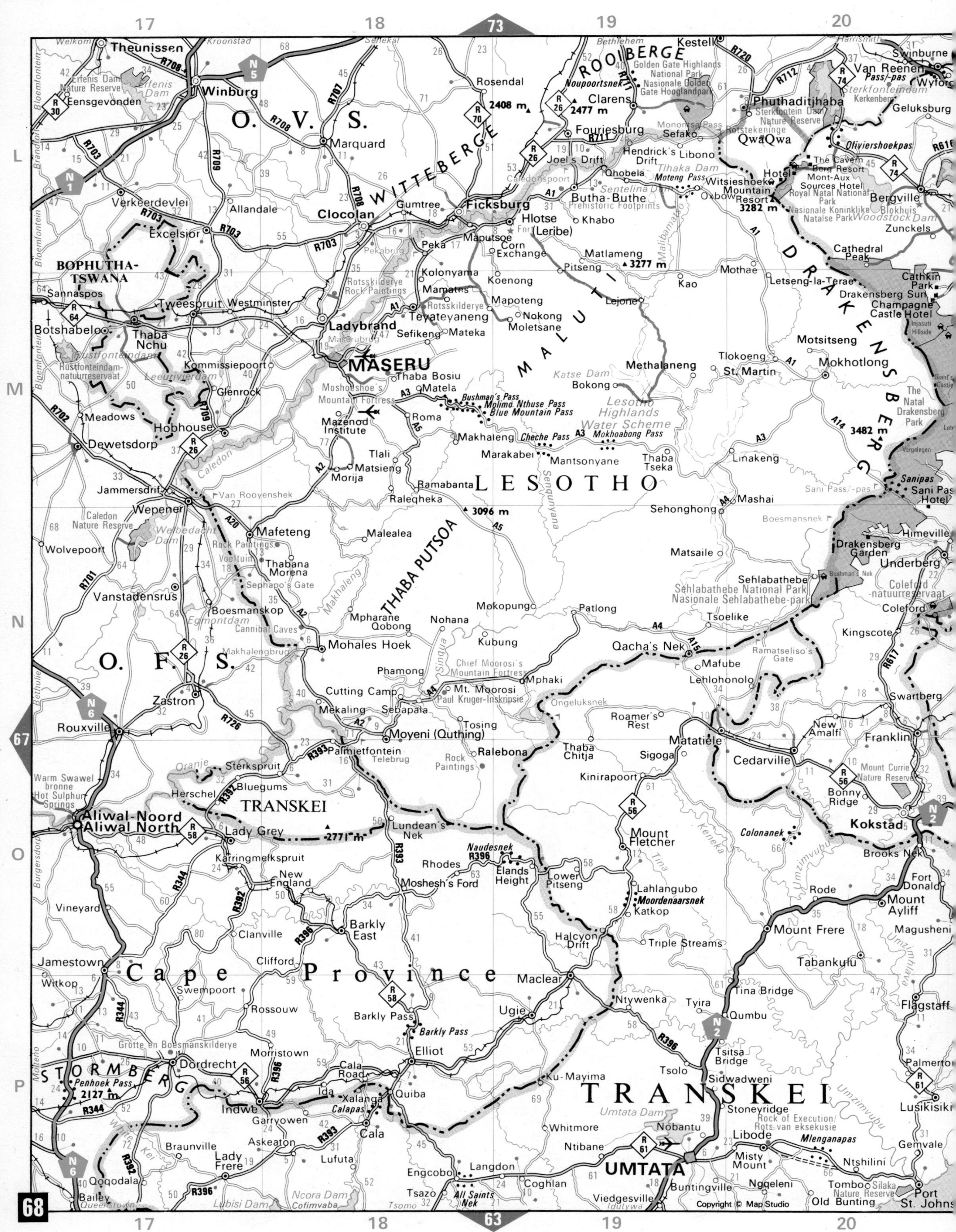

17
18
73
19
20
L
M
N
O
P
67
63
Welkom
Theunissen
Kroonstad
Senekal
Bethlehem
Kestell
Harrismith
Swinburne
Van Reenen
Pass/-pas
Wyford
Erfenis Dam
Nature Reserve
Erfenis Dam
Eensgevonden
Winburg
O. V. S.
Rosendal
ROOIBERGE
Golden Gate Highlands National Park
Nasionale Golden Gate Hooglandpark
Noupoortsnek
Clarens
2408 m
2477 m
Phuthaditjhaba
Sterkfontein Dam
Nature Reserve
Sterkfonteindam
Kerkenberg
Geluksburg
Fouriesburg
Monontsa Pass
Sefako
Rotstekeninge
QwaQwa
Oliviershoekpas
Marquard
WITTEBERGE
Joel's Drift
Hendrick's Drift
Libono
Tlhaka Dam
The Cavern
Berg Resort
Mont-Aux Sources Hotel
Royal Natal National Park
Nasionale Koninklike Natalse Park
Hotel
Qhobela
Moteng Pass
Witsieshoek Mountain Resort
3282 m
Oxbow
Sentelina Dam
Caledonspoort
Butha-Buthe
Prehistoric Footprints
Bergville
Blokhuis
Woodstock Dam
Verkeerdevlei
Allandale
Clocolan
Gumtree
Ficksburg
Hlotse (Leribe)
Khabo
Zunckels
Excelsior
Pekabrug
Peka
Maputsoe
Corn Exchange
Matlameng
3277 m
Malibamatso
Cathedral Peak
BOPHUTHA-TSWANA
Kolonyama
Koenong
Pitseng
Mothae
Kao
Letseng-la-Terae
Cathkin Park
Drakensberg Sun
Champagne Castle Hotel
Injasuti Hillside
DRAKENSBERG
Rotsskilderye Rock Paintings
Mamates
Rotsskilderye
Mapoteng
Lejone
Sannaspos
Tweespruit
Westminster
Teyateyaneng
Nokong
Moletsane
MALUTI
Botshabelo
Thaba Nchu
Ladybrand
Maserubrug
Sefikeng
Mateka
Motsitseng
Rustfonteindam
Rustfonteindam-natuurreservaat
Kommissiepoort
MASERU
Methalaneng
Tlokoeng
St. Martin
Mokhotlong
Leeuriviersdam
Thaba Bosiu
Katse Dam
Bokong
Giant's Castle
Glenrock
Moshoeshoe's Mountain Fortress
Matela
Bushman's Pass
Molimo Nthuse Pass
Blue Mountain Pass
Lesotho Highlands Water Scheme
The Natal Drakensberg Park
Meadows
Mazenod Institute
Roma
3482 m
Hobhouse
Makhaleng
Cheche Pass
Mokhoabong Pass
Dewetsdorp
Caledon
Marakabei
Mantsonyane
Thaba Tseka
Linakeng
Vergelegen
Tlali
Matsieng
Morija
Sanipas
Sani Pass/-pas
Sani Pass Hotel
Jammersdrif
Ramabanta
LESOTHO
Senqunyana
Van Rooyenshek
Raleqheka
Mashai
Wepener
3096 m
Sehonghong
Caledon Nature Reserve
Welbedacht Dam
Mafeteng
Boesmansnek
Himeville
Wolvepoort
Malealea
Drakensberg Garden
Underberg
Rock Paintings
Voeltuin
THABA PUTSOA
Matsaile
Thabana Morena
Sephapo's Gate
Sehlabathebe
Bushman's Nek
Coleford -natuurreservaat
Vanstadensrus
Sehlabathebe National Park
Nasionale Sehlabathebe-park
Coleford
Boesmanskop
Egmontdam
Cannibal Caves
Mpharane
Qobong
Nohana
Mokopung
Patlong
Tsoelike
Kingscote
Makhalengbrug
Mohales Hoek
Kubung
Qacha's Nek
Ramatseliso's Gate
O. F. S.
Phamong
Chief Moorosi's Mountain Fortress
Mafube
Mphaki
Lehlohonolo
Cutting Camp
Mt. Moorosi
Paul Kruger-Inskripsie
Swartberg
Zastron
Ongeluksnek
Mekaling
Sebapala
Roamer's Rest
New Amalfi
Rouxville
Tosing
Moyeni (Quthing)
Matatiele
Franklin
Palmietfontein
Telebrug
Ralebona
Thaba Chitja
Sigoga
Cedarville
Sterkspruit
Oranje
Rock Paintings
Kinirapoort
Mount Currie Nature Reserve
Warm Swawel bronne
Hot Sulphur Springs
Herschel
Bluegums
TRANSKEI
Bonny Ridge
Aliwal-Noord
Aliwal North
Lady Grey
2771 m
Lundean's Nek
Mount Fletcher
Colonanek
Kokstad
Karringmelkspruit
Naudesnek
Rhodes
Elands Height
Lower Pitseng
Brooks Nek
New England
Moshesh's Ford
Lahlangubo
Moordenaarsnek
Katkop
Fort Donald
Rode
Mount Ayliff
Vineyard
Barkly East
Mount Frere
Clanville
Halcyon Drift
Triple Streams
Magusheni
Jamestown
Clifford
Tabankulu
Cape Province
Maclear
Witkop
Swempoort
Tina Bridge
Rossouw
Barkly Pass
Ugie
Ntywenka
Tyira
Qumbu
Flagstaff
Grotte en Boesmanskilderye
Morristown
Barkly Pass
Elliot
Tsitsa Bridge
Palmerton
STORMBERG
Dordrecht
Cala Road
Tsolo
Penhoek Pass
2127 m
Ida
Quiba
Ku-Mayima
Sidwadweni
Indwe
Xalanga
Calapas
TRANSKEI
Umzimvubu
Lusikisiki
Garryowen
Umtata Dam
Stoneyridge
Rock of Execution/Rots van eksekusie
Cala
Whitmore
Nobantu
Braunville
Askeaton
Lufuta
Ntibane
Libode
Mlenganapas
Gemvale
Lady Frere
Langdon
UMTATA
Misty Mount
Ntshilini
Qoqodala
Engcobo
Coghlan
Buntingville
Ngqeleni
Tombo
Silaka Nature Reserve
Port St. Johns
Bailey
Queenstown
Ncora Dam
Cofimvaba
Lubisi Dam
Tsazo
All Saints Nek
Viedgesville
Idutywa
Old Bunting
Tsomo
Copyright © Map Studio

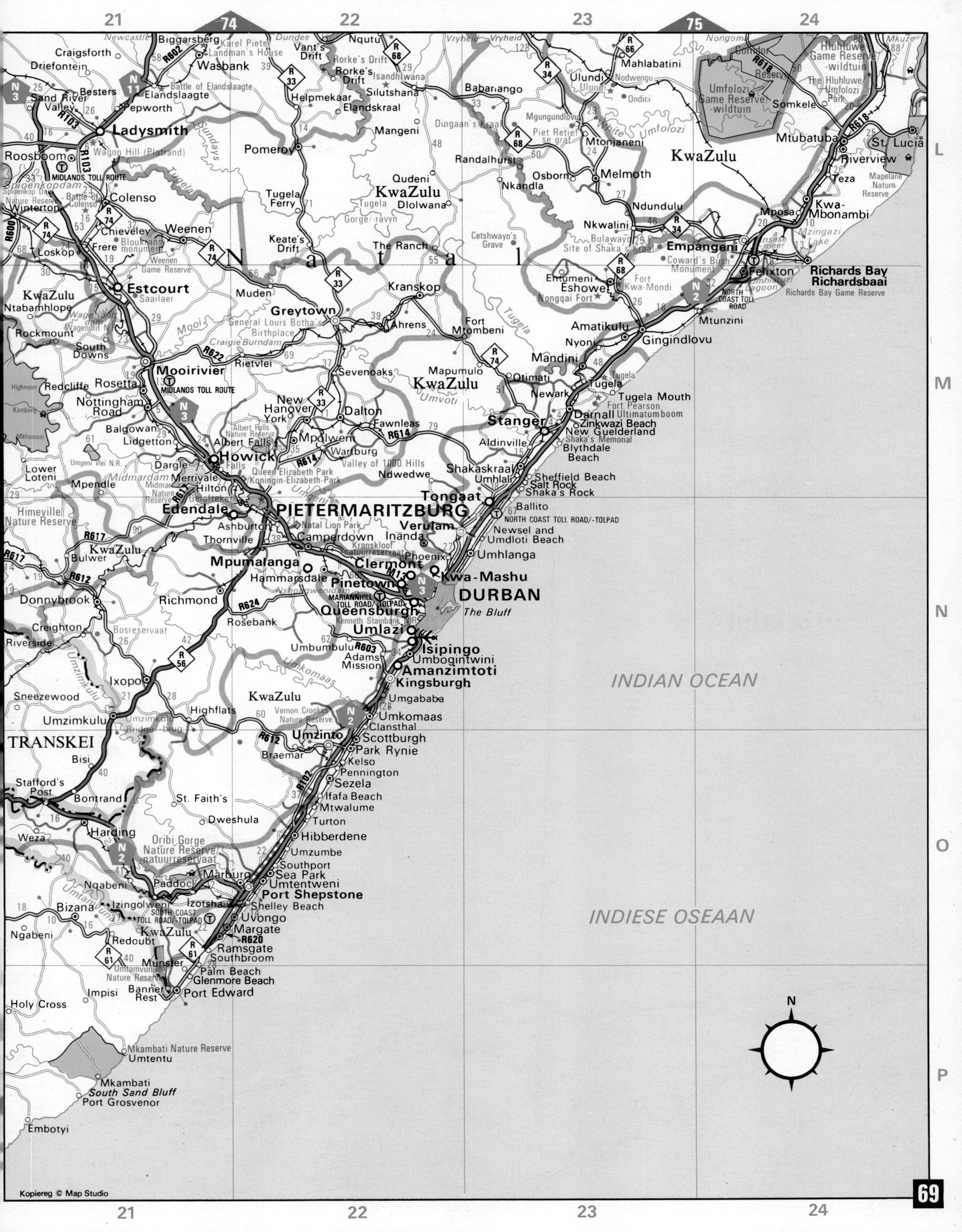
Ladysmith
Estcourt
Mooirivier
Howick
PIETERMARITZBURG
Edendale
Greytown
Stanger
Tongaat
Verulam
DURBAN
Kwa-Mashu
Pinetown
Clermont
Queensburgh
Umlazi
Isipingo
Amanzimtoti
Kingsburgh
Umkomaas
Scottburgh
Umzinto
Port Shepstone
Margate
Ramsgate
Port Edward
Richards Bay
Richardsbaai
Empangeni
Eshowe
Melmoth
Ulundi
Mtubatuba
St. Lucia
Natal
KwaZulu
TRANSKEI
INDIAN OCEAN
INDIESE OSEAAN
L
M
N
O
P
Kopiereg © Map Studio

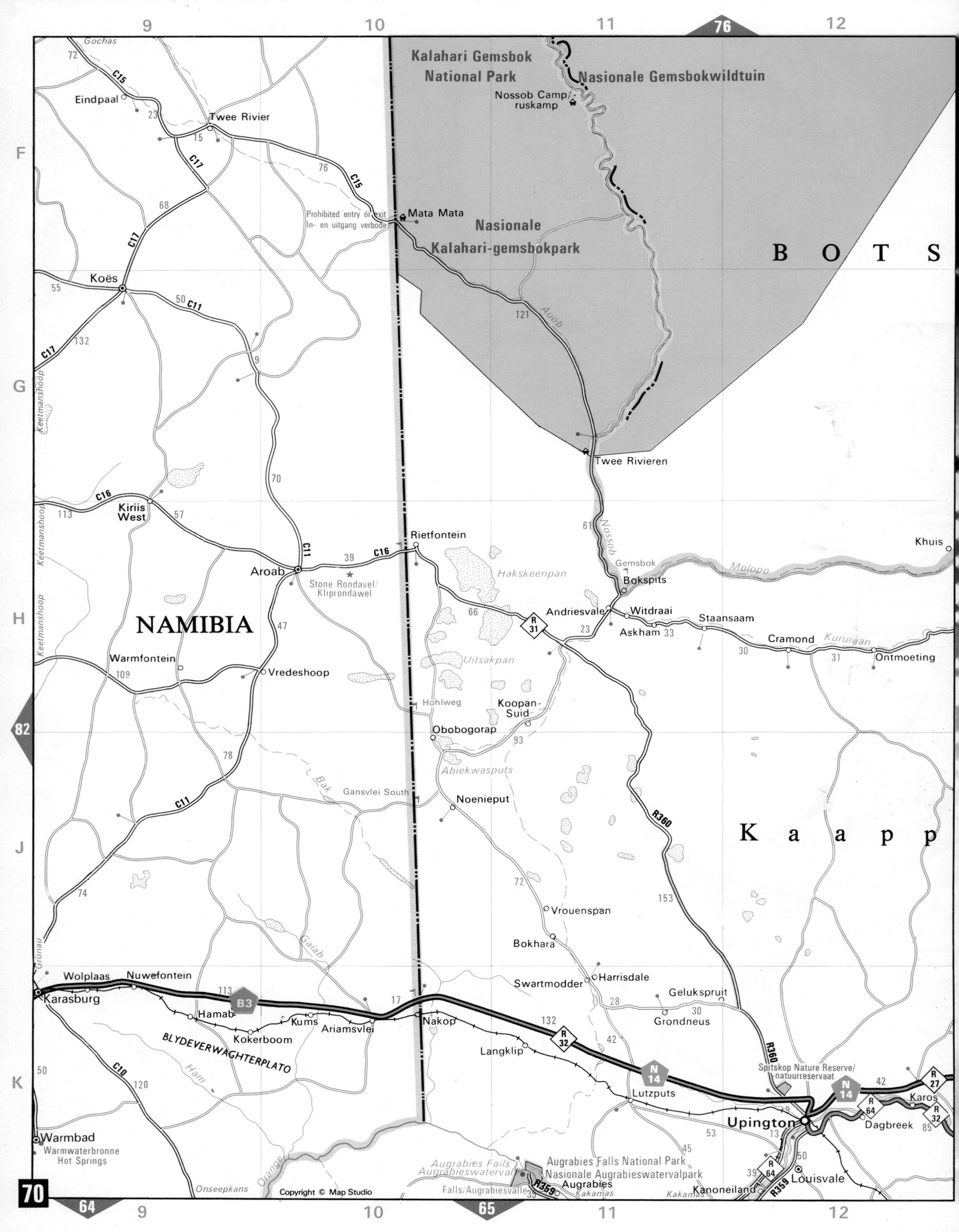

Kalahari Gemsbok National Park
Nasionale Gemsbokwildtuin
Nossob Camp/ruskamp
Mata Mata
Prohibited entry or exit
In- en uitgang verbode
Nasionale Kalahari-gemsbokpark
B O T S
Gochas
Eindpaal
Twee Rivier
Koës
Auob
Twee Rivieren
Kiriis West
Rietfontein
Nossob
Khuis
Gemsbok
Molopo
Hakskeenpan
Bokspits
Aroab
Stone Rondavel/Kliprondawel
Andriesvale
Witdraai
Staansaam
Askham
Cramond
Kuruman
Ontmoeting
NAMIBIA
Warmfontein
Vredeshoop
Uitsakpan
Hohlweg
Koopan-Suid
Obobogorap
Abiekwasputs
Bak
Gansvlei South
Noenieput
Kaapp
Keetmanshoop
Vrouenspan
Bokhara
Gaiab
Grünau
Wolplaas
Nuwefontein
Karasburg
Swartmodder
Harrisdale
Gelukspruit
Hamab
Kums
Ariamsvlei
Nakop
Grondneus
Kokerboom
BLYDEVERWAGHTERPLATO
Langklip
Ham
Spitskop Nature Reserve/natuurreservaat
Lutzputs
Karos
Dagbreek
Upington
Warmbad
Warmwaterbronne Hot Springs
Orange
Augrabies Falls
Augrabieswaterval
Augrabies Falls National Park
Nasionale Augrabieswatervalpark
Augrabies
Louisvale
Kanoneiland
Onseepkans
Falls/Augrabiesvalle
Kakamas
Copyright © Map Studio

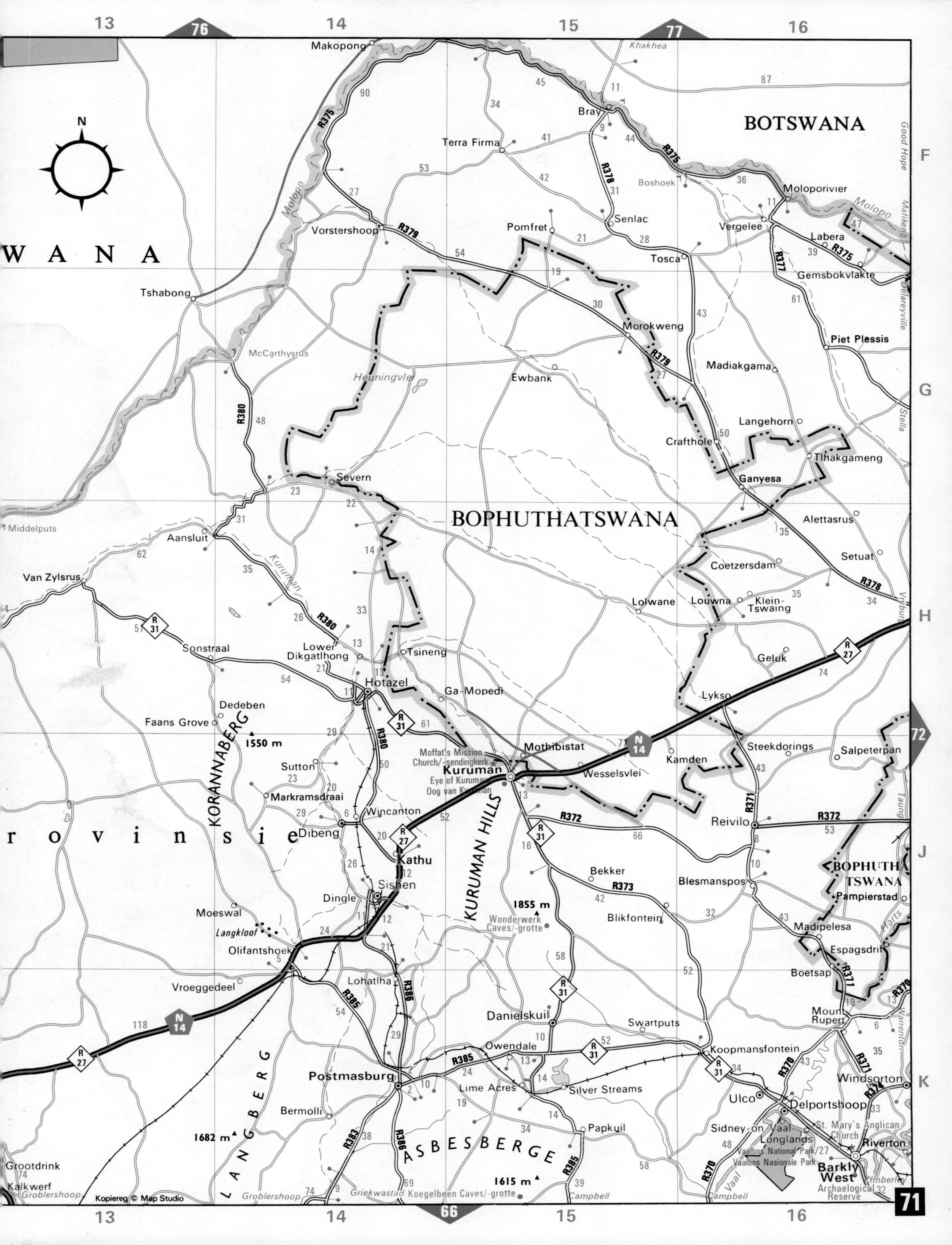

BOTSWANA
WANA
BOPHUTHATSWANA
KORANNABERG
KURUMAN HILLS
LANGBERG
ASBESBERGE
rovinsie
Makopong
Khakhea
Bray
Terra Firma
Boshoek
Moloporivier
Molopo
Senlac
Vorstershoop
Pomfret
Vergelee
Labera
Tosca
Gemsbokvlakte
Tshabong
Morokweng
Piet Plessis
McCarthysrus
Heuningvlei
Ewbank
Madiakgama
Langehorn
Crafthole
Tlhakgameng
Ganyesa
Severn
Middelputs
Aansluit
Alettasrus
Coetzersdam
Setuat
Van Zylsrus
Kuruman
Lolwane
Louwna
Klein-Tswaing
Sonstraal
Lower Dikgatlhong
Tsineng
Geluk
Hotazel
Ga-Mopedi
Lykso
Dedeben
Faans Grove
1550 m
Moffat's Mission Church/-sendingkerk
Kuruman
Eye of Kuruman
Oog van Kuruman
Mothibistat
Wesselsvlei
Kamden
Steekdorings
Salpeterpan
Sutton
Markramsdraai
Wincanton
Reivilo
Dibeng
Kathu
Sishen
Bekker
Blesmanspos
Dingle
1855 m
Wonderwerk Caves/-grotte
Blikfontein
Moeswal
Langkloof
Olifantshoek
Pampierstad
Madipelesa
Espagsdrif
Vroeggedeel
Lohatlha
Boetsap
Danielskuil
Mount Rupert
Swartputs
Owendale
Koopmansfontein
Postmasburg
Lime Acres
Silver Streams
Windsorton
Ulco
Delportshoop
Bermolli
Papkuil
Sidney-on-Vaal
Longlands
St. Mary's Anglican Church
Riverton
Vaalbos National Park/27
Vaalbos Nasionale Park
Barkly West
1682 m
1615 m
Grootdrink
Kalkwerf
Groblershoop
Griekwastad
Koegelbeen Caves/-grotte
Campbell
Vaal
Kimberley
Archaeological Reserve
Good Hope
Mafikeng
Delareyville
Stella
Vryburg
Taung
Harts
Warrenton
R375
R379
R378
R377
R380
R31
R27
N14
R372
R373
R371
R385
R386
R383
R370
R374
13
14
15
16
F
G
H
J
K
76
77
72
66
Kopiereg © Map Studio

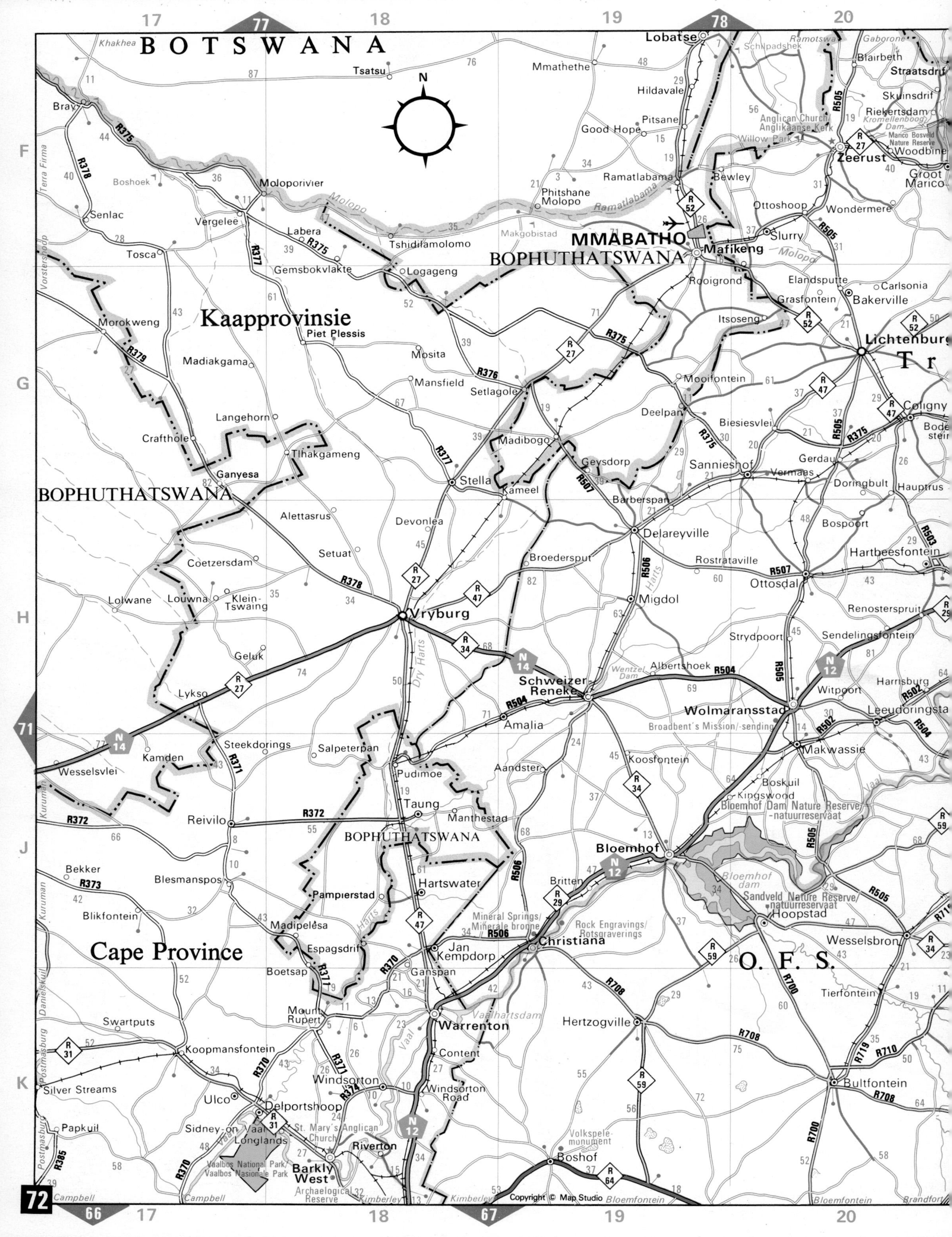
BOTSWANA
Kaapprovinsie
BOPHUTHATSWANA
Cape Province
O. F. S.
MMABATHO
Mafikeng
Lobatse
Zeerust
Lichtenburg
Vryburg
Schweizer-Reneke
Wolmaransstad
Delareyville
Ottosdal
Sannieshof
Bloemhof
Christiana
Hoopstad
Warrenton
Taung
Hartswater
Jan Kempdorp
Barkly West
Boshof
Hertzogville
Bultfontein
Wesselsbron
Makwassie
Leeudoringstad
Copyright © Map Studio

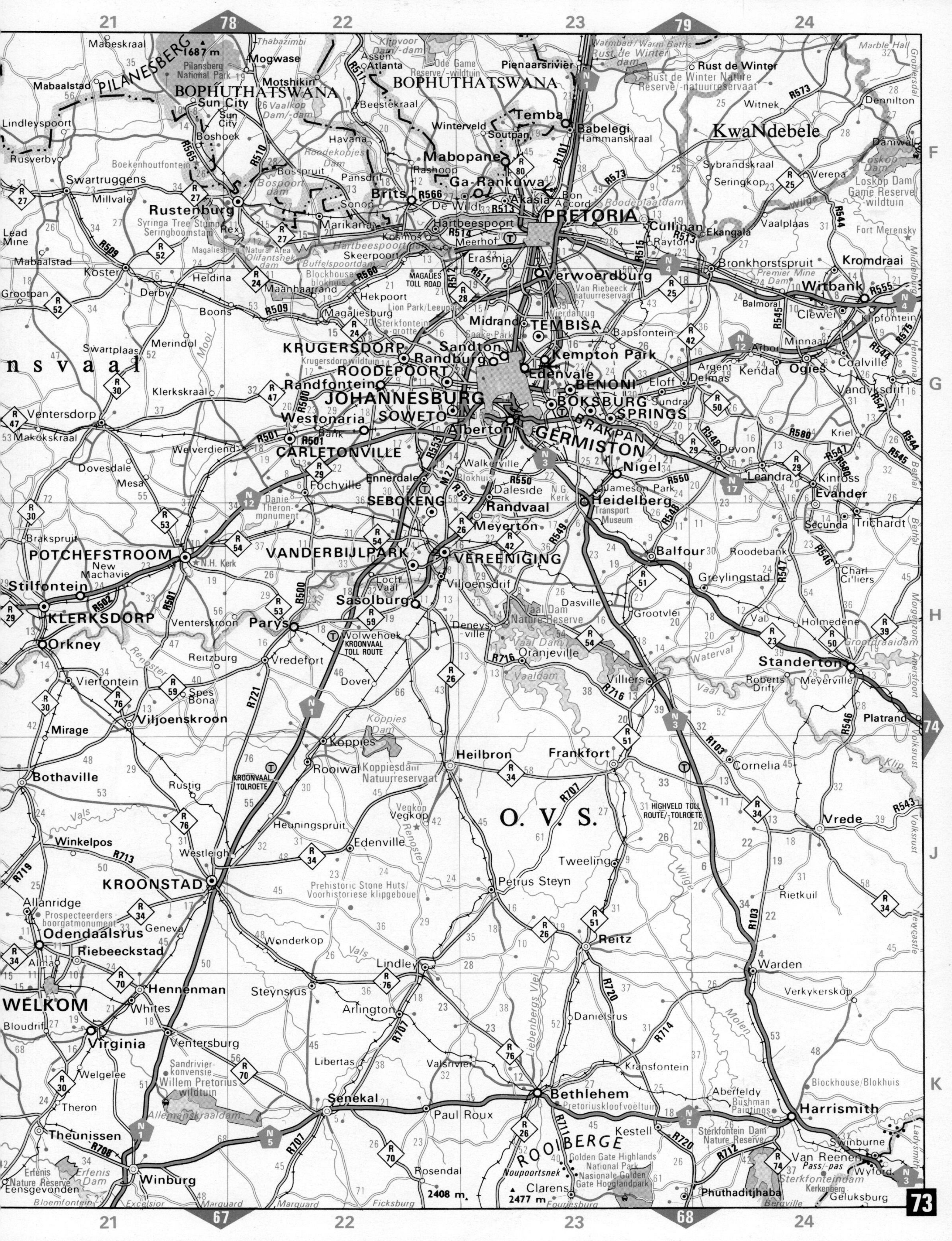

21
22
23
24
78
79
67
68
74
F
G
H
J
K
Mabeskraal
Pilanesberg
1687 m
Pilansberg National Park
Thabazimbi
Mogwase
Klipvoor Dam/-dam
Assen
Atlanta
Ode Game Reserve/-wildtuin
Pienaarsrivier
Warmbad/Warm Baths
Rust de Winter dam
Rust de Winter
Rust de Winter Nature Reserve/-natuurreservaat
Marble Hall
Groblersdal
Mabaalstad
Motshikiri
BOPHUTHATSWANA
Sun City
Beestekraal
Temba
Babelegi
Hammanskraal
Witnek
Dennilton
Lindleyspoort
Vaalkop Dam/-dam
Boshoek
Winterveld
Soutpan
KwaNdebele
Dämwal
Havana
Roodekopjes Dam
Mabopane
Rusverby
Boekenhoutfontein
Bosspruit
Rashoop
Sybrandskraal
Loskop Dam
Swartruggens
Pansdrif
Ga-Rankuwa
Seringkop
Verena
Loskop Dam Game Reserve/-wildtuin
Millvale
Bospoort dam
Brits
Akasia
Bon Accord
Roodeplaatdam
Rustenburg
Sonop
De Wildt
PRETORIA
Syringa Tree Stump/ Seringboomstam
Rex
Marikana
Hartbeespoort
Cullinan
Ekangala
Vaalplaas
Fort Merensky
Lead Mine
Kosmos
Meerhof
Rayton
Hartbeespoort dam
Magaliesburg Natural Area
Olifantsnek dam
Buffelspoortdam
Skeerpoort
Erasmia
Bronkhorstspruit
Kromdraai
Mabaalstad
Koster
Heldina
Blockhouse/ blokhuis
Magalies Toll Road
Verwoerdburg
Premier Mine Dam
Middelburg
Maanhaarrand
Hekpoort
Van Riebeeck natuurreservaat
Witbank
Grootpan
Derby
Balmoral
Clewer
Klipfontein
Boons
Magaliesburg
Lion Park/Leeupark
Wierdabrug
Sterkfontein grotte
Midrand
TEMBISA
Bapsfontein
Merindol
Swartplaas
Snake Park
Minnaar
Mooi
KRUGERSDORP
Sandton
Kempton Park
Arbor
Ogies
Coalville
Krugersdorpwildtuin
Randburg
Edenvale
Argent
Kendal
Hendrina
nsvaal
ROODEPOORT
Delmas
Klerkskraal
Randfontein
BENONI
Eloff
Vandyksdrif
JOHANNESBURG
BOKSBURG
Sundra
Ventersdorp
Westonaria
SOWETO
SPRINGS
Makokskraal
Bank
Alberton
BRAKPAN
Kriel
Welverdiend
CARLETONVILLE
GERMISTON
Devon
Dovesdale
Walkerville
Nigel
Leandra
Kinross
Mesa
Ennerdale
Blokhuis
Fochville
Daleside
N.G. Kerk
Jameson Park
Evander
Danie Theron-monument
SEBOKENG
Randvaal
Heidelberg
Transport Museum
Secunda
Trichardt
Bethal
Brakspruit
Meyerton
VANDERBIJLPARK
VEREENIGING
Balfour
Roodebank
POTCHEFSTROOM
N.H. Kerk
New Machavie
Greylingstad
Charl Ci'liers
Stilfontein
Loch Vaal
Viljoensdrif
Sasolburg
Dasville
Grootvlei
KLERKSDORP
Venterskroon
Parys
Wolwehoek
Kroonvaal Toll Route
Vaal Dam Nature Reserve
Denevs-ville
Val
Holmedene
Morgenzon
Orkney
Reitzburg
Vredefort
Vaal Dam
Oranjeville
Waterval
Grootdraaidam
Amersfoort
Renoster
Vierfontein
Spes Bona
Dover
Vaaldam
Villiers
Standerton
Roberts Drift
Meyerville
Mirage
Viljoenskroon
Koppies Dam
Platrand
Koppies
Heilbron
Frankfort
Cornelia
Klip
Bothaville
Rooiwal
Koppiesdam Natuurreservaat
Kroonvaal Tolroete
Rustig
O. V. S.
Highveld Toll Route/-Tolroete
Vrede
Vals
Vegkop
Heuningspruit
Volksrust
Winkelpos
Edenville
Tweeling
Westleigh
KROONSTAD
Prehistoric Stone Huts/ Voorhistoriese klipgeboue
Petrus Steyn
Wilge
Rietkuil
Allanridge
Prospecteerders-boorgatmonument
Geneva
Newcastle
Odendaalsrus
Wonderkop
Reitz
Riebeeckstad
Lindley
Warden
Alma
WELKOM
Hennenman
Steynsrus
Whites
Arlington
Verkykerskop
Bloudrif
Liebenbergs Vlei
Danielsrus
Molen
Virginia
Ventersburg
Libertas
Valsrivier
Kransfontein
Sandrivier-konvensie
Welgelee
Willem Pretorius-wildtuin
Bethlehem
Pretoriuskloofvoëltuin
Aberfeldy
Bushman Paintings
Blockhouse/Blokhuis
Theron
Senekal
Paul Roux
Harrismith
Allemanskraaldam
Theunissen
Kestell
Sterkfontein Dam Nature Reserve
Swinburne
Ladysmith
ROOIBERGE
Golden Gate Highlands National Park
Nasionale Golden Gate Hooglandpark
Van Reenen Pass/-pas
Wyford
Erfenis Nature Reserve
Erfenis Dam
Rosendal
Noupoortsnek
Sterkfonteindam
Kerkenberg
Winburg
Eensgevonden
Clarens
Phuthaditjhaba
Geluksburg
Bloemfontein
Excelsior
Marquard
Ficksburg
2408 m
2477 m
Fouriesburg
Bergville

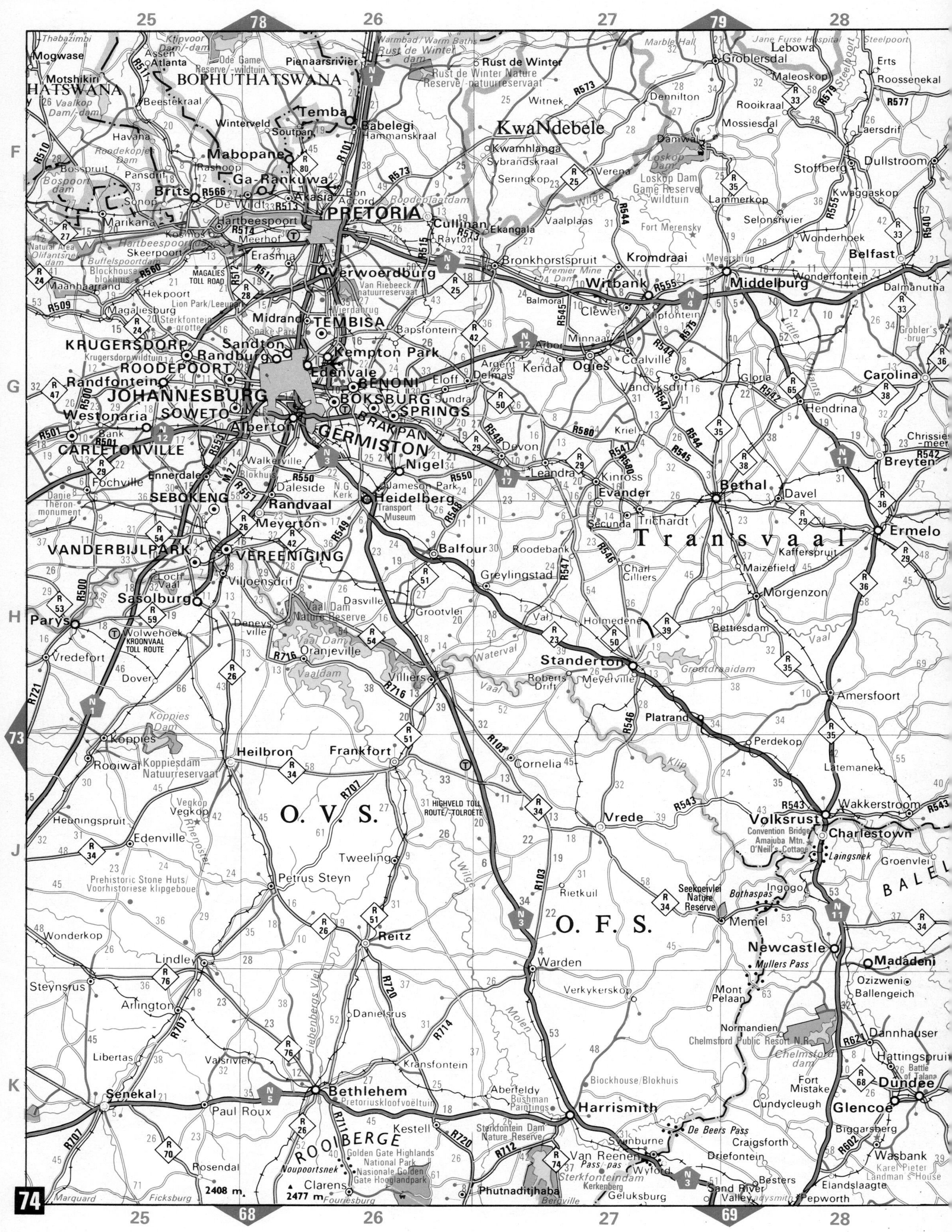

25
78
26
27
79
28
Thabazimbi
Mogwase
Klipvoor Dam/-dam
Assen
Atlanta
Odé Game Reserve/-wildtuin
Pienaarsrivier
Warmbad/Warm Baths
Rust de Winter dam
Rust de Winter
Rust de Winter Nature Reserve/-natuurreservaat
Marble Hall
Groblersdal
Lebowa
Jane Furse Hospital
Steelpoort
Erts
Roossenekal
Motshikiri
BOPHUTHATSWANA
Beestekraal
Vaalkop Dam/-dam
Temba
Babelegi
Hammanskraal
Witnek
Dennilton
Maleoskop
Rooikraal
Mossiesdal
Laersdrif
KwaNdebele
Winterveld
Soutpan
Havana
Roodekopjes Dam
Mabopane
Ga-Rankuwa
Kwamhlanga
Sybrandskraal
Seringkop
Verena
Damwal
Loskop Dam
Loskop Dam Game Reserve/-wildtuin
Stoffberg
Dullstroom
Kwaggaskop
Bosspruit
Bospoort dam
Pansdrif
Rashoop
Brits
De Wildt
Akasia
Bon Accord
Roodeplaatdam
PRETORIA
Cullinan
Rayton
Ekangala
Vaalplaas
Fort Merensky
Lammerkop
Selonsrivier
Wonderhoek
Sonop
Marikana
Hartbeespoort
Kosmos
Meerhof
Hartbeespoortdam
Natural Area Olifantsnek dam
Skeerpoort
Buffelspoortdam
Erasmia
Bronkhorstspruit
Premier Mine Dam
Kromdraai
Meyersbrug
Belfast
Wonderfontein
Blockhouse/blokhuis
Magalies Toll Road
Verwoerdburg
Van Riebeeck Natuurreservaat
Witbank
Middelburg
Dalmanutha
Maanhaarrand
Hekpoort
Lion Park/Leeupark
Wierdabrug
Balmoral
Clewer
Klipfontein
Magaliesburg
Sterkfontein grotte
Midrand
TEMBISA
Snake Park
Bapsfontein
Minnaar
Arbor
Little Olifants
Grobler's brug
KRUGERSDORP
Krugersdorp wildtuin
Randburg
Sandton
ROODEPOORT
Kempton Park
Edenvale
Kendal
Ogies
Coalville
Argent
Delmas
Gloria
Carolina
Randfontein
JOHANNESBURG
BENONI
Eloff
Vandyksdrif
Hendrina
Westonaria
SOWETO
BOKSBURG
Sundra
SPRINGS
Bank
Alberton
BRAKPAN
Kriel
Chrissiesmeer
Breyten
CARLETONVILLE
GERMISTON
Devon
Leandra
Kinross
Walkerville
Blokhuis
Nigel
Fochville
Ennerdale
Daleside
N.G. Kerk
Jameson Park
Evander
Bethal
Davel
Danie Theron-monument
SEBOKENG
Randvaal
Heidelberg
Transport Museum
Secunda
Trichardt
Transvaal
Ermelo
Meyerton
Balfour
Roodebank
Kaffirspruit
VANDERBIJLPARK
VEREENIGING
Loch Vaal
Viljoensdrif
Greylingstad
Charl Cilliers
Maizefield
Sasolburg
Dasville
Grootvlei
Morgenzon
Parys
Wolwehoek
Kroonvaal Toll Route
Deneysville
Vaal Dam Nature Reserve
Vaal Dam
Holmedene
Bettiesdam
Vredefort
Oranjeville
Vaaldam
Waterval
Standerton
Roberts Drift
Meyerville
Grootdraaidam
Dover
Villiers
Amersfoort
Platrand
Koppies Dam
Koppies
Perdekop
Heilbron
Frankfort
Cornelia
Klip
Rooiwal
Koppiesdam Natuurreservaat
Latemanek
Vegkop
Highveld Toll Route/-Tolroete
O. V. S.
Vrede
Wakkerstroom
Volksrust
Heuningspruit
Edenville
Convention Bridge
Amajuba Mtn.
O'Neill's Cottage
Charlestown
Laingsnek
Groenvlei
Tweeling
Wilge
Prehistoric Stone Huts/Voorhistoriese klipgeboue
Petrus Steyn
Rietkuil
Seekoeivlei Nature Reserve
Bothaspas
Ingogo
BALE
Memel
O. F. S.
Wonderkop
Reitz
Newcastle
Lindley
Warden
Mullers Pass
Madadeni
Steynsrus
Ozizweni
Ballengeich
Arlington
Verkykerskop
Mont Pelaan
Danielsrus
Molen
Liebenbergs Vlei
Normandien
Chelmsford Public Resort N.R.
Dannhauser
Hattingspruit
Chelmsford dam
Battle of Talana
Libertas
Valsrivier
Kransfontein
Blockhouse/Blokhuis
Fort Mistake
Dundee
Senekal
Bethlehem
Pretoriuskloofvoëltuin
Aberfeldy
Bushman Paintings
Harrismith
Cundycleugh
Glencoe
Paul Roux
Kestell
Sterkfontein Dam Nature Reserve
De Beers Pass
Swinburne
Biggarsberg
Craigsforth
ROOIBERGE
Golden Gate Highlands National Park
Nasionale Golden Gate Hooglandpark
Noupoortsnek
Van Reenen
Pass/-pas
Wyford
Driefontein
Wasbank
Karel Pieter Landman's House
Rosendal
Sterkfonteindam
Kerkenberg
Besters
Elandslaagte
2408 m
Clarens
2477 m
Phutnaditjhaba
Sand River Valley
Ladysmith
Pepworth
Marquard
Ficksburg
Fouriesburg
Bergville
Geluksburg
F
G
H
J
K
73
68
69

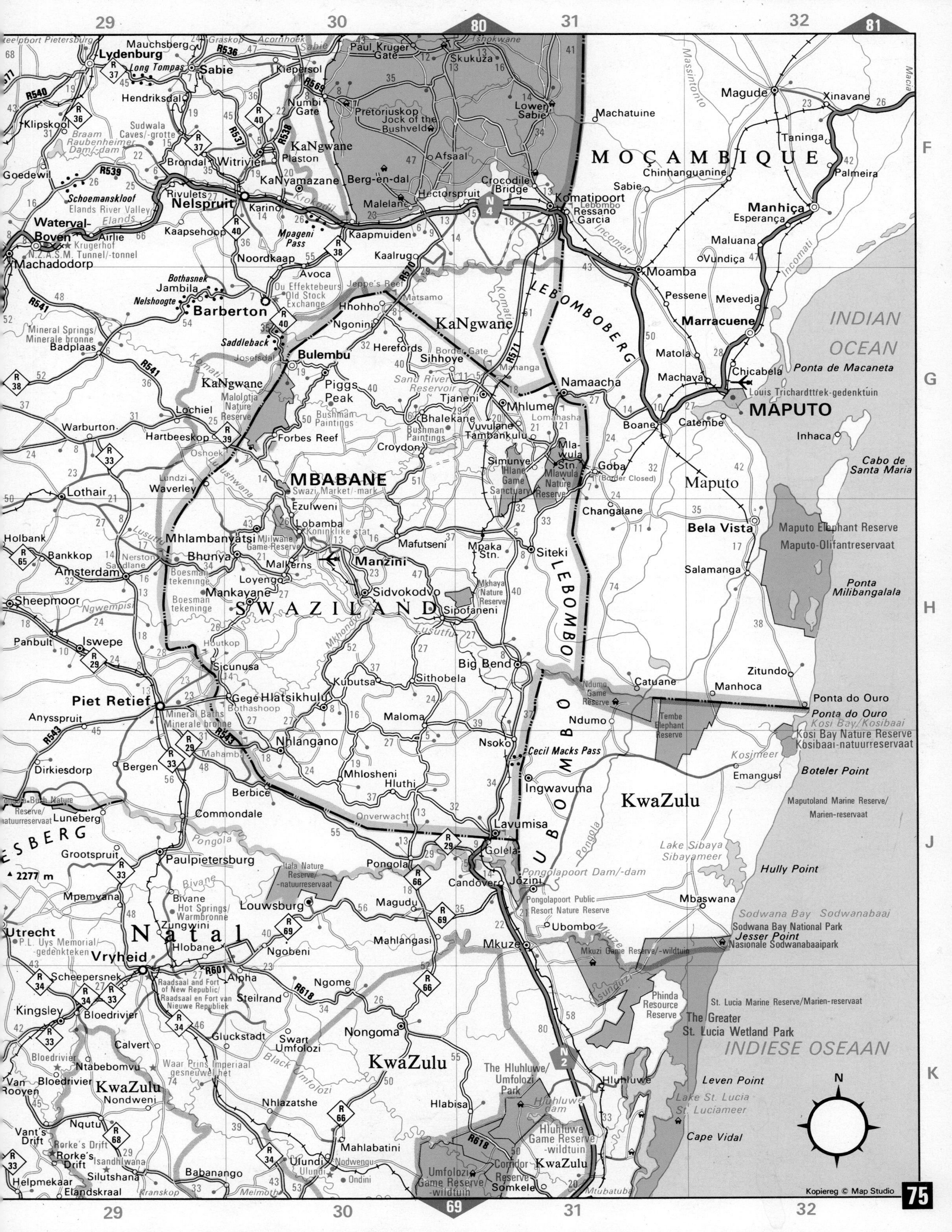
29
30
80
31
32
81
Lydenburg
Mauchsberg
Graskop
Acornhoek
Sabie
Paul Kruger Gate
Tshokwane
Skukuza
Long Tompas
Kiepersol
Hendriksdal
Numbi Gate
Pretoriuskop
Jock of the Bushveld
Lower Sabie
Machatuine
Magude
Xinavane
Massintonto
Klipskool
Braam Raubenheimer Dam/-dam
Sudwala Caves/-grotte
Brondal
Witrivier
Plaston
KaNgwane
Afsaal
Taninga
MOÇAMBIQUE
Chinhanguanine
Palmeira
Goedewil
Schoemanskloof
Elands River Valley
Rivulets
Nelspruit
KaNyamazane
Berg-en-dal
Hectorspruit
Malelane
Crocodile Bridge
Komatipoort
Ressano Garcia
Sabie
Manhiça
Esperança
Waterval-Boven
Airlie
Krugerhof
N.Z.A.S.M. Tunnel/-tonnel
Machadodorp
Karino
Kaapsehoop
Mpageni Pass
Kaapmuiden
Noordkaap
Kaalrug
Maluana
Vundiça
Incomati
Moamba
Bothasnek
Jambila
Nelshoogte
Barberton
Avoca
Ou Effektebeurs/Old Stock Exchange
Jeppe's Reef
Matsamo
Hhohho
Ngonini
LEBOMBOBERG
Pessene
Mevedja
Marracuene
Mineral Springs/ Minerale bronne
Badplaas
Saddleback
Josefsdal
Bulembu
Herefords
Border Gate
Sihhoye
Mananga
Matola
INDIAN OCEAN
KaNgwane
Piggs Peak
Sand River Reservoir
Tjaneni
Mhlume
Namaacha
Machava
Chicabela
Ponta de Macaneta
Louis Trichardttrek-gedenktuin
MAPUTO
Lochiel
Malolotja Nature Reserve
Bushman Paintings
Bhalekane
Vuvulane
Tambankulu
Lomahasha
Boane
Catembe
Inhaca
Warburton
Hartbeeskop
Forbes Reef
Croydon
Mlawula Stn.
Goba
(Border Closed)
Cabo de Santa Maria
Oshoek
Lothair
Lundzi
Waverley
MBABANE
Swazi Market/-mark
Simunye
Hlane Game Sanctuary
Mlawula Nature Reserve
Maputo
Changalane
Ezulweni
Lobamba
Koninklike stat
Holbank
Mhlambanyatsi
Mlilwane Game Reserve
Mafutseni
Mpaka Stn.
Siteki
Bela Vista
Maputo Elephant Reserve
Maputo-Olifantreservaat
Bankkop
Nerston
Sandlane
Bhunya
Manzini
Malkerns
Amsterdam
Boesman tekeninge
Loyengo
LEBOMBO
Salamanga
Ponta Milibangalala
Sheepmoor
Mankayane
Sidvokodvo
Mkhaya Nature Reserve
SWAZILAND
Sipofaneni
Ngwempisi
Panbult
Iswepe
Houtkop
Lusutfu
Mkhondvo
Big Bend
Zitundo
Catuane
Manhoca
Sicunusa
Kubutsa
Sithobela
Piet Retief
Gege
Hlatsikhulu
Bothashoop
Mineral Baths/ Minerale bronne
Ndumo Game Reserve
Tembe Elephant Reserve
Ponta do Ouro
Anysspruit
Maloma
Ndumo
Kosi Bay/Kosibaai
Kosi Bay Nature Reserve
Kosibaai-natuurreservaat
Nhlangano
Nsoko
Cecil Macks Pass
Kosimeer
Emangusi
Dirkiesdorp
Bergen
Mahamba
Mhlosheni
Hluthi
Ingwavuma
Boteler Point
UBOMBO
Berbice
KwaZulu
Maputoland Marine Reserve/ Marien-reservaat
Commondale
Luneberg
Onverwacht
Lavumisa
ESBERG
Pongola
Grootspruit
Paulpietersburg
Golela
Lake Sibaya Sibayameer
2277 m
Itala Nature Reserve/ -natuurreservaat
Bivane
Candover
Jozini
Pongolapoort Dam/-dam
Hully Point
Mpemvana
Hot Springs/ Warmbronne
Louwsburg
Magudu
Pongolapoort Public Resort Nature Reserve
Mbaswana
Zungwini
Utrecht
P.L. Uys Memorial/ -gedenkteken
Natal
Hlobane
Ngobeni
Mahlangasi
Ubombo
Mkuze
Sodwana Bay
Sodwanabaai
Sodwana Bay National Park
Jesser Point
Nasionale Sodwanabaaipark
Vryheid
Mkuzi Game Reserve/-wildtuin
Scheepersnek
Raadsaal and Fort of New Republic/ Raadsaal en Fort van Nieuwe Republiek
Alpha
Ngome
Steilrand
Phinda Resource Reserve
St. Lucia Marine Reserve/Marien-reservaat
Kingsley
Bloedrivier
The Greater St. Lucia Wetland Park
Gluckstadt
Swart Umfolozi
Nongoma
INDIESE OSEAAN
Calvert
Ntabebomvu
Waar Prins Imperiaal gesneuwel het
KwaZulu
The Hluhluwe/ Umfolozi Park
Hluhluwe
Leven Point
Van Rooyen
Bloedrivier
KwaZulu
Nondweni
Black Umfolozi
N
Nhlazatshe
Hlabisa
Hluhluwe dam
Lake St. Lucia
St. Luciameer
Nqutu
Vant's Drift
Rorke's Drift
Isandhlwana
Hluhluwe Game Reserve -wildtuin
Cape Vidal
Mahlabatini
Silutshana
Babanango
Ulundi
Nodwengu
Ondini
Corridor Reserve
KwaZulu
Umfolozi Game Reserve -wildtuin
Somkele
Helpmekaar
Elandskraal
Kranskop
Melmoth
Mtubatuba
Kopiereg © Map Studio
29
30
69
31
32
F
G
H
J
K

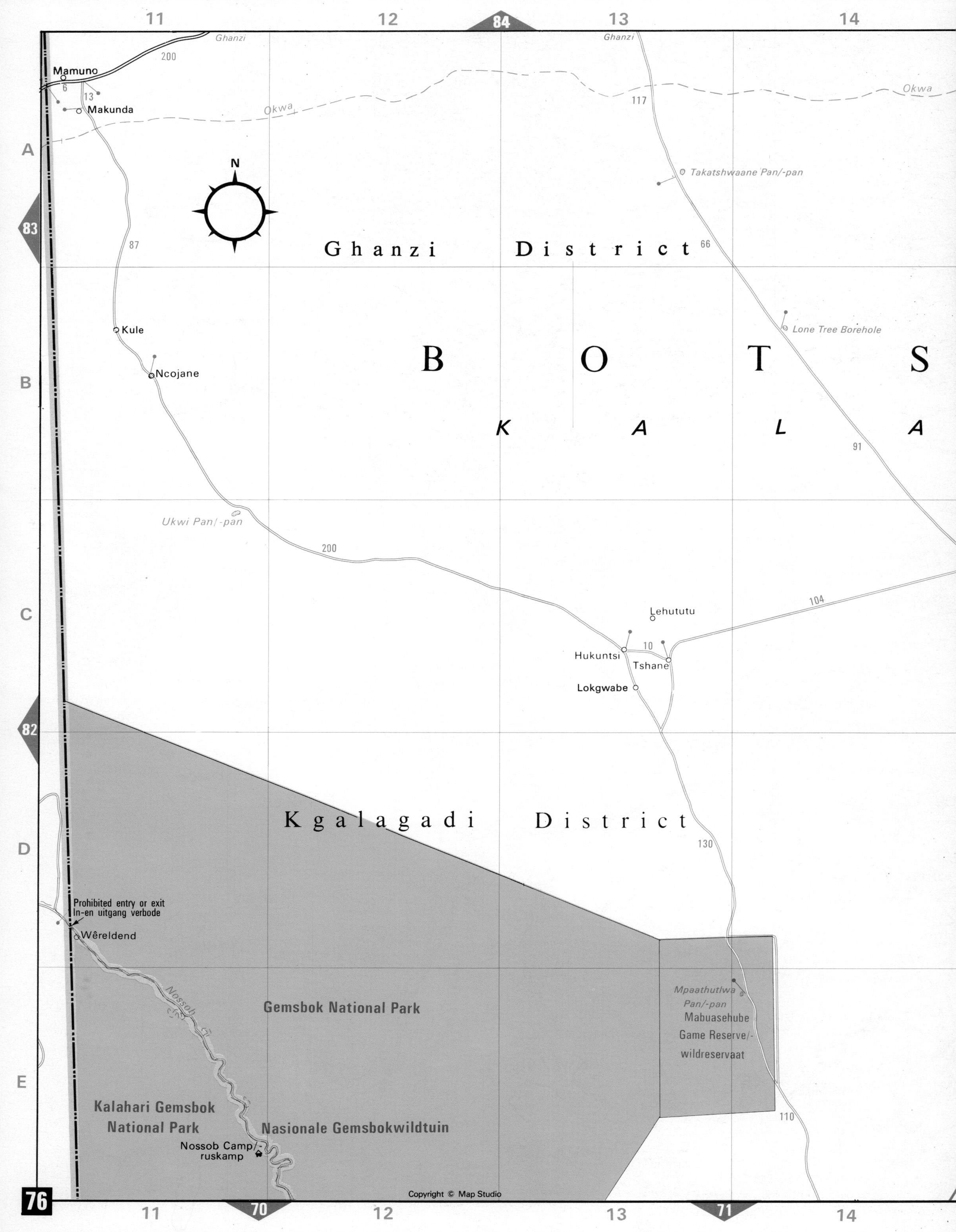

Ghanzi
200
Mamuno
6
13
o Makunda
Okwa
Ghanzi
117
Okwa

A

o Takatshwaane Pan/-pan

N

83

Ghanzi District
66

87

B O T S

Kule o

o Lone Tree Borehole

B

o Ncojane

K A L A

91

Ukwi Pan/-pan
200

104

Lehututu
o

C

10
Hukuntsi • Tshane o

82

Lokgwabe o

Kgalagadi District

130

D

Prohibited entry or exit
In-en uitgang verbode
o Wêreldend

Mpaathutlwa Pan/-pan
Mabuasehube
Game Reserve/-
wildreservaat

Nossob R.

Gemsbok National Park

E

Kalahari Gemsbok
National Park
Nasionale Gemsbokwildtuin
110

Nossob Camp/-
ruskamp

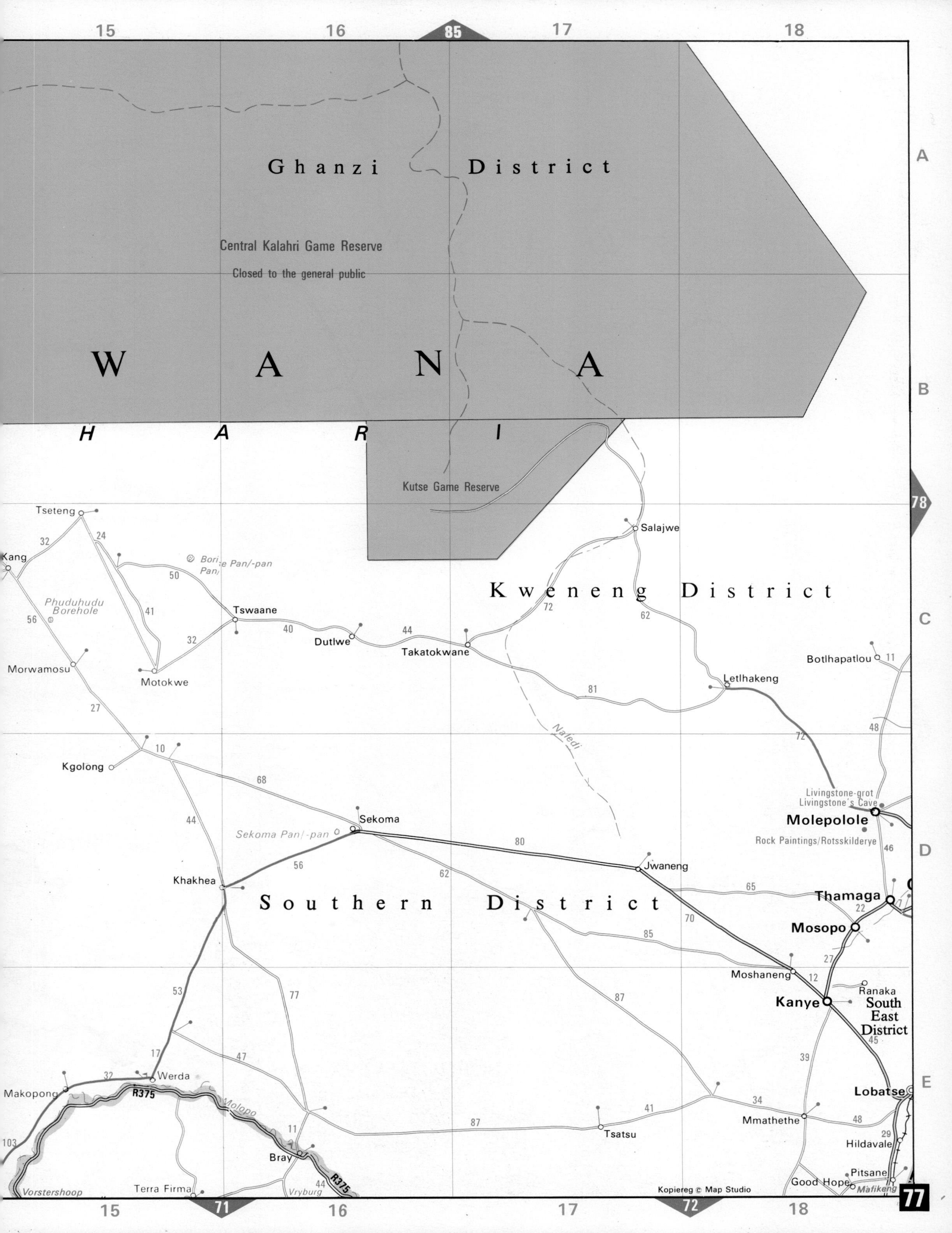

Ghanzi   District

A

Central Kalahri Game Reserve

Closed to the general public

W   A   N   A

B

H   A   R   I

Kutse Game Reserve

78

Tseteng

Kang

32

24

Bori-e Pan/-pan
Pan/

50

Salajwe

Kweneng   District

C

Phuduhudu
Borehole

41

Tswaane

40

44

72

62

56

32

Dutlwe

Takatokwane

Botlhapatlou   11

Morwamosu

Motokwe

81

Letlhakeng

48

27

72

10

Kgolong

68

Naledi

Livingstone-grot
Livingstone's Cave

44

Sekoma Pan/-pan

Sekoma

80

Molepolole

Rock Paintings/Rotsskilderye

46

D

56

62

Jwaneng

65

Thamaga

Khakhea

Southern   District

70

22

Mosopo

85

27

77

87

Moshaneng

12

53

Ranaka

Kanye

South
East
District

17

47

39

45

Makopong

32

R375

Werda

Molopo

34

Mmathethe

48

Lobatse

E

41

29

103

11

Tsatsu

Hildavale

Bray

R375

Pitsane

Vorstershoop

Terra Firma

44

Vryburg

Good Hope

Mafikeng

Kopiereg © Map Studio

77

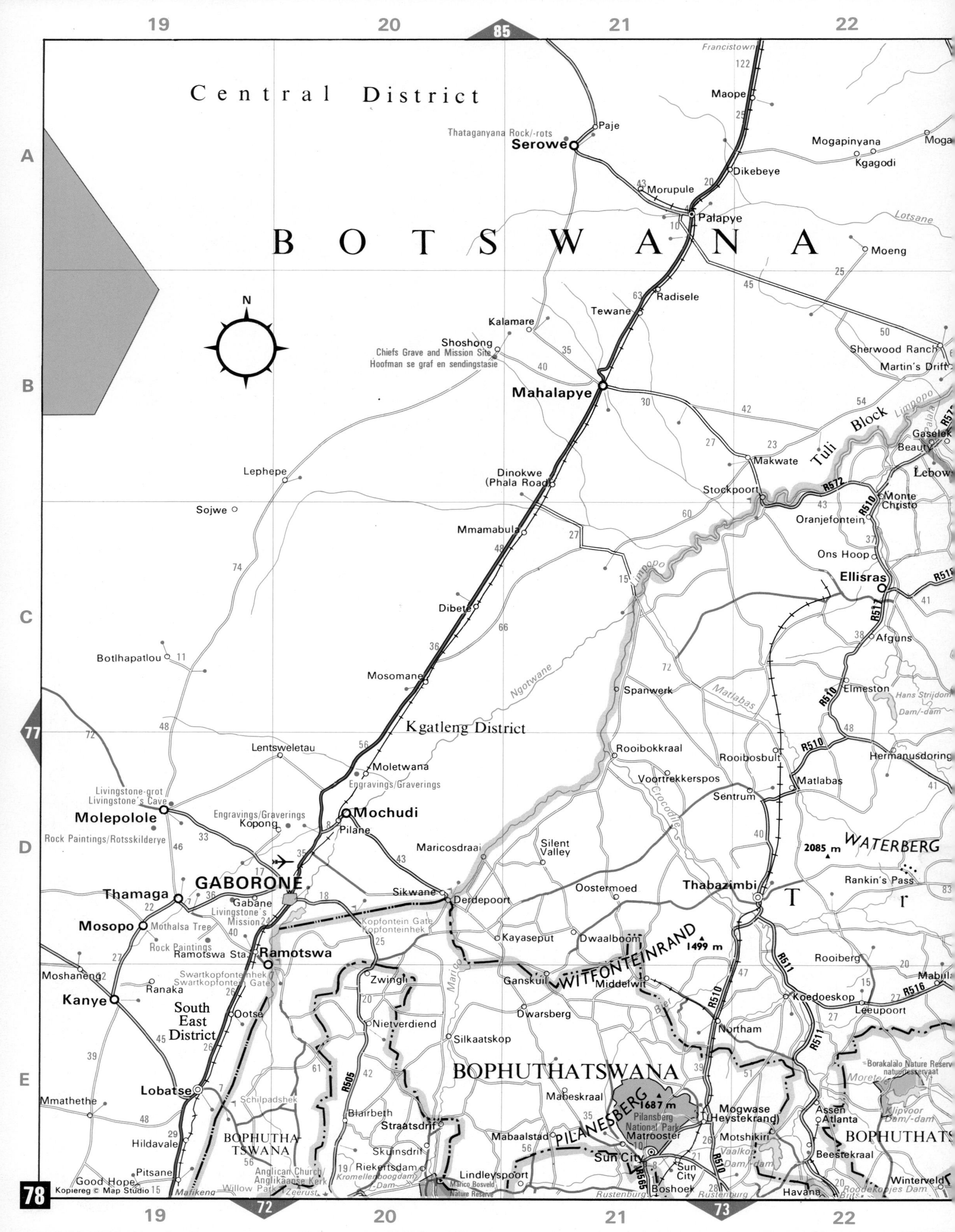

Central District
BOTSWANA
N
Serowe
Paje
Thataganyana Rock/-rots
Francistown
Maope
Mogapinyana
Kgagodi
Dikebeye
Morupule
Palapye
Lotsane
Moeng
Radisele
Tewane
Kalamare
Shoshong
Chiefs Grave and Mission Site
Hoofman se graf en sendingstasie
Mahalapye
Sherwood Ranch
Martin's Drift
Tuli Block
Limpopo
Gaselek
Beauty
Lebow
Makwate
Stockpoort
Dinokwe
(Phala Road)
Lephepe
Sojwe
Mmamabula
R572
R510
Monte Christo
Oranjefontein
Ons Hoop
Ellisras
R517
Afguns
Dibete
Botlhapatlou
Mosomane
Ngotwane
Spanwerk
Matlabas
Elmeston
Hans Strijdom Dam/-dam
Kgatleng District
Lentsweletau
Moletwana
Engravings/Graverings
Rooibokkraal
Rooibosbult
Hermanusdoring
Voortrekkerspos
Crocodile
Matlabas
Sentrum
Livingstone-grot
Livingstone's Cave
Molepolole
Engravings/Graverings
Kopong
Mochudi
Pilane
Rock Paintings/Rotsskilderye
Maricosdraai
Silent Valley
2085 m
WATERBERG
GABORONE
Thamaga
Gabane
Livingstone's Mission
Sikwane
Derdepoort
Oostermoed
Thabazimbi
Rankin's Pass
Mosopo
Mothalsa Tree
Kopfontein Gate
Kopfonteinhek
Kayaseput
Dwaalboom
WITFONTEINRAND
1499 m
Rock Paintings
Ramotswa Sta.
Ramotswa
Rooiberg
Moshaneng
Swartkopfonteinhek
Swartkopfontein Gate
Ranaka
Zwingli
Ganskuil
Middelwit
R511
Mabula
R516
Kanye
South East District
Ootse
Nietverdiend
Dwarsberg
Koedoeskop
Leeupoort
Northam
Marico
Biel
Silkaatskop
BOPHUTHATSWANA
Borakalalo Nature Reserve
natuurreservaat
Moretele
Lobatse
Mmathethe
Schilpadshek
R505
Mabeskraal
1687 m
PILANESBERG
Pilansberg National Park
Mogwase
(Heystekrand)
Assen
Atlanta
Klipvoor Dam/-dam
Blairbeth
Straatsdrif
Mabaalstad
Matrooster
Motshikiri
BOPHUTHATS
Hildavale
BOPHUTHATSWANA
Skuinsdrif
Sun City
Vaalkop Dam/-dam
Beestekraal
Pitsane
Anglican Church/
Anglikaanse Kerk
Riekertsdam
Kromellenboogdam/-Dam
Lindleyspoort
Sun City
Good Hope
Willow Park
Zeerust
Marico Bosveld Nature Reserve
Boshoek
Havana
Winterveld
Roodekopjes Dam
Mafikeng
Rustenburg
R565
Kopiereg © Map Studio
19
20
21
22
A
B
C
D
E
85
77
72
73
83

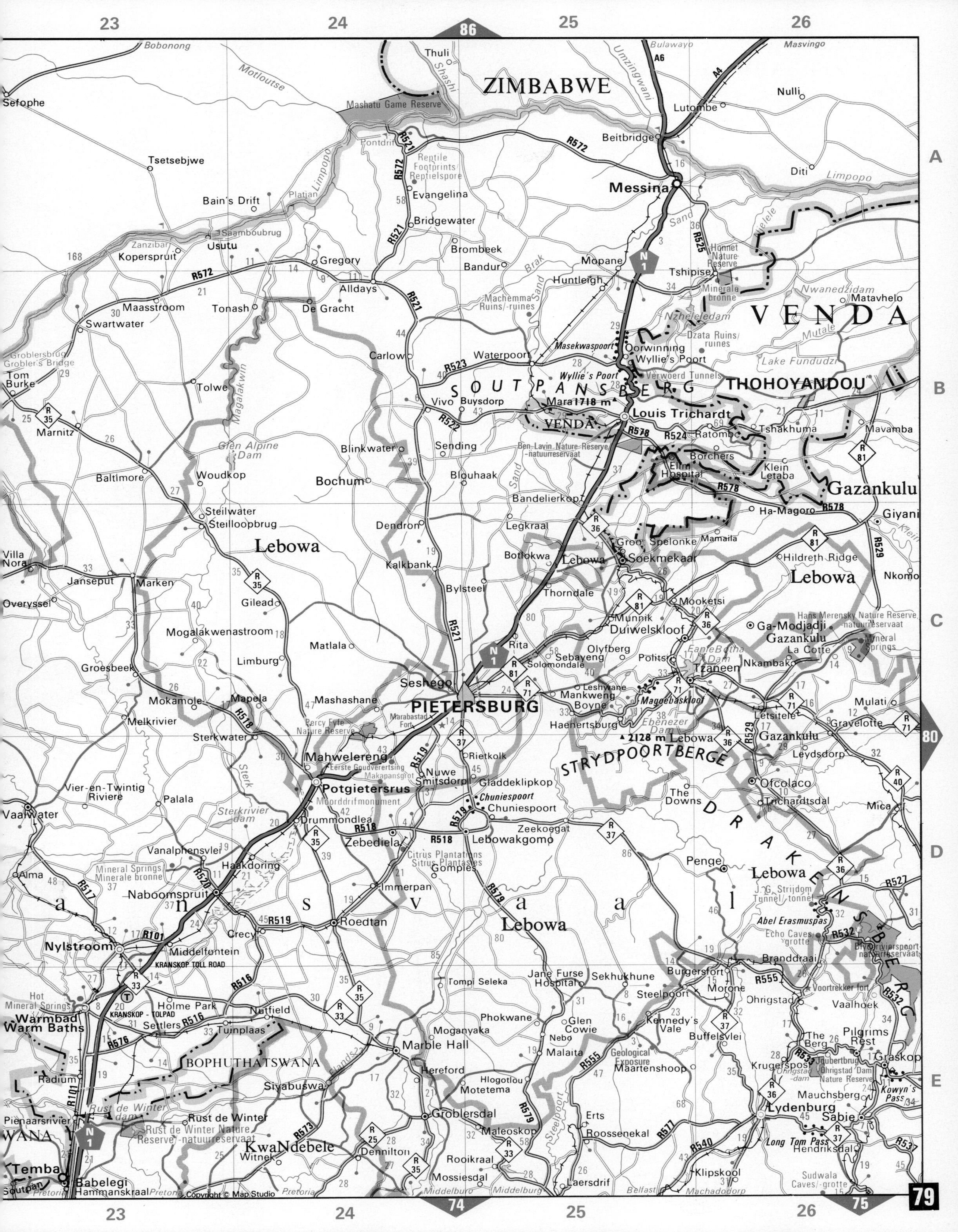
23
24
86
25
26
Bobonong
Motloutse
Sefophe
Thuli
Shashi
ZIMBABWE
Mashatu Game Reserve
Umzingwani
Bulawayo
A6
A4
Masvingo
Nulli
Lutombe
Beitbridge
R572
Pontdrif
R521
Reptile Footprints
Reptielspore
Tsetsebjwe
Limpopo
Platjan
Bain's Drift
Evangelina
Messina
Diti
Limpopo
A
Bridgewater
Saamboubrug
Usutu
Zanzibar
Kopersprult
Brombeek
Bandur
Gregory
Sand
R525
Honnet Nature Reserve
Mopane
Tshipise
Minerale bronne
Alldays
Huntleigh
Brak
Nwanedzidam
Matavhelo
R572
Maasstroom
Tonash
De Gracht
Machemma Ruins/-ruines
Nzheleledam
VENDA
Swartwater
Dzata Ruins/ ruines
Mutale
Masekwaspoort
Oorwinning
Wyllie's Poort
Carlow
Waterpoort
Groblersbrug
Grobler's Bridge
R523
Lake Fundudzi
Verwoerd Tunnels
Tom Burke
SOUTPANSBERG
THOHOYANDOU
B
Tolwe
Vivo
Buysdorp
Mara 1718 m
Louis Trichardt
Magalakwin
R35
R522
VENDA
R578
R524
Ratombo
Tshakhuma
Mavamba
Marnitz
Glen Alpine Dam
Sending
Blinkwater
Ben Lavin Nature Reserve
-natuurreservaat
Borchers
R81
Baltimore
Woudkop
Bochum
Blouhaak
Elim Hospital
Klein Letaba
Gazankulu
Bandelierkop
R578
Steilwater
Steilloopbrug
Dendron
Legkraal
Ha-Magoro
Giyani
R36
Groot Spelonke
Mamaila
Lebowa
R81
R529
Villa Nora
Hildreth Ridge
Janseput
Marken
Kalkbank
Botlokwa
Lebowa
Soekmekaar
Lebowa
Nkomo
R35
Gilead
Bylsteel
Thorndale
Overyssel
Mooketsi
Hans Merensky Nature Reserve
-natuurreservaat
Munnik
Mogalakwenastroom
Duiwelskloof
Ga-Modjadji
C
Gazankulu
Mineral Springs
Matlala
Rita
Olyfberg
Limburg
Politsi
Sebayeng
Solomondale
Ebenezer Dam
La Cotte
Groesbeek
Tzaneen
Nkambako
R521
Seshego
Mankweng
Leshwane
Magoebaskloof
Mokamole
Mapela
Mashashane
PIETERSBURG
Boyne
Mulati
Melkrivier
H518
Percy Fyfe Nature Reserve
Marabastad Fort
Haenertsburg
Letsitele
Gravelotte
Sterkwater
R37
2128 m
Lebowa
Gazankulu
80
Leydsdorp
Mahwelereng
Eerste Goudvertersing
Makapansgrot
R519
Rietkolk
STRYDPOORTBERGE
Nuwe Smitsdorp
Gladdeklipkop
Ofcolaco
R40
Vier-en-Twintig Riviere
Potgietersrus
The Downs
Trichardtsdal
Palala
Moorddrifmonument
Chuniespoort
Chuniespoort
Mica
Vaalwater
Sterkrivier dam
Drummondlea
R579
Sterk
DRAKENSBERG
R518
R518
Zeekoegat
Zebediela
Lebowakgomo
D
Vanalphensvlei
Citrus Plantations
Sitrus Plantasies
Gomples
Penge
Mineral Springs
Minerale bronne
Haakdoring
Lebowa
R36
Alma
R520
J. G. Strijdom Tunnel/-tonnel
R527
R517
Immerpan
Naboomspruit
Abel Erasmuspas
Waterberg
R519
Roedtan
Crecy
Lebowa
Echo Caves/-grotte
R532
Nylstroom
R101
Middelfontein
KRANSKOP TOLL ROAD
Blyderivierspoort-natuurreservaat
Branddraai
R516
Jane Furse Hospital
Sekhukhune
Burgersfort
R33
Tompi Seleka
R555
Ohrigstad
Voortrekker fort
Morone
Hot Mineral Springs
Warmbad
Warm Baths
KRANSKOP - TOLPAD
Holme Park
Nutfield
Steelpoort
Phokwane
Kennedy's Vale
Vaalhoek
Settlers
R516
Tuinplaas
R33
Glen Cowie
R37
Buffelsvlei
The Berg
Pilgrims Rest
R576
Moganyaka
Nebo
Marble Hall
Malaita
Radium
BOPHUTHATSWANA
Geological Exposure
Maartenshoop
Krugerspos
R533
Joubertbrug
Ohrigstad Dam
Graskop
Hereford
Hlogotlou
Motetema
R555
E
Siyabuswa
Ohrigstad dam
Joubertbrug Ohrigstad Dam Nature Reserve
Kowyn's Pass
R101
Rust de Winter dam
Mauchsberg
Groblersdal
R36
Lydenburg
Pienaarsrivier
Rust de Winter
R573
R579
Erts
Sabie
N1
Rust de Winter Nature Reserve/-natuurreservaat
Maleoskop
Roossenekal
R577
R37
R25
Steelpoort
Long Tom Pass
Hendriksdal
R537
KwaNdebele
Dennilton
R540
Witnek
R33
Rooikraal
Klipskool
Temba
R35
Mossiesdal
Sudwala Caves/-grotte
Babelegi
Laersdrif
Hammanskraal
Soutpan
Pretoria
Pretoria
Pretoria
Middelburg
Middelburg
Belfast
Machadodorp
74
75
Copyright © Map Studio
23
24
25
26

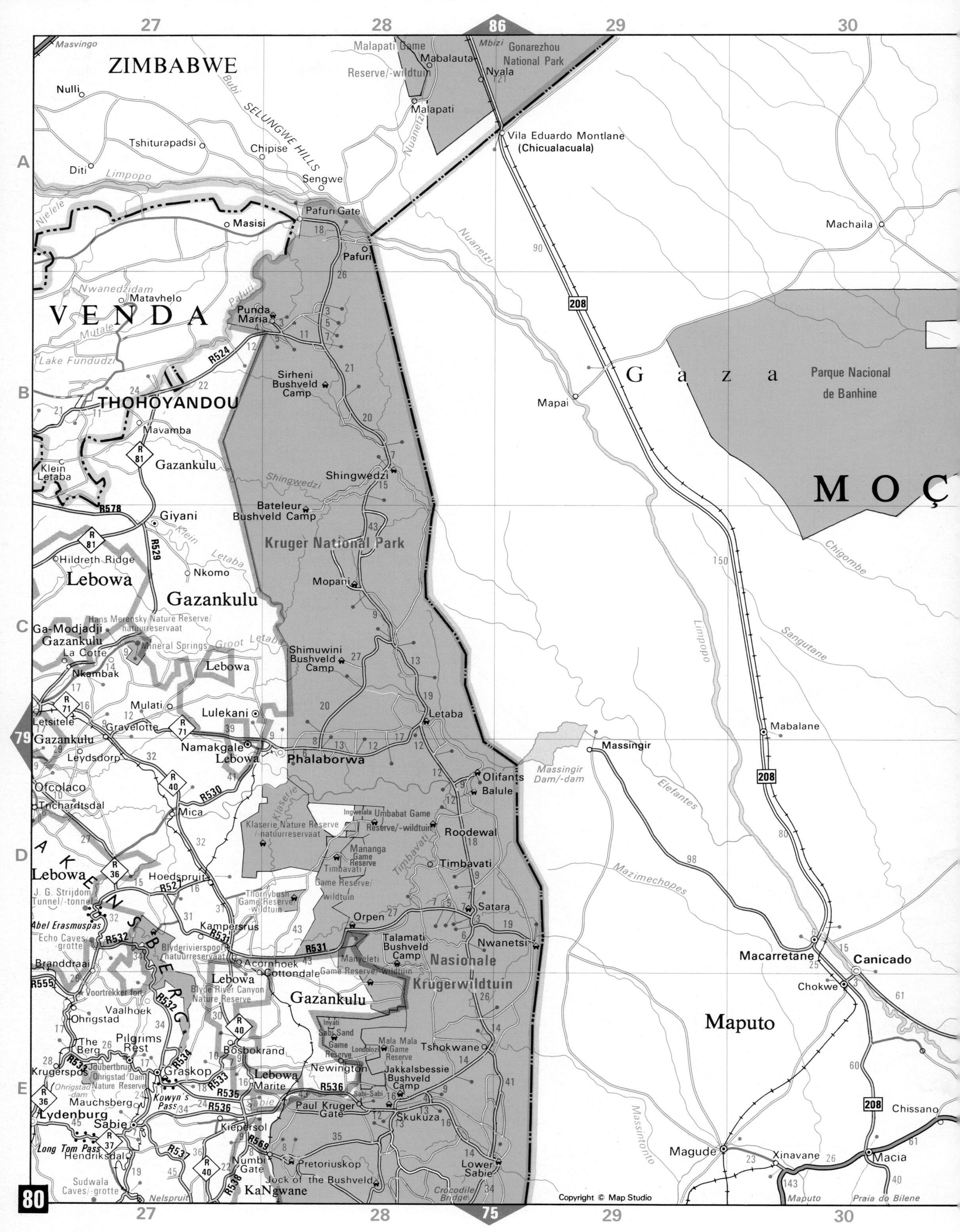
ZIMBABWE
VENDA
Gaza
Parque Nacional de Banhine
MOÇ
Kruger National Park
Nasionale Krugerwildtuin
Lebowa
Gazankulu
Maputo
THOHOYANDOU
Gonarezhou National Park
Malapati Game Reserve/-wildtuin
Malapati
Mabalauta
Nyala
Vila Eduardo Montlane (Chicualacuala)
Nulli
Tshiturapadsi
Chipise
Diti
Sengwe
Pafuri Gate
Pafuri
Masisi
Matavhelo
Punda Maria
Sirheni Bushveld Camp
Mapai
Machaila
Mavamba
Gazankulu
Klein Letaba
Shingwedzi
Bateleur Bushveld Camp
Giyani
Hildreth Ridge
Nkomo
Mopani
Hans Merensky Nature Reserve/-natuurreservaat
Ga-Modjadji
La Cotte
Nkambak
Mineral Springs
Shimuwini Bushveld Camp
Mulati
Lulekani
Letaba
Letsitele
Gravelotte
Namakgale
Phalaborwa
Leydsdorp
Massingir
Massingir Dam/-dam
Mabalane
Ofcolaco
Trichardtsdal
Mica
Olifants
Balule
Klaserie Nature Reserve/-natuurreservaat
Ingwelala
Umbabat Game Reserve/-wildtuin
Roodewal
Manyeleti Game Reserve
Timbavati
Timbavati Game Reserve/-wildtuin
Hoedspruit
J. G. Strijdom Tunnel/-tonnel
Thornybush Game Reserve/-wildtuin
Satara
Orpen
Abel Erasmuspas
Echo Caves/-grotte
Kampersrus
Blyderivierspoort/-natuurreservaat
Talamati Bushveld Camp
Nwanetsi
Acornhoek
Cottondale
Branddraai
Voortrekker fort
Blyde River Canyon Nature Reserve
Ohrigstad
Vaalhoek
Pilgrims Rest
The Berg
Bosbokrand
Inyati
Sabi Sand Game Reserve
Londolozi
Mala Mala Game Reserve
Tshokwane
Krugerspos
Joubertbrug
Ohrigstad Dam Nature Reserve
Graskop
Newington
Jakkalsbessie Bushveld Camp
Marite
Kowyn's Pass
Mauchsberg
Sabi-Sabi
Paul Kruger Gate
Skukuza
Lydenburg
Sabie
Kiepersol
Long Tom Pass
Hendriksdal
Pretoriuskop
Numbi Gate
Lower Sabie
Jock of the Bushveld
Sudwala Caves/-grotte
Nelspruit
KaNgwane
Crocodile Bridge
Macarretane
Canicado
Chokwe
Chissano
Magude
Xinavane
Macia
Praia do Bilene
Limpopo
Nuanetzi
Elefantes
Mazimechopes
Massintonto
Chigombe
Sangutane
Shingwedzi
Letaba
Groot Letaba
Klaserie
Sabie
Mutale
Nwanedzidam
Lake Fundudzi
Bubi
Njelele
Pafuri
Mbizi
SELUNGWE HILLS
DRAKENSBERG
Copyright © Map Studio

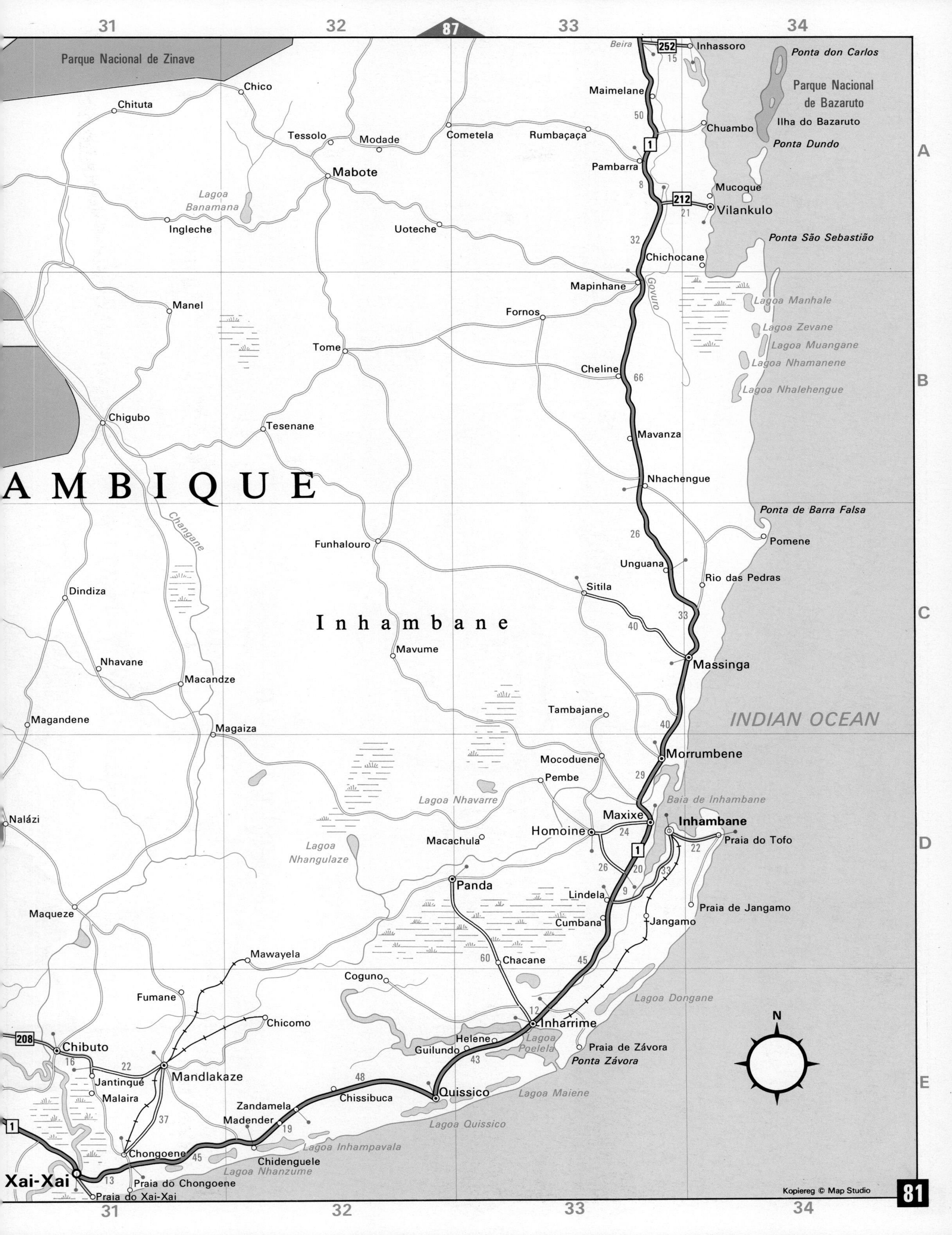

Parque Nacional de Zinave

Chituta

Chico

Tessolo

Modade

Cometela

Rumbaçaça

Beira

Inhassoro

252
15

Ponta don Carlos

Maimelane

50

Parque Nacional de Bazaruto

Chuambo

Ilha do Bazaruto

Mabote

Pambarra

8

Ponta Dundo

212
21

Mucoque

Vilankulo

Uoteche

32

Ponta São Sebastião

Inglesse

Manel

Chichocane

Mapinhane

Govuro

Lagoa Manhale

Fornos

Lagoa Zevane

Tome

Lagoa Muangane

Lagoa Nhamanene

Cheline

66

Lagoa Nhalehengue

Chigubo

Tesenane

Mavanza

Changane

Nhachengue

A M B I Q U E

Ponta de Barra Falsa

26

Pomene

Funhalouro

Unguana

Sitila

Rio das Pedras

Dindiza

40

33

I n h a m b a n e

Nhavane

Mavume

Massinga

Macandze

Magaiza

Tambajane

40

INDIAN OCEAN

Magandene

Morrumbene

Mocoduene

29

Nalázi

Pembe

Baia de Inhambane

Lagoa Nhavarre

Maxixe

Inhambane

Homoine

24

Praia do Tofo

Macachula

1

22

Lagoa
Nhangulaze

26

20

33

Maqueze

Panda

Lindela

9

Praia de Jangamo

60

Cumbana

Jangamo

Chacane

45

Mawayela

Coguno

Lagoa Dongane

Fumane

12

208

Chicomo

Inharrime

Chibuto

Helene

Praia de Závora

16

Guilundo

43

Ponta Závora

Jantingué

22

Mandlakaze

48

Quissico

Lagoa Maiene

Malaira

Chissibuca

37

Zandamela

Lagoa Poelela

1

Madender

19

Lagoa Quissico

Chongoene

45

Chidenguele

Lagoa Inhampavala

Xai-Xai

13

Praia do Chongoene

Lagoa Nhanzume

Praia do Xai-Xai

N

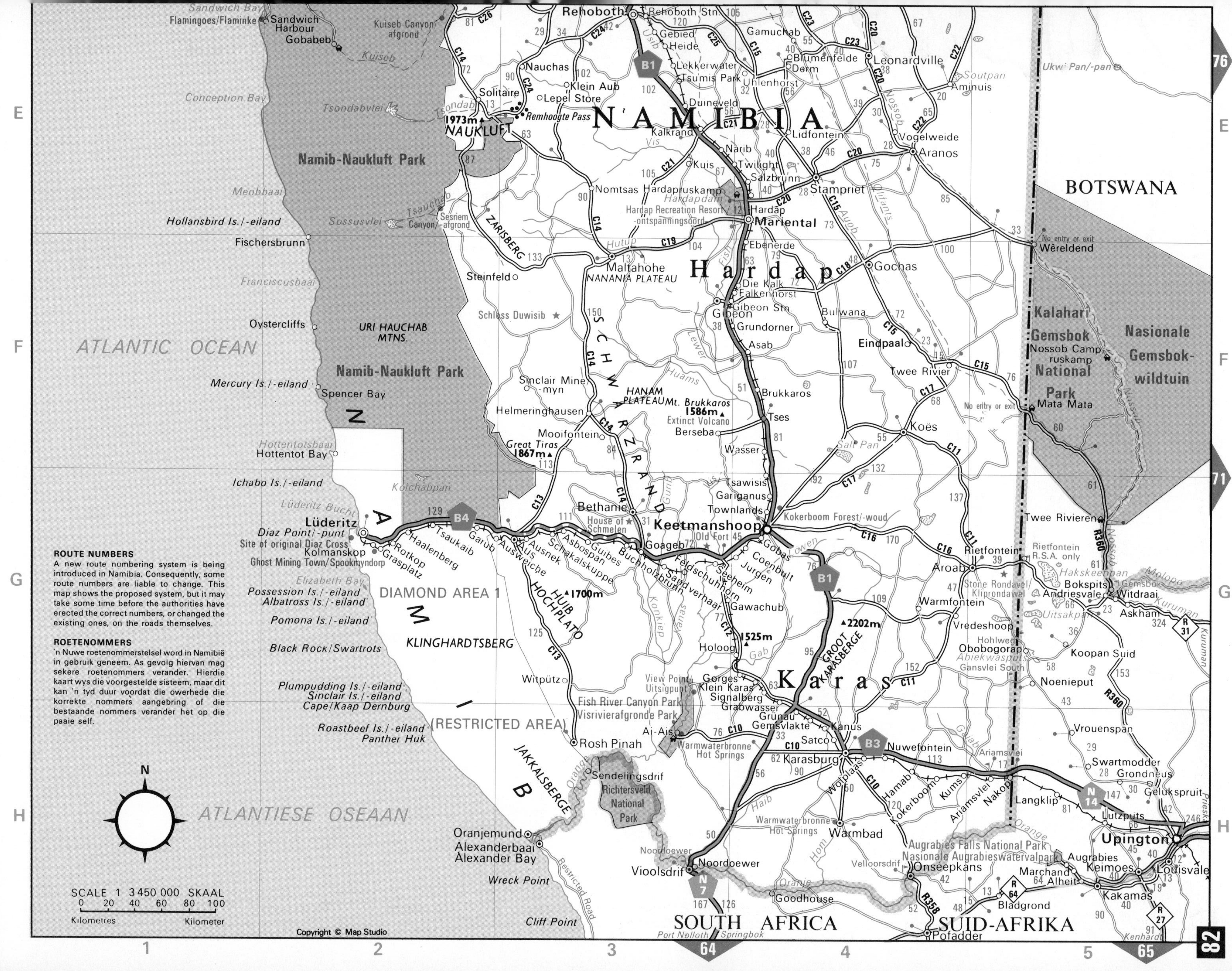

NAMIBIA
Hardap
Karas
BOTSWANA
SOUTH AFRICA
SUID-AFRIKA
ATLANTIC OCEAN
ATLANTIESE OSEAAN
Namib-Naukluft Park
Kalahari Gemsbok National Park
Nasionale Gemsbok-wildtuin
Richtersveld National Park
DIAMOND AREA 1
(RESTRICTED AREA)
Fish River Canyon Park
Visrivierafgronde Park
Augrabies Falls National Park
Nasionale Augrabieswatervalpark
Rehoboth
Mariental
Keetmanshoop
Lüderitz
Upington
Karasburg
Oranjemund
Alexanderbaai
Alexander Bay
Rosh Pinah
Noordoewer
Vioolsdrif
Pofadder
Warmbad
Ai-Ais
Bethanie
Maltahöhe
Gibeon
Gochas
Aranos
Stampriet
Aroab
Koës
Solitaire
Sesriem
Helmeringhausen
Aus
Goageb
Tses
Berseba
Gobabeb
Sandwich Harbour
Spencer Bay
Hottentot Bay
Wêreldend
Mata Mata
Twee Rivieren
Nossob Camp
Kakamas
Keimoes
Onseepkans
Nakop
Nuwefontein
Grünau
Klein Karas
ROUTE NUMBERS
A new route numbering system is being introduced in Namibia. Consequently, some route numbers are liable to change. This map shows the proposed system, but it may take some time before the authorities have erected the correct numbers, or changed the existing ones, on the roads themselves.
ROETENOMMERS
'n Nuwe roetenommerstelsel word in Namibië in gebruik geneem. As gevolg hiervan mag sekere roetenommers verander. Hierdie kaart wys die voorgestelde sisteem, maar dit kan 'n tyd duur voordat die owerhede die korrekte nommers aangebring of die bestaande nommers verander het op die paaie self.
N
SCALE 1 3 450 000 SKAAL
0 20 40 60 80 100
Kilometres Kilometer

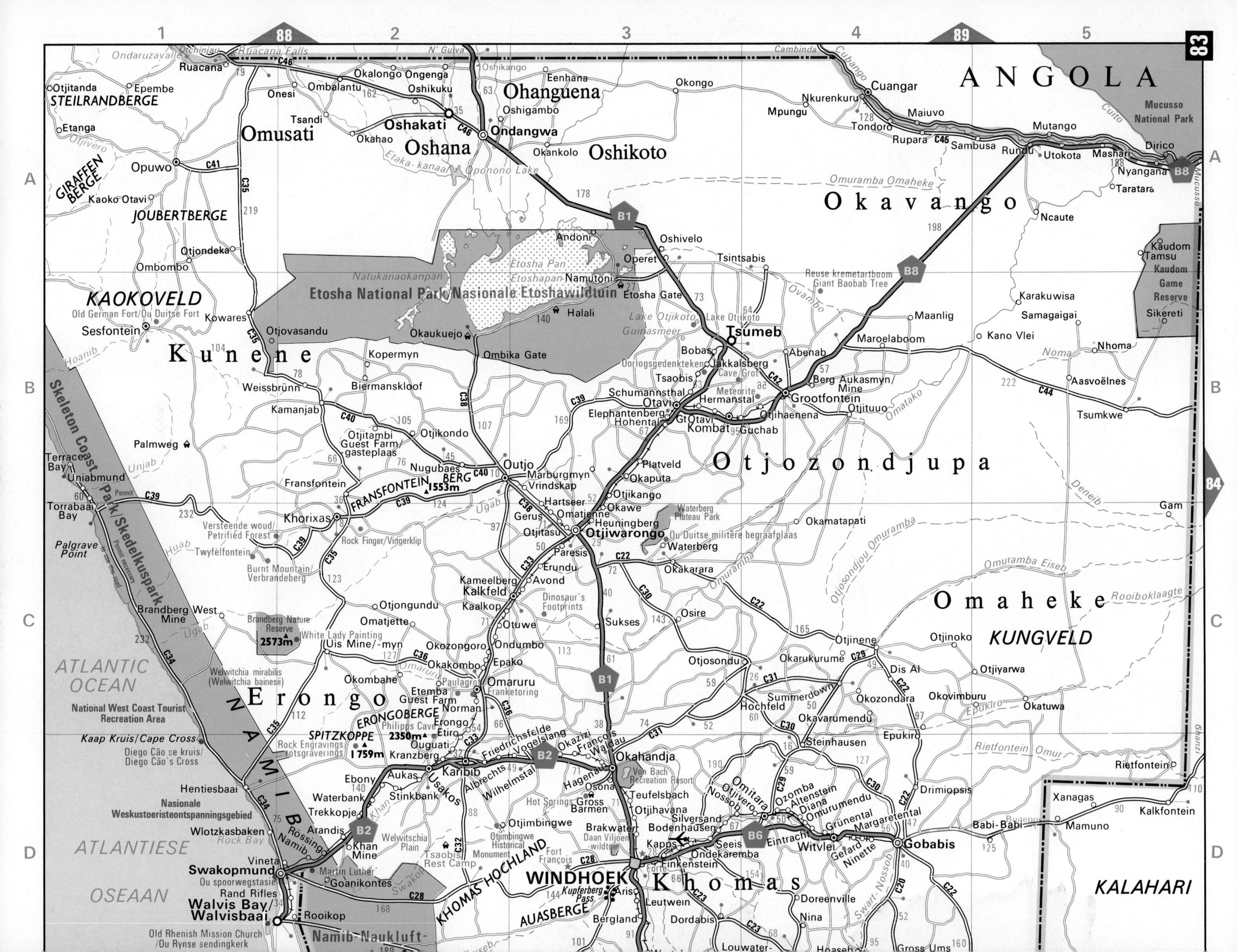

ANGOLA
Omusati
Oshana
Ohanguena
Oshikoto
Okavango
Kunene
Otjozondjupa
Erongo
Omaheke
Khomas
NAMIB
KAOKOVELD
KUNGVELD
KALAHARI
STEILRANDBERGE
GIRAFFENBERGE
JOUBERTBERGE
ERONGOBERGE
AUASBERGE
KHOMAS HOCHLAND
SPITZKOPPE 1759m
FRANSFONTEIN BERG 1553m
ATLANTIC OCEAN
ATLANTIESE OSEAAN
Skeleton Coast Park/Skedelkuspark
Etosha National Park/Nasionale Etoshawildtuin
Etosha Pan
Mucusso National Park
Kaudom Game Reserve
Brandberg Nature Reserve 2573m
National West Coast Tourist Recreation Area
Nasionale Weskustoeristeontspanningsgebied
Namib-Naukluft-
Ruacana
Ruacana Falls
Opuwo
Oshakati
Ondangwa
Tsumeb
Grootfontein
Otavi
Outjo
Khorixas
Otjiwarongo
Okahandja
Karibib
Usakos
Omaruru
Swakopmund
Walvis Bay/Walvisbaai
Hentiesbaai
WINDHOEK
Gobabis
Rundu
Cuangar
Okaukuejo
Halali
Namutoni
Sesfontein
Tsumkwe
Rietfontein
Kalkfontein
Mamuno
Xanagas
Terrace Bay
Torrabaai Bay
Palgrave Point
Kaap Kruis/Cape Cross
Waterberg Plateau Park
88
89
84
A
B
C
D
1
2
3
4
5

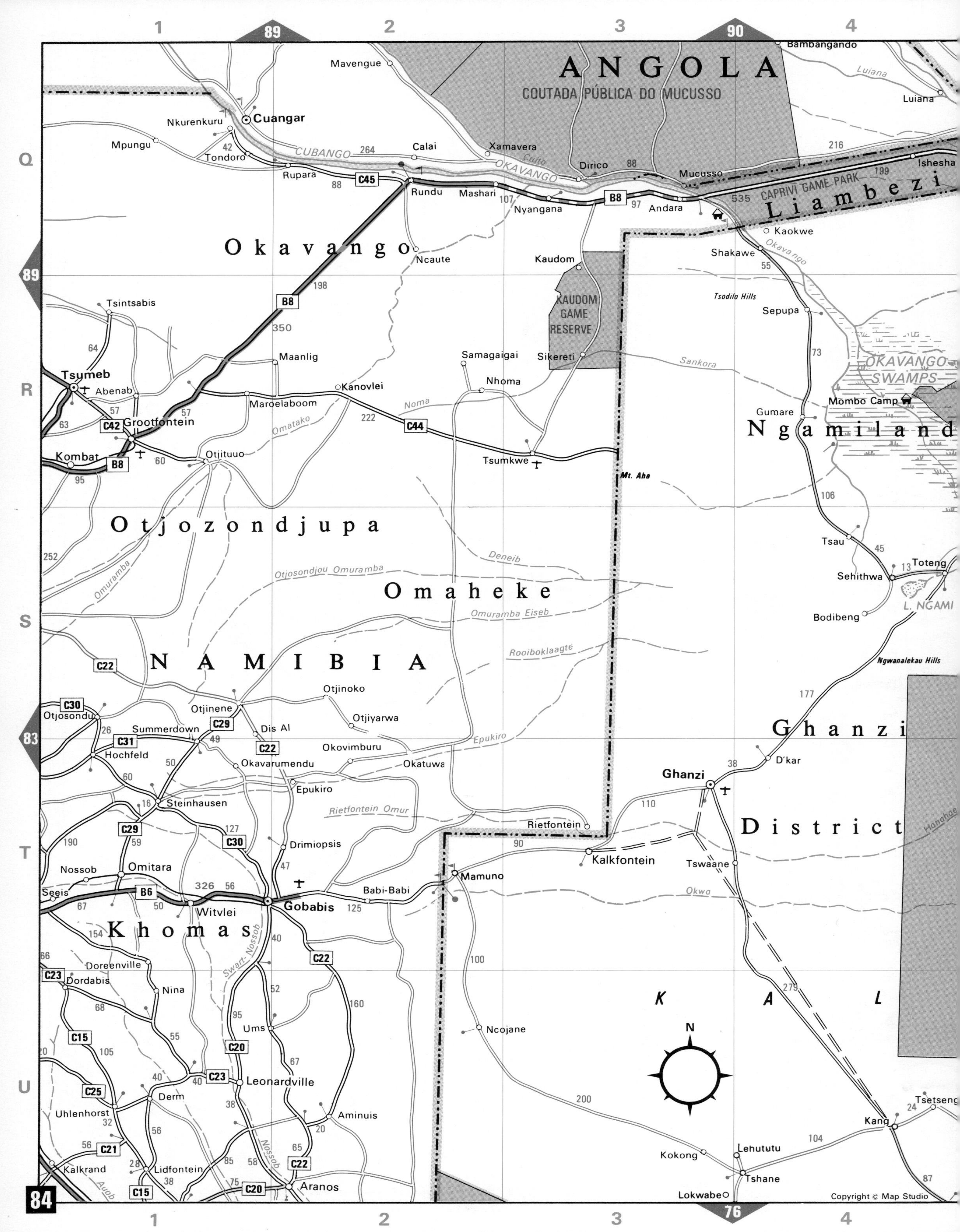

ANGOLA
COUTADA PÚBLICA DO MUCUSSO
Cuangar
Nkurenkuru
Mpungu
Tondoro
Calai
Xamavera
Dirico
Mucusso
Bambangando
Luiana
Ishesha
CAPRIVI GAME PARK
Liambezi
CUBANGO
OKAVANGO
Cuito
Rupara
Rundu
Mashari
Nyangana
Andara
Kaokwe
Shakawe
Okavango
Ncaute
Kaudom
KAUDOM GAME RESERVE
Tsodilo Hills
Sepupa
Tsintsabis
Maanlig
Samagaigai
Sikereti
Sankora
OKAVANGO SWAMPS
Tsumeb
Abenab
Kanovlei
Nhoma
Mombo Camp
Maroelaboom
Noma
Gumare
Grootfontein
Omatako
Ngamiland
Kombat
Otjituuo
Tsumkwe
Mt. Aha
Otjozondjupa
Tsau
Deneib
Toteng
Sehithwa
Otjosondjou Omuramba
Omaheke
L. NGAMI
Omuramba
Omuramba Eiseb
Bodibeng
Rooiboklaagte
NAMIBIA
Ngwanalekau Hills
Otjinoko
Otjinene
Otjosondu
Otjiyarwa
Summerdown
Dis Al
Ghanzi
Hochfeld
Okovimburu
Epukiro
D'kar
Okavarumendu
Okatuwa
Ghanzi
Steinhausen
Rietfontein Omur
District
Hanahae
Rietfontein
Drimiopsis
Kalkfontein
Tswaane
Nossob
Omitara
Mamuno
Seeis
Babi-Babi
Okwa
Witvlei
Gobabis
Khomas
Swart-Nossob
Doreenville
Dordabis
Nina
K A L
Ums
Ncojane
N
Leonardville
Uhlenhorst
Derm
Aminuis
Kang
Tsetseng
Kokong
Lehututu
Kalkrand
Lidfontein
Nossob
Auob
Aranos
Tshane
Lokwabe
Copyright © Map Studio

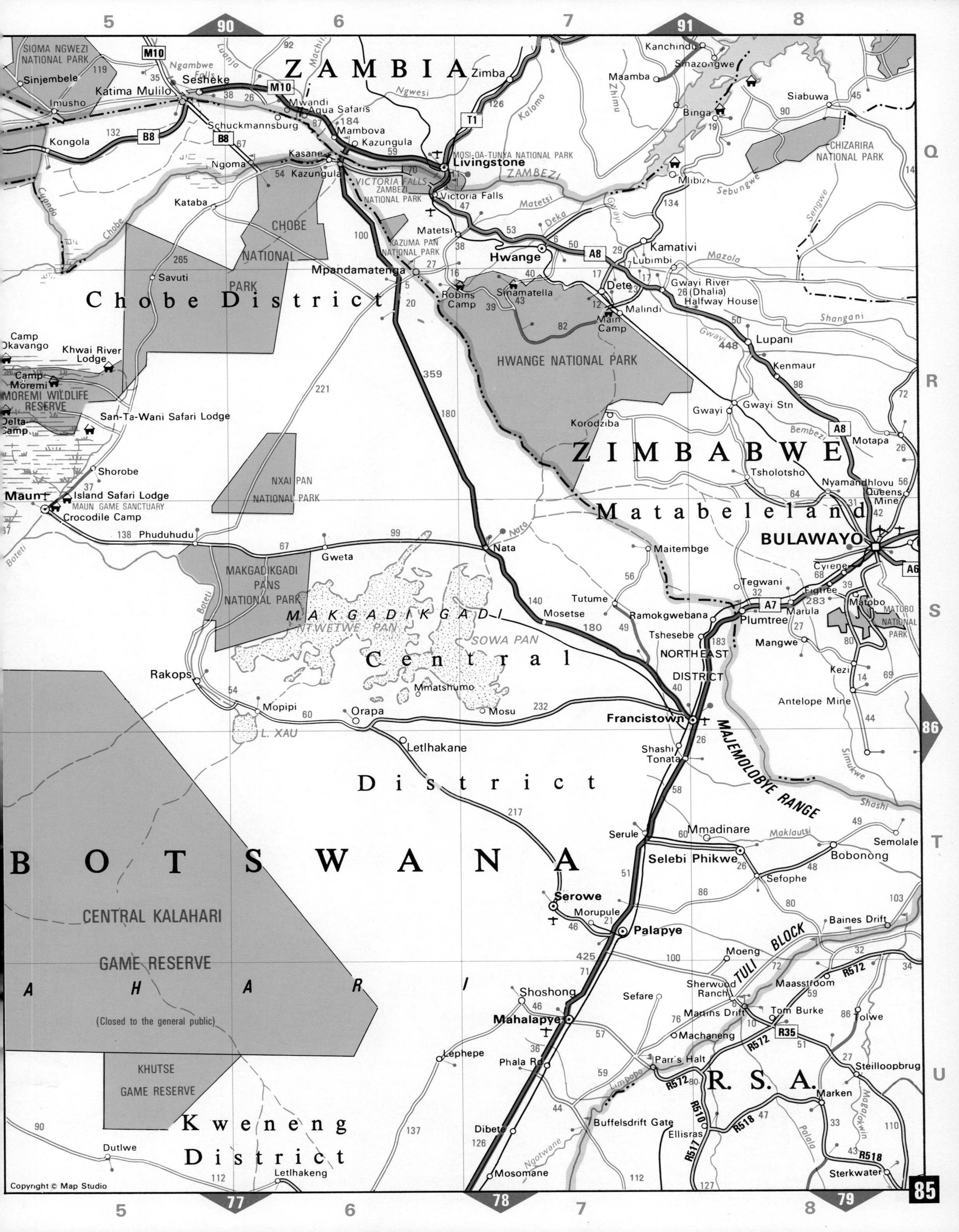
ZAMBIA
ZIMBABWE
BOTSWANA
R.S.A.
Chobe District
Matabeleland
Central District
Kweneng District
NORTH EAST DISTRICT
SIOMA NGWEZI NATIONAL PARK
CHOBE NATIONAL PARK
HWANGE NATIONAL PARK
NXAI PAN NATIONAL PARK
MAKGADIKGADI PANS NATIONAL PARK
MOREMI WILDLIFE RESERVE
MAUN GAME SANCTUARY
CHIZARIRA NATIONAL PARK
MOSI-OA-TUNYA NATIONAL PARK
VICTORIA FALLS ZAMBEZI NATIONAL PARK
KAZUMA PAN NATIONAL PARK
MATOBO NATIONAL PARK
CENTRAL KALAHARI GAME RESERVE
(Closed to the general public)
KHUTSE GAME RESERVE
MAKGADIKGADI
NTWETWE PAN
SOWA PAN
L. XAU
MAJEMOLOBYE RANGE
TULI BLOCK
Livingstone
Victoria Falls
Hwange
Kasane
Kazungula
Maun
Nata
Francistown
BULAWAYO
Plumtree
Selebi Phikwe
Serowe
Palapye
Mahalapye
Copyright © Map Studio

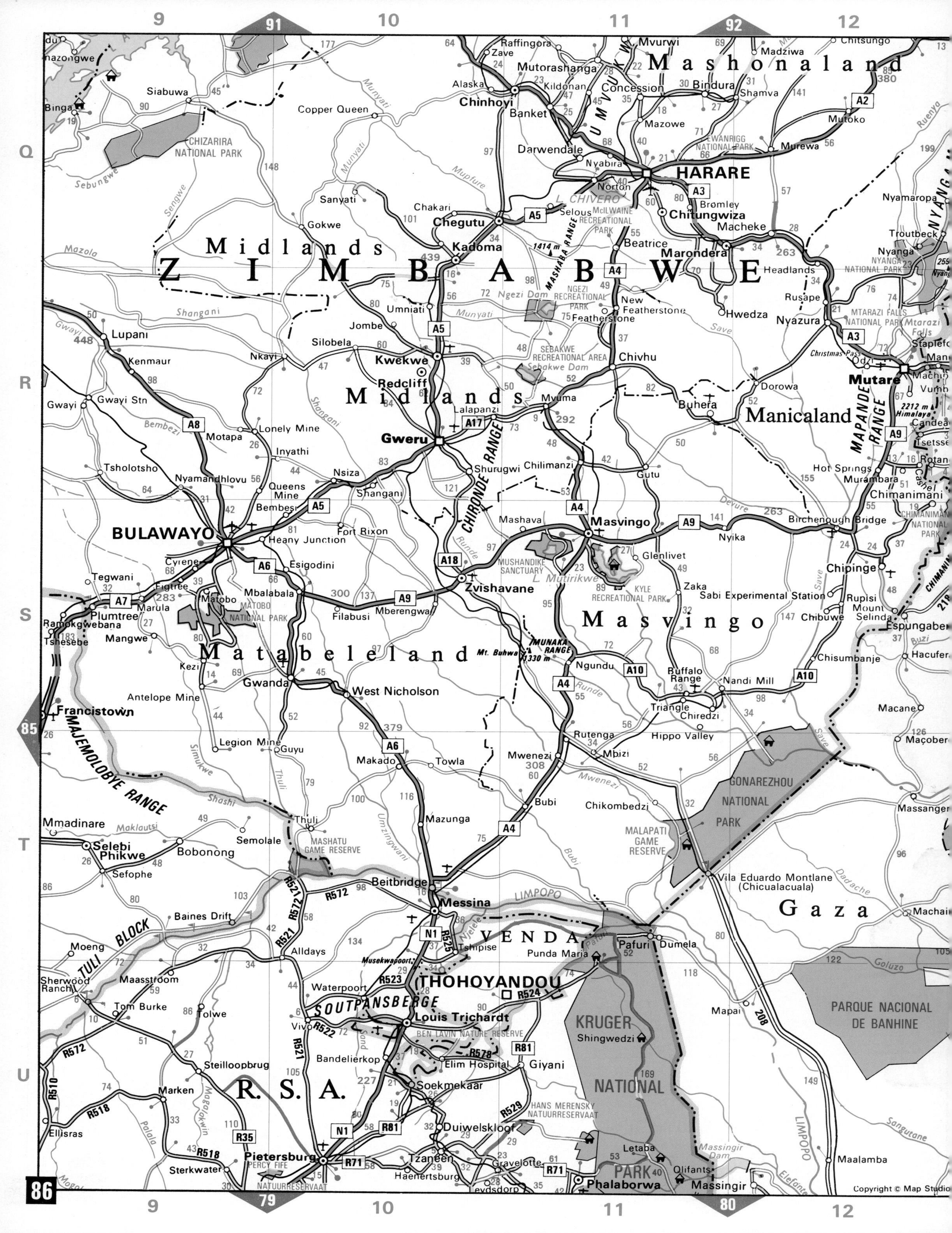

Z I M B A B W E
Mashonaland
Midlands
Manicaland
Masvingo
Matabeleland
Gaza
R. S. A.
VENDA
HARARE
BULAWAYO
Binga
Siabuwa
CHIZARIRA NATIONAL PARK
Copper Queen
Sanyati
Gokwe
Chakari
Chegutu
Kadoma
Raffingora
Zave
Mutorashanga
Alaska
Chinhoyi
Banket
Kildonan
Concession
Mvurwi
Bindura
Shamva
Madziwa
Mazowe
Chitsungo
Mutoko
Murewa
EWANRIGG NATIONAL PARK
Darwendale
Nyabira
Norton
L. CHIVERO
Selous
McILWAINE RECREATIONAL PARK
Chitungwiza
Bromley
Macheke
Marondera
Beatrice
MASHABA RANGE
New Featherstone
Featherstone
Hwedza
Headlands
Rusape
Nyazura
Troutbeck
Nyanga
NYANGA NATIONAL PARK
Nyamaropa
MTARAZI FALLS NATIONAL PARK
Christmas Pass
Odzi
Mutare
Dorowa
Buhera
MAPANDE RANGE
Chivhu
Umniati
Jombe
Silobela
Kwekwe
Redcliff
Nkayi
Lupani
Kenmaur
Gwayi
Gwayi Stn
Motapa
Lonely Mine
Inyathi
Tsholotsho
Nyamandhlovu
Queens Mine
Bembesi
Nsiza
Shangani
Gweru
Lalapanzi
Mvuma
Shurugwi
Chilimanzi
Gutu
NGEZI RECREATIONAL PARK
SEBAKWE RECREATIONAL AREA
CHIRONDE RANGE
Mashava
Masvingo
Nyika
Birchenough Bridge
Hot Springs
Murambara
Chimanimani
CHIMANIMANI NATIONAL PARK
Chipinge
Rupisi
Mount Selinda
Espungabera
Chibuwe
Sabi Experimental Station
Glenlivet
Zaka
KYLE RECREATIONAL PARK
L. Mutirikwe
MUSHANDIKE SANCTUARY
Zvishavane
Fort Rixon
Heany Junction
Esigodini
Cyrene
Tegwani
Figtree
Matobo
MATOBO NATIONAL PARK
Mbalabala
Filabusi
Mberengwa
Plumtree
Marula
Ramokgwebana
Tshesebe
Mangwe
Kezi
Gwanda
West Nicholson
Antelope Mine
Francistown
MAJEMOLOBYE RANGE
Legion Mine
Guyu
Makado
Towla
Mt. Buhwa 1330 m
MUNAKA RANGE
Ngundu
Buffalo Range
Nandi Mill
Chisumbanje
Hacufera
Triangle
Chiredzi
Hippo Valley
Rutenga
Mbizi
Mwenezi
Bubi
Chikombedzi
GONAREZHOU NATIONAL PARK
MALAPATI GAME RESERVE
Vila Eduardo Montlane (Chicualacuala)
Macane
Maçobere
Massangena
Mmadinare
Selebi Phikwe
Bobonong
Semolale
Thuli
MASHATU GAME RESERVE
Sefophe
Mazunga
Beitbridge
Messina
Baines Drift
TULI BLOCK
Moeng
Alldays
Tshipise
Punda Maria
Pafuri
Dumela
Sherwood Ranch
Maasstroom
Tom Burke
Tolwe
Waterpoort
THOHOYANDOU
SOUTPANSBERGE
Louis Trichardt
BEN LAVIN NATURE RESERVE
Vivo
Bandelierkop
Elim Hospital
Giyani
KRUGER NATIONAL PARK
Shingwedzi
Mapai
PARQUE NACIONAL DE BANHINE
Steilloopbrug
Marken
Soekmekaar
HANS MERENSKY NATUURRESERVAAT
Duiwelskloof
Ellisras
Pietersburg
PERCY FIFE NATUURRESERVAAT
Sterkwater
Tzaneen
Haenertsburg
Gravelotte
Letaba
Olifants
Massingir
Phalaborwa
Maalamba
Machaila
LIMPOPO
Copyright © Map Studio

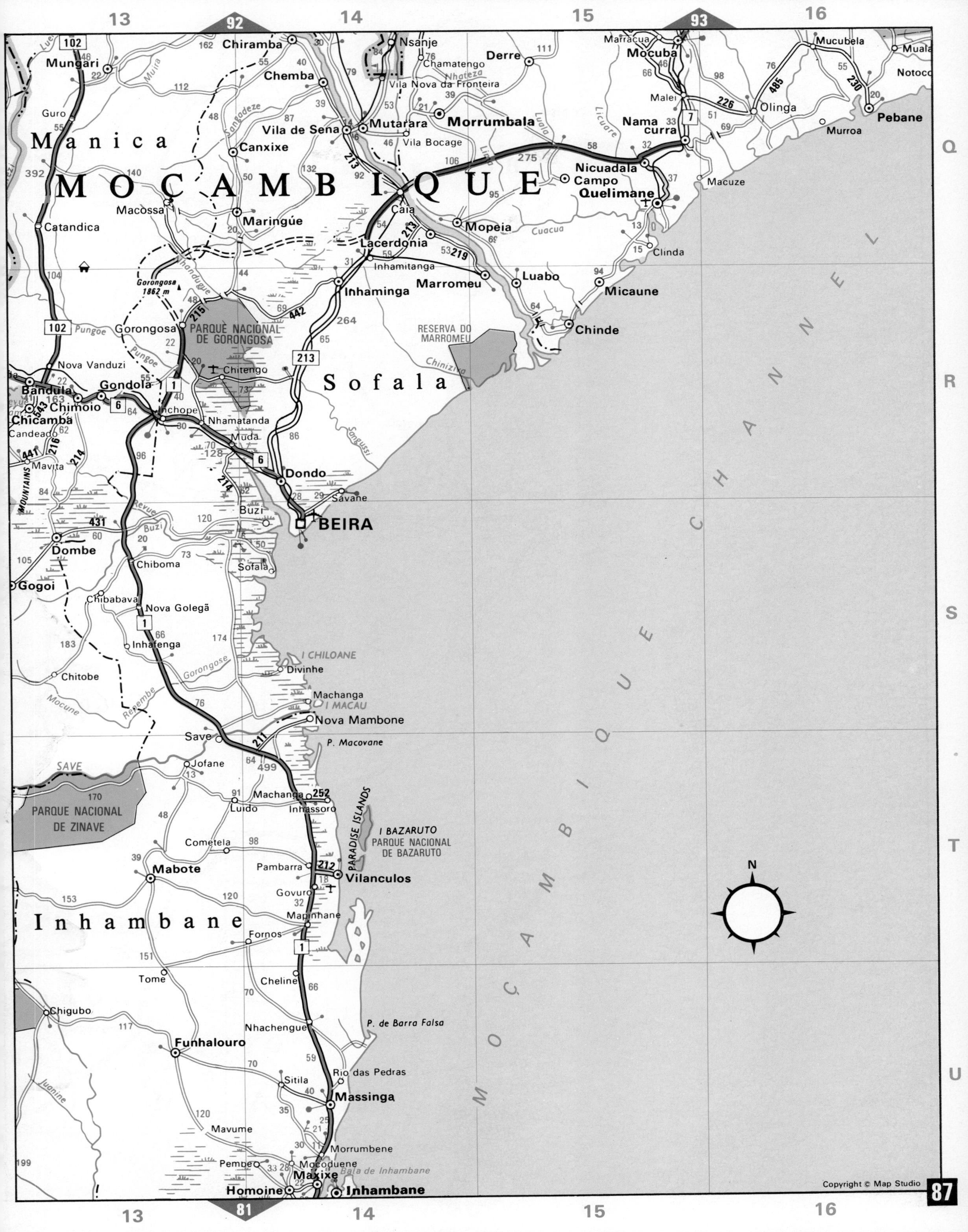

MOÇAMBIQUE
Manica
Sofala
Inhambane
MOÇAMBIQUE CHANNEL
Chiramba
Mungari
Chemba
Nsanje
Chamatengo
Vila Nova da Fronteira
Derre
Mocuba
Mucubela
Muala
Notoco
Malei
Olinga
Pebane
Murroa
Nama curra
Vila de Sena
Mutarara
Morrumbala
Vila Bocage
Canxixe
Guro
Catandica
Macossa
Maringúe
Nicuadala
Campo
Quelimane
Macuze
Caia
Mopeia
Lacerdonia
Inhamitanga
Marromeu
Luabo
Micaune
Chinde
Clinda
Inhaminga
Gorongosa 1862 m
Gorongosa
PARQUE NACIONAL DE GORONGOSA
RESERVA DO MARROMEU
Nova Vanduzi
Chitengo
Bandula
Gondola
Chimoio
Chicamba
Candeado
Inchope
Nhamatanda
Muda
Mavita
Dondo
Savane
BEIRA
Buzi
Dombe
Sofala
Chiboma
Gogoi
Chibabava
Nova Golegã
Inhafenga
Chitobe
I CHILOANE
Divinhe
Machanga
I MACAU
Nova Mambone
P. Macovane
Save
Jofane
PARQUE NACIONAL DE ZINAVE
Luido
Machanga
Inhassoro
PARADISE ISLANDS
I BAZARUTO
PARQUE NACIONAL DE BAZARUTO
Cometela
Mabote
Pambarra
Vilanculos
Govuro
Mapinhane
Fornos
Tome
Cheline
Chigubo
Nhachengue
P. de Barra Falsa
Funhalouro
Sitila
Rio das Pedras
Massinga
Mavume
Morrumbene
Pembe
Mocoduene
Maxixe
Baía de Inhambane
Homoine
Inhambane
N
Copyright © Map Studio

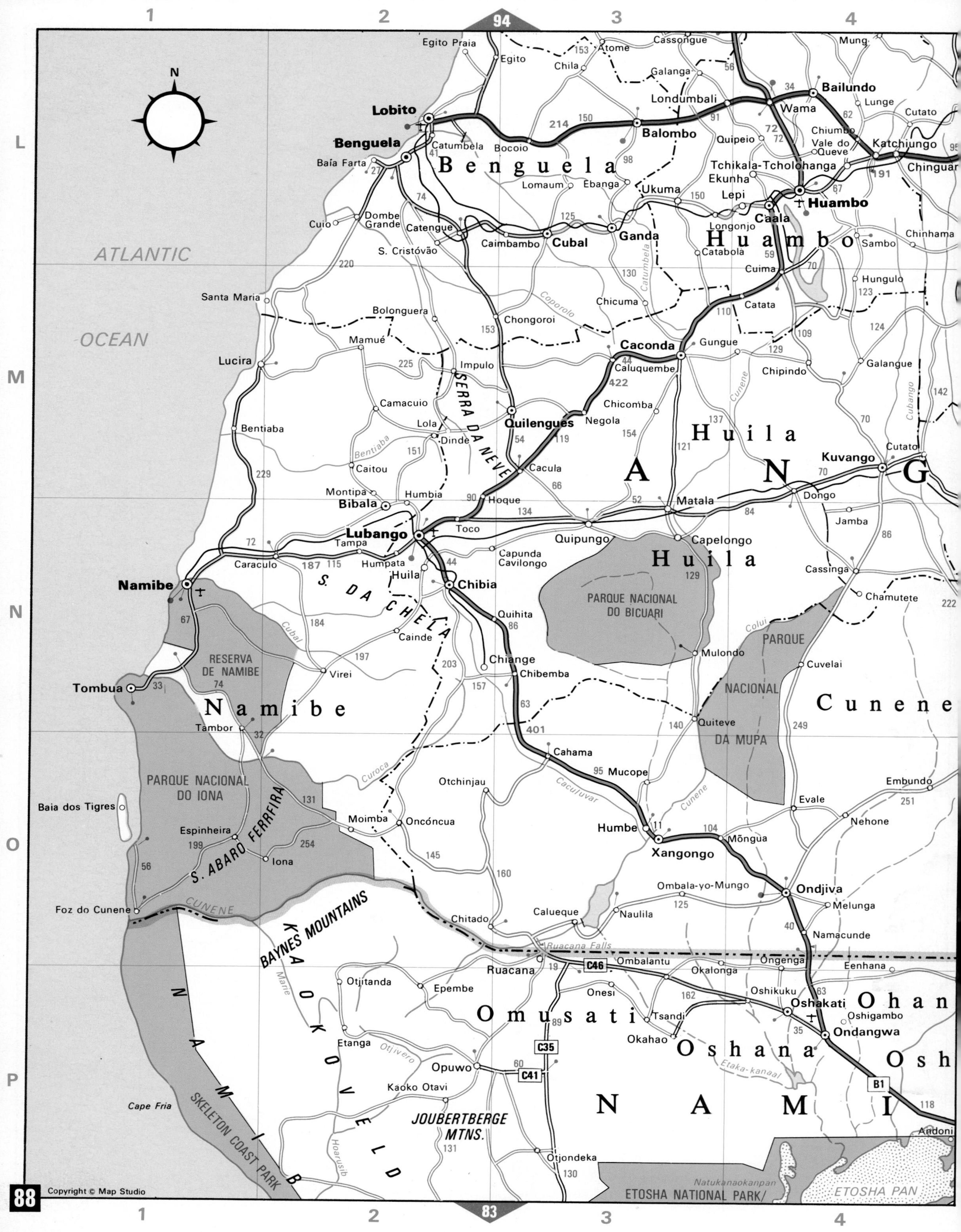
94
1
2
3
4
L
M
N
O
P
N
ATLANTIC
OCEAN
Lobito
Benguela
Baía Farta
Egito Praia
Egito
Chila
Atome
Cassongue
Galanga
Londumbali
Bailundo
Mung
Wama
Lunge
Cutato
Chiumbo
Vale do Queve
Katchiungo
Chinguar
Balombo
Quipeio
Catumbela
Bocoio
Benguela
Lomaum
Ebanga
Tchikala-Tcholohanga
Ekunha
Ukuma
Lepi
Huambo
Caala
Longonjo
Cuio
Dombe Grande
Catengue
Caimbambo
Cubal
Ganda
Huambo
Catabola
Sambo
Chinhama
S. Cristóvão
Cuima
Hungulo
Santa Maria
Bolonguera
Chongoroi
Chicuma
Catata
Mamué
Caconda
Gungue
Galangue
Lucira
Impulo
Caluquembe
Chipindo
SERRA DA NEVE
Camacuio
Chicomba
Negola
Quilengues
Lola
Dinde
Bentiaba
Huila
Caitou
Cacula
A
N
G
Kuvango
Cutato
Montipa
Bibala
Humbia
Hoque
Matala
Dongo
Jamba
Lubango
Toco
Quipungo
Capelongo
Tampa
Caraculo
Humpata
Huila
Capunda Cavilongo
Huila
Namibe
Chibia
S. DA CHELA
Cassinga
Chamutete
Quihita
PARQUE NACIONAL DO BICUARI
Caínde
Chiange
Mulondo
PARQUE
Cuvelai
RESERVA DE NAMIBE
Virei
Chibemba
NACIONAL
Tombua
Namibe
Quiteve
Cunene
Tambor
DA MUPA
Cahama
PARQUE NACIONAL DO IONA
Mucope
Otchinjau
Embundo
Baia dos Tigres
S. ABARO FERRFIRA
Moimba
Oncóncua
Evale
Nehone
Espinheira
Humbe
Mõngua
Iona
Xangongo
Ombala-yo-Mungo
Ondjiva
Foz do Cunene
Melunga
BAYNES MOUNTAINS
Chitado
Calueque
Naulila
Namacunde
Ruacana Falls
Ruacana
Ombalantu
Okalonga
Ongenga
Eenhana
Otjitanda
Epembe
Onesi
Oshikuku
Oshakati
Ohan
KAOKOVELD
Omusati
Tsandi
Oshigambo
Okahao
Oshana
Ondangwa
Etanga
Opuwo
Osh
NAMIB
Kaoko Otavi
NAMI
Cape Fria
SKELETON COAST PARK
JOUBERTBERGE MTNS.
Andoni
Otjondeka
ETOSHA NATIONAL PARK
ETOSHA PAN
83
Copyright © Map Studio

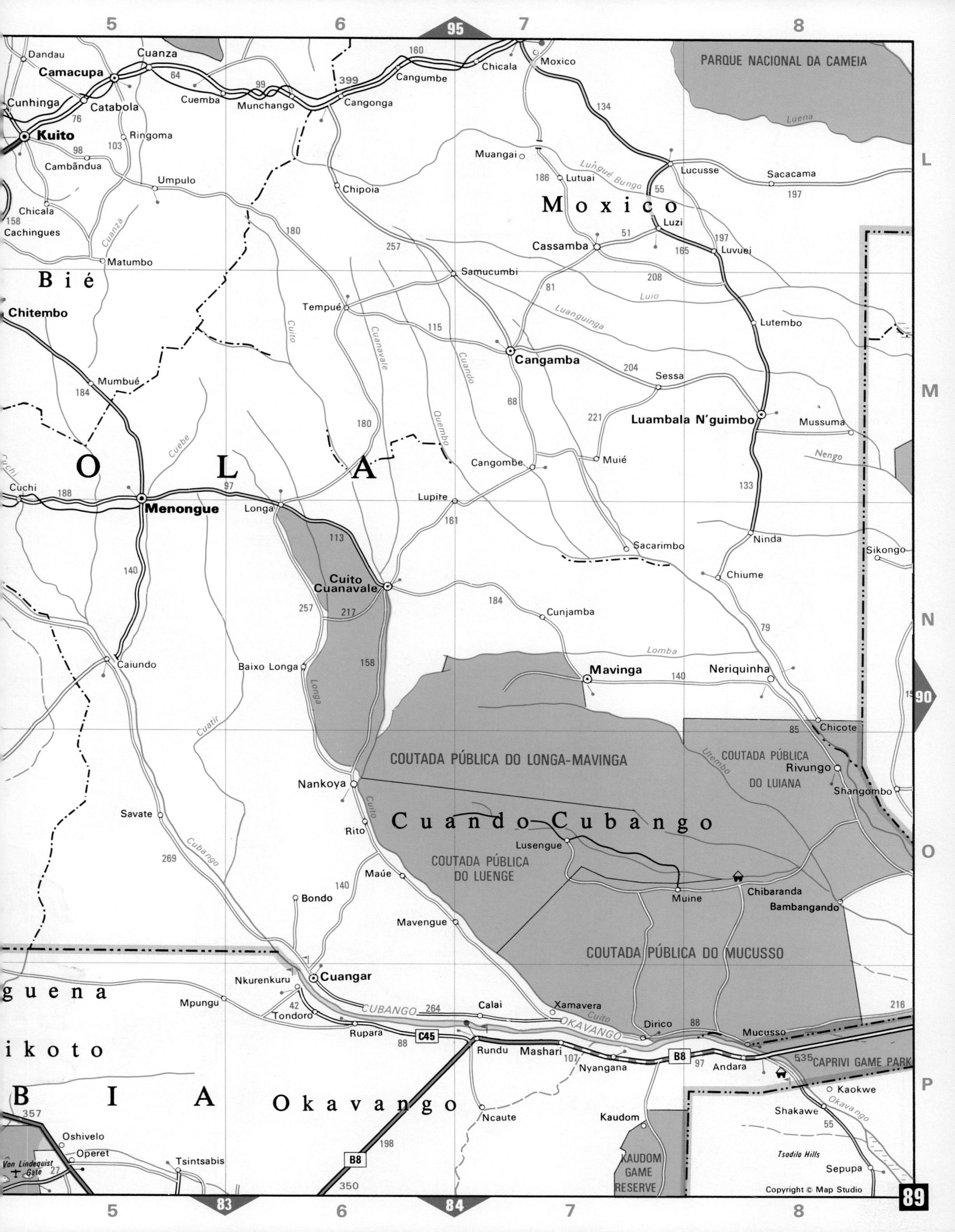

PARQUE NACIONAL DA CAMEIA
Moxico
Bié
O L A
Cuando Cubango
COUTADA PÚBLICA DO LONGA-MAVINGA
COUTADA PÚBLICA DO LUIANA
COUTADA PÚBLICA DO LUENGE
COUTADA PÚBLICA DO MUCUSSO
CAPRIVI GAME PARK
KAUDOM GAME RESERVE
guena
ikoto
B I A
Okavango
Camacupa
Cuanza
Dandau
Cunhinga
Catabola
Kuito
Ringoma
Cuemba
Munchango
Cangonga
Cangumbe
Chicala
Moxico
Cambãndua
Umpulo
Chipoia
Muangai
Lutuai
Lucusse
Sacacama
Chicala
Cachingues
Matumbo
Luzi
Cassamba
Luvuei
Samucumbi
Tempué
Chitembo
Lutembo
Cangamba
Sessa
Mumbué
Luambala N'guimbo
Mussuma
Muié
Cangombe
Cuchi
Menongue
Longa
Lupire
Sacarimbo
Ninda
Sikongo
Chiume
Cuito Cuanavale
Cunjamba
Caiundo
Baixo Longa
Mavinga
Neriquinha
Chicote
Rivungo
Shangombo
Nankoya
Savate
Rito
Lusengue
Maúe
Bondo
Muine
Chibaranda
Bambangando
Mavengue
Cuangar
Nkurenkuru
Mpungu
Tondoro
Calai
Xamavera
Rupara
Dirico
Mucusso
Rundu
Mashari
Nyangana
Andara
Kaokwe
Shakawe
Ncaute
Kaudom
Oshivelo
Operet
Von Lindequist Gate
Tsintsabis
Tsodilo Hills
Sepupa
Luena
Lungué Bungo
Luio
Luanguinga
Cuito
Cuanavale
Cuando
Quembo
Nengo
Cuebe
Lomba
Longa
Cuatir
Utembo
Cubango
CUBANGO
OKAVANGO
Okavango
C45
B8
399
Copyright © Map Studio

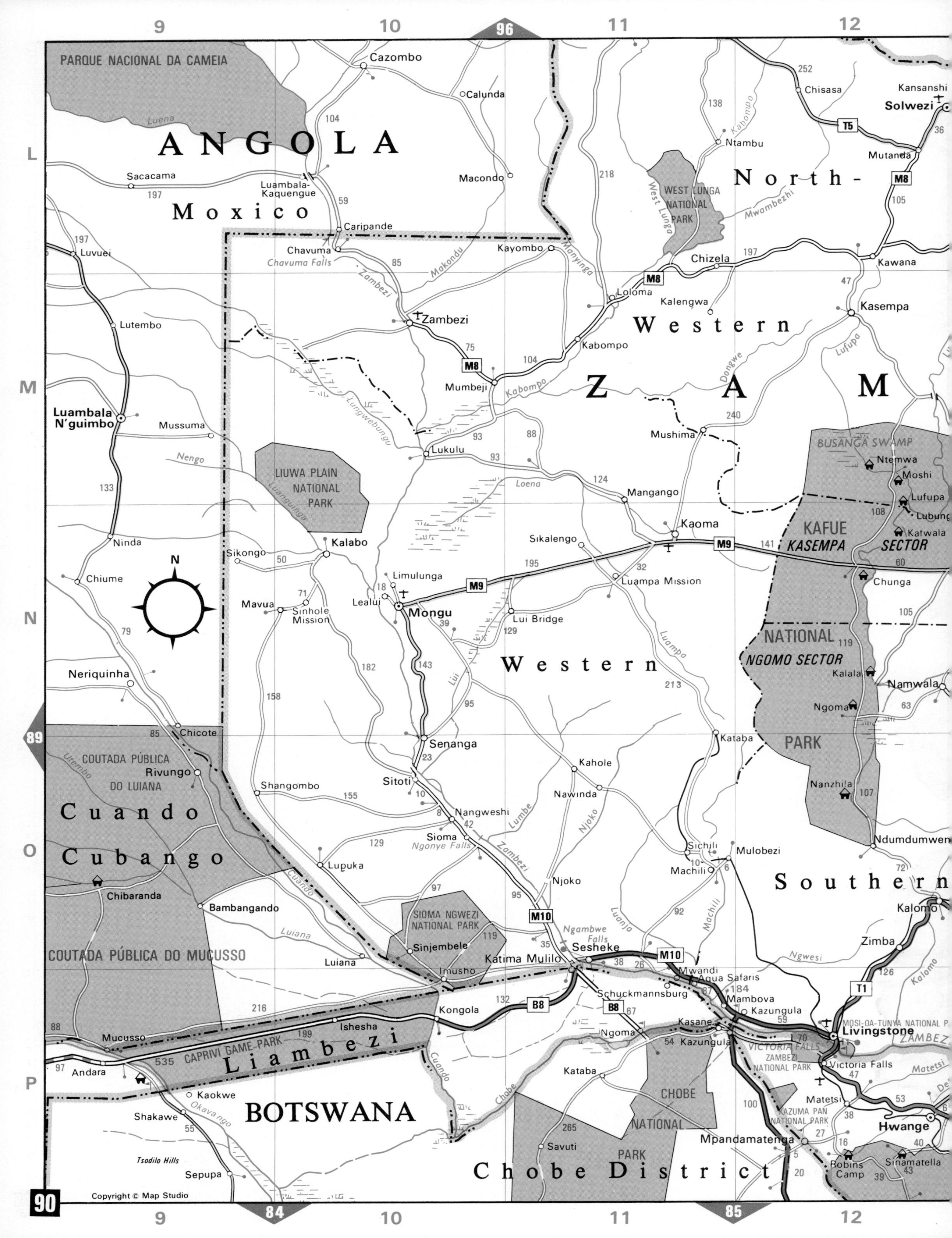

PARQUE NACIONAL DA CAMEIA

Cazombo

Calunda

Luena

104

Chisasa

Kansanshi
Solwezi

138

252

Ntambu

T5

Mutanda

A N G O L A

North-

Sacacama

197

Luambala-
Kaquengue

59

Macondo

218

West Lunga

WEST LUNGA
NATIONAL
PARK

M8

105

Moxico

Caripande

M o x i c o

197

Luvuei

Chavuma

Chavuma Falls

85

Mokondu

Kayombo

Manyinga

Mwambezi

Chizela

197

Kawana

W e s t e r n

Lutembo

Zambezi

M8

Loloma

Kalengwa

47

Kasempa

Zambezi

75

104

Kabompo

Z   A   M

Luambala
N'guimbo

Mussuma

Mumbeji

Kabompo

240

Mushima

Dongwe

Lufupa

BUSANGA SWAMP

Ntemwa

Moshi

Nengo

93

88

KAFUE

Lufupa

Lubung

Lukulu

93

Loena

124

Mangango

KASEMPA

SECTOR

108

Katwala

133

LIUWA PLAIN
NATIONAL
PARK

Luanguinga

Kaoma

M9

141

60

Chunga

Ninda

Sikongo

50

Kalabo

Sikalengo

195

32

Luampa Mission

105

Chiume

71

Limulunga

M9

Luampa

NATIONAL

119

79

N

Mavua

Sinhole
Mission

18

Lealui

Mongu

39

Lui Bridge

129

NGOMO SECTOR

Kalala

Namwala

Neriquinha

W e s t e r n

213

63

Ngoma

158

182

143

Lui

95

Nanzhila

107

89

Chicote

85

COUTADA PÚBLICA
DO LUIANA

Rivungo

Shangombo

155

Senanga

23

Sitoti

10

Kahole

Nawinda

Kataba

PARK

Ndumdumwen

Utembo

C u a n d o

Nangweshi

8

42

Lumbe

Njoko

Sichili

Machili

10

Mulobezi

6

72

Cubango

Chibaranda

Sioma

Ngonye Falls

129

Zambezi

S o u t h e r n

Lupuka

97

95

Njoko

92

Kalomo

COUTADA PÚBLICA DO MUCUSSO

Bambangando

Luiana

SIOMA NGWEZI
NATIONAL PARK

119

M10

Ngambwe
Falls

35

Sesheke

M10

Luanja

Zimba

Sinjembele

Luiana

Imusho

Katima Mulilo

38

26

Mwandi

Aqua Safaris

Machili

126

T1

216

132

B8

B8

67

184

Mambova

59

Mucusso

199

Ishesha

CAPRIVI GAME PARK

Liambezi

Kongola

Schuckmannsburg

Kazungula

Kasane

70

MOSI-OA-TUNYA NATIONAL P.

Livingstone

88

535

54

Kazungula

VICTORIA FALLS

ZAMBEZI

97

Andara

Okavango

Kaokwe

Ngoma

Kataba

CHOBE

NATIONAL

100

ZAMBEZI
NATIONAL
PARK

Victoria Falls

47

KAZUMA PAN
NATIONAL PARK

Matetsi

53

Shakawe

55

B O T S W A N A

Savuti

265

PARK

Mpandamatenga

27

5

20

16

Robins
Camp

Hwange

38

Sinamatella

40

43

Tsodilo Hills

Sepupa

C h o b e   D i s t r i c t

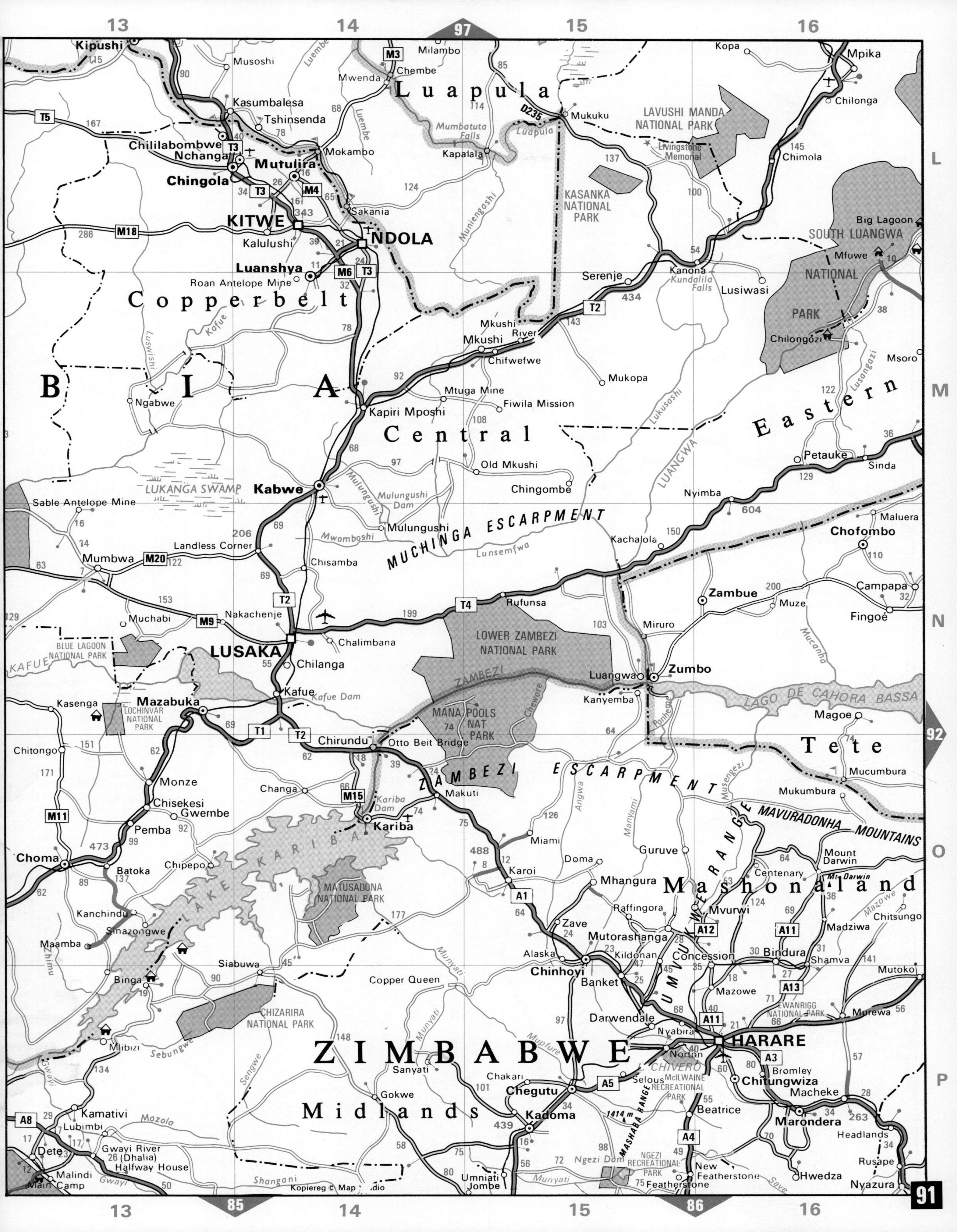
13
14
15
16
97
L
M
N
O
P
92
85
86
Kipushi
Musoshi
Milambo
Chembe
Mwenda
Kopa
Mpika
Chilonga
Luapula
Kasumbalesa
Tshinsenda
Mokambo
Chililabombwe
Nchanga
Mutulira
Chingola
Mukuku
LAVUSHI MANDA NATIONAL PARK
Livingstone Memorial
Mumbatuta Falls
Kapalala
Chimola
KASANKA NATIONAL PARK
Sakania
KITWE
NDOLA
Kalulushi
Luanshya
Roan Antelope Mine
Copperbelt
Big Lagoon
SOUTH LUANGWA NATIONAL PARK
Mfuwe
Serenje
Kanona
Kundalila Falls
Lusiwasi
Chilongozi
Mkushi River
Mkushi
Chifwefwe
Mukopa
Msoro
B I A
Ngabwe
Mtuga Mine
Fiwila Mission
Kapiri Mposhi
Central
Eastern
Petauke
Sinda
Old Mkushi
Chingombe
LUKANGA SWAMP
Kabwe
Mulungushi Dam
Mulungushi
Nyimba
Maluera
Chofombo
Sable Antelope Mine
MUCHINGA ESCARPMENT
Kachalola
Landless Corner
Mumbwa
Chisamba
Campapa
Zambue
Muze
Fingoé
Muchabi
Nakachenje
Rufunsa
Miruro
BLUE LAGOON NATIONAL PARK
LUSAKA
Chalimbana
LOWER ZAMBEZI NATIONAL PARK
Chilanga
Luangwa
Zumbo
Kafue
Kafue Dam
Kanyemba
LAGO DE CAHORA BASSA
Kasenga
LOCHINVAR NATIONAL PARK
Mazabuka
MANA POOLS NAT PARK
Magoe
Chitongo
Chirundu
Otto Beit Bridge
Tete
ZAMBEZI ESCARPMENT
Mucumbura
Monze
Changa
Makuti
Mukumbura
Chisekesi
Gwembe
Kariba Dam
Kariba
MAVURADONHA MOUNTAINS
Pemba
Miami
Guruve
Mount Darwin
Choma
Batoka
Chipepo
Karoi
Doma
Centenary
LAKE KARIBA
MATUSADONA NATIONAL PARK
Mhangura
Mashonaland
Raffingora
Mvurwi
Kanchindu
Sinazongwe
Zave
Chitsungo
Madziwa
Maamba
Mutorashanga
Alaska
Kildonan
Concession
Bindura
Shamva
Siabuwa
Copper Queen
Chinhoyi
Banket
Mutoko
Binga
Mazowe
UMVUKWE RANGE
EWANRIGG NATIONAL PARK
Murewa
CHIZARIRA NATIONAL PARK
Darwendale
Nyabira
Mlibizi
HARARE
Norton
ZIMBABWE
L. CHIVERO
Sanyati
Chakari
Chegutu
Selous
McILWAINE RECREATIONAL PARK
Chitungwiza
Bromley
Gokwe
Macheke
Kamativi
Midlands
Beatrice
Marondera
Lubimbi
Kadoma
MASHABA RANGE
Headlands
Dete
Gwayi River (Dhalia)
Halfway House
Ngezi Dam
NGEZI RECREATIONAL PARK
New Featherstone
Rusape
Malindi
Main Camp
Umniati
Jombe
Featherstone
Hwedza
Nyazura
Kopiereg © Map Studio

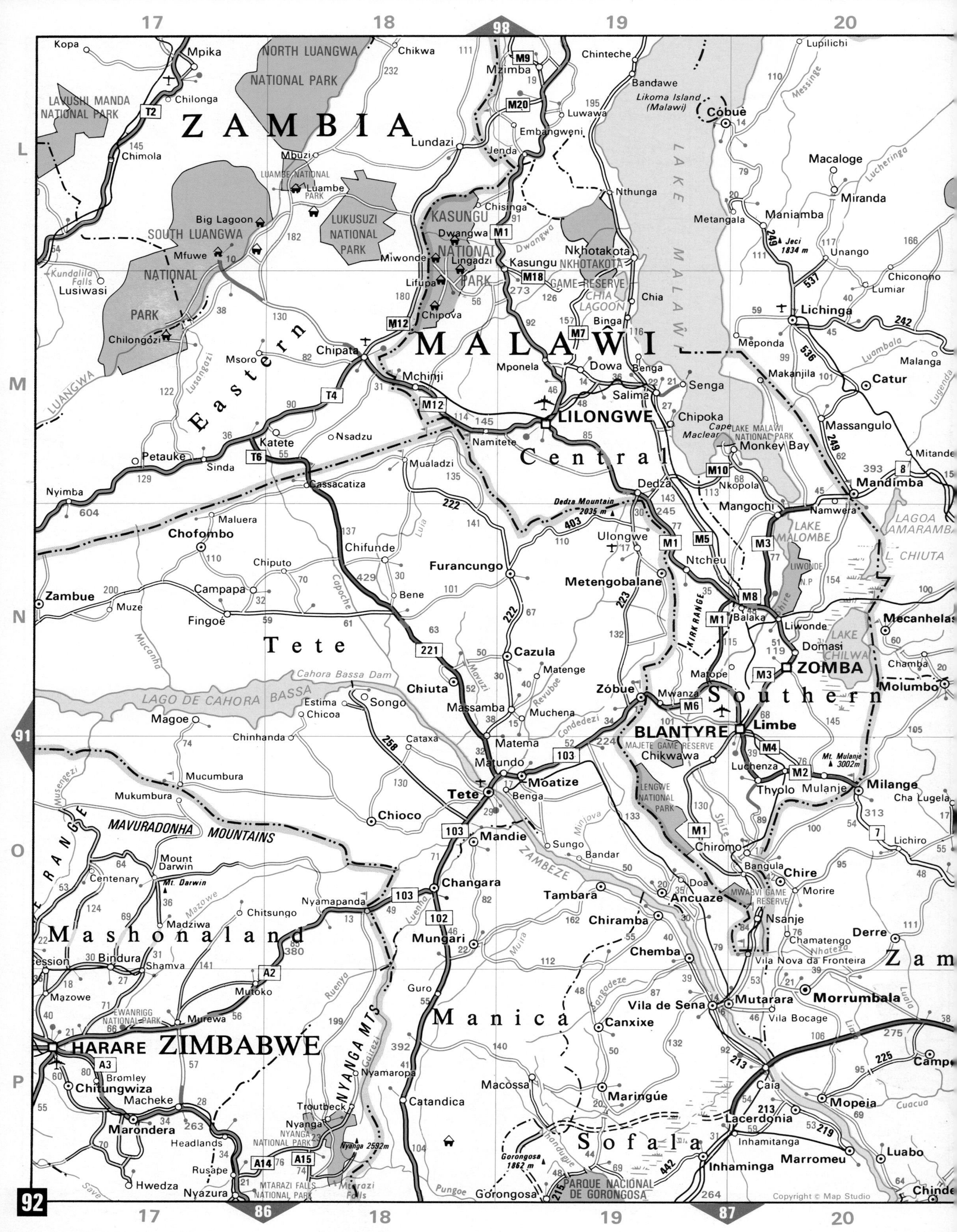

17
18
19
20
98
L
M
N
O
P
91
86
87
ZAMBIA
MALAWI
ZIMBABWE
Eastern
Central
Southern
Tete
Manica
Sofala
Mashonaland
NORTH LUANGWA NATIONAL PARK
LAVUSHI MANDA NATIONAL PARK
LUAMBE NATIONAL PARK
SOUTH LUANGWA NATIONAL PARK
LUKUSUZI NATIONAL PARK
KASUNGU NATIONAL PARK
NKHOTAKOTA GAME RESERVE
LAKE MALAWI
LAKE MALAWI NATIONAL PARK
LAKE MALOMBE
LIWONDE N.P
LAKE CHILWA
LAGOA AMARAMBA
L. CHIUTA
MAJETE GAME RESERVE
LENGWE NATIONAL PARK
MWABVI GAME RESERVE
LAGO DE CAHORA BASSA
Cahora Bassa Dam
MAVURADONHA MOUNTAINS
NYANGA MTS
NYANGA NATIONAL PARK
MTARAZI FALLS NATIONAL PARK
EWANRIGG NATIONAL PARK
PARQUE NACIONAL DE GORONGOSA
KIRK RANGE
ZAMBEZE
Kopa
Mpika
Chilonga
Chimola
Chikwa
Mzimba
Chinteche
Bandawe
Likoma Island (Malawi)
Cóbuè
Lupilichi
Luwawa
Embangweni
Lundazi
Jenda
Mbuzi
Luambe
Big Lagoon
Mfuwe
Kundalila Falls
Lusiwasi
Chilongozi
Chisinga
Dwangwa
Miwonde
Lingadzi
Lifupa
Chipova
Kasungu
Nkhotakota
Nthunga
Metangala
Maniamba
Macaloge
Miranda
Jeci 1834 m
Unango
Chiconono
Lumiar
Lichinga
Meponda
Malanga
Chia
Chia Lagoon
Binga
Chipata
Msoro
Mchinji
Mponela
Dowa
Benga
Salima
Senga
Makanjila
Catur
Katete
Nsadzu
Namitete
LILONGWE
Chipoka
Cape Maclear
Monkey Bay
Massangulo
Mitande
Petauke
Sinda
Nyimba
Cassacatiza
Mualadzi
Dedza
Nkopola
Mangochi
Namwera
Mandimba
Dedza Mountain 2035 m
Maluera
Chofombo
Ulongwe
Ntcheu
Chifunde
Chiputo
Furancungo
Metengobalane
Zambue
Campapa
Muze
Fingoé
Bene
Balaka
Liwonde
Mecanhelas
Cazula
Domasi
ZOMBA
Chamba
Molumbo
Matenge
Matope
Chiuta
Zóbue
Mwanza
Songo
Estima
Chicoa
Massamba
Muchena
Magoe
Chinhanda
Cataxa
Matema
BLANTYRE
Limbe
Chikwawa
Matundo
Moatize
Mucumbura
Mukumbura
Tete
Benga
Chioco
Luchenza
Thyolo
Mulanje
Mt. Mulanje 3002m
Milange
Cha Lugela
Mandie
Sungo
Bandar
Chiromo
Lichiro
Mount Darwin
Mt. Darwin
Centenary
Changara
Bangula
Chire
Morire
Tambara
Doa
Ancuaze
Nyamapanda
Madziwa
Chitsungo
Mungari
Chiramba
Nsanje
Chamatengo
Derre
Chemba
Vila Nova da Fronteira
Bindura
Shamva
Mazowe
Mutoko
Murewa
Guro
Vila de Sena
Mutarara
Morrumbala
Vila Bocage
Canxixe
HARARE
Chitungwiza
Bromley
Macheke
Marondera
Headlands
Rusape
Nyazura
Hwedza
Nyamaropa
Troutbeck
Nyanga
Nyanga 2592m
Mtarazi Falls
Catandica
Macossa
Maringúe
Caia
Mopeia
Campo
Lacerdonia
Inhamitanga
Marromeu
Luabo
Inhaminga
Gorongosa 1862 m
Gorongosa
Chinde
Copyright © Map Studio

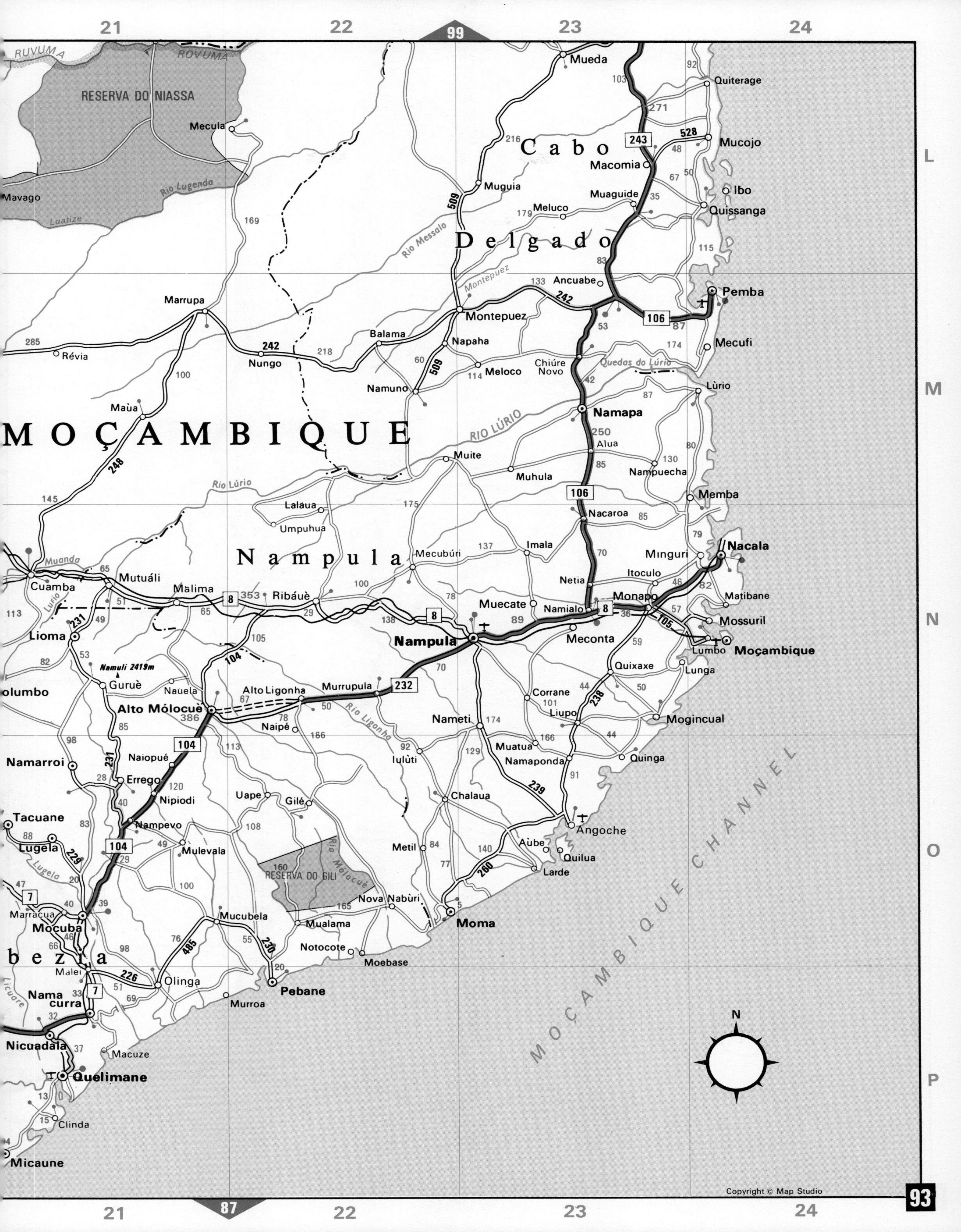

21
22
23
24
99
87
L
M
N
O
P
RUVUMA
ROVUMA
RESERVA DO NIASSA
Mecula
Mavago
Rio Lugenda
Luatize
169
Mueda
Quiterage
271
243
528
Mucojo
Cabo
Macomia
216
Muguia
509
Muaguide
Ibo
Quissanga
179
Meluco
Rio Messalo
Delgado
115
Montepuez
133
Ancuabe
Pemba
242
106
Marrupa
Montepuez
Balama
Napaha
Mecufi
285
Révia
242
Nungo
218
60
Meloco
Chiúre Novo
Quedas do Lúrio
100
Namuno
Lùrio
Maùa
MOÇAMBIQUE
RIO LÚRIO
Namapa
250
Alua
248
Muite
Muhula
Nampuecha
Rio Lúrio
145
Lalaua
175
Umpuhua
Memba
Nacaroa
Nampula
Mecubúri
137
Imala
Nacala
Mìnguri
Muanda
Mutuáli
Cuamba
Malima
8
353
Ribáuè
Netia
Itoculo
Monapo
Matibane
Muecate
Namialo
113
Lúrio
Lioma
231
Mossuril
Nampula
Meconta
105
Lumbo
Moçambique
Quixaxe
Lunga
Namuli 2419m
Guruè
olumbo
Nauela
Alto Ligonha
Murrupula
232
Alto Mólocuè
386
Naipé
Rio Ligonha
Nameti
Corrane
Liupo
238
Mogincual
Namarroi
104
Naiopué
Iulùti
Muatua
Namaponda
Quinga
Errego
Nipiodi
Uape
Gilé
Chalaua
239
Tacuane
Nampevo
Angoche
Lugela
229
Mulevala
Metil
Aùbe
Quilua
Larde
Lugela
RESERVA DO GILI
Rio Mólocuè
260
Nova Nabùri
Marracua
Mocuba
Mucubela
Mualama
Moma
MOÇAMBIQUE CHANNEL
485
230
Notocote
Moebase
bezia
Malei
226
7
Olinga
Pebane
Nama curra
Murroa
Licuare
N
Nicuadala
Macuze
Quelimane
Clinda
Micaune
Copyright © Map Studio

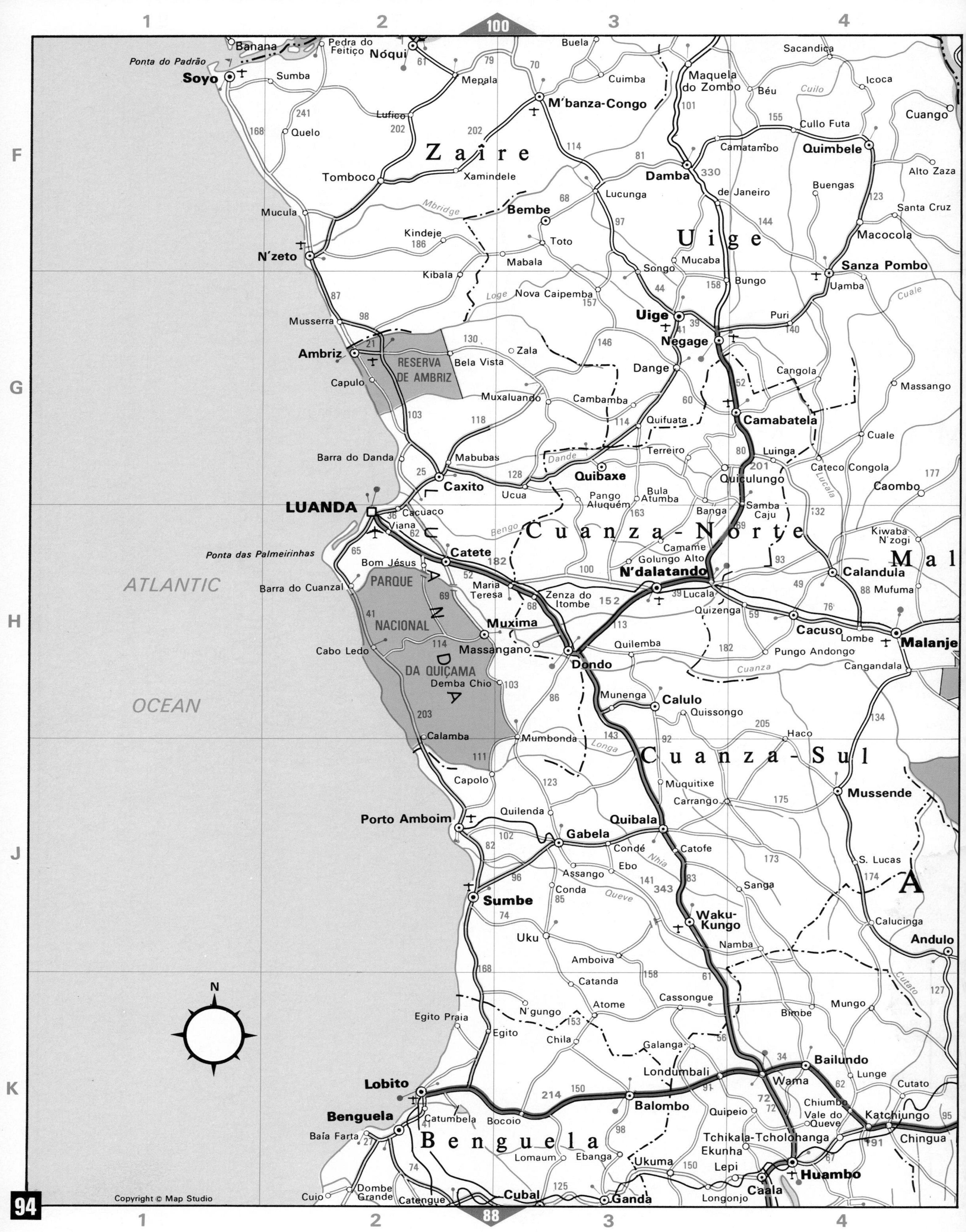
1
2
3
4
100
88
F
G
H
J
K
Banana
Pedra do Feitiço
Nóqui
Buela
Sacandica
Ponta do Padrão
Soyo
Sumba
Mepala
Cuimba
Maquela do Zombo
Béu
Culo
Icoca
M'banza-Congo
Lufico
Cuango
Quelo
Cullo Futa
Camatambo
Quimbele
Zaîre
Damba
Alto Zaza
Tomboco
Xamindele
Lucunga
de Janeiro
Buengas
Mucula
Mbridge
Bembe
Santa Cruz
Kindeje
Toto
Uige
Macocola
N'zeto
Mabala
Mucaba
Songo
Sanza Pombo
Kibala
Bungo
Uamba
Loge
Nova Caipemba
Cuale
Uige
Puri
Musserra
Negage
130
Zala
Ambriz
RESERVA DE AMBRIZ
Bela Vista
Dange
Cangola
Capulo
Massango
Muxaluando
Cambamba
Camabatela
Quifuata
Cuale
Terreiro
Luinga
Barra do Danda
Mabubas
Dande
Quibaxe
Cateco Congola
Quiculungo
Caxito
Bula Atumba
Lucala
Caombo
Ucua
Pango Aluquém
LUANDA
Cacuaco
Banga
Samba Caju
Viana
Bengo
Cuanza-Norte
Kiwaba N'zogi
Ponta das Palmeirinhas
Catete
Camame
Golungo Alto
Bom Jésus
Mal
ATLANTIC
PARQUE NACIONAL DA QUIÇAMA
Barra do Cuanzal
Maria Teresa
Zenza do Itombe
N'dalatando
Lucala
Calandula
Mufuma
Muxima
Quizenga
Cacuso
LUANDA
Lombe
Malanje
Cabo Ledo
Massangano
Quilemba
Pungo Andongo
Dondo
Cangandala
Cuanza
Demba Chio
OCEAN
Munenga
Calulo
Quissongo
Calamba
Mumbonda
Longa
Haco
Cuanza-Sul
Capolo
Muquitixe
Carrango
Mussende
Quilenda
Porto Amboim
Gabela
Quibala
Condé
Catofe
Nhia
S. Lucas
Assango
Ebo
A
Sumbe
Conda
Queve
Sanga
Waku-Kungo
Calucinga
Uku
Namba
Andulo
Amboiva
Catanda
Cutato
Atome
Cassongue
N'gungo
Mungo
Egito Praia
Bimbe
Egito
Chila
Galanga
Bailundo
Londumbali
Lunge
Lobito
Wama
Cutato
Balombo
Chiumbo
Benguela
Catumbela
Bocoio
Quipeio
Vale do Queve
Katchiungo
Baía Farta
Benguela
Tchikala-Tcholohanga
Chingua
Lomaum
Ebanga
Ekunha
Ukuma
Lepi
Huambo
Dombe Grande
Caala
Cuio
Cubal
Catengue
Ganda
Longonjo

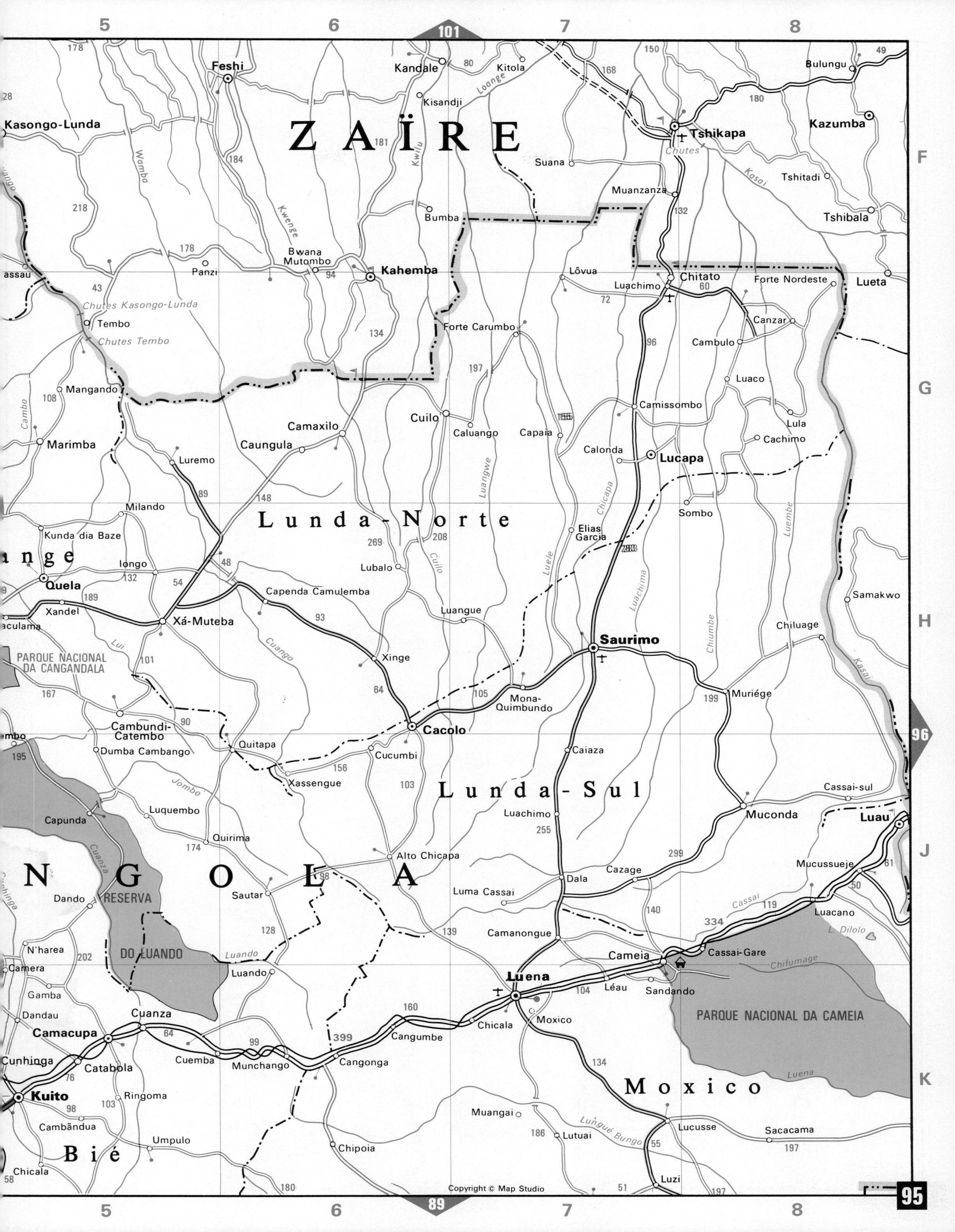

ZAÏRE

Kasongo-Lunda

Feshi

Kandale   Kitola   Bulungu

80   150   49

Kisandji   168   180

178   181   **Tshikapa**   **Kazumba**

28   184   Suana

218   Bumba   Muanzanza   Tshitadi

assau   178   Bwana Mutombo   132   Tshibala

43   94   ⊙ **Kahemba**   Lôvua   Chitato   Forte Nordeste   Lueta

Tembo   Panzi   Luachimo   60

Chutes Kasongo-Lunda   134   Forte Carumbo   72   Canzar

Chutes Tembo   96   Cambulo

Mangando   197   Luaco

108   Camissombo   Lula

Marimba   Camaxilo   Cuilo   Caluango   Capaia   Calonda   Cachimo

Luremo   Caungula   ⊙ **Lucapa**

89   148   Sombo

Milando

ange   Kunda dia Baze   **Lunda-Norte**   Elias Garcia

Iongo   132   48   269   208   Samakwo

Quela   54   Lubalo   Chiluage

189   Xandel   Capenda Camulemba   Luangue

aculama   **Xá-Muteba**   93   **Saurimo**

PARQUE NACIONAL DA CANGANDALA   101   Xinge   Muriége

167   64   105   199

mbo   Cambundi-Catembo   90   Mona-Quimbundo

195   Dumba Cambango   Quitapa   Cucumbi   Caiaza   Cassai-sul

Capunda   156   **Lunda-Sul**   Muconda   **Luau**

Luquembo   Xassengue   103   Luachimo

N G O L A   174   Quirima   255   Mucussueje   61

Dando   **RESERVA**   Alto Chicapa   Cazage   299   50

N'harea   **DO LUANDO**   98   Sautar   Dala   Luacano

202   128   Luma Cassai   140   119

Camera   139   334   L. Dilolo

Gamba   Luando   Camanongue   Cameia   Cassai-Gare

Dandau   **Cuanza**   **Luena**   Léau   Sandando

Camacupa   64   104

Cunhinga   Catabola   99   160   Chicala   Moxico   **PARQUE NACIONAL DA CAMEIA**

76   Cuemba   Munchango   399   Cangonga   Cangumbe

Kuito   98   103   Ringoma   134

Cambãndua   **M o x i c o**

58   Muangai   Lucusse   Sacacama

Biê   Chipoia   186   Lutuai   55   197

Chicala   180   Luzi   51   197

Loange   Kwilu   Chutes   Kasai   Kwenge   Cambo   Lui   Cuango   Cuilo   Luele   Luangwe   Chicapa   Luachima   Chiumbe   Luembe   Kasai   Jombo   Luando   Cuanza   Cassai   Chifumage   Luena   Lungué Bungo

Copyright © Map Studio

F   G   H   96   J   K

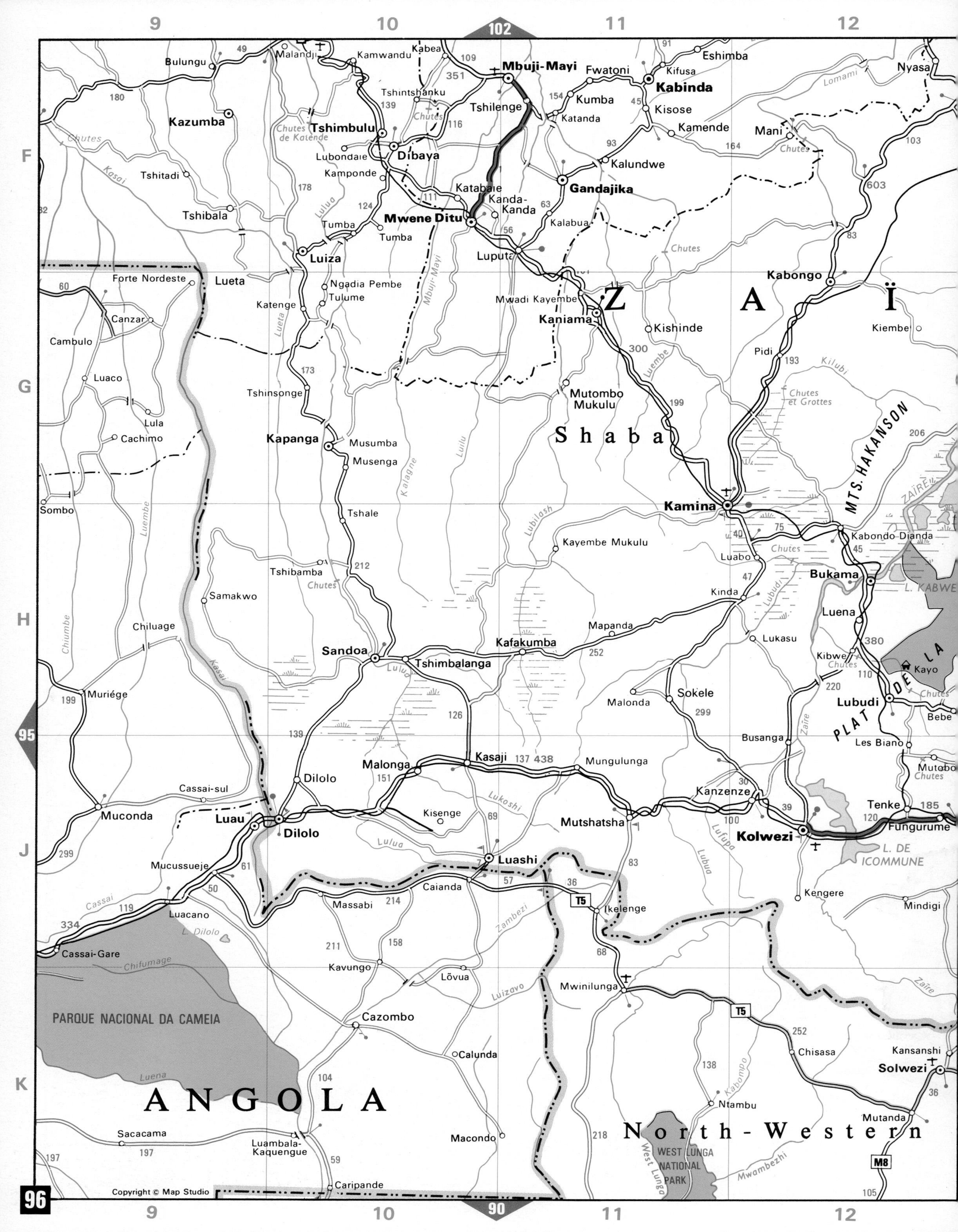

102
Mbuji-Mayi
Kabinda
Tshimbulu
Dibaya
Kazumba
Mwene Ditu
Gandajika
Luiza
Kaniama
Kabongo
Z A Ï
Shaba
Kapanga
Kamina
MTS. HAKANSON
Bukama
Sandoa
Kafakumba
Tshimbalanga
Lubudi
PLAT DE LA
Kasaji
Malonga
Dilolo
Luau
Muconda
Kolwezi
Fungurume
Tenke
Luashi
Mutshatsha
Kanzenze
Cassai-Gare
PARQUE NACIONAL DA CAMEIA
Cazombo
Mwinilunga
Solwezi
ANGOLA
North-Western
WEST LUNGA NATIONAL PARK
95
90
Copyright © Map Studio

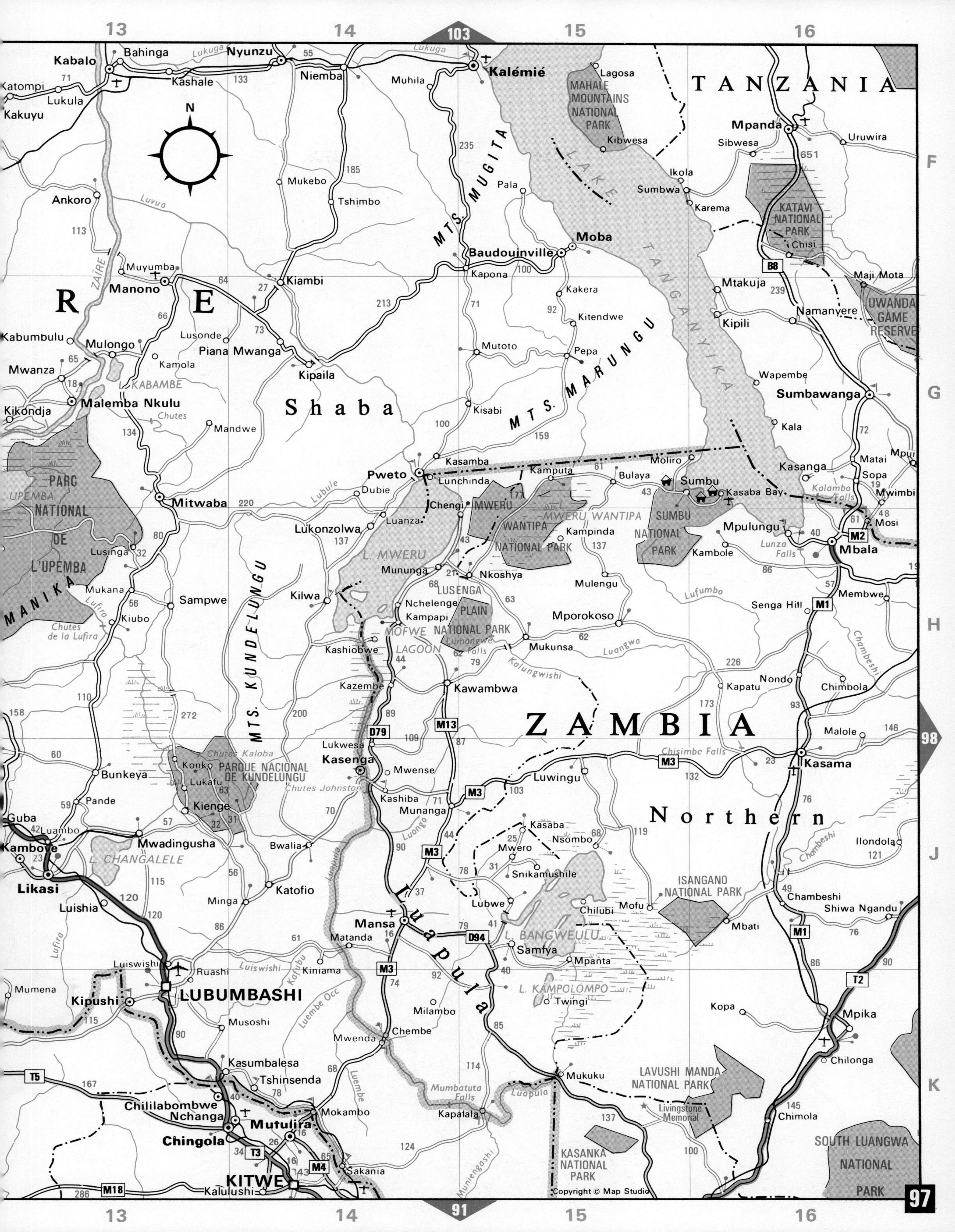

TANZANIA
ZAMBIA
Shaba
Northern
R E
Kabalo
Bahinga
Nyunzu
Kalémié
Niemba
Kashale
Lukugu
Katompi
Lukula
Kakuyu
Muhila
Lagosa
MAHALE MOUNTAINS NATIONAL PARK
Kibwesa
Mpanda
Sibwesa
Uruwira
Mukebo
Tshimbo
MTS. MUGITA
Pala
Ankoro
Luvua
LAKE TANGANYIKA
Ikola
Sumbwa
Karema
KATAVI NATIONAL PARK
Chisi
Moba
Baudouinville
Kapona
Muyumba
Manono
Kiambi
ZAÏRE
Mtakuja
Maji Mota
UWANDA GAME RESERVE
Namanyere
Kipili
Kakera
Kitendwe
Kabumbulu
Mulongo
Lusonde
Piana Mwanga
Kamola
Kipaila
Mutoto
Pepa
MTS. MARUNGU
Mwanza
Malemba Nkulu
Kikondja
L. KABAMBE
Chutes
Mandwe
Kisabi
Wapembe
Sumbawanga
Kala
PARC NATIONAL DE L'UPEMBA
UPEMBA
MANIKA
Pweto
Kasamba
Lunchinda
Dubie
Lubule
Kamputa
Moliro
Bulaya
Sumbu
Kasaba Bay
Kasanga
Matai
Sopa
Mwimbi
Mpui
Kalambo Falls
Mitwaba
Chengi
MWERU WANTIPA NATIONAL PARK
SUMBU NATIONAL PARK
Lukonzolwa
Luanza
Kampinda
L. MWERU
Mpulungu
Mosi
Mbala
Lunza Falls
Kambole
Lusinga
Mununga
Nkoshya
Mulengu
Mukana
Lufira
Kilwa
Nchelenge
Kampapi
LUSENGA PLAIN NATIONAL PARK
MOFWE LAGOON
Lumangwe Falls
Mporokoso
Mukunsa
Luangwa
Lufumbo
Membwe
Senga Hill
Sampwe
Kiubo
Chutes de la Lufira
Kashiobwe
Kalungwishi
Chambeshi
Kazembe
Kawambwa
Kapatu
Nondo
Chimbola
MTS. KUNDELUNGU
Malole
Lukwesa
Kasenga
Mwense
Chisimbe Falls
Kasama
Luwingu
PARQUE NACIONAL DE KUNDELUNGU
Chutes Kaloba
Konko
Lukafu
Kienge
Chutes Johnston
Bunkeya
Pande
Kashiba
Munanga
Kasaba
Nsombo
Guba
Luambo
Kambove
Mwadingusha
L. CHANGALELE
Bwalia
Mwero
Snikamushile
Ilondola
Likasi
Luishia
Minga
Katofio
Luongo
Luapula
ISANGANO NATIONAL PARK
Mofu
Chilubi
Lubwe
Chambeshi
Shiwa Ngandu
Mbati
Mansa
Matanda
L. BANGWEULU
Samfya
Mpanta
Luiswishi
Ruashi
Kiniama
Kafubu
Mumena
Kipushi
LUBUMBASHI
Milambo
L. KAMPOLOMPO
Twingi
Kopa
Mpika
Musoshi
Luembe Occ
Chembe
Mwenda
Chilonga
Kasumbalesa
Tshinsenda
Mukuku
LAVUSHI MANDA NATIONAL PARK
Livingstone Memorial
Mumbatuta Falls
Chililabombwe
Nchanga
Mutulira
Mokambo
Kapalala
Chimola
Chingola
KASANKA NATIONAL PARK
SOUTH LUANGWA NATIONAL PARK
Sakania
Muniengashi
KITWE
Kalulushi
Copyright © Map Studio
13
14
15
16
F
G
H
J
K
103
98
91
B8
M1
M2
M3
M4
M13
M18
D79
D94
T2
T3
T5

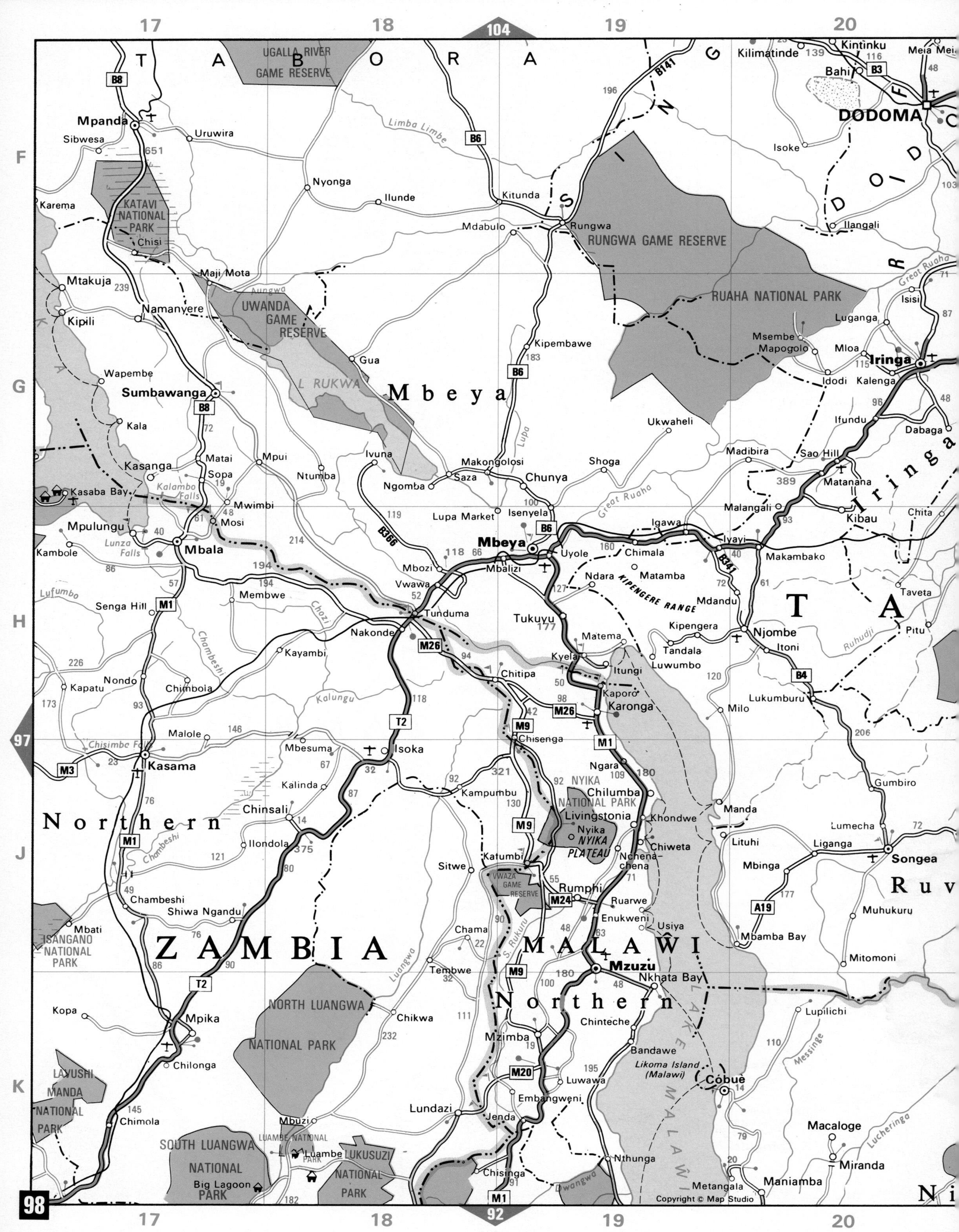

17
18
19
20
104
92
97
F
G
H
J
K
T A B O R A
S I N G I D A
DODOMA
Mbeya
Iringa
T A
Ruv
Northern
ZAMBIA
MALAWI
Northern
UGALLA RIVER GAME RESERVE
KATAVI NATIONAL PARK
UWANDA GAME RESERVE
L RUKWA
RUNGWA GAME RESERVE
RUAHA NATIONAL PARK
NYIKA NATIONAL PARK
NYIKA PLATEAU
VWAZA GAME RESERVE
ISANGANO NATIONAL PARK
NORTH LUANGWA NATIONAL PARK
LAVUSHI MANDA NATIONAL PARK
SOUTH LUANGWA NATIONAL PARK
LUAMBE NATIONAL PARK
LUKUSUZI NATIONAL PARK
KIPENGERE RANGE
LAKE MALAWI
Mpanda
Sibwesa
Uruwira
Nyonga
Ilunde
Kitunda
Mdabulo
Rungwa
Karema
Chisi
Mtakuja
Kipili
Namanyere
Maji Mota
Wapembe
Sumbawanga
Kala
Kasanga
Matai
Sopa
Mpui
Ntumba
Kasaba Bay
Mwimbi
Mosi
Mpulungu
Mbala
Kambole
Lunza Falls
Kalambo Falls
Gua
Kipembawe
Ivuna
Ngomba
Saza
Makongolosi
Chunya
Shoga
Ukwaheli
Lupa Market
Isenyela
Mbeya
Uyole
Mbozi
Vwawa
Mbalizi
Chimala
Matamba
Ndara
Mdandu
Igawa
Iyayi
Makambako
Tukuyu
Matema
Kyela
Itungi
Kipengera
Tandala
Luwumbo
Njombe
Itoni
Tunduma
Nakonde
Senga Hill
Membwe
Kayambi
Kapatu
Nondo
Chimbola
Chitipa
Kaporo
Karonga
Malole
Chisimbe Falls
Kasama
Mbesuma
Isoka
Chisenga
Kalinda
Kampumbu
Ngara
Chilumba
Livingstonia
Khondwe
Chiweta
Nchenachena
Chinsali
Ilondola
Katumbi
Sitwe
Rumphi
Ruarwe
Enukweni
Usiya
Chambeshi
Shiwa Ngandu
Mbati
Chama
Tembwe
Mzuzu
Nkhata Bay
Chikwa
Chinteche
Mzimba
Bandawe
Likoma Island (Malawi)
Cóbuè
Luwawa
Embangweni
Jenda
Lundazi
Mbuzi
Luambe
Big Lagoon
Nthunga
Chisinga
Metangala
Maniamba
Miranda
Macaloge
Kopa
Mpika
Chilonga
Chimola
Kilimatinde
Kintinku
Bahi
Meia Meia
Isoke
Ilangali
Isisi
Luganga
Msembe
Mapogolo
Mloa
Iringa
Idodi
Kalenga
Ifundu
Dabaga
Madibira
Sao Hill
Matanana
Malangali
Kibau
Chita
Taveta
Pitu
Lukumburu
Milo
Gumbiro
Manda
Lumecha
Lituhi
Liganga
Songea
Mbinga
Muhukuru
Mbamba Bay
Mitomoni
Lupilichi
Limba Limbe
Great Ruaha
Lupa
Ruhudji
Chambeshi
Chozi
Lufumbo
Kalungu
Luangwa
S. Rukuru
Dwangwa
Messinge
Lucheringa
Lusewa
B8
B6
B141
B3
B366
B341
B4
M1
M3
M9
M24
M20
M26
T2
A19
Copyright © Map Studio

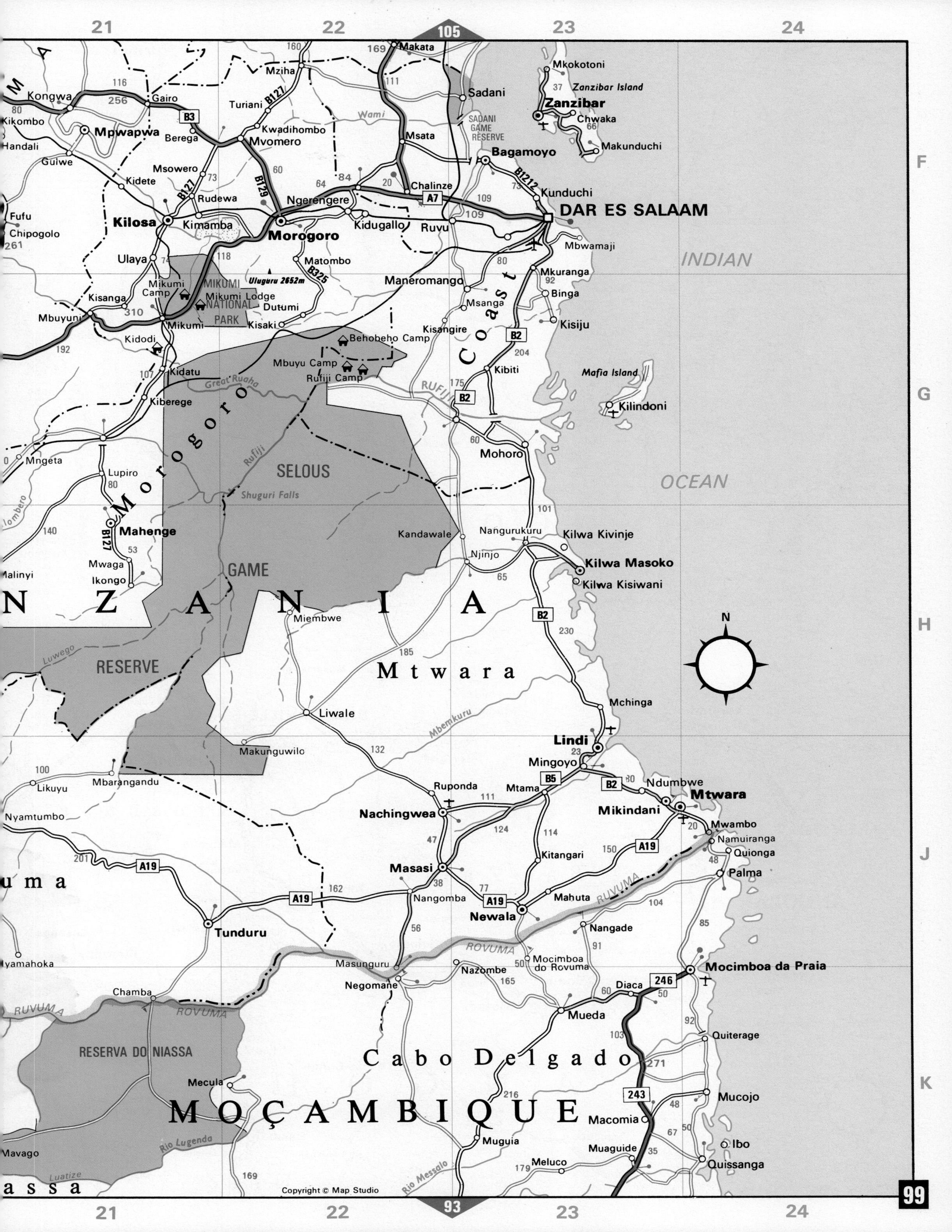

21   22   23   24

Kongwa
Kikombo
Handali
Gulwe
Fufu
Chipogolo

Mpwapwa
Bereza
Msowero
Kidete
Rudewa
Kimamba

Kilosa

Ulaya

Kisanga
Mbuyuni

Kidodi
Kidatu
Kiberege

Mngeta
Lupiro

Mahenge
Mwaga
Ikongo

Malinyi

Mziha
Turiani
Kwadihombo
Mvomero
Ngerengere

Morogoro

Matombo
Dutumi
Kisaki

Mikumi
Camp
MIKUMI
Mikumi Lodge
Mikumi NATIONAL
PARK

Uluguru 2652m

MIKUMI NATIONAL PARK

Mbuyu Camp
Rufiji Camp
Behobeho Camp

Kisangire

Kandawale

Miembwe

Liwale

Makunguwilo

Mbarangandu
Likuyu

Nyamtumbo

Tunduru

Nyamahoka

Chamba

Mavago

Makata
Mziha

Sadani

Msata

Chalinze
Kidugallo
Ruvu

Maneromango

Msanga

Mohoro

Nangurukuru
Njinjo

SELOUS

GAME

RESERVE

Shuguri Falls

M t w a r a

Lindi
Mingoyo

Ruponda
Mtama
Nachingwea

Kitangari
Masasi
Nangomba
Newala
Mahuta

Masunguru
Nazombe
Negomane
Mocimboa
do Rovuma

MOÇAMBIQUE

Cabo Delgado

Mecula

Muguia

Zanzibar
Mkokotoni
Zanzibar Island
Chwaka
Makunduchi

Bagamoyo
Kunduchi

DAR ES SALAAM
Mbwamaji
Mkuranga
Binga
Kisiju

Kibiti

Mafia Island

Kilindoni

Kilwa Kivinje
Kilwa Masoko
Kilwa Kisiwani

Mchinga

Ndumbwe
Mikindani   **Mtwara**
Mwambo
Namuiranga
Quionga
Palma

Nangade

Nangade

Mocimboa da Praia
Diaca

Mueda
Quiterage

Mucojo

Macomia
Muaguide
Meluco
Ibo
Quissanga

RESERVA DO NIASSA

INDIAN

OCEAN

N

Copyright © Map Studio

21   22   23   24

F

G

H

J

K

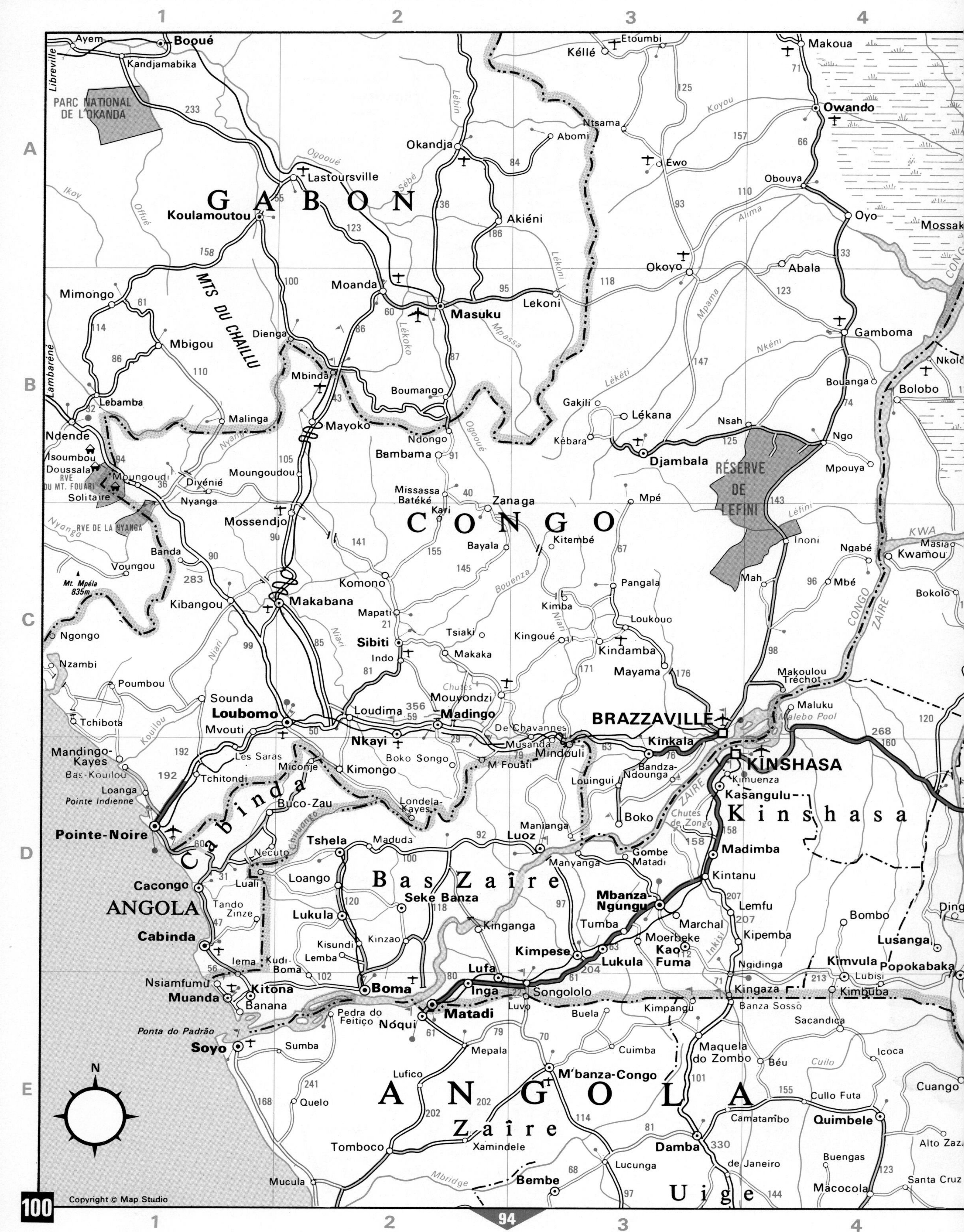
GABON
CONGO
ANGOLA
Cabinda
Bas Zaïre
Kinshasa
Zaïre
Uige
PARC NATIONAL DE L'OKANDA
MTS DU CHAILLU
RÉSERVE DE LEFINI
RVE DE LA NYANGA
RVE DU MT. FOUARI
BRAZZAVILLE
KINSHASA
Pointe-Noire
Loubomo
Koulamoutou
Lastoursville
Okandja
Akiéni
Masuku
Moanda
Lekoni
Owando
Oyo
Makoua
Djambala
Gamboma
Nkayi
Madingo
Sibiti
Makabana
Mossendjo
Mayoko
Boma
Matadi
Muanda
Soyo
Cabinda
Cacongo
M'banza-Congo
Mbanza-Ngungu
Kimpese
Tshela
Lukula
Luozi
Madimba
Damba
Quimbele
Copyright © Map Studio

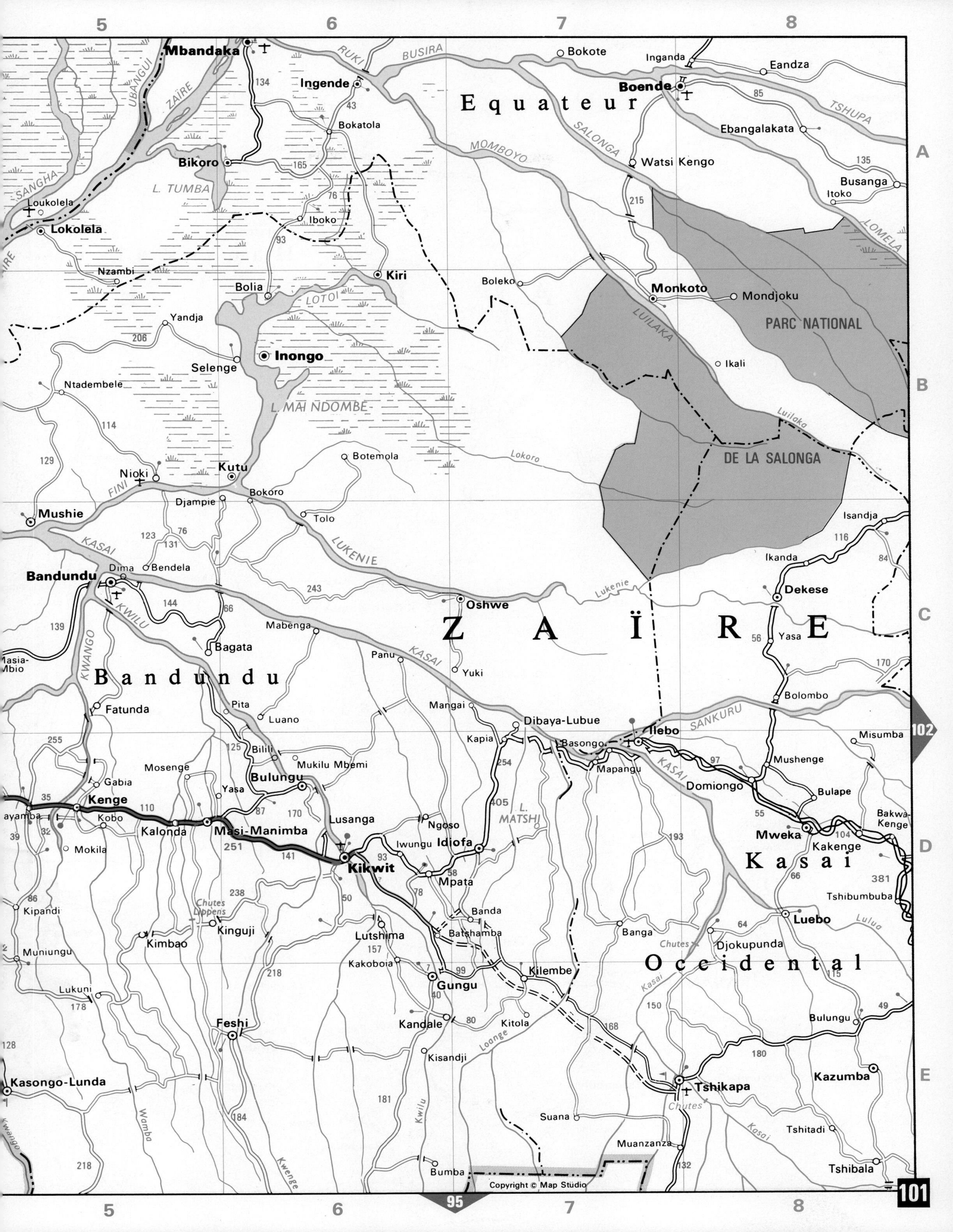

Column/row grid markers: 5, 6, 7, 8 (top and bottom); A, B, C, D, E (right side)

Regions: Equateur, ZAÏRE, Bandundu, BANDUNDU, Kasai, Oceidental, PARC NATIONAL, DE LA SALONGA

Cities, towns and features:

Mbandaka, Ingende, Bokatola, Bikoro, Bokote, Inganda, Boende, Eandza, Ebangalakata, Watsi Kengo, Busanga, Itoko, Loukolela, Lokolela, Nzambi, Iboko, Bolia, Kiri, Boleko, Monkoto, Mondjoku, L. TUMBA, LOTOI, Yandja, Selenge, Inongo, Ikali, Ntadembele, L. MAI NDOMBE, Botemola, Luilaka, Lokoro, Nioki, Kutu, Bokoro, Mushie, Djampie, Tolo, Isandja, Ikanda, Bandundu, Dima, Bendela, KASAI, KWILU, KWANGO, LUKENIE, Bagata, Mabenga, Oshwe, Dekese, Yasa, Bolombo, Masia-Mbio, Panu, Yuki, Mangai, Kapia, Dibaya-Lubue, Basongo, Ilebo, SANKURU, Misumba, Mapangu, Mushenge, Bulape, Fatunda, Pita, Luano, Bilili, Mukilu Mbemi, Kapia, Domiongo, Mosenge, Gabia, Yasa, Bulungu, Ngoso, Iwungu, Idiofa, L. MATSHI, Mweka, Kakenge, Bakwa-Kenge, Kenge, Kobo, Kalonda, Masi-Manimba, Lusanga, Mpata, Banga, Tshibumbuba, Mokila, Kikwit, Banda, Batshamba, Luebo, Djokupunda, Chutes Lippens, Kinguji, Kimbao, Lutshima, Kakoboia, Kilembe, Banga, Kipandi, Muniungu, Gungu, Kandale, Kitola, Lukuni, Feshi, Kisandji, Loange, Bulungu, Kazumba, Kasongo-Lunda, Tshikapa, Suana, Muanzanza, Tshitadi, Bumba, Tshibala, Wamba, Kwenge, Kwilu, Kasai, Lulua

Numbers (distances): 134, 43, 165, 76, 93, 85, 135, 215, 206, 114, 129, 123, 131, 76, 144, 66, 243, 139, 255, 125, 87, 170, 35, 110, 251, 141, 93, 38, 78, 50, 238, 7, 99, 40, 80, 157, 218, 181, 184, 128, 218, 178, 168, 150, 180, 49, 15, 64, 66, 381, 104, 55, 97, 193, 56, 84, 116, 170, 405, 254, 32, 39, 86, 102, 95, 101, 132, 254

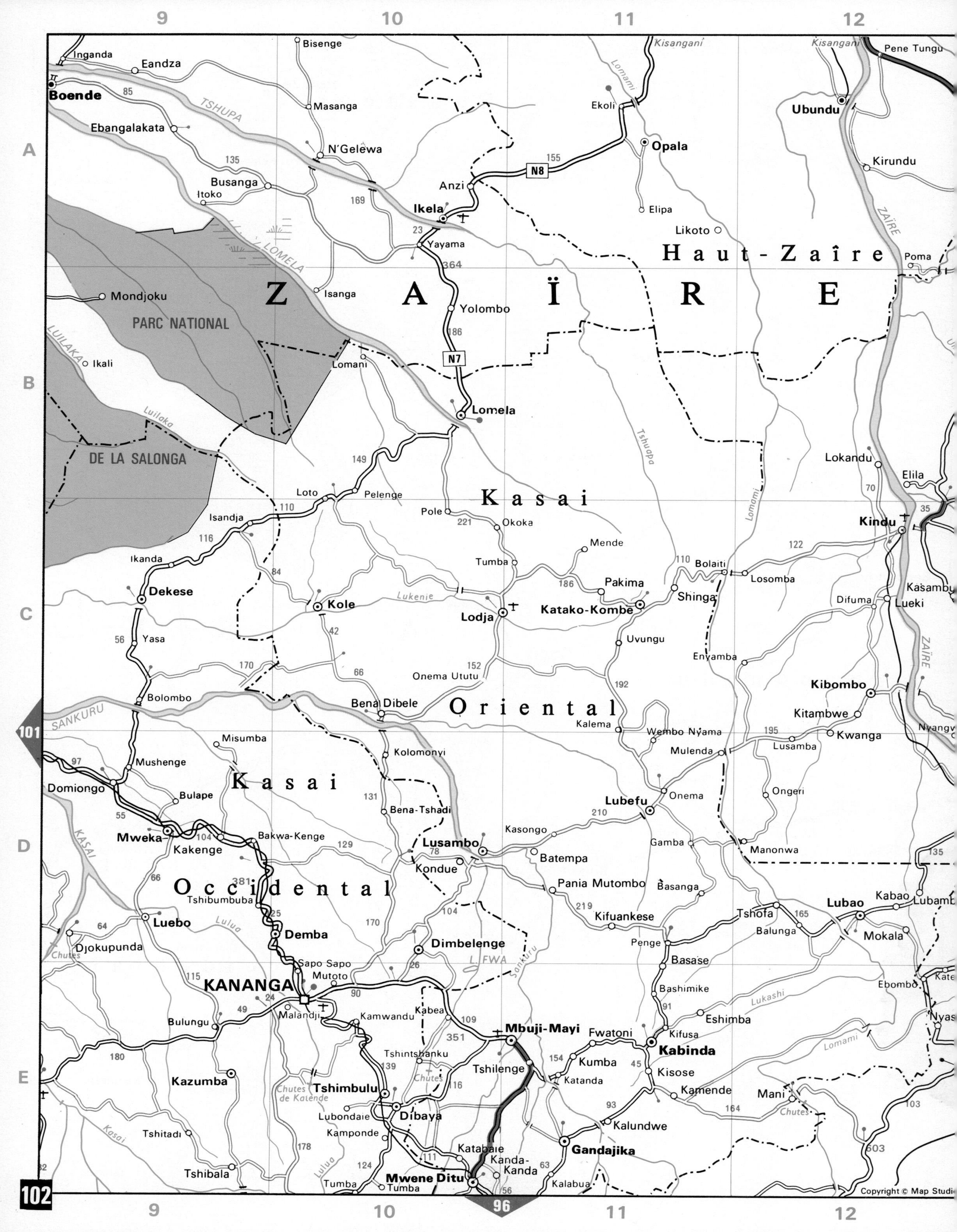

9
10
11
12
A
B
C
D
E
Z A Ï R E
Haut-Zaïre
Kasai Oriental
Kasai Occidental
PARC NATIONAL
DE LA SALONGA
Inganda
Eandza
Boende
Bisenge
Masanga
Ebangalakata
N'Gelewa
Busanga
Itoko
TSHUPA
LOMELA
Ikela
Yayama
Anzi
N8
Ekoli
Opala
Elipa
Likoto
Kisangani
Lomami
Ubundu
Pene Tungu
Kirundu
ZAÏRE
Poma
Mondjoku
Isanga
Yolombo
N7
Lomani
LUILAKA
Ikali
Luilaka
Lomela
Tshuapa
Lokandu
Elila
Kindu
Loto
Pelenge
Pole
Okoka
Isandja
Ikanda
Dekese
Tumba
Mende
Pakima
Kole
Lukenie
Lodja
Katako-Kombe
Shinga
Bolaiti
Losomba
Difuma
Lueki
Kasambu
Yasa
Uvungu
Enyamba
Onema Ututu
Kibombo
Bolombo
SANKURU
Bena Dibele
Kalema
Wembo Nyama
Mulenda
Kitambwe
Kwanga
Lusamba
Nyangw
Misumba
Kolomonyi
Domiongo
Mushenge
Bulape
Bena-Tshadi
Lubefu
Onema
Ongeri
Mweka
Kakenge
Bakwa-Kenge
KASAI
Lusambo
Kasongo
Batempa
Gamba
Manonwa
Kondue
Pania Mutombo
Basanga
Tshibumbuba
Luebo
Lulua
Demba
Dimbelenge
Kifuankese
Tshofa
Lubao
Kabao
Lubamb
Djokupunda
Chutes
Penge
Balunga
Mokala
Sapo Sapo
Mutoto
L. FWA
Sankuru
Basase
Ebombo
Kate
KANANGA
Malandji
Kamwandu
Kabea
Bashimike
Lukashi
Eshimba
Bulungu
Mbuji-Mayi
Fwatoni
Kifusa
Kabinda
Nyas
Tshintshanku
Tshilenge
Kumba
Kazumba
Tshimbulu
Chutes de Katende
Katanda
Kisose
Kamende
Mani
Dibaya
Lubondaie
Kamponde
Kalundwe
Tshitadi
Kasai
Gandajika
Katabaie
Kanda-Kanda
Tshibala
Mwene Ditu
Tumba
Kalabua
101
96
Copyright © Map Studio

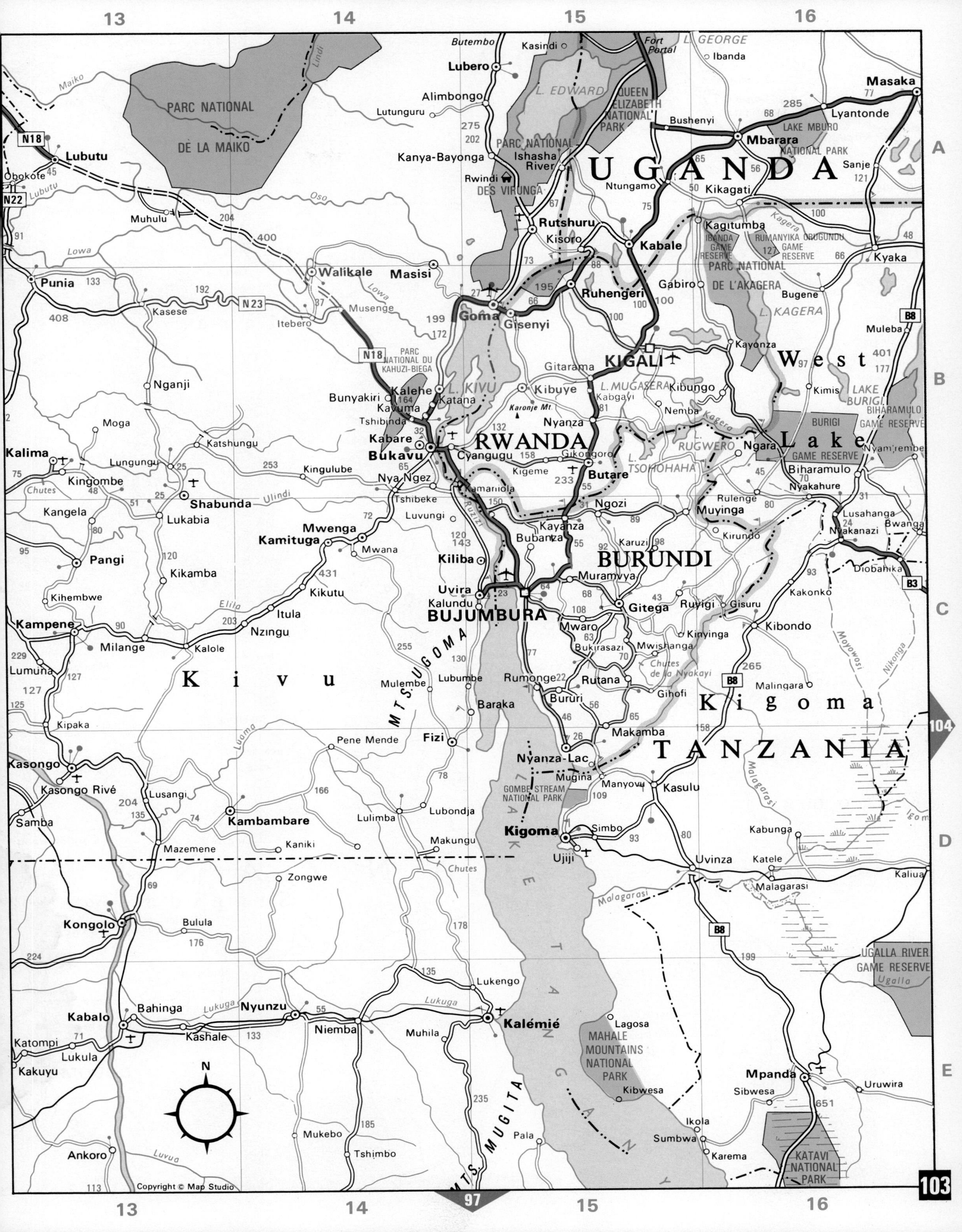

UGANDA
RWANDA
BURUNDI
TANZANIA
Kivu
Kigoma
West Lake
KIGALI
BUJUMBURA
PARC NATIONAL DE LA MAIKO
PARC NATIONAL DES VIRUNGA
QUEEN ELIZABETH NATIONAL PARK
LAKE MBURO NATIONAL PARK
PARC NATIONAL DE L'AKAGERA
PARC NATIONAL DU KAHUZI-BIEGA
BURIGI LAKE GAME RESERVE
BIHARAMULO GAME RESERVE
GOMBE STREAM NATIONAL PARK
MAHALE MOUNTAINS NATIONAL PARK
UGALLA RIVER GAME RESERVE
KATAVI NATIONAL PARK
L. EDWARD
L. GEORGE
L. KIVU
L. KAGERA
MTS. UGOMA
MTS. MUGITA
Bukavu
Goma
Gisenyi
Uvira
Kigoma
Kalémié
Kabalo
Kongolo
Kasongo
Masaka
Mbarara
Kabale
Ruhengeri
Butare
Gitega
Copyright © Map Studio

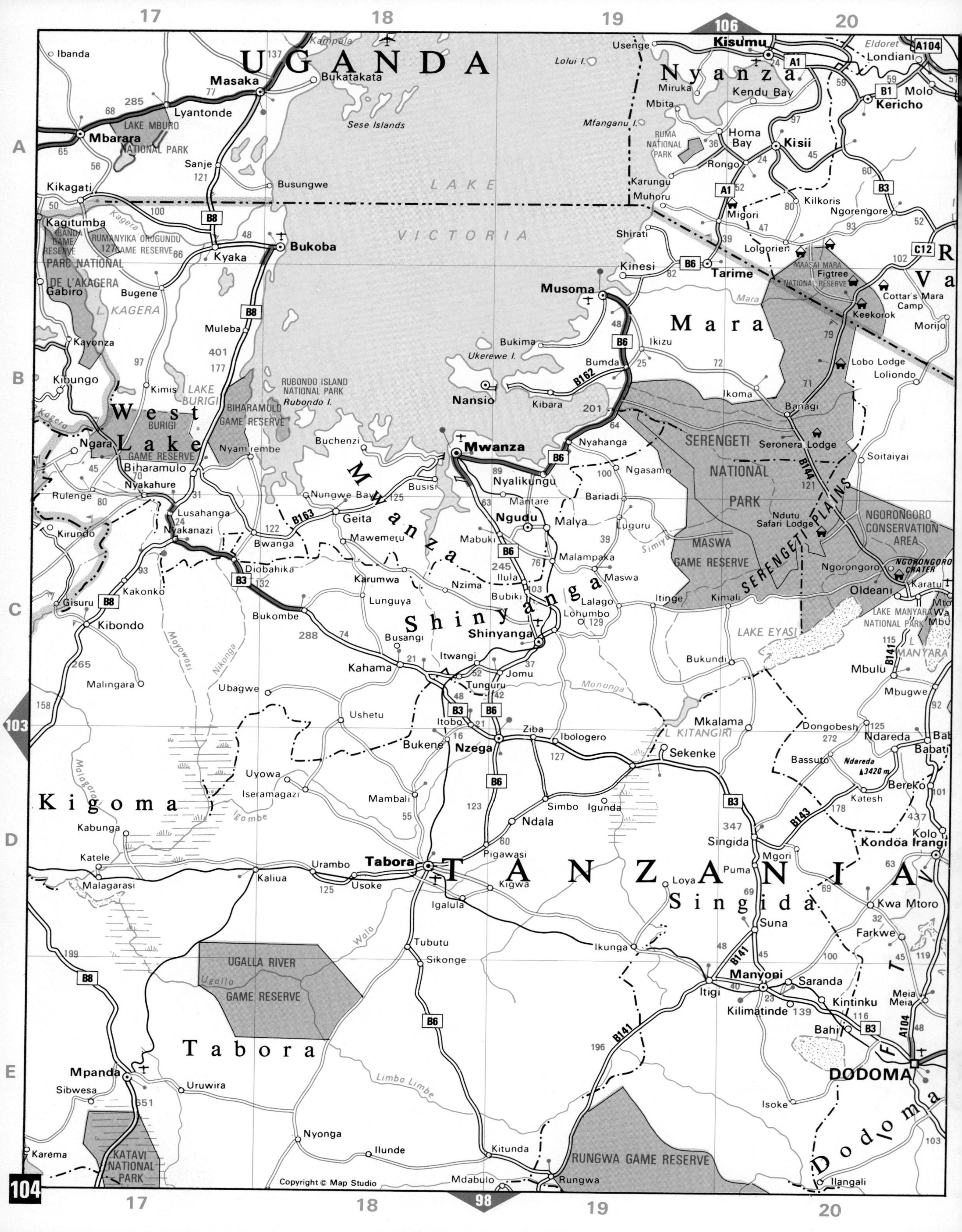
UGANDA
TANZANIA
LAKE VICTORIA
Nyanza
Mara
Mwanza
Shinyanga
West Lake
Kigoma
Tabora
Singida
Dodoma
Masaka
Mbarara
Lyantonde
Bukatakata
Sese Islands
Lake Mburo National Park
Kikagati
Kagitumba
Bukoba
Kyaka
Rumanyika Orugundu Game Reserve
Parc National de l'Akagera
Gabiro
L. Kagera
Muleba
Kayonza
Kibungo
Rubondo Island National Park
Lake Burigi
Biharamulo Game Reserve
Ngara
Biharamulo
Nyakahure
Rulenge
Kirundo
Gisuru
Kibondo
Kisumu
Kericho
Kisii
Homa Bay
Migori
Tarime
Musoma
Ukerewe I.
Nansio
Mwanza
Ngudu
Geita
Serengeti National Park
Seronera Lodge
Ngorongoro Conservation Area
Ngorongoro Crater
Maswa Game Reserve
Lake Eyasi
Shinyanga
Kahama
Nzega
Tabora
Singida
Manyoni
Itigi
Ugalla River Game Reserve
Mpanda
Katavi National Park
Rungwa Game Reserve
DODOMA
Kondoa Irangi
Babati
Mbulu
Copyright © Map Studio

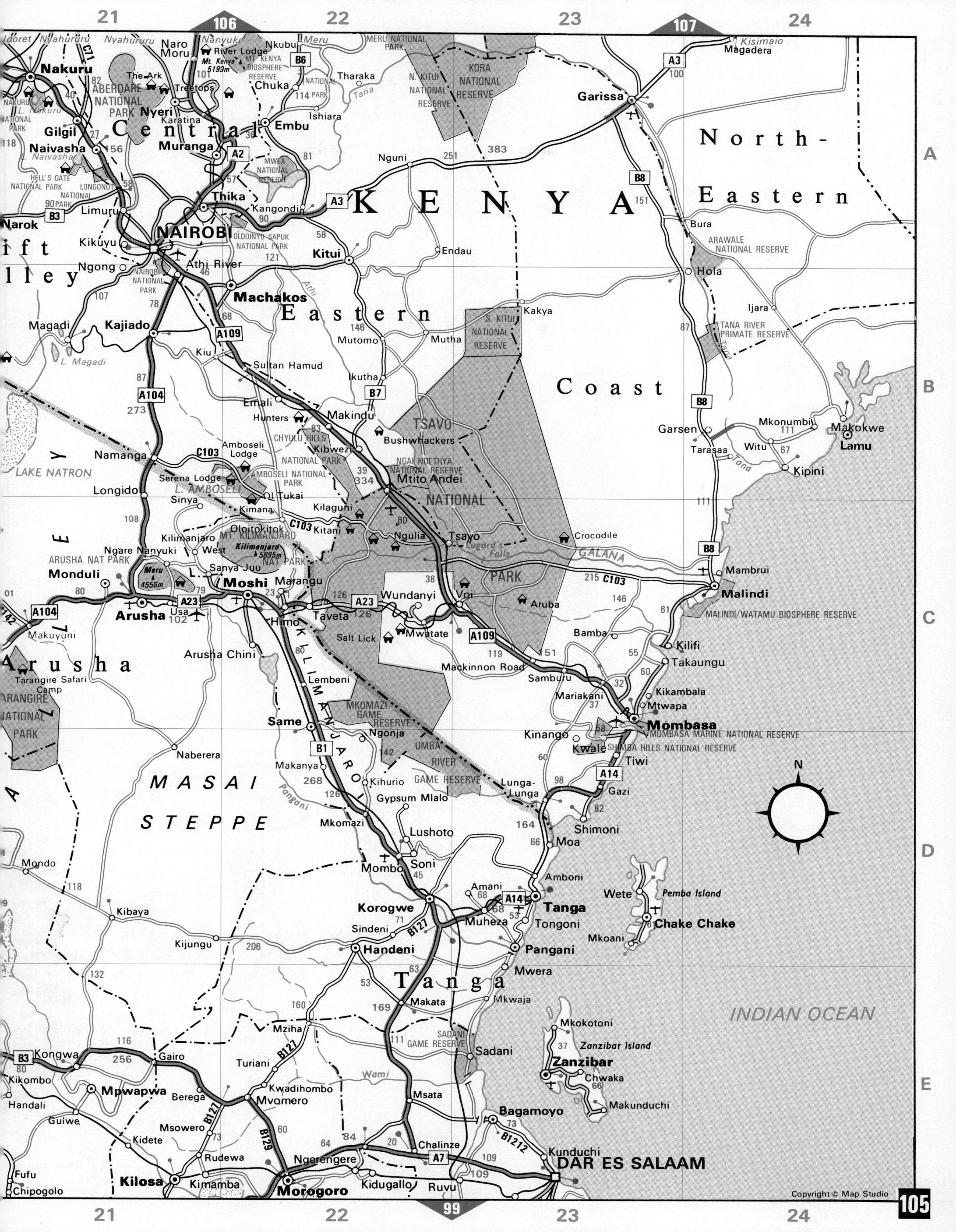

21
106
22
23
107
24
A
B
C
D
E
KENYA
Central
Rift Valley
Eastern
North-Eastern
Coast
Arusha
Tanga
MASAI STEPPE
INDIAN OCEAN
Nakuru
Nyahururu
Naro Moru
River Lodge
Mt. Kenya 5193m
MT. KENYA BIOSPHERE RESERVE
Nkubu
Meru
MERU NATIONAL PARK
Tharaka
Chuka
The Ark
Treetops
ABERDARE NATIONAL PARK
Nyeri
Karatina
Embu
Ishiara
Gilgil
Naivasha
L. Naivasha
L. Nakuru
Muranga
MWEA NATIONAL RESERVE
HELL'S GATE NATIONAL PARK
LONGONOT NATIONAL PARK
Thika
Kangondi
Limuru
Narok
NAIROBI
Kikuyu
Ngong
Athi River
NAIROBI NATIONAL PARK
OLDOINYO SAPUK NATIONAL PARK
Kitui
Endau
Machakos
Magadi
L. Magadi
Kajiado
Kiu
Sultan Hamud
Mutomo
Mutha
Kakya
S. KITUI NATIONAL RESERVE
Ikutha
Emali
Hunters
Makindu
TSAVO
Bushwhackers
CHYULU HILLS NATIONAL PARK
Kibwezi
NGAI NDETHYA NATIONAL RESERVE
Namanga
Amboseli Lodge
LAKE NATRON
Serena Lodge
AMBOSELI NATIONAL PARK
L. AMBOSELI
Longido
Ol Tukai
Sinya
Kimana
Mtito Andei
NATIONAL
Kilaguni
Kitani
Ngulia
Tsavo
Lugard's Falls
Crocodile
GALANA
Oloitokitok
MT. KILIMANJARO
Kilimanjaro 5895m
NAT PARK
Kilimanjaro West
Ngare Nanyuki
ARUSHA NAT PARK
Meru 4556m
Monduli
Sanya Juu
Moshi
Marangu
Arusha
Usa
Himo
Taveta
Wundanyi
Voi
PARK
Aruba
Mwatate
Salt Lick
Makuyuni
Arusha Chini
KILIMANJARO
Lembeni
Mackinnon Road
Tarangire Safari Camp
TARANGIRE NATIONAL PARK
Same
MKOMAZI GAME RESERVE
Ngonja
UMBA RIVER GAME RESERVE
Naberera
Makanya
Kihurio
Pangani
Gypsum Mlalo
Mkomazi
Lushoto
Mombo
Soni
Mondo
Kibaya
Korogwe
Amani
Tanga
Muheza
Tongoni
Sindeni
Handeni
Pangani
Mwera
Kijungu
Makata
Mkwaja
SADANI GAME RESERVE
Sadani
Mziha
Turiani
Wami
Kongwa
Gairo
Kikombo
Mpwapwa
Berega
Kwadihombo
Mvomero
Handali
Gulwe
Msowero
Kidete
Rudewa
Msata
Bagamoyo
Chalinze
Ngerengere
Kunduchi
DAR ES SALAAM
Fufu
Chipogolo
Kilosa
Kimamba
Morogoro
Kidugallo
Ruvu
Garissa
Kisimaio
Magadera
KORA NATIONAL RESERVE
N. KITUI NATIONAL RESERVE
Nguni
Bura
ARAWALE NATIONAL RESERVE
Hola
Ijara
TANA RIVER PRIMATE RESERVE
Tana
Garsen
Tarasaa
Witu
Mkonumbi
Makokwe
Lamu
Kipini
Mambrui
Malindi
MALINDI/WATAMU BIOSPHERE RESERVE
Bamba
Kilifi
Takaungu
Samburu
Mariakani
Kikambala
Mtwapa
Mombasa
MOMBASA MARINE NATIONAL RESERVE
Kinango
Kwale
SHIMBA HILLS NATIONAL RESERVE
Tiwi
Lunga-Lunga
Gazi
Shimoni
Moa
Amboni
N
Wete
Pemba Island
Chake Chake
Mkoani
Mkokotoni
Zanzibar Island
Zanzibar
Chwaka
Makunduchi
A2
A3
A104
A109
A23
A14
A7
B1
B3
B6
B7
B8
B127
B129
B1212
C103
99

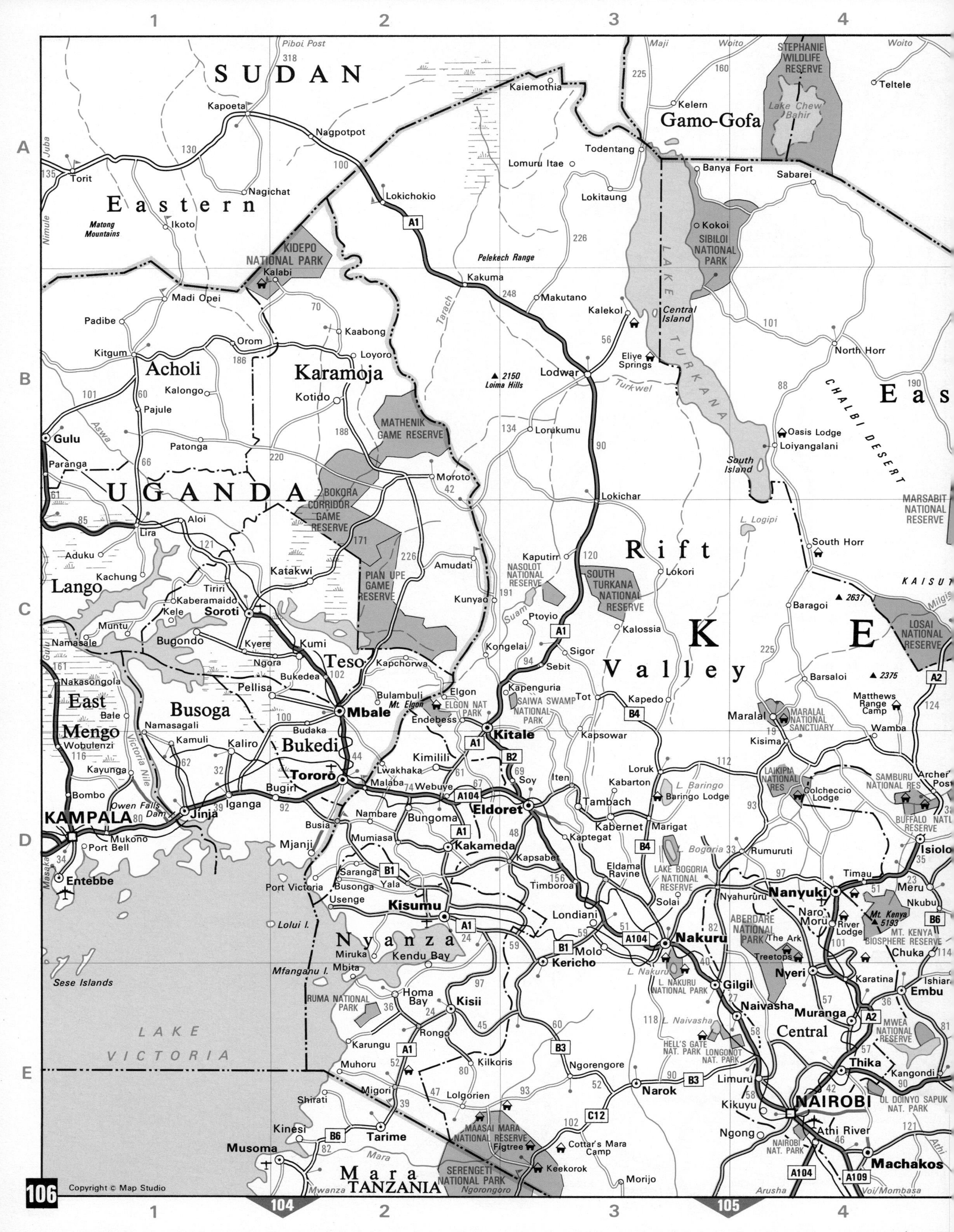
1
2
3
4
A
B
C
D
E
SUDAN
Piboi Post
Kaiemothia
Kapoeta
Nagpotpot
Juba
Torit
Nagichat
Eastern
Matong Mountains
Ikoto
Nimule
Lokichokio
A1
KIDEPO NATIONAL PARK
Kalabi
Madi Opei
Padibe
Kaabong
Orom
Kitgum
Loyoro
Acholi
Karamoja
Kalongo
Kotido
Pajule
Gulu
Aswa
MATHENIK GAME RESERVE
Patonga
Paranga
UGANDA
Moroto
BOKORA CORRIDOR GAME RESERVE
Aloi
Lira
Aduku
Kachung
Lango
Tiriri
Kaberamaido
Kele
Soroti
Katakwi
PIAN UPE GAME RESERVE
Amudati
Muntu
Namasale
Bugondo
Kyere
Kumi
Ngora
Teso
Kapchorwa
Bukedea
Nakasongola
East Mengo
Bale
Busoga
Pellisa
Bulambuli
Mt Elgon
Elgon
ELGON NAT PARK
Mbale
Endebess
Namasagali
Kamuli
Budaka
Kaliro
Bukedi
Wobulenzi
Kayunga
Victoria Nile
Tororo
Lwakhaka
Malaba
Webuye
Kimilili
Bombo
Owen Falls Dam
Jinja
Iganga
Bugiri
KAMPALA
Mukono
Port Bell
Entebbe
Masaka
Busia
Nambare
Bungoma
Mumiasa
Kakameda
Mjanji
Saranga
Busonga
Yala
Port Victoria
Usenge
Kisumu
Lolui I.
Nyanza
Miruka
Mbita
Kendu Bay
Mfanganu I.
Sese Islands
RUMA NATIONAL PARK
Homa Bay
Kisii
Rongo
Karungu
LAKE VICTORIA
Muhoru
Kilkoris
Migori
Lolgorien
Shirati
Kinesi
Tarime
Musoma
Mara
TANZANIA
Mwanza
MAASAI MARA NATIONAL RESERVE
Figtree
SERENGETI NATIONAL PARK
Ngorongoro
Keekorok
Cottar's Mara Camp
Morijo
Narok
Ngorengore
Kericho
Molo
Londiani
Timboroa
Kapsabet
Eldoret
Kitale
Kapenguria
SAIWA SWAMP NATIONAL PARK
Kapsowar
Soy
Iten
Tot
Kapedo
Sigor
Sebit
Kongelai
Ptoyio
Kalossia
Kunyao
Suam
NASOLOT NATIONAL RESERVE
SOUTH TURKANA NATIONAL RESERVE
Kaputirr
Lokori
Rift Valley
K
E
Lokichar
Lorukumu
Lodwar
Turkwel
Loima Hills
2150
Kakuma
Makutano
Pelekech Range
Tarach
Lomuru Itae
Lokitaung
Todentang
Kalekol
Eliye Springs
Central Island
LAKE TURKANA
South Island
L. Logipi
Maji
Woito
Kelern
Gamo-Gofa
STEPHANIE WILDLIFE RESERVE
Lake Chew Bahir
Teltele
Banya Fort
Sabarei
Kokoi
SIBILOI NATIONAL PARK
North Horr
CHALBI DESERT
Eas
Oasis Lodge
Loiyangalani
MARSABIT NATIONAL RESERVE
South Horr
KAISUT
Baragoi
2637
LOSAI NATIONAL RESERVE
Milgis
Barsaloi
2375
Matthews Range Camp
Maralal
MARALAL NATIONAL SANCTUARY
Wamba
Kisima
Loruk
Kabarton
L. Baringo
Baringo Lodge
Tambach
Kabernet
Marigat
Kaptegat
L. Bogoria
LAKE BOGORIA NATIONAL RESERVE
Rumuruti
Eldama Ravine
Solai
Nyahururu
LAIKIPIA NATIONAL RES
Colcheccio Lodge
SAMBURU NATIONAL RES
Archer's Post
BUFFALO NATL RESERVE
Isiolo
Timau
Nanyuki
Meru
Nkubu
Naro Moru
River Lodge
Mt. Kenya 5193
MT. KENYA BIOSPHERE RESERVE
ABERDARE NATIONAL PARK
The Ark
Treetops
Nyeri
Chuka
Karatina
Ishiara
Embu
Nakuru
L. Nakuru
L. NAKURU NATIONAL PARK
Gilgil
Naivasha
L. Naivasha
HELL'S GATE NAT. PARK
LONGONOT NAT. PARK
Muranga
Central
MWEA NATIONAL RESERVE
Thika
Kangondi
Limuru
Kikuyu
NAIROBI
OL DOINYO SAPUK NAT. PARK
Ngong
Athi River
NAIROBI NAT. PARK
Athi
Machakos
Arusha
Voi/Mombasa
A1
A2
A104
A109
B1
B2
B3
B4
B6
C12

104
105

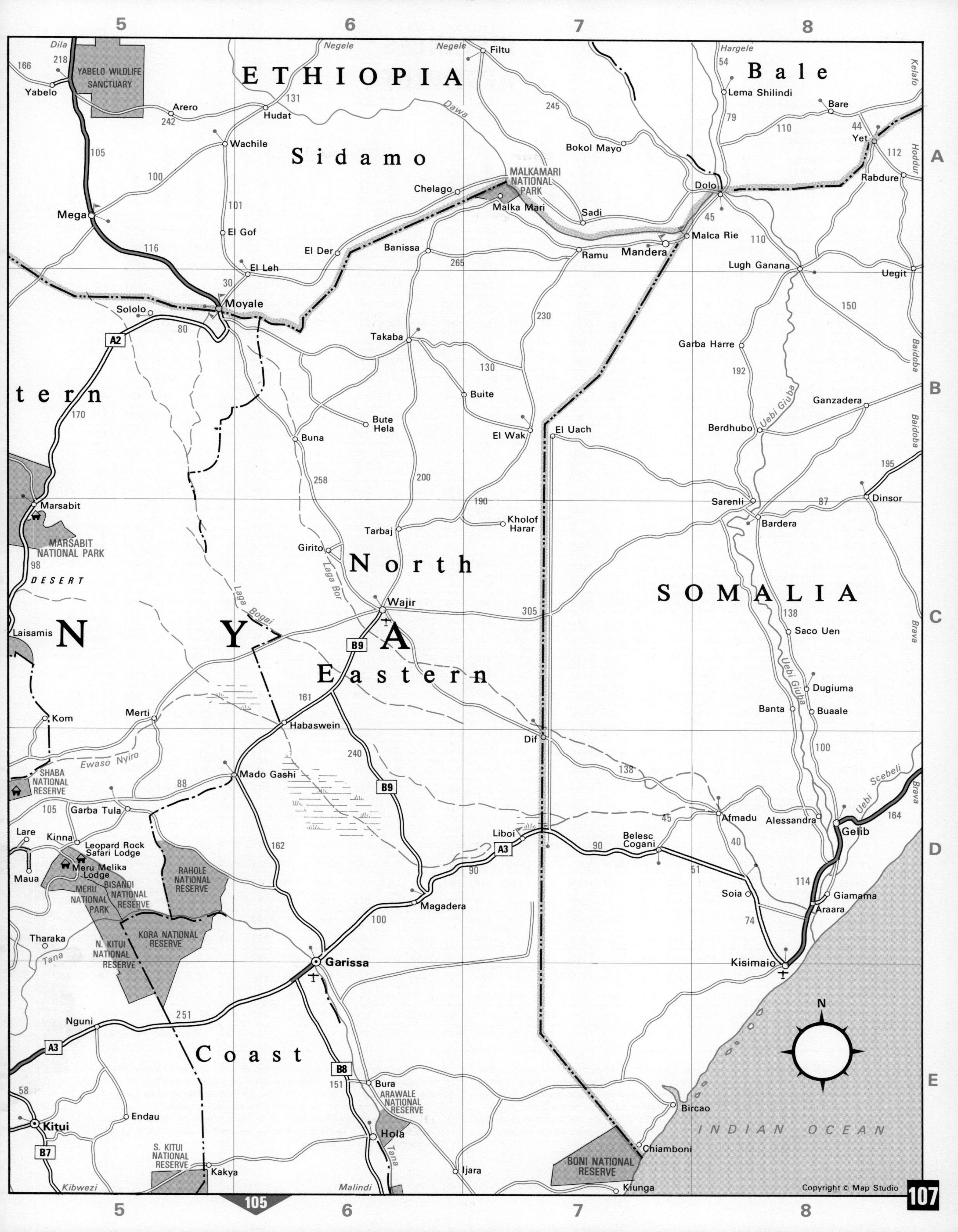

ETHIOPIA

Sidamo

Bale

Dila
166
218
Dila
5
Negele
6
Negele
Filtu
7
Hargele
54
8

YABELO WILDLIFE SANCTUARY
Yabelo
Arero
242
131
Hudat
Wachile
Lema Shilindi
Bare
79
110
Yet
44
A
105
100
Bokol Mayo
Rabdure
112
Hoddur

Mega
101
El Gof
Chelago
MALKAMARI NATIONAL PARK
Malka Mari
Sadi
Dolo
45
Malca Rie
110
116
El Der
Banissa
Ramu
Mandera
Lugh Ganana
Uegit

El Leh
30
265
230
150
Kelafo
Baidoba

Sololo
Moyale
80
Takaba
Garba Harre
192

A2
130
El Wak
El Uach
Berdhubo
Uebi Giuba
Ganzadera
Baidoba

tern
170
Buna
Buite
SOMALIA
195

Marsabit
258
200
190
Sarenli
87
Dinsor

MARSABIT NATIONAL PARK
98
DESERT
Tarbaj
Kholof Harar
Bardera
138
Brava

N
Girito
North
305
Saco Uen

Laisamis
Wajir
Dugiuma

Kom
Merti
161
B9
A
Eastern
Banta
Buaale

Habaswein
138
100

SHABA NATIONAL RESERVE
Mado Gashi
240
Dif
Afmadu
Alessandra
Scebeli

Garba Tula
88
B9
138
45
40
Gelib
164
Brava

Lare
Kinna
Leopard Rock Safari Lodge
162
Liboi
A3
Belesc Cogani
51
Soia
114
Giamama

Maua
Meru Melika Lodge
MERU NATIONAL PARK
BISANDI NATIONAL RESERVE
RAHOLE NATIONAL RESERVE
90
Magadera
74
Araara

Tharaka
KORA NATIONAL RESERVE
N. KITUI NATIONAL RESERVE
100
Garissa
Kisimaio
N

Nguni
251
Coast
A3
58
B8
Bura
151
ARAWALE NATIONAL RESERVE
Bircao

Kitui
B7
S. KITUI NATIONAL RESERVE
Kakya
Hola
Tana
Malindi
Ijara
BONI NATIONAL RESERVE
Chiamboni
INDIAN OCEAN

Endau
Kibwezi
105
Kiunga

NYA
Ewaso Nyiro
Laga Bogai
Laga Bor
Dawa

Copyright © Map Studio
107

DISTANCES
AFSTANDE

APPROXIMATE DISTANCES IN KILOMETRES / BENADERDE AFSTANDE IN KILOMETER	BLOEMFONTEIN	BULAWAYO	CAPE TOWN/KAAPSTAD	DAR ES SALAAM	DURBAN	EAST LONDON/OOS-LONDEN	GABORONE	HARARE	JOHANNESBURG	KIMBERLEY	LILONGWE	LUBUMBASHI	LUSAKA	MAFIKENG	MAPUTO	MASERU	MBABANE	NAIROBI	PORT ELIZABETH	PRETORIA	UMTATA	WINDHOEK
ARUSHA	4181	2978	5185	691	4371	4765	3686	2659	3783	4255	1832	2273	2171	4070	4041	4276	4124	276	4921	3788	4719	5647
BEIRA	1806	854	2810	2837	1996	2390	1574	554	1408	1880	1174	1552	1042	1569	1101	1838	1686	3282	2483	1350	2281	3209
BLANTYRE	2125	1043	3129	2027	2315	2709	1751	604	1727	2199	364	1602	1092	1888	1675	2157	2005	2472	2802	1624	2600	2743
BLOEMFONTEIN	●	1266	1004	4012	634	584	622	1521	398	177	2025	2520	2009	464	897	157	677	4457	677	456	570	1593
BULAWAYO	1266	●	2270	2923	1456	1850	708	439	868	1340	1407	1437	927	1029	1063	1298	1146	3368	1943	810	1741	1700
CAPE TOWN/KAAPSTAD	1004	2270	●	5016	1753	1099	1501	2525	1402	962	3493	3524	3013	1343	1900	1160	1680	5461	769	1460	1314	1500
COLESBERG	226	1492	778	4238	860	488	848	1747	624	292	2715	2746	2236	672	1123	383	903	4683	451	682	517	1573
DAR ES SALAAM	4012	2923	5016	●	4192	4596	3631	2490	3614	4086	1663	2104	2002	3775	3809	4044	3892	967	4689	3556	4487	5415
DODOMA	3747	2658	4751	468	3937	4331	3865	2225	3412	3821	1398	1839	1737	3510	3544	3779	3627	710	4424	3291	4222	5150
DURBAN	634	1456	1753	4192	●	674	979	1711	578	811	2679	2710	2199	821	625	590	562	4647	984	636	439	2227
EAST LONDON/OOS-LONDEN	584	1850	1079	4596	674	●	1206	2105	982	780	3073	3104	2593	1048	1301	630	1238	5041	310	1040	235	1987
ELDORET	4767	3678	5771	1277	4957	5351	4885	3245	4432	4841	2418	3063	2757	4656	4968	4807	4730	310	4050	4311	5238	6170
GABORONE	622	708	1501	3631	979	1206	●	1147	358	538	2115	2139	1629	158	957	702	719	4575	1299	350	1192	1735
GEORGE	773	2039	438	4785	1319	645	1361	2294	1171	762	3262	3293	2783	1203	1670	913	1450	5230	335	1229	880	1887
GRAAFF-REINET	424	1690	787	4436	942	395	1012	1945	822	490	2913	2944	2434	854	1321	599	1101	4881	291	880	503	1697
GRAHAMSTOWN	601	1867	899	4613	854	180	1223	2122	999	667	3090	3121	2611	1065	1478	692	1418	5058	130	1057	415	1856
HARARE	1521	439	2525	2490	1711	2105	1147	●	1123	1595	968	998	488	1284	1318	1553	1401	2935	2198	1065	1996	2139
JOHANNESBURG	398	868	1402	3614	578	982	358	1123	●	472	2091	2122	1611	287	599	438	361	4122	1075	58	869	1801
KEETMANSHOOP	1088	1856	995	4910	1722	1482	1230	2295	1296	911	3263	3293	2783	1072	1895	1245	1657	5355	1445	1354	1561	505
KIMBERLEY	177	1340	962	4086	811	780	538	1595	472	●	2563	2594	2084	380	1071	334	833	4531	743	530	747	1416
KITWE	2358	1276	3362	1943	2548	2942	1978	837	1960	2433	1098	161	349	2122	2156	2390	2238	2388	3035	1902	2833	2977
LADYSMITH	410	1232	1413	3970	236	752	755	1487	356	587	2455	2486	1976	597	567	366	386	4415	1062	414	517	2008
LILONGWE	2025	1407	3493	1663	2679	3073	2115	968	2091	2563	●	1259	749	2252	2039	2521	2369	2108	3166	2033	2964	3107
LIVINGSTONE	1714	448	2718	3377	1904	2298	1156	887	1316	1788	1855	1885	1375	1477	1511	1746	1594	2743	2391	1258	2189	1370
LUBUMBASHI	2519	1437	3523	2104	2709	3103	2139	998	2121	2594	1259	●	510	2283	2317	2551	2399	2549	3196	2063	2994	3138
LUSAKA	2009	927	3013	2002	2199	2593	1629	488	1611	2084	749	510	●	1773	1807	2041	1889	2447	2686	1553	2484	2628
MAFIKENG	464	1029	1343	3775	821	1048	158	1284	287	380	2252	2283	1773	●	886	544	648	4346	1141	294	1034	1577
MAPUTO	897	1063	1900	3809	625	1301	957	1318	599	1071	2039	2317	1807	886	●	853	223	4658	1609	583	1064	2400
MARSABIT	4975	3886	5979	1485	5165	5559	5093	3453	4640	5049	2626	3067	2965	4864	5176	5015	4938	518	4258	4519	5446	6378
MASERU	157	1298	1160	4044	590	630	702	1553	438	334	2521	2552	2041	544	853	●	633	4497	822	488	616	1750
MBABANE	677	1146	1680	3892	562	1238	719	1401	361	833	2369	2400	1889	648	223	633	●	4420	1548	372	1003	2162
MBEYA	3121	2032	4125	891	3301	3705	2740	1745	2723	3195	772	1213	1111	3010	3322	3161	3084	1336	3798	2665	3592	4524
MESSINA	928	338	1932	3084	1118	1512	696	593	530	1002	1561	1775	1082	691	725	960	808	3529	1605	472	1403	2331
MOMBASA	4336	3253	5340	542	4516	4920	3955	2814	3938	4410	1987	2428	2326	4225	4537	4376	4299	484	5013	3880	4807	5739
NAIROBI	4457	3368	5461	967	4647	5041	4575	2935	4122	4531	2108	2549	2447	4346	4658	4497	4420	●	3740	4001	4928	5860
NELSPRUIT	757	830	1762	3969	707	1226	672	1085	355	827	2053	2084	1574	635	244	713	173	4414	1434	322	976	2156
PIETERMARITZBURG	555	1367	1674	4113	79	595	900	1622	499	732	2590	2621	2111	742	706	511	640	4558	905	557	360	2148
PIETERSBURG	717	549	1721	3295	897	1301	485	804	319	791	1772	1803	1293	580	605	749	515	3740	1394	261	1192	2120
PORT ELIZABETH	677	1943	769	4689	984	310	1299	2198	1075	743	3166	3197	2686	1141	1609	822	1548	5134	●	1133	545	1950
PRETORIA	456	810	1460	3556	636	1040	350	1065	58	530	2033	1864	1553	294	583	488	372	4001	1133	●	928	1859
UMTATA	570	1741	1314	4487	439	235	1192	1996	869	747	2964	2995	2484	1034	1064	616	1003	4928	545	928	●	2066
UPINGTON	588	1601	894	4410	1222	982	730	1856	796	411	2824	2855	2345	572	1395	745	1157	4855	945	854	1061	1005
WELKOM	153	1126	1156	3872	564	737	479	1381	258	294	2349	2380	1870	321	813	249	451	4317	830	316	718	1679
WINDHOEK	1593	1700	1500	5415	2227	1987	1735	2139	1801	1416	3107	3138	2628	1577	2400	1750	2162	5860	1950	1859	2066	●

Although the greatest care has been taken in compiling this kilometre table and in ensuring that the road distances given conform to the latest information available, no responsibility for errors can be accepted by the publishers, who would welcome any suggested amendments. The kilometres indicate the shortest distance between any two places over tarred roads wherever possible.

To find the distance between any two places in the table read down and across the respective connecting columns. An example is given above in which the distance between Cape Town and Pretoria is shown as 1460 kilometres.

Hoewel die grootste sorgvuldigheid geneem is met die opstel van hierdie kilometerafstandtabel, kan die uitgewers geen verantwoordelikheid aanvaar vir onjuisthede nie en sal hulle enige voorstelle vir wysiging vir toekomstige uitgawes verwelkom. Die kilometerafstande dui die kortste afstand aan tussen enige twee plekke oor geteerde paaie waar ook moontlik.

Om die afstand tussen twee plekke in die rooster te vind, lees dwars en af langs die verbindende kolomme. 'n Voorbeeld word hierbo gegee wat die afstand tussen Kaapstad en Pretoria aangegee as 1460 kilometer.

INDEX TO PLACE NAMES

INDEKS VAN PLEKNAME

A place names index to the map section shows a page number and grid reference to each town e.g. Cape Town........square T2 page **60**

Vir elke stad en dorp van die kaartgedeelte word 'n bladsynommer en roosterverwysing in die inhoud van plekname aangegee. b.v. Kaapstad........blok T2 bladsy **60**

ABBREVIATIONS

C.P. - Cape Province
Moc. - Mocambique
O.F.S. - Orange Free State
Tvl - Transvaal

AFKORTINGS

C.P. - Kaapprovinsie
Moc. - Mosambiek
O.F.S. - Oranje-Vrystaat
Tvl. - Transvaal

Madiakgama G17 **72**
Madibira G20 **98**
Madibogo G19 **72**
Madimba D3 **100**
Madingou C2 **100**
Madipelesa J18 **72**
Mado Gashi D6 **107**
Maduds D2 **100**
Madziwa Q12 **86**
Mafeteng N17 **68**
Mafikeng F19 **72**
Mafube N19 **68**
Mafutseni H30 **75**
Magadera D6 **107**
Magadi B21 **105**
Magaiza D31 **81**
Magaliesburg G22 **73**
Magandene C31 **81**
Magoe N16 **91**
Magude E29 **80**
Magudu J30 **75**
Magusheni O20 **68**
Mah C4 **100**
Mahalapye B21 **78**
Mahenge H21 **99**
Mahlabatini K30 **75**
Mahlangasi J30 **75**
Mahuta J23 **99**
Mahwelereng D24 **79**
Maimelane A33 **81**
Maitembge S7 **85**
Maiuvo A4 **83**
Maizefield H28 **74**
Maji Mota G16 **97**
Makabana C2 **100**
Makado T10 **86**
Makaka C2 **100**
Makamba D15 **103**
Makambako H20 **98**
Makanjila M20 **92**
Makanya D22 **105**
Makata F22 **99**
Makhaleng M18 **68**
Makindu B22 **105**
Makokskraal G21 **73**
Makokwe B24 **105**
Makongolosi G18 **98**
Makopong E15 **77**
Makoua A4 **100**
Makoulou
Tréchot C4 **100**
Makunda A11 **76**
Makunduchi F23 **99**
Makungu D14 **103**
Makunguwilo J22 **99**
Makutano B3 **106**
Makuyuni C21 **105**
Makwassie J20 **72**
Makwate B22 **78**
Malaba D2 **106**
Malagarasi D17 **104**
Malaira E31 **81**
Malaita E25 **79**
Malaka Mari A7 **107**
Malampaka C19 **104**
Malandji E10 **102**
Malanga M20 **92**
Malangali H20 **98**
Malanje H4 **94**
Malapati A28 **80**
Malca Rie A8 **107**
Malealea N18 **68**
Malei Q15 **87**
Malelane F30 **75**
Malemba Nkulu G13 **97**
Maleoskop E25 **79**
Malgas T5 **61**
Malima N21 **93**
Malindi,
Kenya C24 **105**
Malindi,
Zimbabwe R7 **85**
Malinga B1 **100**
Malingara C17 **104**
Malinyi H21 **99**
Malkerns H30 **75**
Malmesbury S2 **60**
Malole H16 **97**
Maloma H30 **75**
Malonda H11 **96**
Malonga J10 **96**
Malova C33 **81**
Maltahöhe F3 **82**
Maluana F32 **75**
Maluera N16 **91**
Maluku C4 **100**
Malvernia A31 **81**
Malya C19 **104**
Mamaila C26 **79**
Mamates M18 **68**
Mambali D18 **104**
Mambova O6 **85**
Mambrui C24 **105**
Mamre S2 **60**
Mamué M2 **88**
Mamuno T2 **84**
Manda J20 **98**
Mandera A7 **107**
Mandie O18 **92**
Mandimba M20 **92**
Mandingo-Kayes D1 **100**
Mandini M23 **69**
Mandlakaze E31 **81**
Mandwe G13 **97**
Manel B31 **81**
Maneromango G23 **99**
Mangai C7 **101**
Mangando G5 **95**
Mangango M11 **90**
Mangeni L22 **69**
Mangochi N20 **92**
Mangwe S9 **86**
Manhica F32 **75**
Manhoca H32 **75**
Mani E12 **102**
Maniamba L20 **92**
Manianga D3 **100**
Manica R12 **86**
Mankayane H30 **75**
Mankweng C25 **79**
Manono G13 **97**
Manonwa D12 **102**
Mansa J14 **97**
Mansfield G18 **72**
Mantare C19 **104**
Manthestad J18 **72**
Mantsonyane M19 **68**
Manubi S15 **63**
Manyanga D3 **100**
Manyoni E20 **104**
Manyovu D15 **103**
Manzini H30 **75**
Maope A22 **79**
Mapai U12 **86**
Mapanda H11 **96**
Mapangu D7 **101**
Mapati C2 **100**
Mapela C24 **79**
Mapinhane T14 **87**
Mapogolo G20 **98**
Mapoteng M19 **68**
Mapumulo M23 **69**
Maputo G32 **75**
Maputsoe L18 **68**
Maquela do
Zombo E3 **100**
Maqueze D31 **81**
Mara B25 **79**
Marakabei M19 **68**
Maralal C4 **106**
Marangu C22 **105**
Marble Hall E24 **79**
Marburg O22 **69**
Marburg Mine B3 **83**
Marburgmyn B3 **83**
Marchal D3 **100**
Marchand L6 **65**
Margaretental D4 **83**
Margate O22 **69**
Maria Teresa H3 **94**
Mariakani C23 **105**
Maricosdraai D20 **78**
Mariental E4 **82**
Marigat D3 **106**
Marikana F22 **73**
Marimba G5 **95**
Maringúe Q13 **87**
Marite E27 **80**
Marken C23 **79**
Markramsdraai J14 **71**
Marnitz B23 **79**
Maroelaboom B4 **83**
Marondera Q11 **86**
Marquard L18 **68**
Marracua Q15 **87**
Marracuene G32 **75**
Marromeu R15 **87**
Marrupa M21 **93**
Marsabit C5 **107**
Martin's Drift B22 **78**
Marula S9 **86**
Marydale M9 **66**
Masaka A17 **104**
Masange A10 **102**
Masasi J22 **99**
Maseru M18 **68**
Mashai M20 **68**
Mashari A5 **83**
Mashashane C24 **79**
Mashava S11 **86**
Masia C4 **100**
Masia-Mbio C5 **101**
Masisi,
South Africa A27 **80**
Masisi, Zaïre B14 **103**
Masi-Manimba D5 **101**
Massabi J10 **96**
Massamba N19 **92**
Massangano H3 **94**
Massangena T12 **86**
Massango G4 **94**
Massangulo M20 **92**
Massau F5 **95**
Massinga U14 **87**
Massingir D29 **80**
Masuku B2 **100**
Masunguru J22 **99**
Masvingo S11 **86**
Maswa C19 **104**
Mata Mata F10 **70**
Matadi E2 **100**
Matai G16 **97**
Matala N3 **88**
Matamba H19 **98**
Matanana G20 **98**
Matanda J14 **97**
Matatiele O19 **68**
Matavhelo B26 **79**
Mateka M18 **68**
Matela's M18 **68**
Matema,
Tanzania H19 **98**
Matema,
Zimbabwe N18 **92**
Matenge N19 **92**
Matetsi O6 **85**
Matibane N24 **93**
Matjiesfontein S5 **61**
Matjiesrivier S7 **61**
Matlabas D22 **78**
Matlala C24 **79**
Matlameng L19 **68**
Matobo S9 **86**
Matola G32 **75**
Matombo F22 **99**
Matope N19 **92**
Matroosberg S4 **60**
Matrooster E21 **78**
Matsaile N19 **68**
Matsap L10 **66**
Matsieng M18 **68**
Matumbo L5 **89**
Matundo O19 **92**
Maua D5 **107**
Maùa M21 **93**
Mauchsberg E26 **79**
Maúe O6 **89**
Maun S5 **85**
Mavago L21 **93**
Mavamba B26 **79**
Mavanza B33 **81**
Mavengue O6 **89**
Mavinga N7 **89**
Mavita R13 **87**
Mavume C32 **81**
Mawayela D32 **81**
Mawemeru C18 **104**
Maxixe D33 **81**
Mayama C3 **100**
Mayamba D5 **101**
Mayoko B2 **100**
Mazabuka N13 **91**
Mazemene D13 **103**
Mazenod Inst. M18 **68**
Mazeppa Bay S15 **63**
Mazowe Q11 **86**
Mazunga T10 **86**
Mbabane G30 **75**
Mbala H16 **97**
Mbalabala S10 **86**
Mbale C2 **106**
Mbalizi H19 **98**
Mbamba Bay J20 **98**
Mbandaka A6 **101**
Mbanza-Ngungu D3 **100**
Mbarangandu J21 **99**
Mbarara A17 **104**
Mbaswana J32 **75**
Mbati J16 **97**
Mbé C4 **100**
Mbesuma J18 **98**
Mbevengwa S10 **86**
Mbeya H19 **98**
Mbigou B1 **100**
Mbinda B2 **100**
Mbinga J20 **98**
Mbita E2 **106**
Mbizi T11 **86**
Mbozi H18 **98**
Mbugwe C20 **104**
Mbuji-Mayi E11 **102**
Mbulu C20 **104**
Mbuyu Camp G22 **99**
Mbuyuni G21 **99**
Mbuzi L18 **92**
Mbwamaji F23 **99**
McGregor T4 **60**
Mchinga H23 **99**
Mchinji M18 **92**
Mdabulo F19 **98**
Mdandu H19 **98**
Mdantsane S14 **63**
Meadows M17 **68**
Mecanhelas N20 **92**
Meconta N23 **93**
Mecubúri N22 **93**
Mecúfi M24 **93**
Mecula L22 **93**
Meerhof F23 **73**
Mega A5 **107**
Meia Meia E20 **104**
Mekaling N18 **68**
Melkbosstrand T2 **60**
Melkrivier C23 **79**
Melmoth L23 **69**
Meloco M23 **93**
Meltonwold P10 **66**
Meluco L23 **93**
Melunga O4 **88**
Memba M24 **93**
Membwe H16 **97**
Memel J28 **74**
Mende C11 **102**
Menongue N5 **89**
Mepala E2 **100**
Meponda M20 **92**
Merindol G21 **73**
Merriman P11 **66**
Merrivale M21 **69**
Merti C5 **107**
Meru D4 **106**
Merweville R6 **61**
Mesa G21 **73**
Mesklip N3 **64**
Messina T10 **86**
Metangala L20 **92**
Metengobalane N19 **92**
Methalaneng M19 **68**
Metil O22 **93**
Meyerton H23 **73**
Meyerville H27 **74**
Mgori D20 **104**
Mgwali S14 **63**
Mhangura O15 **91**
Mhlambanyatsi H30 **75**
Mhlosheni J30 **75**
Mhlume G31 **75**
Miami O15 **91**
Mica D26 **79**
Micaune R15 **87**
Miconje D2 **100**
Middelburg, C.P. P13 **67**
Middelburg, Tvl. G28 **74**
Middeldrift S13 **63**
Middelfontein D23 **79**
Middelpos Q4 **60**
Middelton S12 **62**
Middelwit E21 **78**
Midrand G23 **73**
Miembwe H22 **99**
Migdol H19 **72**
Migori E2 **106**
Miharamulo B17 **104**
Mikindani J23 **99**
Mikumi G21 **99**
Mikumi Camp G21 **99**
Mikumi Lodge G21 **99**
Milambo K14 **97**
Milando H5 **95**
Milange O20 **92**
Milange C13 **103**
Miller S9 **62**
Millvale F21 **73**
Milnerton T2 **60**
Milo H20 **98**
Mimongo B1 **100**
Mindigi J12 **96**
Mindouli D3 **100**
Minga J14 **97**
Mingoyo J23 **99**
Minguri N24 **93**
Minnaar G27 **74**
Mirage J21 **73**
Miranda L20 **92**
Miruka D2 **106**
Miruro N15 **91**
Misgund T8 **61**
Missassa Batéké B2 **100**
Misty Mount Q16 **63**
Misumba D8 **101**
Mitande M20 **92**
Mitomoni J20 **98**
Mitwaba G13 **97**
Mjanji D2 **106**
Mkalama C20 **104**
Mkambati P21 **69**
Mkoani D23 **105**
Mkokotoni F23 **99**
Mkomazi D22 **105**
Mkonumbi B24 **105**
Mkuranga F23 **99**
Mkushi M15 **91**
Mkushi River M15 **91**
Mkuze J31 **75**
Mkwaja E23 **105**
Mlawula Stn. G31 **75**
Mlibizi O7 **85**
Mloa G20 **98**
Mmabatho F19 **72**
Mmadinare T9 **86**
Mmamabula C21 **78**
Mmathethe E18 **77**
Mmatshumo S6 **85**
Mngeta G21 **99**
Moa D23 **105**
Moamba G31 **75**
Moanda B2 **100**
Moatize O19 **92**
Moba F15 **97**
Moçambique N24 **93**
Mochudi D20 **78**
Mocimboa da
Praia K24 **99**
Mocimboa do
Rovuma J23 **99**
Mocoduene D33 **81**
Mocuba Q15 **87**
Modade A32 **81**
Modderrivier L13 **67**
Moebase O22 **93**
Moeng A22 **78**
Moerbeke D3 **100**
Moeswal J14 **71**
Mofu J15 **97**
Moga B13 **103**
Mogalakwena-
stroom C23 **79**
Moganyaka E24 **79**
Mogapi A22 **78**
Mogapinyana A22 **78**
Mogincual N23 **93**
Mogwase
(Heystekrand) E21 **78**
Mohale's Hoek N18 **68**
Mohambe E32 **81**
Mohoro G23 **99**
Moimba O2 **88**
Mokala D12 **102**
Mokambo L14 **91**
Mokamole C23 **79**
Mokhotlong M20 **68**
Mokila D5 **101**
Mokopung N19 **68**
Molenrivier T8 **61**
Molepolole D18 **77**
Moletsane M19 **68**
Moletwana D20 **78**
Moliro G16 **97**
Molo D3 **106**
Moloporivier F16 **71**
Molteno P15 **67**
Molumbo N20 **92**
Moma O22 **93**
Mombasa C23 **105**
Mombo D22 **105**
Monapo N23 **93**
Mona-Quimbundo H7 **95**
Mondjoku B8 **101**
Mondo D21 **105**
Monduli C21 **105**
Mongu N10 **90**
Mõngua O4 **88**
Monkey Bay M20 **92**
Monkoto B7 **101**
Mont Aux-Sources
Hotel L20 **68**
Mont Pelaan K27 **74**
Montagu T4 **60**
Monte Christo B22 **78**
Montepuez M23 **93**
Montipa M2 **88**
Monze O13 **91**
Mooifontein,
Namibia F3 **82**
Mooifontein,
Tvl. G19 **72**
Mooirivier M21 **69**
Mooketsi C25 **79**
Moordkuil T3 **60**
Moorreesburg S2 **60**
Mopane A25 **79**
Mopani C28 **80**
Mopeia Q14 **87**
Mopipi S6 **85**
Morgan's Bay S15 **63**
Morgenzon H28 **74**
Morija M18 **68**
Morijo E3 **106**
Morire O20 **92**
Morogoro F22 **99**
Morokweng G15 **71**
Morone E26 **79**
Moroto B2 **106**
Morristown P18 **68**
Morrumbala Q14 **87**
Morrumbene U14 **87**
Mortimer R12 **62**
Morupule A21 **78**
Morwamosu C15 **77**
Mosenge D5 **101**
Mosetse S7 **85**
Moshaneng E18 **77**
Moshesh's Ford O18 **68**
Moshi C22 **105**
Mosi H16 **97**
Mosita G18 **72**
Mosomane C20 **78**
Mosopo D18 **77**
Mossaka A4 **100**
Mossel Bay T7 **61**
Mosselbaai T7 **61**
Mossendjo C2 **100**
Mossiesdal E25 **79**
Mossuril N24 **93**
Motapa R9 **86**
Motetema E25 **79**
Mothae L20 **68**
Mothibistat J15 **71**
Motloutse A26 **80**
Motokwe C15 **77**
Motshikiri E22 **78**
Motsitseng M20 **68**
Moungoudi B1 **100**
Moungoudou B2 **100**
Mount Ayliff O20 **68**
Mount Darvin O16 **91**
Mount Fletcher O19 **68**
Mount Frere O20 **68**
Mount Rupert K18 **72**
Mount Selinda S12 **86**
Mount Stewart S10 **62**
Mouyondzi C2 **100**
Moxico K7 **95**
Moyale B5 **107**
Moyeni (Quthing) N18 **68**
Mpaka Stn. H31 **75**
Mpanda E17 **104**
Mpandamatenga R6 **85**
Mpanta J15 **97**
Mpata D6 **101**
Mpé B3 **100**
Mpemvana J29 **75**
Mpendle M21 **69**
Mpetu S15 **63**
Mpharane N18 **68**
Mpika K16 **97**
Mpolweni M22 **69**
Mponela M19 **92**
Mporokoso H15 **97**
Mposa L24 **69**
Mpouya B4 **100**
Mpui G16 **97**
Mpulungu H16 **97**
Mpumalanga N22 **69**
Mpungu A40 **83**
Mpwapwa F21 **99**
Mqanduli R16 **63**
Msanga G23 **99**
Msata F22 **99**
Msembe G20 **98**
Msoro M16 **91**
Msowero F21 **99**
Mtakuja G16 **97**
Mtama J23 **99**
Mtito Andei B22 **105**
Mto Wa Mbu C20 **104**
Mtonjaneni L23 **69**
Mtubatuba L24 **69**
Mtuga Mine M14 **91**
Mtunzini M24 **69**
Mtwalume O22 **69**
Mtwapa C23 **105**
Mtwara J23 **99**
Mt. Moorosi N18 **68**
Muaguide L23 **93**
Mualadzi M18 **92**
Mualama O22 **93**
Muanda E1 **100**
Muangai K7 **95**
Muanzanza E7 **101**
Muatua O23 **93**
Mucaba F3 **94**
Muchabi N13 **91**
Muchena N19 **92**
Mucojo L24 **93**
Muconda J8 **95**
Mucope O3 **88**
Mucoque A34 **81**
Mucubela Q16 **87**
Muculá F2 **94**
Mucumbura O16 **91**
Mucusso P8 **89**
Mucussueje J8 **95**
Muda R13 **87**
Muden M22 **69**
Muecate N23 **93**
Mueda K23 **99**
Mufuma H4 **94**
Mugina D15 **103**
Muguia L23 **93**
Muheza D23 **105**
Muhila E14 **103**
Muhoru E2 **106**
Muhukuru J20 **98**
Muhula M23 **93**
Muhulu A13 **103**
Muié M7 **89**
Muine O7 **89**
Muite M22 **93**
Muizenberg T2 **60**
Mukana H13 **97**
Mukebo F14 **97**
Mukilu Mbembi D6 **101**
Mukono D1 **106**
Mukopa M15 **91**
Mukuku K15 **97**
Mukumbura O16 **91**
Mukunsa H15 **97**
Mulanje O20 **92**
Mulati C26 **79**
Muleba B17 **104**
Mulembe C14 **103**
Mulenda D11 **102**
Mulengu H15 **97**
Mulevala O21 **93**
Mulobezi O11 **90**
Mulondo N3 **88**
Mulungo G13 **97**
Mumbeji M10 **90**
Mumbonda H3 **94**
Mumbué M5 **89**
Mumbwa N13 **91**
Mumena K13 **97**
Mumiasa D2 **106**
Munanga J14 **97**
Munchango K6 **95**
Munenga H3 **94**
Mungari Q13 **87**
Mungo K4 **94**
Mungulunga J11 **96**
Muniungu D5 **101**
Munnik C25 **79**
Munster P21 **69**
Muntu C1 **106**
Mununga H14 **97**
Munyu R15 **63**
Muquitixe J3 **94**
Murambara R12 **86**
Muramvya C15 **103**
Muranga E4 **106**
Murewa Q12 **86**
Muriége H8 **95**

Murraysburg R9 **62**
Murroa O16 **87**
Murrupula N22 **93**
Musanda D3 **100**
Musenga G10 **96**
Musenge B14 **103**
Mushenge D8 **101**
Mushie C5 **101**
Mushima M11 **90**
Musoma E1 **106**
Musoshi K13 **97**
Mussende J4 **94**
Musserra G2 **94**
Mussuma M8 **89**
Musumba G10 **96**
Mutanda K12 **96**
Mutango D5 **83**
Mutarara O14 **87**
Mutare R12 **86**
Mutha B22 **105**
Mutobo J12 **96**
Mutoko O12 **86**
Mutombo
Mukulu G11 **96**
Mutomo B22 **105**
Mutorashanga O11 **86**
Mutorashanga O15 **91**
Mutoto G15 **97**
Mutoto E10 **102**
Mutshatsa J11 **96**
Mutuáli N21 **93**
Mutulira L14 **91**
Muxaluando G3 **94**
Muxima H2 **94**
Muyumba F13 **97**
Muze N16 **91**
Mvomero F22 **99**
Mvouti C1 **100**
Mvurwi O16 **91**
Mwadi Kayembe G11 **96**
Mwadingusha J13 **97**
Mwaga H21 **99**
Mwambo J24 **99**
Mwana C14 **103**
Mwandi O6 **85**
Mwanza,
Malawi N19 **92**
Mwanza,
Zaïre G13 **97**
Mwanza B18 **104**
Mwaro C15 **103**
Mwatate C22 **105**
Mweka D8 **101**
Mwenda K14 **97**
Mwenezi T11 **86**
Mwenga C14 **103**
Mwense J14 **97**
Mwera E23 **105**
Mwero J15 **97**
Mwimbi G16 **97**
Mwinilunga K11 **96**
Mwishanga C15 **103**
Mynfontein O12 **66**
Mziha F22 **99**
Mzimba L19 **92**
Mzuzu J19 **98**
M'Fouati D2 **100**
M'banza-Congo E3 **100**

N

Nababeep M3 **64**
Naberra D21 **105**
Nabies L6 **65**
Naboomspruit D23 **79**
Nacala N24 **93**
Nacaroa N23 **93**
Nachingwea J22 **99**
Nagichat A1 **106**
Nagpotpot A2 **106**
Naiopué O21 **93**
Naipé N22 **93**
Nairobi E4 **106**
Naivasha E4 **106**
Nakachenje N13 **91**
Nakasongola C1 **106**
Nakonde H18 **98**
Nakop H5 **82**
Nakuru D3 **106**
Nalázi D31 **81**
Namaacha G31 **75**
Namacunde O4 **88**
Namacurra O15 **87**
Namakgale D27 **80**
Namanga B21 **105**
Namanyere G16 **97**
Namapa M23 **93**
Namaponda O23 **93**
Namarroi O21 **93**
Namasagali C1 **106**
Namasale C1 **106**
Namba J4 **94**
Nambare D2 **106**
Nameti N23 **93**
Namialo N23 **93**
Namib D2 **83**
Namibe N1 **88**
Namies M4 **64**
Namitete M18 **92**
Nampevo O21 **93**
Nampuecha M23 **93**
Nampula N23 **93**
Namuiranga J24 **99**
Namuno M22 **93**
Namutoni B3 **83**
Namwala N12 **90**
Namwera M20 **92**
Nandi Mill S11 **86**
Nangade J23 **99**
Nangomba J22 **99**
Nangurukuru H23 **99**
Nangweshi O10 **90**
Nankoya O6 **89**
Nansio B18 **104**
Nanyuki D4 **106**
Napaha M22 **93**
Napier U4 **60**
Narib E3 **82**
Nariep O3 **64**
Naro Moru D4 **106**
Narok E3 **106**
Nata S7 **85**
Nature's Valley T8 **61**
Nauchas E3 **82**
Nauela N21 **93**
Naulila O3 **88**
Nawinda O11 **90**
Nazombe J23 **99**
Ncanaha T12 **62**
Ncaute A5 **83**
Nchanga L13 **91**
Nchelenge H14 **97**
Nchenachena J19 **98**
Ncojane B11 **76**
Ncora R14 **63**
Ndala D19 **104**
Ndara H19 **98**
Ndareda D20 **104**
Ndende B1 **100**
Ndola L14 **91**
Ndongo B2 **100**
Ndumbwe J23 **99**
Ndumdumwense
Hill O12 **90**
Ndumo H31 **75**
Ndundulu L23 **69**
Ndwedwe M22 **69**
Nebo E25 **79**
Necuto D1 **100**
Negage G3 **94**
Negola M3 **88**
Negomane K22 **99**
Nehone O4 **88**
Neilersdrif L7 **65**
Nelspoort O8 **61**
Nelspruit F30 **75**
Nemba B15 **103**
Neriquinha N8 **89**
Netia N23 **93**
New Amalfi N20 **68**
New England O18 **68**
New
Featherstone R11 **86**
New
Guelderland M23 **69**
New Hanover M22 **69**
New Machavie H21 **73**
Newala J23 **99**
Newark M23 **69**
Newcastle J28 **74**
Newington E28 **80**
Newsel Beach N23 **69**
Ngabé C4 **100**
Ngabeni O21 **68**
Ngabwe M13 **91**
Ngadia Pembe G10 **96**
Nganji B13 **103**
Ngara,
Tanzania B17 **104**
Ngara,
Zambia J19 **98**
Ngare Nanyuki C21 **105**
Ngasamo B19 **104**
Ngerengere F22 **99**
Ngidinga D3 **100**
Ngo B4 **100**
Ngobeni J30 **75**
Ngoma O6 **85**
Ngomba G18 **98**
Ngome K30 **75**
Ngong E4 **106**
Ngongo C1 **100**
Ngonini G30 **75**
Ngonja D22 **105**
Ngora C1 **106**
Ngorengore E3 **106**
Ngorongoro C20 **104**
Ngoso D6 **101**
Ngozi C15 **103**
Ngqeleni O16 **63**
Ngqungqu R16 **63**
Ngudu C19 **104**
Ngulia C22 **105**
Ngundu S11 **86**
Nguni E5 **107**
Nhachengue U14 **87**
Nhachengue B33 **81**
Nhamatanda R13 **87**
Nhavane C31 **81**
Nhlangano J30 **75**
Nhlazatshe K30 **75**
Nhoma B5 **83**
Nicuadala O15 **87**
Niekerkshoop M10 **66**
Niemba E14 **103**
Nietverdiend E20 **78**
Nieuwoudtville P4 **64**
Nieu-Bethesda R10 **62**
Nigel G23 **73**
Nigramoep M2 **64**
Nina D4 **83**
Ninda N8 **89**
Ninette D4 **83**
Nioki B5 **101**
Nipiodi O21 **93**
Njinjo H23 **99**
Njoko O11 **90**
Njombe H20 **98**
Nkambako C26 **79**
Nkandla L23 **69**
Nkau N19 **68**
Nkayi R10 **86**
Nkayi C2 **100**
Nkhotakota L19 **92**
Nkolo B4 **100**
Nkomo C26 **79**
Nkopola M20 **92**
Nkoshya H15 **97**
Nkubu D4 **106**
Nkurenkuru P6 **89**
Nkurenkuru A4 **83**
Nkwalini L23 **69**
Nobantu P20 **68**
Nobokwe R14 **63**
Noenieput G5 **82**
Nohana N18 **68**
Nokong M19 **68**
Noll T8 **61**
Nomtsas E3 **82**
Nondo H16 **97**
Nondweni K29 **75**
Nongoma K30 **75**
Noordhoek T2 **60**
Noordkaap F30 **75**
Noordkuil R2 **60**
Noordoewer H3 **82**
Nóqui E2 **100**
Norman C2 **83**
Normandien K28 **74**
North Horr B4 **106**
Northam E21 **78**
Norton O11 **86**
Norvalspont O14 **67**
Nossob D3 **83**
Nossob Camp F11 **70**
Notintsila R16 **63**
Notocote O22 **93**
Nottingham
Road M21 **69**
Noupoort P13 **67**
Nova Caipemba G3 **94**
Nova Golega S13 **87**
Nova Mambone S14 **87**
Nova Nabùri O22 **93**
Nova Vanduzi R13 **87**
Nqabara R16 **63**
Nqabeni O21 **69**
Nqamakwe R15 **63**
Nqutu K29 **75**
Nsadzu M18 **92**
Nsah B4 **100**
Nsanje O20 **92**
Nsiamfumu E1 **100**
Nsiza R10 **86**
Nsoko J30 **75**
Nsombo J15 **97**
Ntabamhlope M21 **69**
Ntabebomvu K29 **75**
Ntadembele B5 **101**
Ntambu K11 **96**
Ntcheu N19 **92**
Nthunga L19 **92**
Ntibane P19 **68**
Ntsama A3 **100**
Ntseshe R15 **63**
Ntshilini O16 **63**
Ntumba G18 **98**
Ntungamo A15 **103**
Ntywenka P19 **68**
Nugubaes B2 **83**
Nulli A26 **79**
Numbi Gate E28 **80**
Nungo M22 **93**
Nungwe Bay B18 **104**
Nutfield E24 **79**
Nuwe Smitsdorp D24 **79**
Nuwefontein H4 **82**
Nuwerus P3 **64**
Nuy T3 **60**
Nwanetsi D29 **80**
Nya Ngezi B14 **103**
Nyabira O11 **86**
Nyahanga B19 **104**
Nyahururu D3 **106**
Nyakahure B17 **104**
Nyakanazi C17 **104**
Nyala A28 **80**
Nyalikungu B19 **104**
Nyamahoka J21 **99**
Nyamandhlovu R9 **86**
Nyamapanda O18 **92**
Nyamaropa O12 **86**
Nyamtumbo J21 **99**
Nyanga,
Congo B1 **100**
Nyanga, Moç O12 **86**
Nyangana P7 **89**
Nyangwe C12 **102**
Nyanza B15 **103**
Nyanza-Lac D15 **103**
Nyarembe B17 **104**
Nyasa E12 **102**
Nyazura R12 **86**
Nyeri E4 **106**
Nyika,
Tanzania J19 **98**
Nyika,
Zimbabwe S11 **86**
Nyimba M16 **91**
Nylstroom D23 **79**
Nyokana R15 **63**
Nyonga F18 **98**
Nyoni M23 **69**
Nyunzu E14 **103**
Nzambi,
Congo C1 **100**
Nzambi, Zaïre B5 **101**
Nzega D18 **104**
Nzima C18 **104**
Nzingu C14 **103**
N'Gelewa A10 **102**
N'dalatando H3 **94**
N'gungo K3 **94**
N'harea J5 **95**
N'zeto F2 **94**

O

Oatlands S10 **62**
Obobogorap G5 **82**
Obokote A13 **103**
Obouya A4 **100**
Odendaalsrus J21 **73**
Ofcolaco D26 **79**
Ogies G27 **74**
Ohrigstad E26 **79**
Okahandja C3 **83**
Okakarara C3 **83**
Okakombo C2 **83**
Okalonga O3 **88**
Okalongo A2 **83**
Okandja A2 **100**
Okaputa B2 **83**
Okarukurume C4 **83**
Okaukuejo B4 **83**
Okavarumendu C4 **83**
Okawe C3 **83**
Okazizi D3 **83**
Okiep M3 **64**
Okoka C11 **102**
Okombahe C2 **83**
Okonzongoro C2 **83**
Okovimburu C5 **83**
Okoyo B3 **100**
Okozondara C4 **83**
Ol Tukai B22 **105**
Old Bunting R16 **63**
Old Mkushi M15 **91**
Old Morley R16 **63**
Oldeani C20 **104**
Olifants D28 **80**
Olifantshoek J14 **71**
Olinga O16 **87**
Oloitokitok C22 **105**
Olyfberg C25 **79**
Omaruru C2 **83**
Omatjenne C3 **83**
Omatjette C2 **83**
Ombalantu A2 **83**
Ombala-yo-Mungo O3 **88**
Ombika B2 **83**
Ombombo A1 **83**
Omdraaisvlei N11 **66**
Omitara D4 **83**
Omurumendu D4 **83**
Onconcua O2 **88**
Ondangwa A2 **83**
Ondekaremba D3 **83**
Ondersteldorings N6 **65**
Ondjiva O4 **88**
Ondumbo C2 **83**
Onema D11 **102**
Onema Ututu C10 **102**
Onesi A2 **83**
Ongandjera A2 **83**
Ongenga A2 **83**
Ongeri D12 **102**
Onrus U3 **60**
Ons Hoop C22 **78**
Onseepkans L5 **65**
Ontmoeting H12 **70**
Oorwinning B25 **79**
Oosgam S6 **61**
Oostermoed D21 **78**
Oos-Londen S14 **63**
Ootse E19 **78**
Opala A11 **102**
Operet A3 **83**
Opuwo A1 **83**
Orania M12 **66**
Oranjefontein C22 **78**
Oranjemund H3 **82**
Oranjerivier M12 **66**
Oranjeville H23 **73**
Orapa S6 **85**
Orkney H21 **73**
Orom B1 **106**
Orpen D28 **80**
Osborn L23 **69**
Oshakati A2 **83**
Oshigambo A3 **83**
Oshikuku A2 **83**
Oshivelo P5 **89**
Oshivelo A3 **83**
Oshwe C7 **101**
Osire C3 **83**
Osona D3 **83**
Otavi B3 **83**
Otchinjau O2 **88**
Otimati M23 **69**
Otjianda A1 **83**
Otjihaenena B4 **83**
Otjihavana D3 **83**
Otjikango B3 **83**
Otjikondo B2 **83**
Otjimbingwe D2 **83**
Otjinene C4 **83**
Otjinoko C4 **83**
Otjitambi Guest
Farm B2 **83**
Otjitambigaste-
plaas B2 **83**
Otjitanda P2 **88**
Otjitasu C3 **83**
Otjituuo B4 **83**
Otjiwarongo C3 **83**
Otjiyarwa C5 **83**
Otjondeka A1 **83**
Otjongundu C2 **83**
Otjosondu C3 **83**
Otjovasandu B1 **83**
Otokota A5 **83**
Ottosdal H20 **72**
Ottoshoop F10 **72**
Otuwe C2 **83**
Oudtshoorn S7 **61**
Ouguati D2 **83**
Oukraal U3 **60**
Outjo B2 **83**
Overyssel C23 **79**
Oviston O14 **67**
Owando A4 **100**
Owendale K15 **71**
Oxbow L19 **68**
Oyo A4 **100**
Oyster Bay U10 **62**
Oystercliffs F2 **82**
Ozizweni K28 **74**
Ozombo D4 **83**

P

Paarl T3 **60**
Pacaltsdorp T7 **61**
Paddock O21 **69**
Padibe B1 **106**
Pafuri A28 **80**
Pafuri Gate A28 **80**
Paje A21 **78**
Pajule B1 **106**
Pakima C11 **102**
Pala F15 **97**
Palala D23 **79**
Palapye A21 **78**
Paleisheuwel R2 **60**
Palm Beach P21 **69**
Palma J24 **99**
Palmeira F32 **75**
Palmerton P20 **68**
Palmietfontein O18 **68**
Palmwag B1 **83**
Pambarra A33 **81**
Pampierstad J18 **72**
Pampoenpoort O10 **66**
Panbult H29 **75**
Panda D32 **81**
Pande J13 **97**
Pangala C3 **100**
Pangani D23 **105**
Pangi C13 **103**
Pango Aluquém G3 **94**
Pania Mutombo D11 **102**
Pansdrift F22 **73**
Panu C6 **101**
Panzi F5 **95**
Papendorp O1 **60**
Papiesvlei U3 **60**
Papkuil K15 **71**
Paranga B1 **106**
Paresis C3 **83**
Park Rynie O22 **69**
Parow T2 **60**
Parys H22 **73**
Patensie T10 **62**
Paterson T12 **62**
Patlong N19 **68**
Patonga B1 **106**
Paul Kruger Gate/
-hek E28 **80**
Paul Roux K22 **73**
Paulpietersburg J29 **75**
Pearly Beach U3 **60**
Pearston S11 **62**
Pebane O16 **87**
Peddie T13 **63**
Pedra do Feitico E2 **100**
Peka L18 **68**
Pelenge B10 **102**
Pella L4 **64**
Pellisa C1 **106**
Pemba, Moç M24 **93**
Pemba,
Zambia O13 **91**
Pembe D33 **81**
Pene Mende D14 **103**
Pene Tungu A12 **102**
Penge D26 **79**
Penge (Zaïre) D11 **102**
Pennington O22 **69**
Pepa G15 **97**
Pepworth L21 **69**
Perdekop J28 **74**
Petauke M16 **91**
Peternoster R1 **60**
Petersburg R11 **62**
Petrus Steyn J23 **73**
Petrusburg L14 **67**
Petrusville N13 **67**
Phalaborwa D28 **80**
Phalaborwe U11 **86**
Phamong N18 **68**
Philadelphia T2 **60**
Philippolis N14 **67**
Philippolis Road N14 **67**
Philipstown N13 **67**
Phitshane
Molopo F19 **72**
Phoenix N22 **69**
Phokwane E25 **79**
Phuduhudu S5 **85**
Phuthaditjhaba L20 **68**
Piana Mwanga G14 **97**
Pidi G12 **96**
Pienaarsrivier E23 **79**
Piet Plessis G18 **72**
Piet Retief H29 **75**
Pieter Meintjies S4 **60**
Pietermaritzburg N22 **69**
Pietersburg C25 **79**
Pigawasi D19 **104**
Piggs Peak G30 **75**
Piketberg R2 **60**
Pilane D20 **78**
Pilgrims Rest E26 **79**
Pinetown N22 **69**
Pita C6 **101**
Pitsane E18 **77**
Pitseng M19 **68**
Pitu H20 **98**
Plaston F30 **75**
Platbakkies N4 **64**
Plathuis S5 **61**
Platrand H27 **74**
Platveld B3 **83**
Plettenberg Bay T8 **61**
Plettenbergbaai T8 **61**
Plooysburg L12 **66**
Plumtree S9 **86**
Pniel T3 **60**
Pofadder M5 **65**
Pole C10 **102**
Politsi C25 **79**
Poma A12 **102**
Pomene C34 **81**
Pomeroy L22 **69**
Pomfret F15 **71**
Pongola J30 **75**
Ponte-Noire D1 **100**
Ponto do Ouro H32 **75**
Pools R2 **60**
Popokabaka D4 **100**
Port Alfred T13 **63**
Port Beaufort U5 **61**
Port Bell D1 **106**
Port Edward P21 **69**
Port Elizabeth U11 **62**
Port Grosvenor P21 **69**
Port Nolloth M1 **64**
Port Shepstone O22 **69**
Port St. Johns P20 **68**
Port Victoria D2 **106**
Porterville S3 **60**
Porto Amboim J2 **94**
Post Chalmers R11 **62**
Postmasburg K14 **71**
Potchefstroom H21 **73**
Potfontein N12 **66**
Potgietersrus D24 **79**
Potsdam S14 **63**
Poumbou C1 **100**
Poupan N12 **66**
Praia de
Jangamo D34 **81**
Praia de Závora E33 **81**
Praia do
Chongoene E31 **81**
Praia do Tofo D34 **81**
Praia do Xai-Xai E31 **81**
Pretoria F23 **73**
Pretoriuskop E28 **80**
Prieska M10 **66**
Prince Albert S7 **61**
Prince Albert
Road R6 **61**
Prince Alfred
Hamlet S3 **60**
Pringle Bay U2 **60**
Priors N14 **67**
Protem T4 **60**
Ptoyio C3 **106**
Pudimoe J18 **72**
Puma D20 **104**
Punda Maria B28 **80**
Pungo Andongo H4 **94**
Punia B13 **103**

Puri G4 **94**
Putsonderwater M8 **65**
Pweto G14 **97**

Q

Qabane N19 **68**
Qachas Nek N19 **68**
Qamata R14 **63**
Qhobela L19 **68**
Qobong N18 **68**
Qoboqobo S15 **63**
Qolora Mouth S15 **63**
Qombolo R14 **63**
Qoqodala Q13 **63**
Qora Mouth S15 **63**
Qudeni L22 **69**
Queens Mine R9 **86**
Queensburgh N22 **69**
Queenstown R13 **63**
Quela H5 **95**
Quelimane Q15 **87**
Quelo E2 **100**
Quiba P18 **68**
Quibala J3 **94**
Quibaxe G3 **94**
Quiculungo G3 **94**
Quifuata G3 **94**
Quihita N3 **88**
Quilemba H3 **94**
Quilenda J3 **94**
Quilengues M3 **88**
Quilua Q23 **93**
Quimbele F4 **94**
Quinga Q23 **93**
Quionga J24 **99**
Quipeio K4 **94**
Quipungo N3 **88**
Quirima J5 **95**
Quissanga L24 **93**
Quissico E32 **81**
Quissongo H3 **94**
Quitapa J6 **95**
Quiterage L24 **93**
Quiteve N3 **88**
Quixaxe N23 **93**
Quizenga H4 **94**
Quko S15 **63**
Qumbu P20 **68**

R

Rabdure A8 **107**
Radisele B21 **78**
Radium E23 **79**
Raffingora Q11 **86**
Raffingora Q15 **91**
Rakops S5 **85**
Ralebona Q18 **68**
Raleqheka M18 **68**
Ramabanta M18 **68**
Ramatlabama F19 **72**
Ramotswa D19 **78**
Ramotswa Stn. D19 **78**
Ramsgate Q21 **69**
Ramu A7 **107**
Ranaka E18 **77**
Rand Rifles D2 **83**
Randalhurst L23 **69**
Randburg G23 **73**
Randfontein G22 **73**
Randvaal G26 **74**
Rankin's Pass D22 **78**
Rashoop F22 **73**
Ratelfontein Q2 **60**
Ratombo B26 **79**
Rawsonville T3 **60**
Rayton F23 **73**
Redcliff R10 **86**
Redcliffe M21 **69**
Reddersburg M15 **67**
Redelinghuys R2 **60**
Redoubt Q21 **69**
Reebokrand N13 **67**
Rehoboth E3 **82**
Rehoboth Stn. E3 **82**
Reitz J23 **73**
Reitzburg H21 **73**
Reivilo J17 **72**
Renosterskop Q8 **61**
Renosterspruit H20 **72**
Rensburg H23 **73**
Ressano Garcia F31 **75**
Restvale Q8 **61**
Révia M21 **93**
Rex F22 **73**
Rhodes Q18 **68**
Ribáuè N22 **93**
Richards Bay M24 **69**
Richardsbaai M24 **69**
Richmond, C.P. P12 **66**
Richmond, Natal N21 **69**
Riebeeck Kasteel S3 **60**
Riebeeckstad J21 **73**
Riebeeck-Oos T12 **62**
Riebeeck-Wes S2 **60**
Riekertsdam E20 **78**
Rietbron R8 **61**
Rietfontein, C.P. H10 **70**
Rietfontein, Namibia D5 **83**
Riethuiskraal T6 **67**
Rietkolk D25 **79**
Rietkuil J27 **74**
Rietpoel T4 **60**
Rietpoort Q3 **64**
Rietvlei M22 **69**
Ringoma K5 **95**
Rio das Pedras U14 **87**
Rio das Pedras C34 **81**
Rita C25 **79**
Ritchie L13 **67**
Rito Q6 **89**
Riversdal T6 **61**
Riversdale T6 **61**
Riverside N21 **69**
Riverton K18 **72**
Riverview L24 **69**
Riviersonderend T4 **60**
Rivulets F29 **75**
Rivungo Q8 **89**
Roamer's Rest N19 **68**
Roan Antelope Mine M14 **91**
Roberts Drift H27 **74**
Robertson T4 **60**
Rockmount M21 **69**
Rode Q20 **68**
Rodenbeck M15 **67**
Roedtan D24 **79**
Roma M18 **68**
Rondevlei T7 **61**
Rongo E2 **106**
Roodebank H27 **74**
Roodepoort G22 **73**
Roodewal D28 **80**
Rooiberg D22 **78**
Rooibokkraal D21 **78**
Rooibosbult D22 **78**
Rooigrond G20 **72**
Rooikop D2 **83**
Rooikraal E25 **79**
Rooipan M13 **67**
Rooiwal J22 **73**
Roosboom L21 **69**
Roossenekal E25 **79**
Rorke's Drift L22 **69**
Rosebank N22 **69**
Rosedene Q7 **61**
Rosendal L18 **68**
Rosetta M21 **69**
Rosh Pinah H3 **82**
Rosmead P13 **67**
Rössing D2 **83**
Rossouw P17 **68**
Rostrataville H19 **72**
Rotanda R12 **86**
Rothmere R16 **63**
Rotkop G2 **82**
Rouxpos S5 **61**
Rouxville N17 **68**
Ruacana Q3 **88**
Ruarwe J19 **98**
Ruashi K13 **97**
Rudewa F21 **99**
Rufiji Camp G22 **99**
Rufunsa N15 **91**
Ruhengeri B15 **103**
Ruitersbos T6 **61**
Rulenge C17 **104**
Rumbaçaça A33 **81**
Rumonge C15 **103**
Rumphi J19 **98**
Rumuruti D4 **106**
Rundu P7 **89**
Rungwa F19 **98**
Rupara P6 **89**
Rupisi S12 **86**
Ruponda J22 **99**
Rusape R12 **86**
Rust S2 **60**
Rust De Winter E23 **79**
Rustenburg F22 **73**
Rustig J21 **73**
Rusverby F21 **73**
Rutana C15 **103**
Rutenga T11 **86**
Rutshuru A15 **103**
Ruvu F23 **99**
Ruyigi C15 **103**
Rwindi A15 **103**

S

Sekhukhune E25 **79**
Saaifontein Q6 **61**
Sabarei A4 **106**
Sabi Experimental Stn. S12 **86**
Sabie, Moç F31 **75**
Sabie, Tvl. E26 **79**
Sable Antelope Mine N13 **91**
Sacacama K8 **95**
Sacandica E4 **100**
Sacarimbo N7 **89**
Saco Uen C8 **107**
Sada R13 **63**
Sadani F23 **99**
Sadi A7 **107**
Sakania L14 **91**
Sakrivier Q6 **65**
Salajwe C17 **77**
Salamanga H32 **75**
Saldanha S1 **60**
Salem T13 **63**
Salima M19 **92**
Salpeterpan J18 **72**
Salt Lake M12 **66**
Salt Lick C22 **105**
Salt Rock M23 **69**
Salzbrunn E4 **82**
Samagaigai B5 **83**
Samakwo H9 **96**
Samba D13 **103**
Samba Caju G4 **94**
Samburu C23 **105**
Samusa A5 **83**
Same C22 **105**
Samfya J15 **97**
Sampwe H13 **97**
Samucumbi M7 **89**
Sand River Valley L21 **69**
Sandano K7 **95**
Sandberg R2 **60**
Sandoa H10 **96**
Sandton G23 **73**
Sandverhaar G3 **82**
Sandvlakte T10 **62**
Sandwich Bay E2 **82**
Sanga J4 **94**
Sani Pass Hotel M20 **69**
Sanje A17 **104**
Sannaspos M15 **67**
Sannieshof G20 **72**
Santa Cruz F4 **94**
Santa Maria M1 **88**
Sanya Juu C21 **105**
Sanyati Q10 **86**
Sanza Pombo G4 **94**
Sao Hill G20 **98**
Sapo Sapo E10 **102**
Saranda E20 **104**
Saranga D2 **106**
Sarenli C8 **107**
Sasolburg H22 **73**
Satara D28 **80**
Satco H4 **82**
Sauer R2 **60**
Saurimo H7 **95**
Sautar J6 **95**
Savane R14 **87**
Savate Q5 **89**
Save T13 **87**
Savuti R5 **85**
Saza G18 **98**
Scarborough T2 **60**
Schakalskuppe G3 **82**
Scheepersnek K29 **75**
Schmidtsdrif L12 **66**
Schoemanshoek S7 **61**
Schoemansville F22 **73**
Schoombee P14 **67**
Schuckmannsburg Q6 **85**
Schumannsthal B3 **83**
Schweizer-Reneke H19 **72**
Scottburgh Q22 **69**
Sea Park Q22 **69**
Sea View U11 **62**
Sebapala N18 **68**
Sebayeng C25 **79**
Sebit C3 **106**
Sebokeng H25 **74**
Secunda H27 **74**
Sederberg R3 **60**
Sedgefield T7 **61**
Seeheim G3 **82**
Seeis D3 **83**
Seekoegat S7 **61**
Sefako L19 **68**
Sefikeng M18 **68**
Sefophe T9 **86**
Sefophe A23 **79**
Sehithwa S4 **84**
Sehlabathebe N20 **68**
Sehonghong N19 **68**
Seke Banza D2 **100**
Sekenke D19 **104**
Sekoma D16 **77**
Selebi Phikwe T9 **86**
Selebi-Phikwe A25 **80**
Selenge B6 **101**
Selika B25 **80**
Selonsrivier F28 **74**
Selous Q11 **86**
Semolale T9 **86**
Senanga Q10 **90**
Sendelingsdrif H3 **82**
Sendelingsfontein H20 **72**
Sending B24 **79**
Senekal K22 **73**
Senga M19 **92**
Senga Hill H16 **97**
Sengwe A28 **80**
Senlac F15 **71**
Sentrum D22 **78**
Sepupa R4 **84**
Serenje M15 **91**
Seringkop F24 **73**
Serowe A21 **78**
Serule T7 **85**
Sesfontein B1 **83**
Seshego C24 **79**
Sesheke Q5 **85**
Sessa M7 **89**
Setlagole G19 **72**
Settlers E23 **79**
Setuat H18 **72**
Sevenoaks M22 **69**
Severn G14 **71**
Seweweekspoort S6 **61**
Seymour S13 **63**
Sezela Q22 **69**
Shabunda C13 **103**
Shakaskraal M23 **69**
Shakawe Q4 **84**
Shaka's Rock M23 **69**
Shamva Q12 **86**
Shamva Q16 **91**
Shangani R10 **86**
Shangombo Q8 **89**
Shannon M15 **67**
Shashi T7 **85**
Sheepmoor H29 **75**
Sheffield Beach M23 **69**
Sheldon S12 **62**
Shelley Beach Q22 **69**
Sherborne P13 **67**
Sherwood Ranch U9 **86**
Sherwood Ranch B22 **78**
Shimoni D23 **105**
Shimuwini C28 **80**
Shinga C11 **102**
Shingwedzi B28 **80**
Shinyanga C19 **104**
Shirati E2 **106**
Shiwa Ngandu J16 **97**
Shoga G19 **98**
Shorobe R5 **85**
Shoshong B20 **78**
Shurugwi R10 **86**
Siabuwa Q9 **86**
Sibiti C2 **100**
Sibwesa F16 **97**
Sibwesa E17 **104**
Sichili Q11 **90**
Sicunusa H30 **75**
Sidney-on-Vaal K17 **72**
Sidvokodvo H30 **75**
Sidwadweni P19 **68**
Signalberg G4 **82**
Sigoga Q19 **68**
Sigor C3 **106**
Sihhoya G30 **75**
Sikalengo N11 **90**
Sikereti A5 **83**
Sikonge E18 **104**
Sikongo N9 **90**
Sikwane D20 **78**
Silent Valley D21 **78**
Silkaatskop E20 **78**
Silobela R10 **86**
Silutshana L22 **69**
Silver Sand D3 **83**
Silver Streams K15 **71**
Simbo D15 **103**
Simbo D19 **104**
Simonstad T2 **60**
Simon's Town T2 **60**
Sinazongwe Q13 **91**
Sinclair Mine/-myn F3 **82**
Sinda M16 **91**
Sindeni D22 **105**
Singida D20 **104**
Sinhole Mission N10 **90**
Sinjembele Q5 **85**
Sinksabrug T7 **61**
Sinya C21 **105**
Sioma Q10 **90**
Sipofaneni H30 **75**
Sir Lowry's Pass T3 **60**
Sirheni B28 **80**
Sishen J14 **71**
Siteki H31 **75**
Sithobela H30 **75**
Sitila C33 **81**
Sitoti Q10 **90**
Sittingbourne S14 **63**
Sitwe J18 **98**
Siyabuswa E24 **79**
Skeerpoort F22 **73**
Skerpioenpunt L9 **66**
Skipskop U4 **60**
Skoenmakerskop U11 **62**
Skuinsdrif E20 **78**
Skukuza E28 **80**
Slangrivier U10 **62**
Slurry F20 **72**
Smithfield N15 **67**
Smitskraal T10 **62**
Sneeukraal Q7 **61**
Sneezewood N21 **69**
Snikamushile J15 **97**
Sodium N11 **66**
Soebatsfontein N2 **64**
Soekmekaar U10 **86**
Soekmekaar C25 **79**
Sofala S14 **87**
Soia D8 **107**
Soitaiyai B20 **104**
Sojwe C19 **78**
Sokele H11 **96**
Solai D3 **106**
Solitaire E2 **82**
Sololo B5 **107**
Solomondale C25 **79**
Solwezi K12 **96**
Sombo G8 **95**
Somerset East S11 **62**
Somerset West T3 **60**
Somerset-Oos S11 **62**
Somerset-Wes T3 **60**
Somkele L24 **69**
Songea J20 **98**
Songo, Angola F3 **94**
Songo, Moç N18 **92**
Songololo E3 **100**
Soni D22 **105**
Sonop F22 **73**
Sonstraal H13 **71**
Sopa G16 **97**
Soroti C1 **106**
Sounda C1 **100**
South Downs M21 **69**
South Horr C4 **106**
Southbroom Q21 **69**
Southeyville R14 **63**
Southpoort Q22 **69**
Southwell T13 **63**
Soutpan, O.F.S. L15 **67**
Soutpan, Tvl. E23 **79**
Soweto G22 **73**
Soy D3 **106**
Soyo E1 **100**
Spanwerk C21 **78**
Speelmanskraal T8 **61**
Spencer Bay F2 **82**
Spes Bona H21 **73**
Spitskopvlei R11 **62**
Spoegrivier N3 **64**
Spring Valley R12 **62**
Springbok M3 **64**
Springfontein N14 **67**
Springs G23 **73**
Spruitdrif Q2 **60**
Spytfontein L13 **67**
Squamans F31 **75**
Staansaam H11 **70**
Stafford's Post Q21 **69**
Stampriet E4 **82**
Standerton H27 **74**
Stanford U3 **60**
Stanger M23 **69**
Stapleford R12 **86**
Steekdorings J17 **72**
Steelpoort E25 **79**
Steilloopbrug C23 **79**
Steilrand K30 **75**
Steilwater C23 **79**
Steinfeld F3 **82**
Steinhausen D4 **83**
Steinkopf M2 **64**
Stekaar Q12 **66**
Stella G18 **72**
Stellenbosch T3 **60**
Sterkspruit Q18 **68**
Sterkstroom P15 **67**
Sterkwater C24 **79**
Sterling P8 **65**
Steynsburg P14 **67**
Steynsrus K22 **73**
Steytlerville T10 **62**
Stilbaai-Oos T6 **61**
Stilbaai-Wes U6 **61**
Stilfontein H21 **73**
Stinkbank D2 **83**
Stockpoort B22 **78**
Stoffberg F28 **74**
Stofvlei N4 **64**
Stompneusbaai R1 **60**
Stoneyridge P20 **68**
Stormberg P15 **67**
Stormsrivier U9 **62**
Stormsvlei T4 **60**
Straatsdrif E20 **78**
Strand T2 **60**
Strandfontein Q1 **60**
Struisbaai U4 **60**
Strydenburg N12 **66**
Strydpoort H20 **72**
Studtis T9 **62**
Stutterheim S14 **63**
St. Faith's Q21 **69**
St. Helenabaai K1 **60**
St. Lucia Estuary L24 **69**
St. Mark's R14 **63**
St. Martin M19 **68**
Suana E7 **101**
Sukses C3 **83**
Sulton Hamud B22 **105**
Sumba E2 **100**
Sumbawanga G16 **97**
Sumbe J2 **94**
Sumbu G16 **97**
Sumbwa F15 **97**
Summerdown C4 **83**
Summerstrand U12 **62**
Sun City E21 **78**
Suna D20 **104**
Sundra G23 **73**
Sungo Q19 **92**
Sutherland R5 **61**
Sutton J14 **71**
Suurberg T12 **62**
Suurbraak T5 **61**
Swaershoek S11 **62**
Swakopmund D2 **83**
Swart Umfolozi K30 **75**
Swartberg N20 **68**
Swartkops U12 **62**
Swartmodder K11 **70**
Swartplaas G21 **73**
Swartputs K15 **71**
Swartruggens F21 **73**
Swartwater B23 **79**
Swellendam T4 **60**
Swempoort P17 **68**
Swinburne K27 **74**
Sybrandskraal F24 **73**
Syfergat P15 **67**
S. Cristovão L2 **88**
S. Lucas J4 **94**

T

Tabankulu Q22 **68**
Tabora D18 **104**
Tacuane Q21 **93**
Tafelberg P14 **67**
Tainton S15 **63**
Takaba B6 **107**
Takatokwane C17 **77**
Takatshawane A13 **77**
Takaungu C23 **105**
Talamati D28 **80**
Taleni R15 **63**
Tambach D3 **106**
Tambajane C33 **81**
Tambankulu G31 **75**
Tambara Q19 **92**
Tambor N1 **88**
Tampa N2 **88**
Tamsu A5 **83**
Tandala H19 **98**
Tando-Zinze D1 **100**
Tanga D23 **105**
Taninga F32 **75**
Tarasaa B24 **105**
Taratara A5 **83**
Tarbaj C6 **107**
Tarime E2 **106**
Tarkastad R12 **62**
Taung J18 **72**
Taveta, Kenya C22 **105**
Taveta, Tanzania H20 **98**
Tchibota C1 **100**
Tchikala-Tcholohanga K4 **94**
Tchitondi D1 **100**
Tegwani S9 **86**
Teltele A4 **106**
Temba E23 **79**
Tembisa G23 **73**
Tembo G5 **95**
Tembwe J18 **98**
Tempué M6 **89**
Tenke J12 **96**
Terra Firma E15 **77**
Terreiro G3 **94**
Tesenane B32 **81**
Tessolo A32 **81**
Tete Q18 **92**
Teufelsbach D3 **83**
Teviot P17 **67**
Tewane B21 **78**
Teyateyaneng M18 **68**
Teza L24 **69**
Thaba Bosiu M18 **68**
Thaba Chitja Q19 **68**
Thaba Nchu M17 **68**
Thaba Tseka M19 **68**
Thabana Morena N18 **68**
Thabazimbi D22 **78**
Thamaga D18 **77**
Tharaka D5 **107**
The Berg E26 **79**
The Crags T8 **61**
The Downs D25 **79**
The Haven R16 **63**
The Heads T8 **61**
The Ranch L22 **69**
Theron K21 **73**
Theunissen K21 **73**
Thika E4 **106**
Thohoyandou U10 **86**
Thohoyandou B29 **81**
Thorndale C25 **79**
Thornville N22 **69**
Three Sisters Q8 **61**
Thuli T10 **86**
Thyolo Q20 **92**
Tierfontein K20 **72**
Timau D4 **106**
Timbavati D28 **80**
Timboroa D3 **106**
Tina Bridge P20 **68**
Tiriri C1 **106**
Tiwi D23 **105**
Tjaneni G31 **75**
Tlalis M18 **68**
Tlhakgameng G18 **72**
Tlokoeng M20 **68**
Toco N2 **88**
Todentang A3 **106**
Tolo C6 **101**
Tolwe U9 **86**
Tom Burke U9 **86**
Tombo Q16 **63**

STRIP ROUTES

These strip maps are a representation of features to be found en route' and are not drawn to scale. Kilometre distances are given in red figures, depending on direction of travel.

Left map (Nairobi – Iringa):

NAIROBI — 0 km / 950
Athi River — 27 / 923
A109
51
Mombasa
Kajiado — 78 / 872
Magadi
A104
87
METO HILLS
KENYA
Amboseli National Park
Namanga — 165 / 785
TANZANIA
29
L. Amboseli
Longido
82
A23
Moshi
ARUSHA — 276 / 674
74
8
A104
Ngorongoro Oldeani/
Lake Manyara National Park — 350 / 600
Makuyuni
L. Manyara
92
Tarangire National Park
Babati — 442 / 508
79
Singida
Kolo
23
Kondoa — 544 / 406
Mondo
29
Handeni
Karema
Kwa Mtoro
A104
89
Meia Meia
48
Hombolo
Bahi — B3
Manyoni
58
36
B3
49
Kongwa
Buigiri
DODOMA — 710 / 240
140
Mtera Reservoir
Great Ruaha
Makatapora — 850 / 100
100
Ruaha National Park
A104
A7
Morogoro/ Dar-es-Salaam
IRINGA — 950 / 0 km
Mbeya

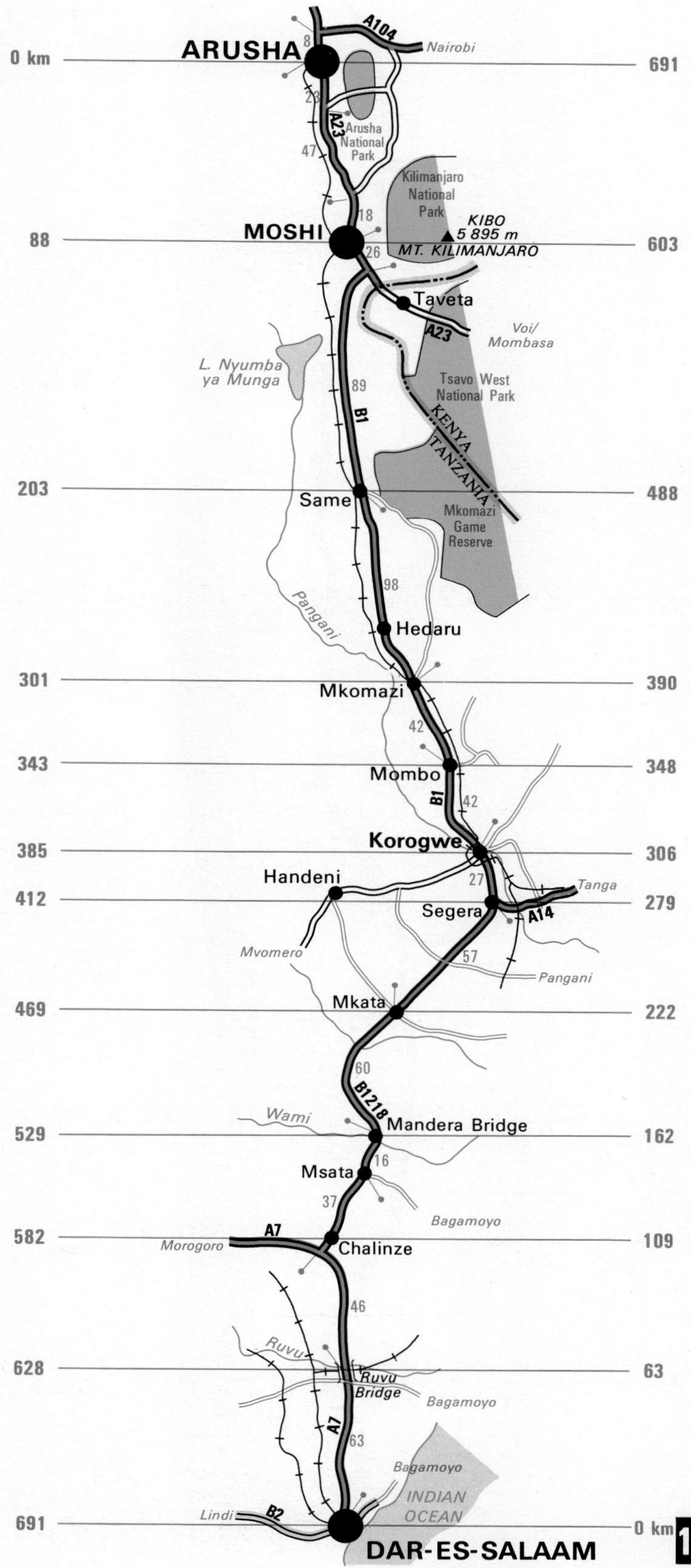

Right map (Arusha – Dar-es-Salaam):

ARUSHA — 0 km / 691
A104
8
Nairobi
29
A23
Arusha National Park
47
Kilimanjaro National Park
18
KIBO ▲ 5 895 m
MT. KILIMANJARO
MOSHI — 88 / 603
26
Taveta
A23
Voi/ Mombasa
89
L. Nyumba ya Munga
Tsavo West National Park
B1
KENYA
TANZANIA
Same — 203 / 488
Pangani
98
Mkomazi Game Reserve
Hedaru
Mkomazi — 301 / 390
42
Mombo — 343 / 348
B1
42
Korogwe — 385 / 306
27
Tanga
Handeni — 412 / 279
Segera
A14
Mvomero
57
Pangani
Mkata — 469 / 222
60
B1/21/8
Wami
Mandera Bridge — 529 / 162
Msata
16
37
Bagamoyo
A7
Morogoro
Chalinze — 582 / 109
46
Ruvu
Ruvu Bridge — 628 / 63
Bagamoyo
A7
63
Bagamoyo
INDIAN OCEAN
Lindi — B2
DAR-ES-SALAAM — 691 / 0 km

117

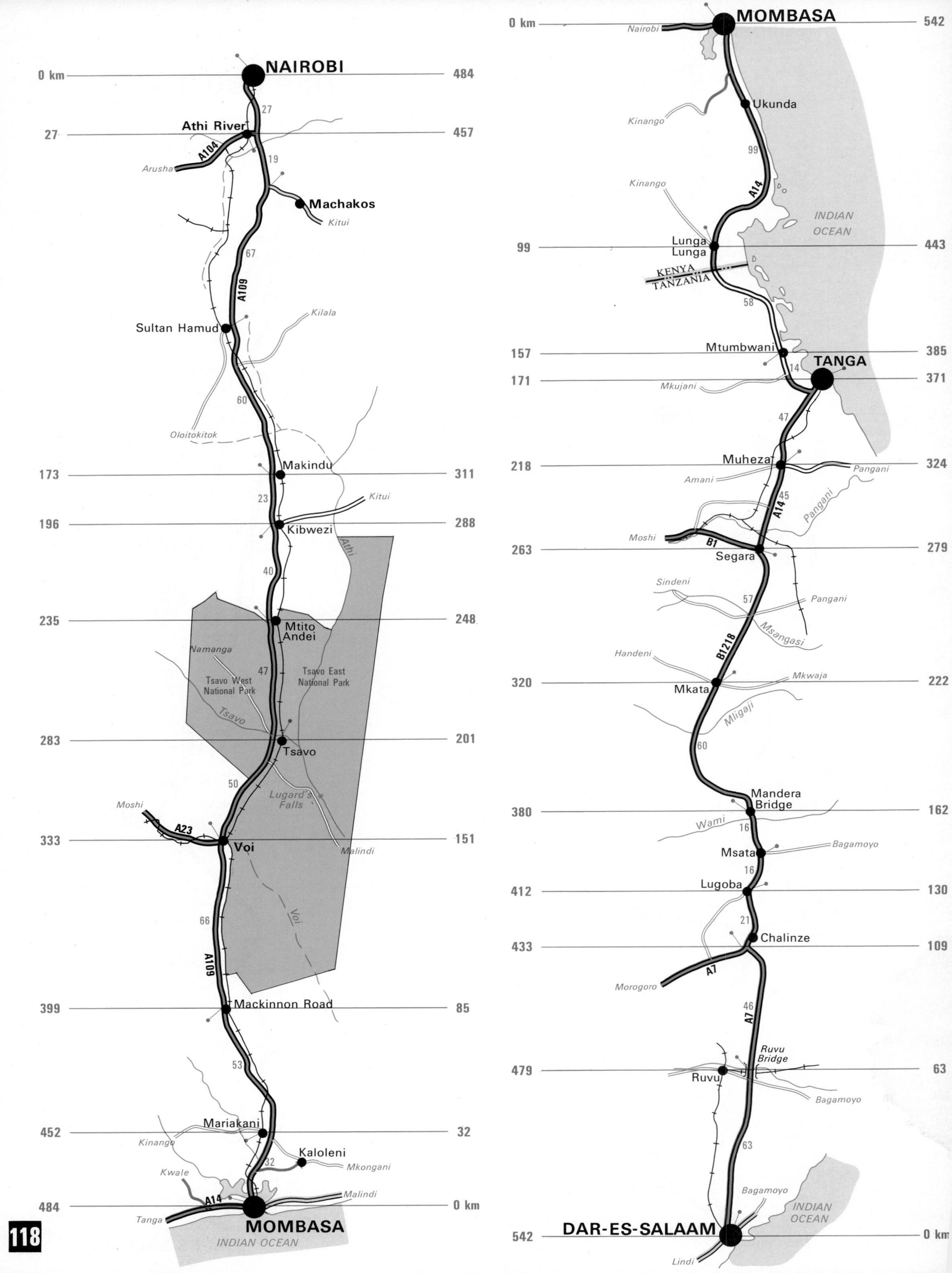

NAIROBI — **MOMBASA**

km	Place	km
0 km	NAIROBI	484
27	Athi River	457
	Machakos	
	Sultan Hamud	
173	Makindu	311
196	Kibwezi	288
235	Mtito Andei	248
283	Tsavo	201
333	Voi	151
399	Mackinnon Road	85
452	Mariakani	32
	Kaloleni	
484	MOMBASA	0 km

A104 · Arusha
A109
27 · 19
67
60
Kilala
Oloitokitok
23 · Kitui
40
Athi
Namanga · 47 · Tsavo East National Park
Tsavo West National Park · Tsavo
50 · Lugard's Falls
Moshi · A23 · Malindi
66
A109
53
Kinango · 32 · Mkongani
Kwale · Malindi
A14 · Tanga
INDIAN OCEAN

MOMBASA — **DAR-ES-SALAAM**

km	Place	km
0 km	MOMBASA	542
	Ukunda	
99	Lunga Lunga	443
157	Mtumbwani	385
171	TANGA	371
218	Muheza	324
263	Segara	279
320	Mkata	222
380	Mandera Bridge	162
	Msata	
412	Lugoba	130
433	Chalinze	109
479	Ruvu	63
542	DAR-ES-SALAAM	0 km

Nairobi
Kinango
A14 · 99
Kinango
KENYA · TANZANIA
58
14 · Mkujani
47
Amani · Pangani
Moshi · A14 · 45 · Pangani
B1 · Sindeni · Pangani
57
Handeni · B1218 · Mkwaja
Msangasi
Mligaji
60
Wami · 16 · Bagamoyo
16
21
Morogoro · A7
46 · Ruvu Bridge
A7
Bagamoyo
63
Bagamoyo
Lindi · INDIAN OCEAN

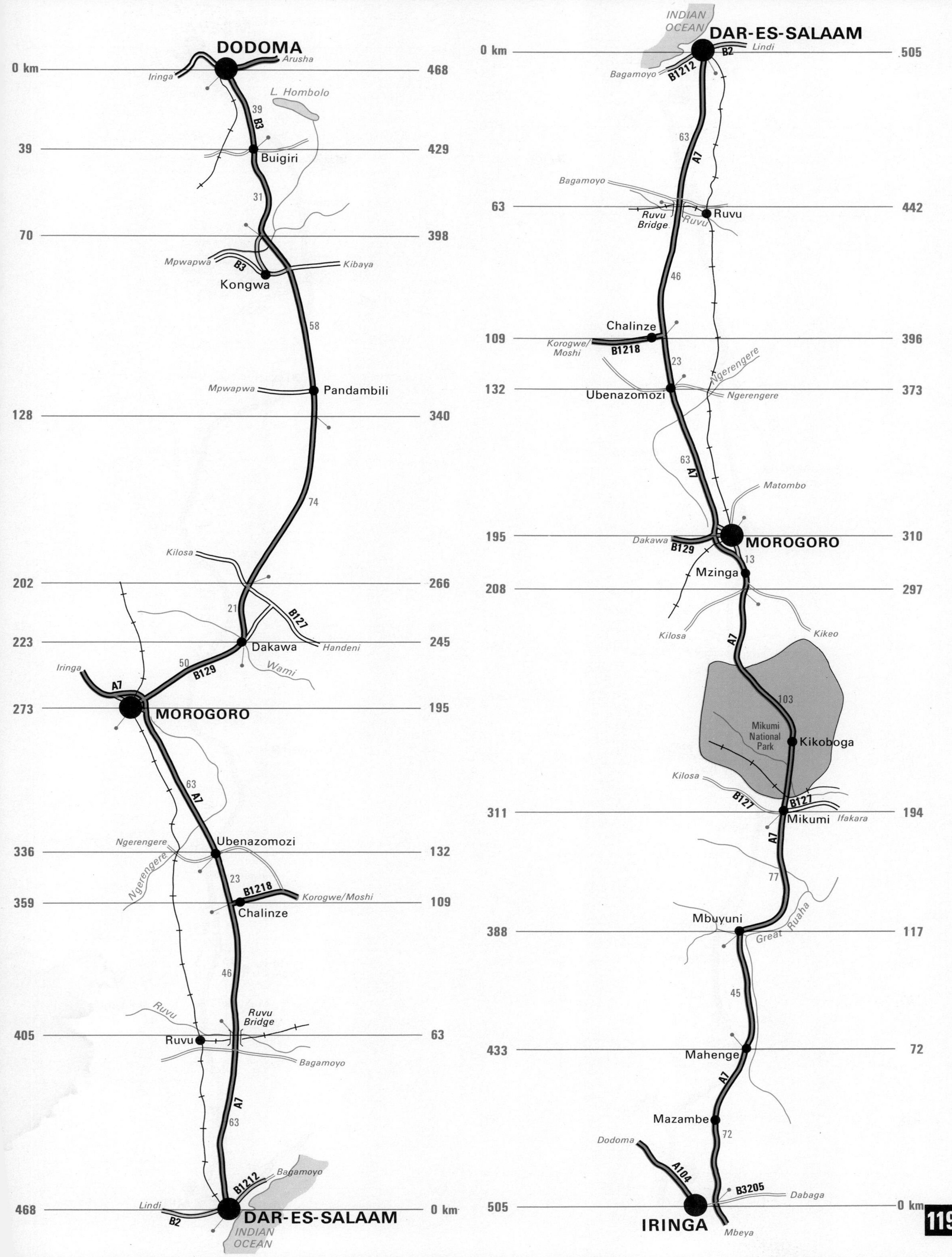

DODOMA

Arusha
Iringa
0 km   468

39 **B3**
39   429
Buigiri

31

70   398

L. Hombolo

Mpwapwa **B3** *Kibaya*
Kongwa

58

Mpwapwa Pandambili
128   340

74

Kilosa
202   266

21 **B127**
223   245
Dakawa *Handeni*
50 **B129** *Wami*

Iringa **A7**
273   195
MOROGORO

63 **A7**

Ngerengere Ubenazomozi
336   132
Ngerengere
23 **B1218**
359   109
Chalinze *Korogwe/Moshi*

46

Ruvu *Ruvu Bridge*
405   63
Ruvu
Bagamoyo
A7
63

B1212 *Bagamoyo*
468   0 km
Lindi **B2** **DAR-ES-SALAAM**
INDIAN OCEAN

INDIAN OCEAN
DAR-ES-SALAAM
0 km **B2** *Lindi*   505
Bagamoyo **B1212**

63 **A7**

Bagamoyo
63   442
Ruvu Bridge *Ruvu* Ruvu

46

Chalinze
109   396
Korogwe/Moshi **B1218**
23 *Ngerengere*
132   373
Ubenazomozi *Ngerengere*

63 **A7**

Matombo
Dakawa **B129**
195   310
MOROGORO
13
Mzinga
208   297
Kilosa **A7** *Kikeo*

103

Mikumi National Park Kikoboga
Kilosa **B127** **B127**
311   194
Mikumi *Ifakara*
A7

77
Great Ruaha
Mbuyuni
388   117

45

Mahenge
433   72

A7

Mazambe
72
Dodoma **A104** **B3205** *Dabaga*
505   0 km
IRINGA
Mbeya

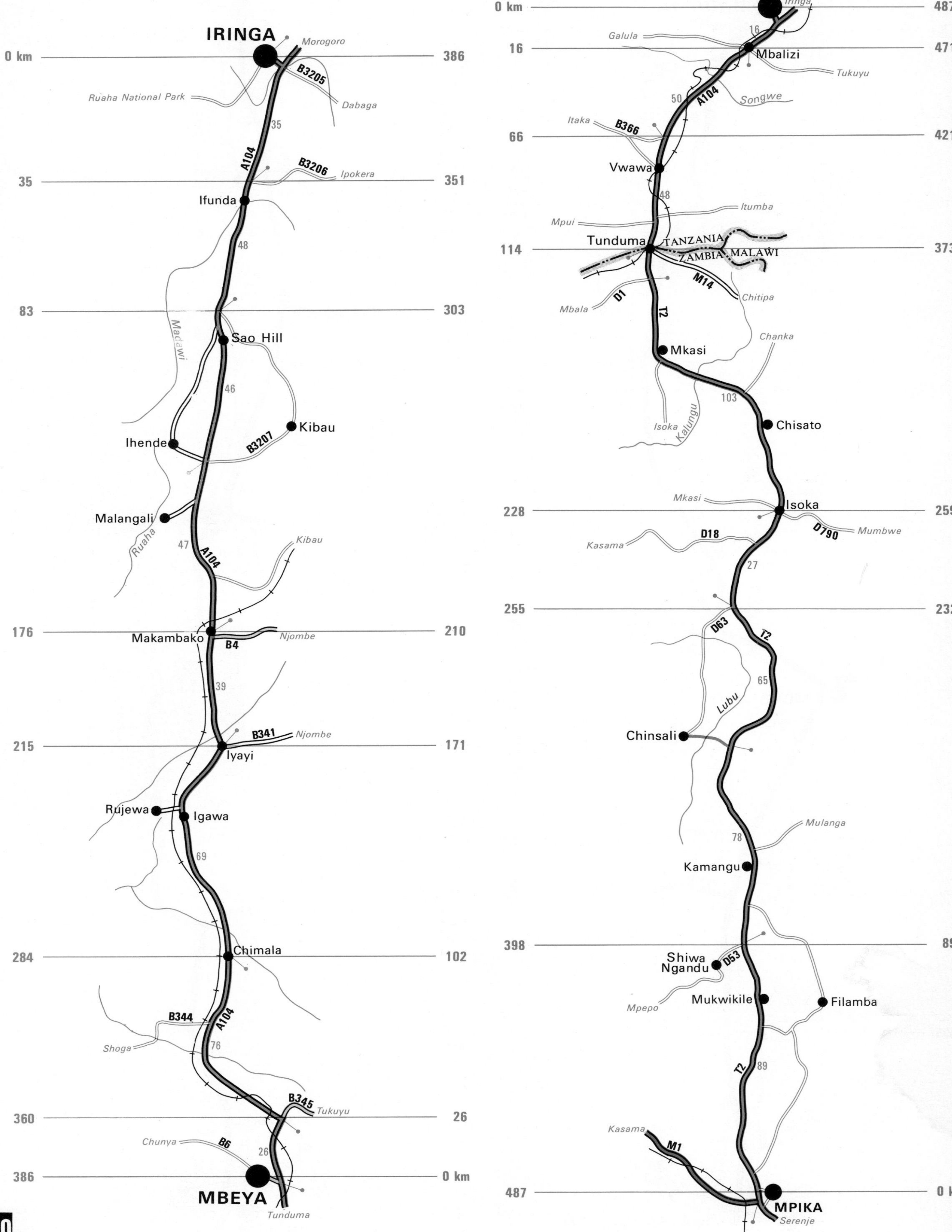

IRINGA

0 km | Morogoro | 386
B3205
Ruaha National Park | Dabaga
35
A104 | B3206 | Ipokera
35 | | 351
Ifunda
48
Macawi
83 | | 303
Sao Hill
46
Ihende | B3207 | Kibau
Malangali
Ruaha
47 | A104 | Kibau
176 | Njombe | 210
Makambako | B4
39
215 | B341 | Njombe | 171
Iyayi
Rujewa | Igawa
69
284 | Chimala | 102
B344 | A104
Shoga | 76
360 | B345 | Tukuyu | 26
Chunya | B6 | 26
386 | | 0 km

MBEYA
Tunduma

MBEYA

0 km | Iringa | 487
16 | Galula | Mbalizi | 471
| Tukuyu
50 | A104 | Songwe
66 | Itaka | B366 | 421
Vwawa
48
Mpui | Itumba
Tunduma | TANZANIA | 373
114 | ZAMBIA MALAWI
D1 | M14 | Chitipa
Mbala | T2 | Chanka
Mkasi
103
Isoka | Kalungu
Chisato
Mkasi
228 | D18 | D790 | Mumbwe | 259
Kasama
27
255 | D63 | T2 | 232
65
Chinsali | Lubu
78 | Mulanga
Kamangu
398 | | 89
Shiwa | D53
Ngandu
Mpepo | Mukwikile | Filamba
T2 | 89
Kasama
487 | M1 | 0 km
Serenje

MPIKA

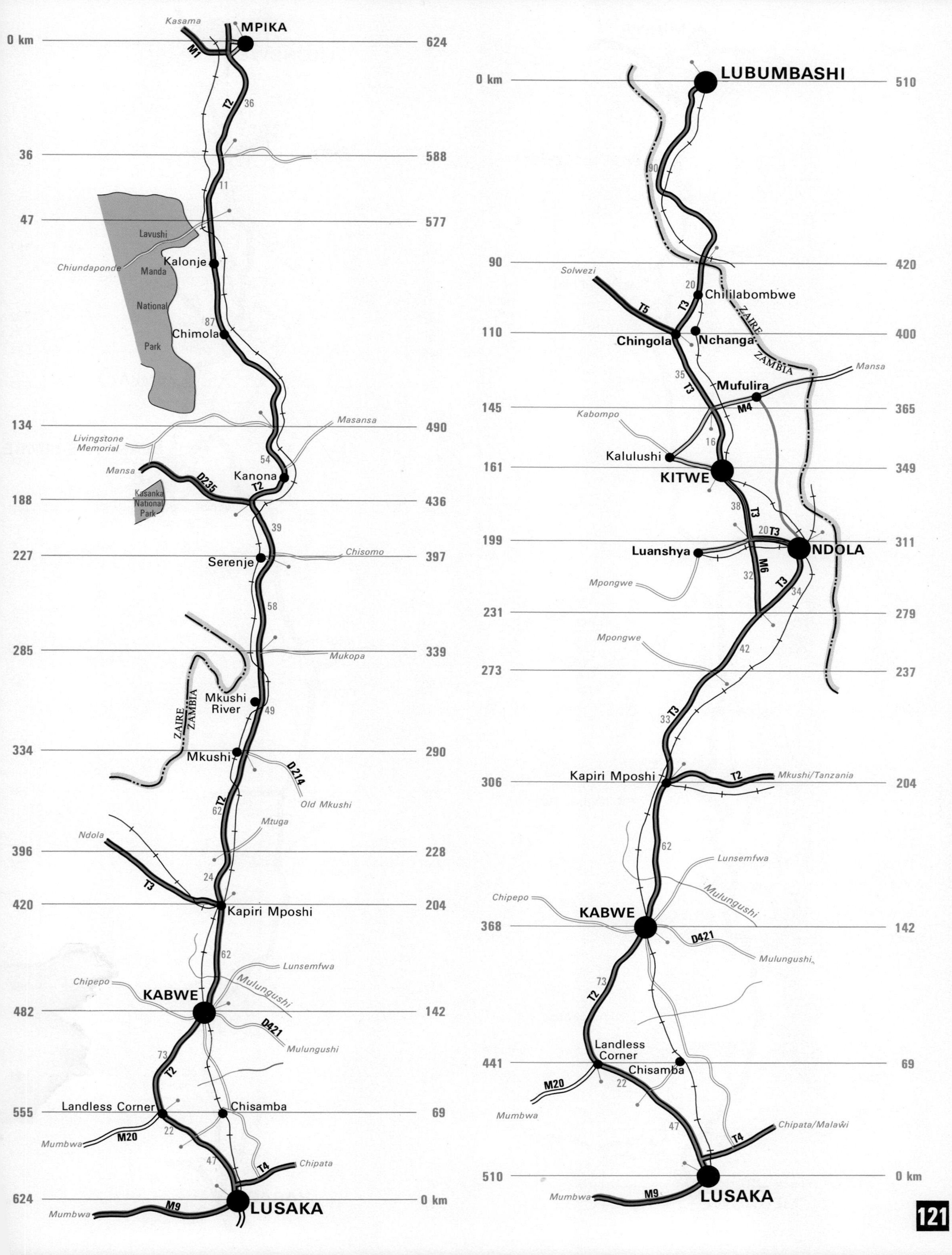
MPIKA
Kasama
M1
T2
Lavushi
Manda
National
Park
Chiundaponde
Kalonje
Chimola
Livingstone Memorial
Masansa
Mansa
D235
Kanona
Kasanka National Park
Serenje
Chisomo
Mukopa
ZAIRE
ZAMBIA
Mkushi River
Mkushi
D214
Old Mkushi
Mtuga
Ndola
T3
Kapiri Mposhi
Lunsemfwa
Chipepo
KABWE
Mulungushi
D421
Landless Corner
Chisamba
M20
Mumbwa
T4
Chipata
M9
LUSAKA
LUBUMBASHI
Solwezi
T5
Chililabombwe
Chingola
Nchanga
Mansa
Mufulira
M4
Kabompo
Kalulushi
KITWE
Luanshya
NDOLA
M6
Mpongwe
Mkushi/Tanzania
Chipata/Malawi

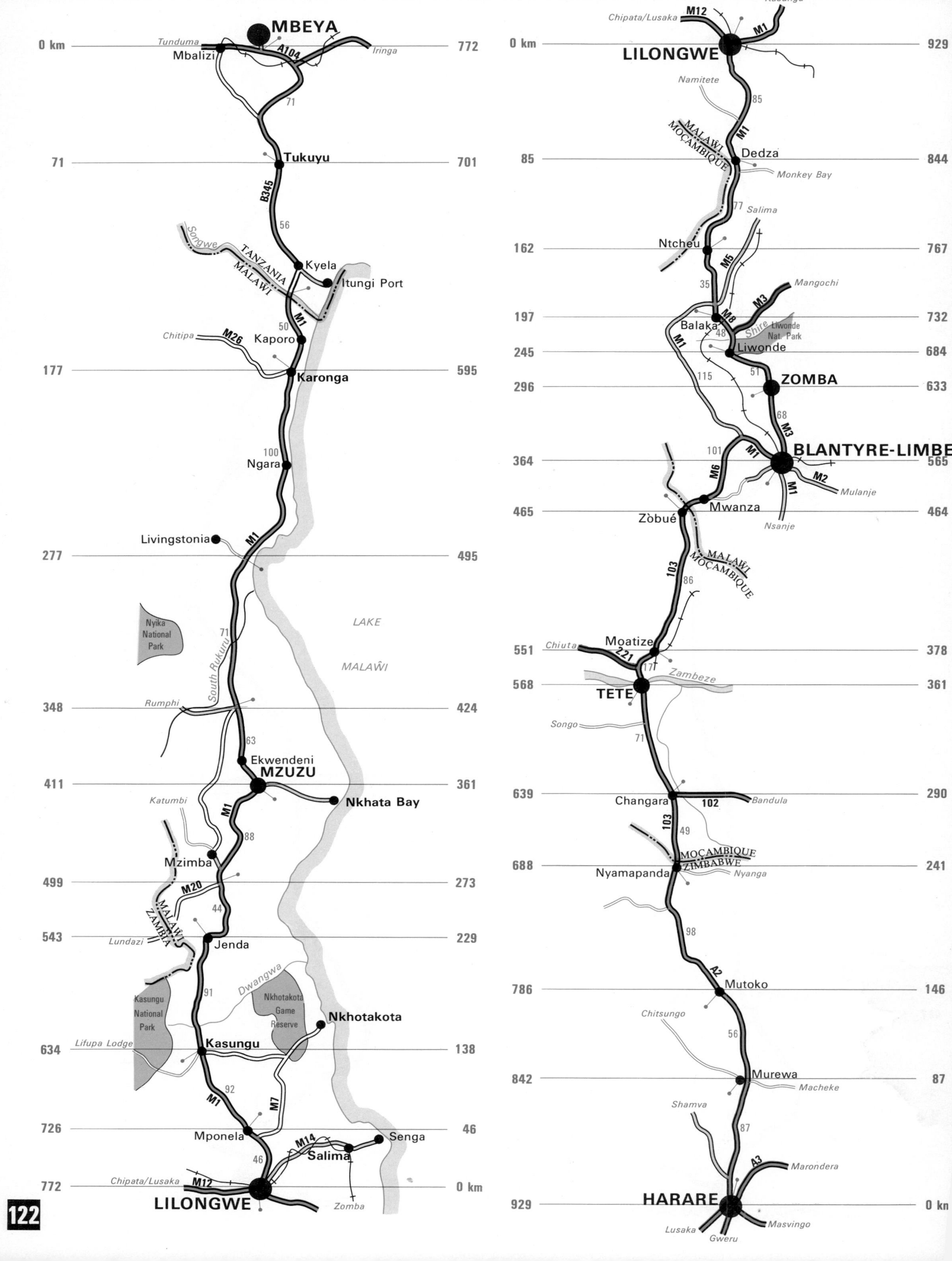

MBEYA

0 km	Tunduma · Mbalizi · *Iringa* · A104	772
71	**Tukuyu** · B345 · 71	701
	56	
	Songwe · TANZANIA · MALAWI · Kyela	
	Itungi Port · M1	
	50	
	Chitipa · M26 · Kaporo	
177	**Karonga**	595
	100	
	Ngara	
277	Livingstonia · M1	495
	Nyika National Park · 71 · *South Rukuru* · LAKE MALAWI	
348	*Rumphi*	424
	63	
411	Ekwendeni · **MZUZU**	361
	Katumbi · M1 · **Nkhata Bay**	
	88	
	Mzimba	
499	M20 · 44	273
543	*Lundazi* · MALAWI ZAMBIA · Jenda	229
	Dwangwa · 91 · Nkhotakota Game Reserve · **Nkhotakota**	
	Kasungu National Park · *Lifupa Lodge*	
634	**Kasungu**	138
	M1 · 92 · M7	
726	Mponela · M14 · Senga	46
	46 · **Salima** · *Zomba*	
772	*Chipata/Lusaka* · M12 · **LILONGWE**	0 km

LILONGWE

0 km	*Chipata/Lusaka* · M12 · M1 · *Kasungu*	929
	Namitete · 85 · M1	
85	MALAWI MOÇAMBIQUE · Dedza · *Monkey Bay*	844
	77 · *Salima*	
162	Ntcheu · M5	767
	35 · M3 · *Mangochi*	
197	M8 · Balaka · 48 · *Liwonde Nat. Park* · *Shire*	732
245	M1 · Liwonde · 51	684
296	115 · **ZOMBA**	633
	68 · M3	
	101 · M1 · **BLANTYRE-LIMBE**	
364	M6 · M2 · M1 · *Mulanje*	565
465	Zóbué · Mwanza · *Nsanje*	464
	103 · MALAWI MOÇAMBIQUE · 86	
551	*Chiuta* · Moatize · 221	378
568	17 · *Zambeze* · **TETE**	361
	Songo · 71	
639	Changara · 102 · *Bandula*	290
	103 · 49	
688	MOÇAMBIQUE ZIMBABWE · Nyamapanda · *Nyanga*	241
	98	
786	A2 · Mutoko	146
	Chitsungo · 56	
842	*Shamva* · Murewa · *Macheke*	87
	87 · A3 · *Marondera*	
929	**HARARE** · *Lusaka* · *Gweru* · *Masvingo*	0 km

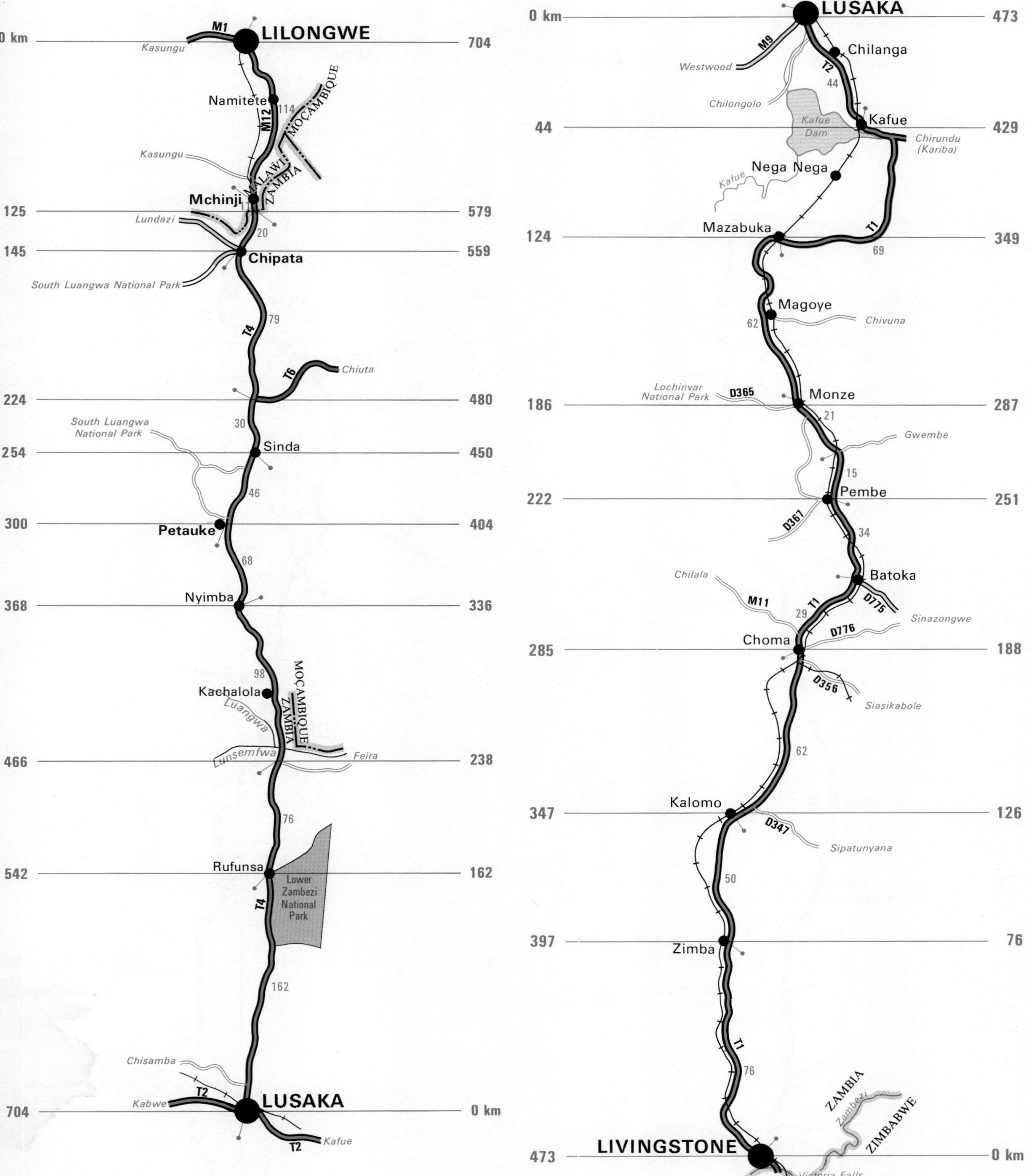

LILONGWE

0 km — LILONGWE — 704
M1
Kasungu

Namitete — 114
M12
MOÇAMBIQUE
Kasungu
MALAWI
ZAMBIA

125 — Mchinji — 579
Lundazi 20

145 — Chipata — 559
South Luangwa National Park
T4 79

224 — — 480
T6 *Chiuta*

South Luangwa National Park 30
254 — Sinda — 450
46

300 — Petauke — 404
68

368 — Nyimba — 336
98
MOÇAMBIQUE
ZAMBIA
Kachalola
Luangwa
Lunsemfwa *Feira*
466 — — 238
76

542 — Rufunsa — 162
T4 Lower Zambezi National Park
162

Chisamba
Kabwe T2
704 — LUSAKA — 0 km
T2 *Kafue*

LUSAKA

0 km — LUSAKA — 473
M9 Chilanga
Westwood T2
44
Chilongolo *Kafue Dam*
44 — Kafue — 429
Chirundu (Kariba)
Nega Nega
Kafue
124 — Mazabuka — 349
T1 69

62 Magoye
Chivuna

Lochinvar National Park D365
186 — Monze — 287
21
Gwembe
15
222 — Pembe — 251
D367
34

Chilala
M11 T1 Batoka
29 D775
Choma D776 *Sinazongwe*
285 — Choma — 188
D356
Siasikabole
62

347 — Kalomo — 126
D347 *Sipatunyana*
50

397 — Zimba — 76
T1
76

ZAMBIA
Zambezi
ZIMBABWE
473 — LIVINGSTONE — 0 km
Victoria Falls

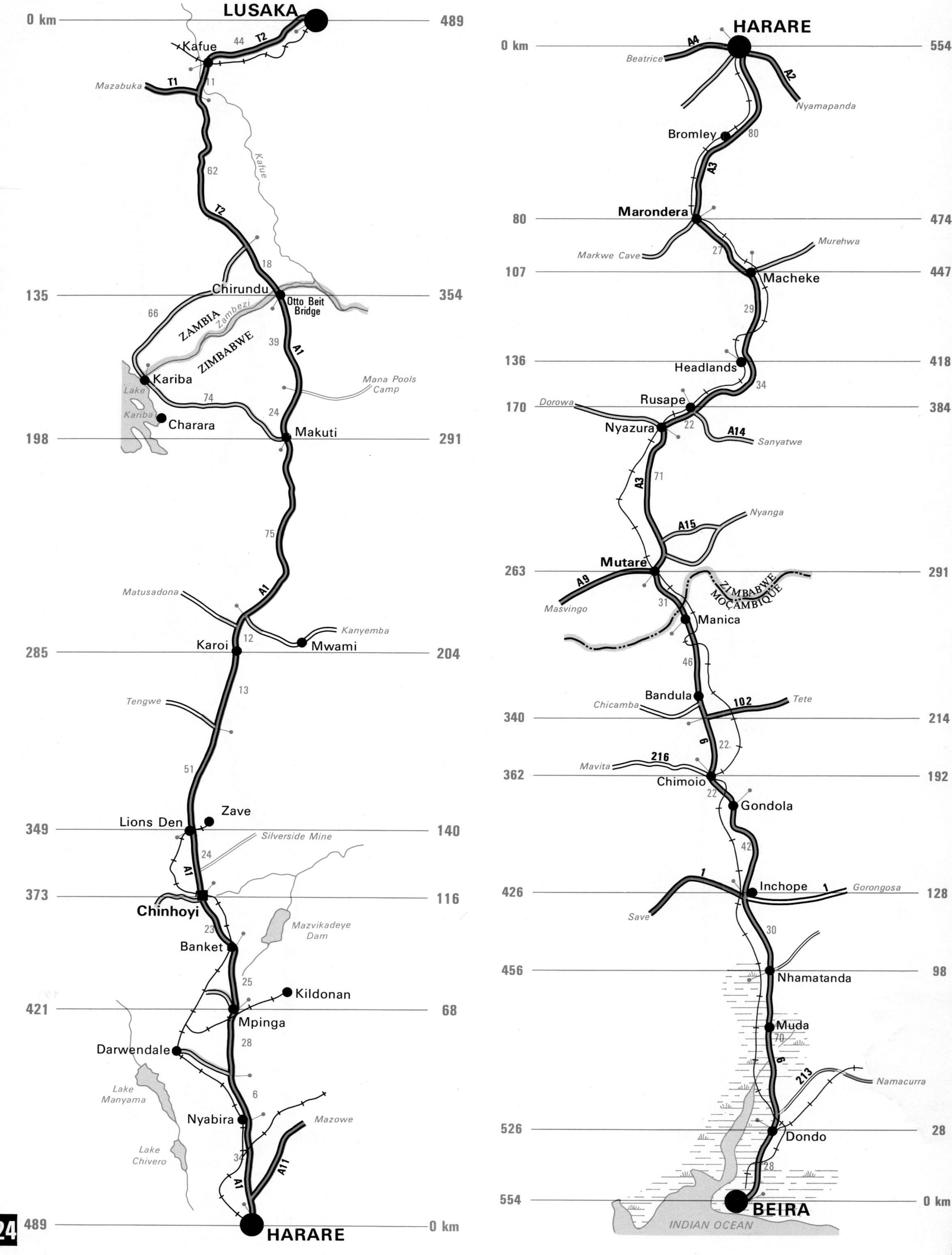

LUSAKA

0 km — 489

Kafue 44 T2
T1 11
Mazabuka

62 Kafue

T2

18

135 — Chirundu — 354
Otto Beit Bridge
66 Zambezi
ZAMBIA
39
ZIMBABWE A1

Kariba
74 Mana Pools Camp
24
198 — Charara — 291
Makuti
Lake Kariba

75

A1

Matusadona
12 Kanyemba
285 — Karoi — 204
Mwami

13

Tengwe

51

Lions Den Zave
349 — — 140
Silverside Mine
24

A1

373 — **Chinhoyi** — 116
23
Banket Mazvikadeye Dam

25
Kildonan
421 — Mpinga — 68
28
Darwendale

Lake Manyama 6

Nyabira Mazowe
34
Lake Chivero A1 A11

124 489 — **HARARE** — 0 km

HARARE

0 km — 554
A4
Beatrice A2
Nyamapanda

Bromley 80
A3

80 — **Marondera** — 474
Markwe Cave 27 Murehwa
107 — Macheke — 447
29
136 — Headlands — 418
34
170 — Rusape — 384
Dorowa 22
Nyazura A14
Sanyatwe
A3 71

A15 Nyanga
263 — **Mutare** — 291
A9
Masvingo 31 **ZIMBABWE**
MOÇAMBIQUE
Manica
46
Bandula **102** Tete
340 — — 214
Chicamba
9 22
216
362 — Chimoio — 192
Mavita 22
Gondola
42

1 Inchope **1** Gorongosa
426 — — 128
Save 30

456 — Nhamatanda — 98
Muda
70
9
213 Namacurra

526 — Dondo — 28
28

554 — **BEIRA** — 0 km
INDIAN OCEAN

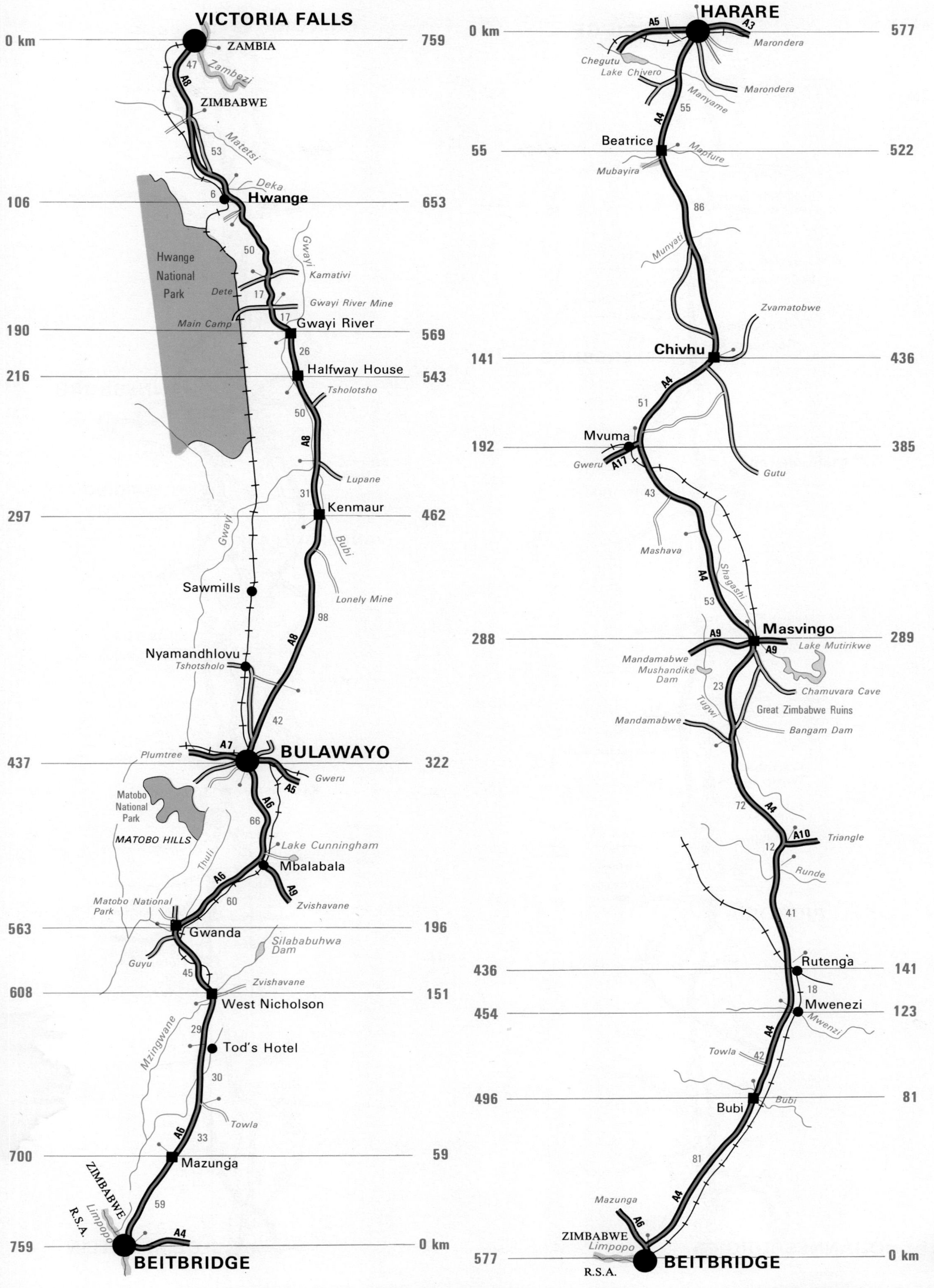

VICTORIA FALLS

0 km	ZAMBIA	759
	Zambezi	
	47 A8	
	ZIMBABWE	
	53	
	Matetsi	
	Deka	
106	6 **Hwange**	653
	Hwange National Park	
	50 *Gwayi*	
	Kamativi	
	Dete 17 *Gwayi River Mine*	
	Main Camp 17	
190	**Gwayi River**	569
	26	
216	**Halfway House**	543
	Tsholotsho	
	50	
	A8	
	Lupane	
	31	
297	**Kenmaur**	462
	Bubi	
	Gwayi *Lonely Mine*	
	Sawmills 98	
	A8	
	Nyamandhlovu	
	Tshotsholo	
	42	
437	*Plumtree* A7 **BULAWAYO**	322
	A6 A5 *Gweru*	
	Matobo National Park	
	MATOBO HILLS 66	
	Lake Cunningham	
	A6 **Mbalabala** A9	
	Thuli 60 *Zvishavane*	
	Matobo National Park	
563	**Gwanda** *Silababuhwa Dam*	196
	Guyu 45 *Zvishavane*	
608	**West Nicholson**	151
	Mzingwane 29	
	• **Tod's Hotel**	
	30	
	Towla	
	A6 33	
700	**Mazunga**	59
	ZIMBABWE 59	
	Limpopo R.S.A. A4	
759	**BEITBRIDGE**	0 km

HARARE

0 km	A5 A3	577
	Chegutu *Marondera*	
	Lake Chivero *Manyame*	
	Mubayira *Marondera*	
	A4 55	
55	**Beatrice** *Mapfure*	522
	86	
	Munyati	
	Zvamatobwe	
141	**Chivhu**	436
	A4	
	51	
	Mvuma *Gutu*	
192	*Gweru* A17	385
	43 *Shagashi*	
	Mashava A4	
	53	
288	A9 **Masvingo** *Lake Mutirikwe*	289
	Mandamabwe A9	
	Mushandike Dam	
	23 *Chamuvara Cave*	
	Tugwi **Great Zimbabwe Ruins**	
	Mandamabwe *Bangam Dam*	
	72 A4	
	A10 *Triangle*	
	12 *Runde*	
	41	
436	**Rutenga**	141
	18	
454	**Mwenezi**	123
	A4 *Mwenezi*	
	Towla 42	
496	**Bubi** *Bubi*	81
	81	
	Mazunga A4	
	ZIMBABWE A6	
	Limpopo	
577	R.S.A. **BEITBRIDGE**	0 km

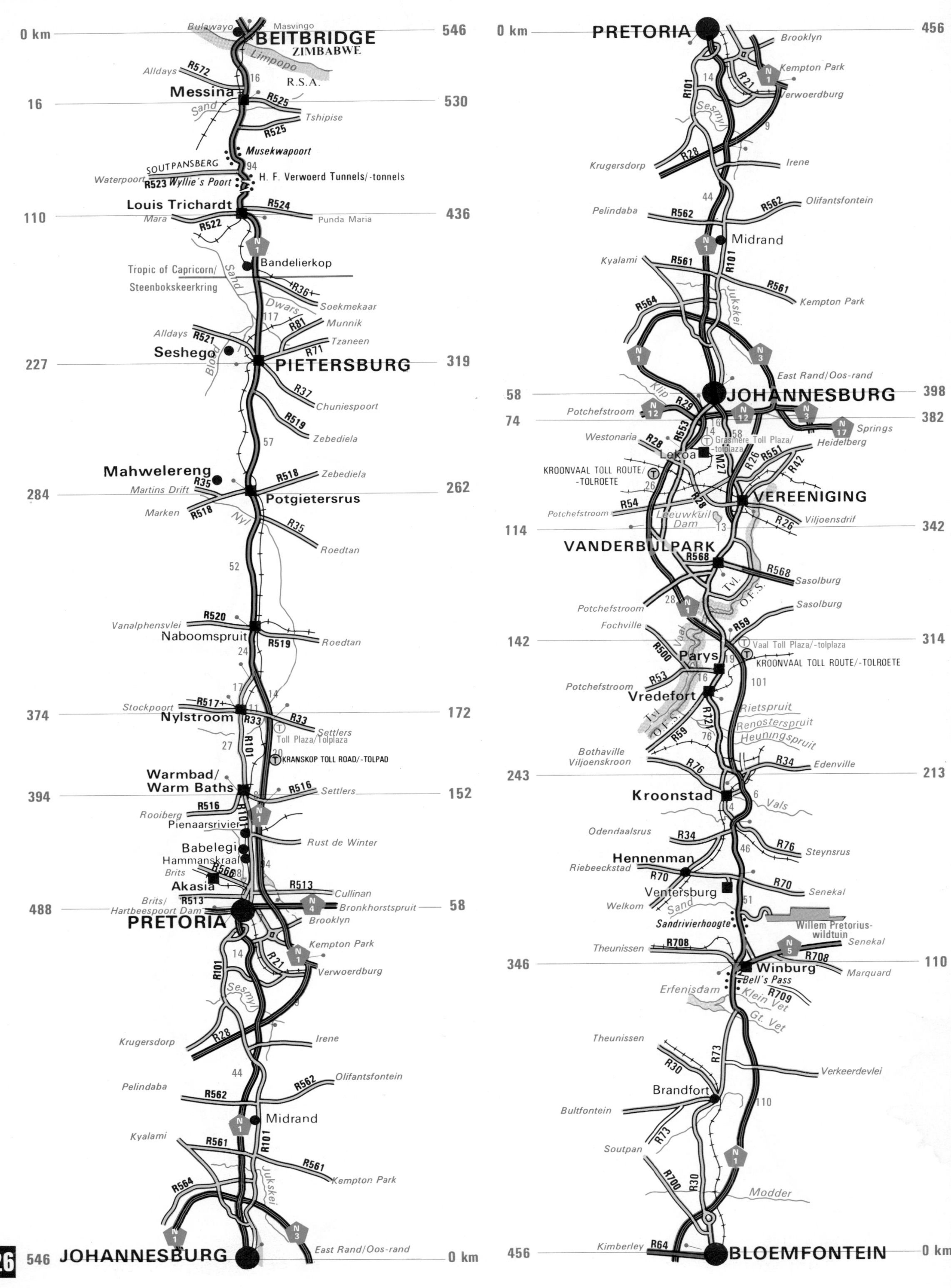

Left map (Beitbridge — Johannesburg):

0 km — Bulawayo, Masvingo — **BEITBRIDGE** / ZIMBABWE — 546
Limpopo, R.S.A.
Alldays R572 — 16
16 — Sand — **Messina** — R525 — 530
R525 — Tshipise
Musekwapoort
SOUTPANSBERG — 94
Waterpoort — R523 Wyllie's Poort — H. F. Verwoerd Tunnels/-tonnels
110 — **Louis Trichardt** — R524 — 436
Mara — R522 — Punda Maria
N1
Bandelierkop
Tropic of Capricorn/ Steenbokskeerkring — R36
Dwars — Soekmekaar
117 — R81 — Munnik
Alldays R521 — R71 — Tzaneen
227 — **Seshego** — **PIETERSBURG** — 319
Bloe — R37 — Chuniespoort
R519 — Zebediela
57
Mahwelereng — R518 — Zebediela
284 — Martins Drift R35 — R518 — **Potgietersrus** — 262
Marken — R518 — R35 — Roedtan
Nyl
52
R520
Vanalphensvlei — **Naboomspruit** — R519 — Roedtan
24
17 — 14
374 — Stockpoort R517 — 11 — R33 — 172
Nylstroom — R33 — T — Settlers
27 — R101 — Toll Plaza/Tolplaza
20 — T KRANSKOP TOLL ROAD/-TOLPAD
Warmbad/ Warm Baths — R516 — Settlers
394 — 9 — 152
Rooiberg — R516 — R101
Pienaarsrivier — N1
Babelegi — Rust de Winter
Hammanskraal
Brits — R566 — 34
Akasia — R513 — Cullinan
Brits/ — R513 — N4 — Bronkhorstspruit — 58
488 — Hartbeespoort Dam — Brooklyn
PRETORIA
Kempton Park
R101 — 14 — R21 — N1
Verwoerdburg
Sesmyl
Krugersdorp — R28 — Irene
44
Pelindaba — R562 — R562 — Olifantsfontein
Midrand — N1
Kyalami — R561 — R101 — R561 — Kempton Park
R564 — Jukskei

126 — 546 — **JOHANNESBURG** — East Rand/Oos-rand — 0 km — N1 — N3

Right map (Pretoria — Bloemfontein):

0 km — **PRETORIA** — Brooklyn — 456
14 — Kempton Park — N1
R101 — R21 — Verwoerdburg
Sesmyl — 9
Krugersdorp — R28
Irene
44
Pelindaba — R562 — R562 — Olifantsfontein
Midrand — N1
Kyalami — R561 — R101 — Kempton Park
R564 — R561
Jukskei
N1 — N3
East Rand/Oos-rand
58 — Klip — R29 — **JOHANNESBURG** — 398
74 — Potchefstroom — N12 — R553 — Grasmere Toll Plaza/ — N12 — N3 — 382
Westonaria — R28 — -tolplaza — 58 — N17 — Springs
16 — R26 — R551 — Heidelberg
Lekoa — M21 — R42
KROONVAAL TOLL ROUTE/ — T
-TOLROETE — 26 — R28 — **VEREENIGING**
R54 — Leeuwkuil Dam
Potchefstroom — Viljoensdrif
114 — **VANDERBIJLPARK** — R26 — 342
R568 — Tvl. — R568 — Sasolburg
O.F.S.
28 — N1 — Sasolburg
Potchefstroom — R59
Fochville — Vaal Toll Plaza/-tolplaza — T
142 — R500 — **Parys** — R53 — KROONVAAL TOLL ROUTE/-TOLROETE — 314
Potchefstroom — 16 — 101
Vredefort — R721
Tvl. — Rietspruit
O.F.S. — Renosterspruit
R59 — 76 — Heuningspruit
Bothaville — R76 — R34 — Edenville
Viljoenskroon
243 — R76 — 213
Kroonstad — Vals
4 — 6
Odendaalsrus — R34 — R76 — Steynsrus
46
Riebeeckstad — **Hennenman** — R70 — Senekal
Welkom — **Ventersburg** — R70
Sand — 51
Sandrivierhoogte — Willem Pretorius- wildtuin
Theunissen — R708 — N5 — Senekal
346 — **Winburg** — R708 — 110
Bell's Pass — Marquard
Erfenisdam — Klein Vet — R709
Gt. Vet
Theunissen — R30 — R73 — Verkeerdevlei
Brandfort
Bultfontein — 110
R73
Soutpan — N1
R100 — R30 — Modder
456 — Kimberley — R64 — **BLOEMFONTEIN** — 0 km

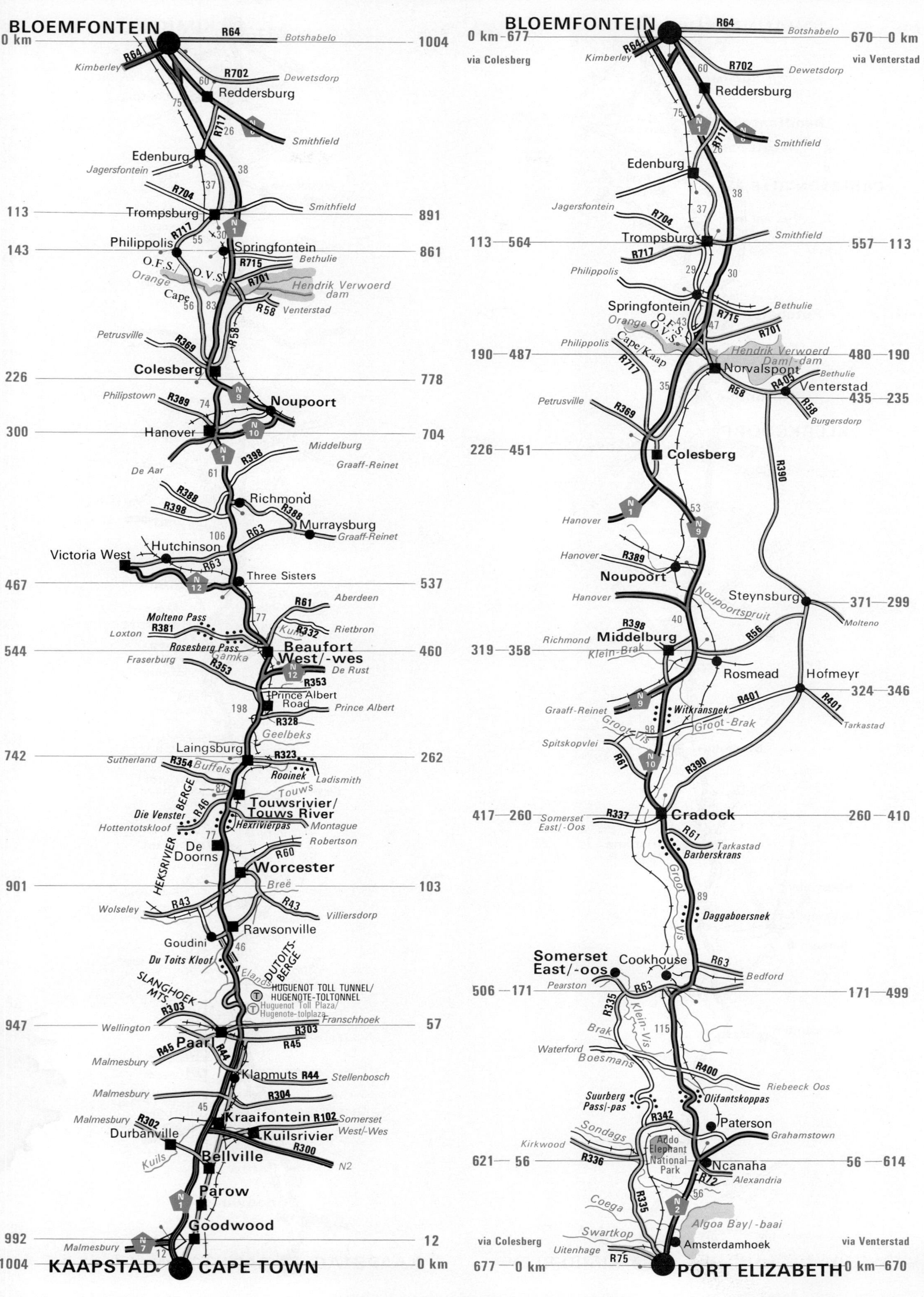

BLOEMFONTEIN

0 km — R64 — Botshabelo — 1004

R64 Kimberley

60 R702 Dewetsdorp

Reddersburg

75

R717 26 N1

Smithfield

Edenburg

38

Jagersfontein R704

37 Smithfield

113 — Trompsburg — 891

R717 X 30

55 Springfontein

143 — Philippolis — 861

O.F.S./ O.V.S R715 Bethulie

Orange R701

Cape 56 83 Hendrik Verwoerd dam

R58 Venterstad

Petrusville R369

Colesberg

226 — — 778

Philipstown R389 74 N9

Noupoort

300 — Hanover — 704

N10

N1

De Aar 61 R398 Middelburg

Graaff-Reinet

R388 Richmond

R398 R388

R63 Murraysburg

106 Graaff-Reinet

Hutchinson

Victoria West R63

467 — N12 Three Sisters — 537

R61 Aberdeen

Molteno Pass 77 R332 Rietbron

Loxton R381 Kuru

Roseberg Pass Gamka

544 — Fraserburg R353 Beaufort West/-wes — 460

N12 De Rust

R353

Prince Albert Road Prince Albert

198 R328

R328 Geelbeks

Laingsburg R323

742 — Sutherland R354 Buffels — 262

Rooinek Ladismith

82 Touws

Die Venster R46 Touwsrivier/ Touws River

Hottentotskloof 77 Hexrivierpas Montague

De Doorns Robertson

R60

Worcester

901 — Breë — 103

Wolseley R43 R43 Villiersdorp

Rawsonville

Goudini 46

Du Toits Kloof DUTOITS-BERGE

Eland HUGUENOT TOLL TUNNEL/ HUGENOTE-TOLTONNEL

SLANGHOEK MTS T Huguenot Toll Plaza/ Hugenote-tolplaza

R303 Franschhoek

947 — Wellington R303 — 57

R45 Paarl R45

R44

Malmesbury Klapmuts R44 Stellenbosch

Malmesbury R304

45

Malmesbury R302 Kraaifontein R102 Somerset West/-Wes

Durbanville Kuilsrivier

Kuils R300

Bellville N2

N1 Parow

Goodwood

992 — Malmesbury N7 — 12

12

1004 — KAAPSTAD CAPE TOWN — 0 km

BLOEMFONTEIN

0 km—677 R64 Botshabelo 670—0 km

via Colesberg R64 Kimberley via Venterstad

60 R702 Dewetsdorp

Reddersburg

75

R717 26 N1

Smithfield

Edenburg

38

Jagersfontein R704

37 Smithfield

113—564 Trompsburg 557—113

R717

Philippolis 29 30

Springfontein R715 Bethulie

O.F.S./ 43 47

Orange O.V.S R701

Philippolis Cape/Kaap Hendrik Verwoerd Dam/-dam

190—487 Norvalspont 480—190

R58 Bethulie

R405 Venterstad

Petrusville R369 35 R58 Burgersdorp

435—235

226—451 Colesberg R390

N1 53

Hanover N9

Hanover R389

Noupoort Steynsburg

371—299

Hanover Noupoortspruit Molteno

R398 40 R56

319—358 Richmond Middelburg

Klein-Brak Rosmead Hofmeyr

N9 R401 324—346

Graaff-Reinet Witkransnek R401 Tarkastad

Groot-Vis 98 Groot-Brak

Spitskopvlei N10

R61 R390

417—260 Somerset R337 Cradock 260—410

East/-Oos R61 Tarkastad

Barberskrans

Groot-Vis

89

Daggaboersnek

Somerset Cookhouse R63

East/-oos Bedford

506—171 Pearston R63 171—499

R335 Klein-Vis

Brak 115

Waterford R400

Boesmans Riebeeck Oos

Suurberg R342 Olifantskoppas

Pass/-pas Paterson

Kirkwood Sondags Grahamstown

R336 Addo Ncanaha

621—56 Elephant R72 Alexandria 56—614

National

Park 56

Coega N2

R335 Algoa Bay/-baai

via Colesberg Swartkop via Venterstad

Uitenhage R75 Amsterdamhoek

677—0 km PORT ELIZABETH 0 km—670

127

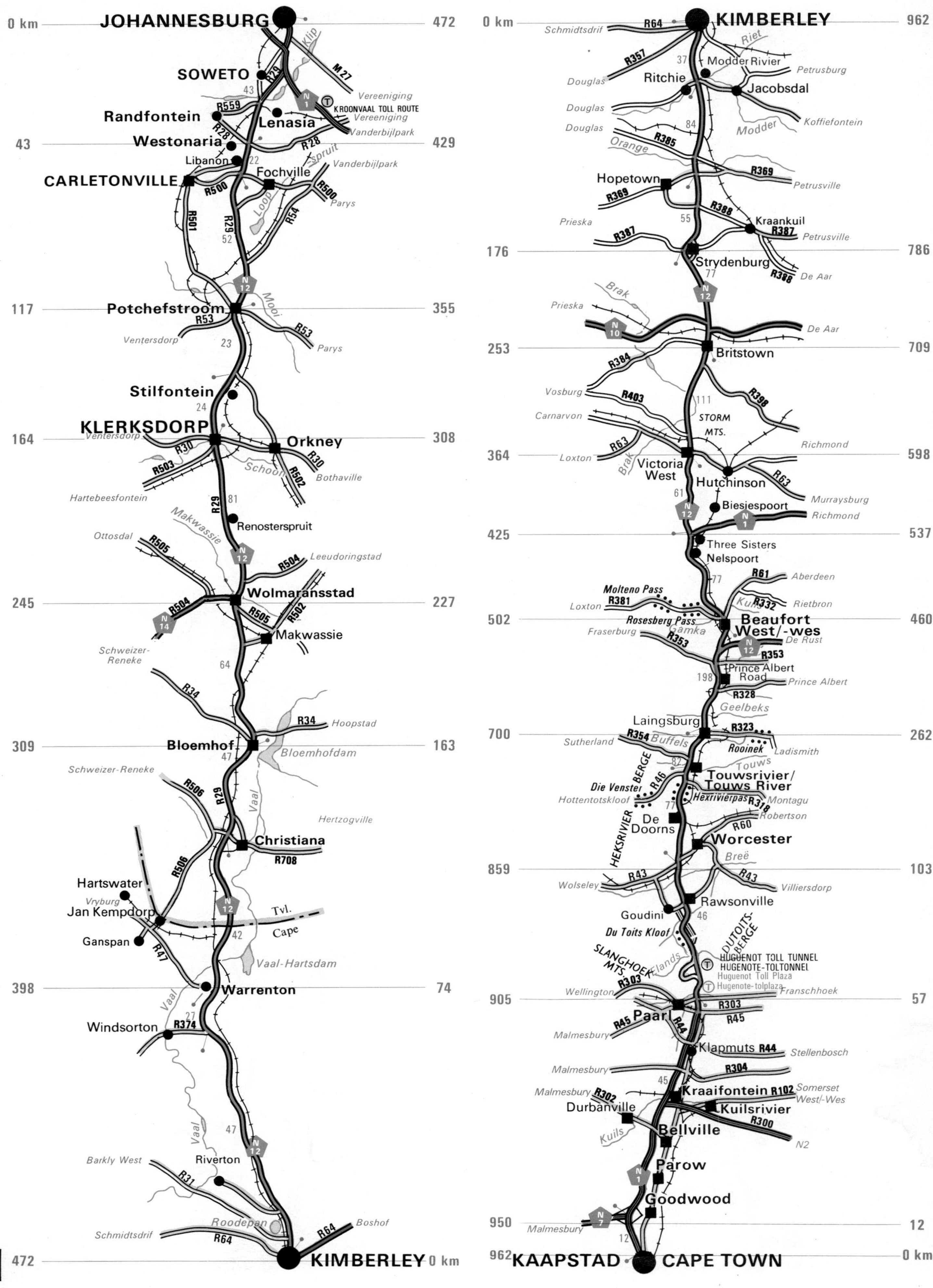

JOHANNESBURG 0 km | 472
SOWETO
M 27
R29 43
N1
Kroonvaal Toll Route
Vereeniging
R559 Vereeniging
Randfontein R28 Lenasia Vanderbijlpark
Westonaria 43 | 429
Libanon 22 Spruit Vanderbijlpark
CARLETONVILLE Fochville
R500 Parys R500
R501 R29 52 R54
N12
Potchefstroom 117 | 355
R53 R53
Ventersdorp 23 Parys
Stilfontein
24
KLERKSDORP 164 | 308
Ventersdorp R30 Orkney R30
R503 Schoon R502 Bothaville
Hartebeesfontein R29 81
Makwassie
Ottosdal R505 Renosterspruit
N12 R504 Leeudoringstad
Wolmaransstad 245 | 227
R504 R505 R502
N14 Makwassie
Schweizer-Reneke 64
R34
R34 Hoopstad
Bloemhof 309 | 163
47 Bloemhofdam
Schweizer-Reneke
R506 R29 Vaal Hertzogville
Christiana
R506 R708
Hartswater
Vryburg N12 Tvl.
Jan Kempdorp Cape
Ganspan R47 42
Vaal-Hartsdam
Warrenton 398 | 74
27
Windsorton R374
Vaal
47
N12
Barkly West Riverton
R31
Roodepan Boshof
Schmidtsdrif R64 R64
472 KIMBERLEY 0 km

KIMBERLEY 0 km | 962
Schmidtsdrif R64 Riet
R357 37 Modder Rivier Petrusburg
Ritchie Jacobsdal
Douglas Koffiefontein
Douglas Modder
Douglas Orange R385 84
R369
Hopetown R369 Petrusville
R388 Kraankuil
Prieska R387 55 R387 Petrusville
176 Strydenburg 786
De Aar R398
N12
Prieska Brak
N10 De Aar
253 | 709
R384 Britstown
Vosburg R403 111 R398
Carnarvon STORM MTS. Richmond
R63 364 | 598
Loxton Brak Victoria West Hutchinson R63 Richmond
61
N12 Biesiespoort Murraysburg
N1 Richmond
425 | 537
Three Sisters
Nelspoort
77 R61 Aberdeen
Molteno Pass R332 Rietbron
Loxton R381 Kuils
Rosesberg Pass Gamka
502 Beaufort West/-wes 460
Fraserburg R353 De Rust
N12
R353
Prince Albert Road Prince Albert
198 R328
Geelbeks
Laingsburg
700 R354 Buffels R323 262
Sutherland Rooinek Ladismith
82 Touws
Touwsrivier/Touws River
Die Venster R46 Hexrivierpas R318 Montagu
Hottentotskloof 77 Robertson
De Doorns R60
Worcester
859 | 103
Bree
Wolseley R43 R43 Villiersdorp
Rawsonville
Goudini 46
Du Toits Kloof DUTOITS-BERGE
SLANGHOEK MTS. HUGUENOT TOLL TUNNEL
Wellington HUGENOTE-TOLTONNEL
R303 Huguenot Toll Plaza
905 Huguenote-tolplaza Franschhoek 57
R45 Paarl R303
Malmesbury R45
Klapmuts R44 Stellenbosch
Malmesbury R304
45
Malmesbury R302 Kraaifontein R102 Somerset West/-Wes
Durbanville Kuilsrivier
Bellville R300
Kuils N2
N1 Parow
Goodwood
950 | 12
Malmesbury N7
962 KAAPSTAD CAPE TOWN 0 km

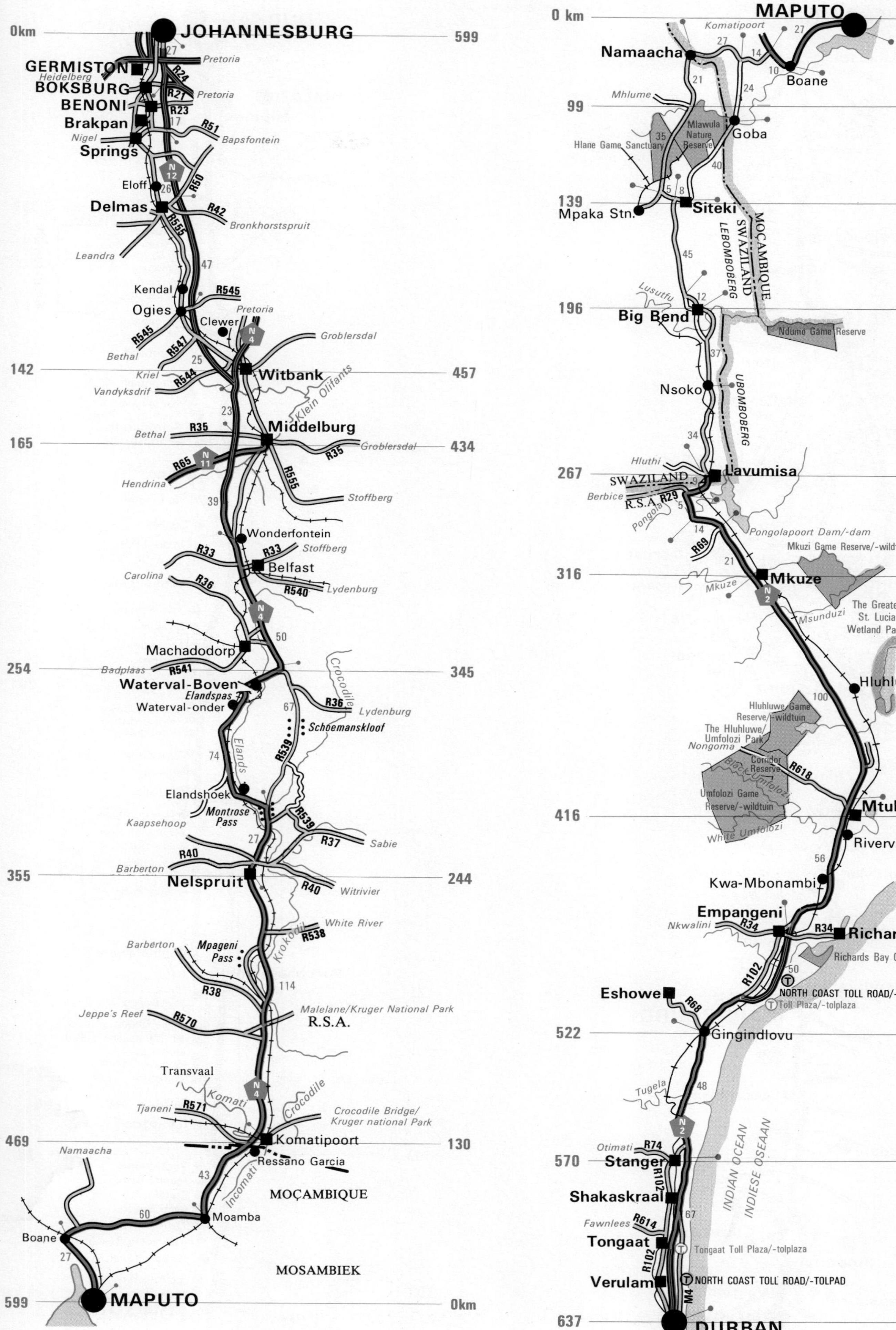
JOHANNESBURG
GERMISTON
BOKSBURG
BENONI
Brakpan
Springs
Delmas
Witbank
Middelburg
Wonderfontein
Belfast
Machadodorp
Waterval-Boven
Waterval-onder
Elandshoek
Nelspruit
Komatipoort
Ressano Garcia
Moamba
Boane
MAPUTO
R.S.A.
MOÇAMBIQUE
MOSAMBIEK
Namaacha
Goba
Siteki
Mpaka Stn.
Big Bend
Nsoko
Lavumisa
SWAZILAND
Mkuze
Hluhluwe
Mtubatuba
Riverview
Kwa-Mbonambi
Empangeni
Richards Bay/-baai
Eshowe
Gingindlovu
Stanger
Shakaskraal
Tongaat
Verulam
DURBAN
INDIAN OCEAN
INDIESE OSEAAN
NORTH COAST TOLL ROAD/-TOLPAD
Tongaat Toll Plaza/-tolplaza

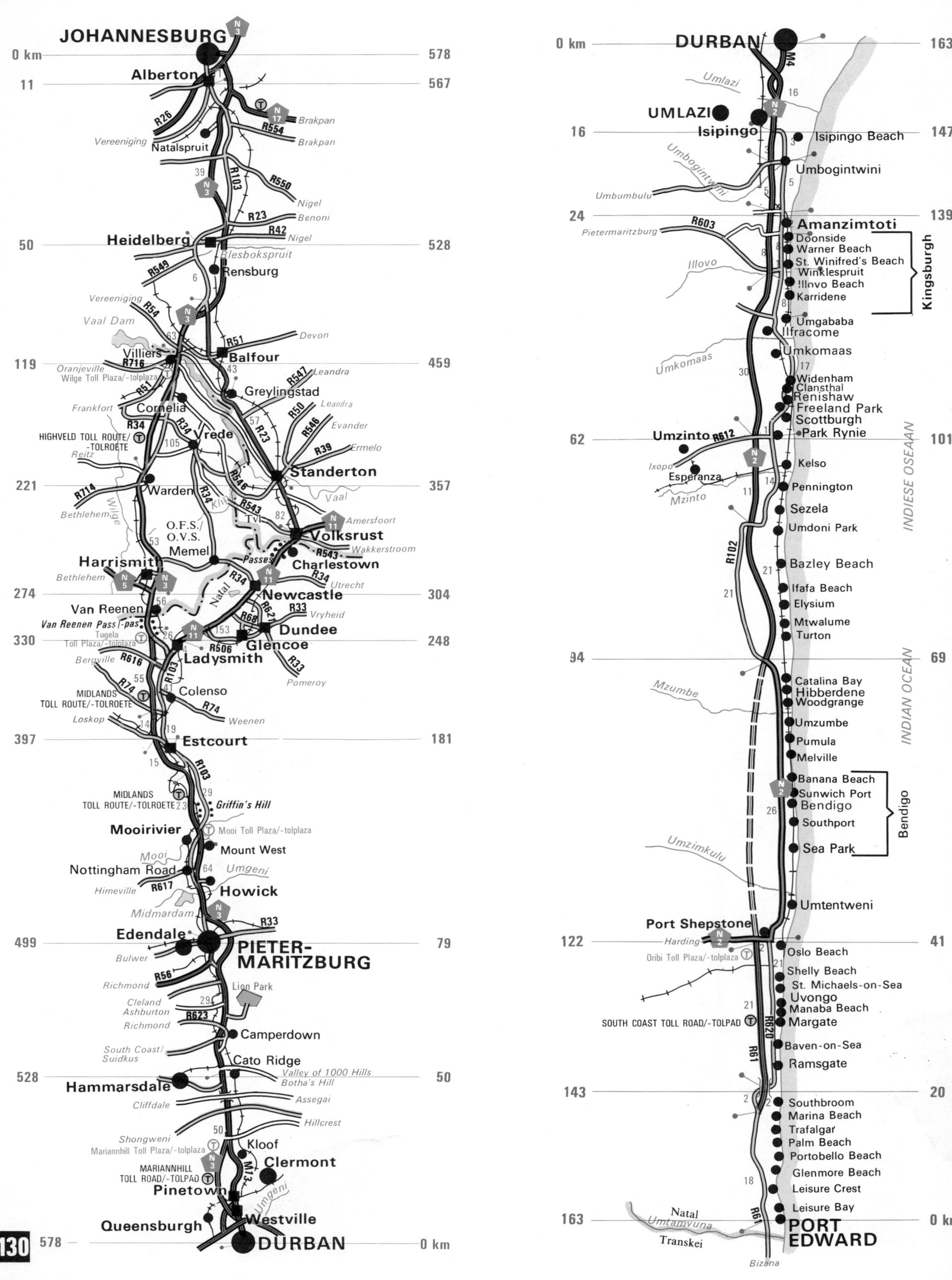

JOHANNESBURG

0 km   578

Alberton

11   567

R26   R17   *Brakpan*
R554   *Brakpan*

Vereeniging   Natalspruit

39   R103   R550

R23   *Nigel*

R42   *Nigel*

Heidelberg

50   528

R549   *Blesbokspruit*

Rensburg

6

Vereeniging   R54

Vaal Dam   R716

R51   *Devon*

Villiers   **Balfour**

119   459

Oranjeville
Wilge Toll Plaza/-tolplaza   43

R547   *Leandra*

Greylingstad

Frankfort   Cornelia

57   R23   R50   *Leandra*

R34   R34   R546   *Evander*

HIGHVELD TOLL ROUTE/-TOLROETE   Vrede   *Ermelo*

105   R39

Reitz   **Standerton**

221   357

R714   Warden   R34   R46   *Vaal*

Bethlehem   *Wilge*

Klip   82   R543   *Amersfoort*

O.F.S./   *Tvl*   **Volksrust**

O.V.S.   R543   *Wakkerstroom*

Memel   **Charlestown**

Harrismith   *Passes*   R34   *Utrecht*

Bethlehem   N5   N3   *Natal*   R34

274   304

56   **Newcastle**

Van Reenen   R62   R33   *Vryheid*

Van Reenen Pass/-pas   R68

Tugela   153   **Dundee**

330   *Toll Plaza/-tolplaza*   26   R506   **Glencoe**   248

Bergville   R616   R103   **Ladysmith**   R33

55   R74   Colenso   *Pomeroy*

MIDLANDS   41
TOLL ROUTE/-TOLROETE   R74

Loskop   14   *Weenen*

19

397   **Estcourt**   181

15   R103

MIDLANDS   29
TOLL ROUTE/-TOLROETE   23   *Griffin's Hill*

Mooirivier

Mooi Toll Plaza/-tolplaza

Mooi   **Mount West**

Nottingham Road   64   *Umgeni*

Himeville   R617

Midmardam   **Howick**

N3   R33

Edendale

499   **PIETER-**   79
Bulwer   **MARITZBURG**

R56   *Lion Park*

Richmond   29

Cleland
Ashburton   R623

Richmond   **Camperdown**

South Coast/
Suidkus   **Cato Ridge**

528   *Valley of 1000 Hills*   50
  Botha's Hill

Hammarsdale

Cliffdale   *Assegai*

Hillcrest

50

Shongweni   **Kloof**
Mariannhill Toll Plaza/-tolplaza

MARIANNHILL   N3   **Clermont**
TOLL ROAD/-TOLPAD   M13

Pinetown

Umgeni

130   578   **Queensburgh**   **Westville**

      DURBAN   0 km

DURBAN

0 km   163

Umlazi   16

UMLAZI

Isipingo   N2

16   3   Isipingo Beach   147

Umbogintwini   Umbogintwini

Umbumbulu   5

24   R603   **Amanzimtoti**   139

Pietermaritzburg   8   Doonside

Illovo   Warner Beach

St. Winifred's Beach

Winklespruit   *Kingsburgh*

Illovo Beach

8   Karridene

Umgababa
Ilfracome

Umkomaas

Umkomaas   30   17

Widenham
Clansthal
Renishaw

Freeland Park
Scottburgh
Park Rynie

62   **Umzinto**   R612   101

Ixopo   N2   Kelso

Esperanza   14

Mzinto   11   Pennington

Sezela

Umdoni Park

R102   21   Bazley Beach

21   Ifafa Beach

Elysium

Mtwalume
Turton

94   69

Mzumbe   Catalina Bay
Hibberdene
Woodgrange

Umzumbe

Pumula
Melville

Banana Beach

N2   Sunwich Port

Bendigo   *Bendigo*

26   Southport

Sea Park

Umtentweni

Port Shepstone

122   *Harding*   N2   41

Oribi Toll Plaza/-tolplaza   Oslo Beach

21   Shelly Beach

St. Michaels-on-Sea

Uvongo

Manaba Beach

21   Margate

SOUTH COAST TOLL ROAD/-TOLPAD   R620

Baven-on-Sea

R61   Ramsgate

143   2   20

Southbroom
Marina Beach
Trafalgar
Palm Beach
Portobello Beach
Glenmore Beach

18   Leisure Crest

Leisure Bay

163   *Natal*   R61   0 km

Umtamvuna   **PORT**
Transkei   **EDWARD**
Bizana

INDIESE OSEAAN

INDIAN OCEAN

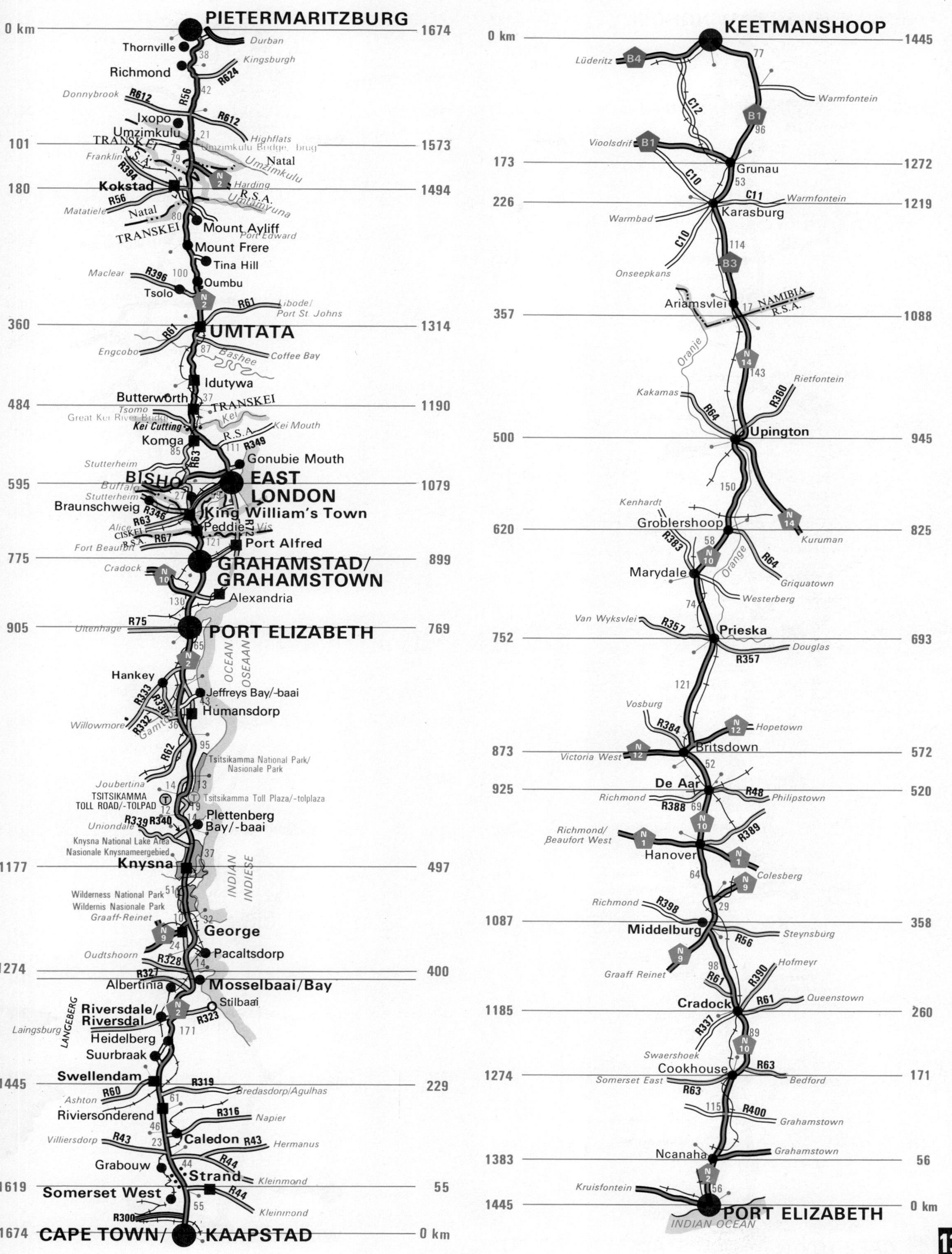

PIETERMARITZBURG 0 km   1674

Thornville   *Durban*

Richmond   *Kingsburgh*

38

R624

Donnybrook R612 R56

R612

Ixopo

Umzimkulu   *Highflats*

101   1573

TRANSKEI   *Umzimkulu Bridge, brug* 21

Franklin   **R.S.A.** 79   *Natal*

R394   *Umzimkulu*

180   **Kokstad**   *Harding* **N2**   1494

R56   **R.S.A.**

Matatiele   *Natal*   *Umtamvuna*

TRANSKEI 80

Mount Ayliff

Port Edward

Mount Frere

Tina Hill

Maclear R396 100   Qumbu

Tsolo   **N2**

R61   *Libode/*

360   R61   *Port St. Johns*   1314

R61   **UMTATA**

Engcobo 81   *Bashee*   *Coffee Bay*

Idutywa

484   Butterworth 37   **TRANSKEI**   1190

Tsomo   *Kei*

Great Kei River Bridge

Kei Cutting   *Kei Mouth*

Komga 85   **R.S.A.**

R63 111 R349

Stutterheim   Gonubie Mouth

595   **BISHO**   **EAST**   1079

Buffalo   **LONDON**

Stutterheim 27

Braunschweig   **King William's Town**

R346

Alice R63   Peddie   *Vis*

CISKEI R72

R67 121

Fort Beaufort **R.S.A.**   Port Alfred

775   899

Cradock **N10**   **GRAHAMSTAD/**

    GRAHAMSTOWN

130   Alexandria

905   R75   **PORT ELIZABETH**   769

Uitenhage 65   **N2**

Hankey

R333 R370   Jeffreys Bay/-baai

43   Humansdorp

Willowmore R332 36

R62   *Gam* 95

Tsitsikamma National Park/

    Nasionale Park

Joubertina 14 3

TSITSIKAMMA   T   Tsitsikamma Toll Plaza/-tolplaza

TOLL ROAD/-TOLPAD 12 9

R339 R340   Plettenberg

Uniondale   Bay/-baai

Knysna National Lake Area

Nasionale Knysnameergebied 37

1177   **Knysna**   497

Wilderness National Park 51

Wildernis Nasionale Park

Graaff-Reinet 10 32

N9   George

24

Oudtshoorn R328   Pacaltsdorp

1274   R327 14   400

Albertinia   **Mosselbaai/Bay**

N2   *Stilbaai*

Riversdale/ R323

Riversdal

Laingsburg 171

Heidelberg

Suurbraak

1445   **Swellendam** R319   *Bredasdorp/Agulhas*   229

Ashton R60 61

Riviersonderend R316   *Napier*

46

Villiersdorp R43   Caledon R43   *Hermanus*

23

Grabouw 44   **Strand**   *Kleinmond*

R44

1619   **Somerset West** R44   55

55   *Kleinmond*

R300

1674   **CAPE TOWN/**   **KAAPSTAD**   0 km

KEETMANSHOOP 0 km   1445

Lüderitz B4 77

Warmfontein

C12 B1 96

173   *Vioolsdrif* B1   Grunau   1272

C10 53

226   C11   *Warmfontein*   1219

Warmbad   Karasburg

C10 114

Onseepkans B3

357   Ariamsvlei 17   **NAMIBIA**   1088

    R.S.A.

Oranje **N14**

Kakamas 143   *Rietfontein*

R64 R360

500   Upington   945

150   **N14**

Kenhardt

620   Groblershoop   *Kuruman*   825

R383 58   *Orange*

N10 R64

Marydale   *Griquatown*

74   *Westerberg*

Van Wyksvlei R357

752   Prieska   693

R357   *Douglas*

121

Vosburg

R384   **N12**   *Hopetown*

873   **N12**   *Victoria West*   Britsdown   572

52

925   **De Aar** R48   *Philipstown*   520

Richmond R388 69

N10 R389

Richmond/

Beaufort West **N1**

Hanover **N1**

64   *Colesberg*

N9

Richmond R398 29

1087   Middelburg R56   *Steynsburg*   358

N9   98   *Hofmeyr*

Graaff Reinet R61 R390

Cradock R61   *Queenstown*

1185   260

R337 89

N10

Swaershoek

Cookhouse R63   *Bedford*

1274   *Somerset East* R63   171

115 R400   *Grahamstown*

Ncanaha   *Grahamstown*

1383   56

N2 56

Kruisfontein

1445   **PORT ELIZABETH**   0 km

INDIAN OCEAN

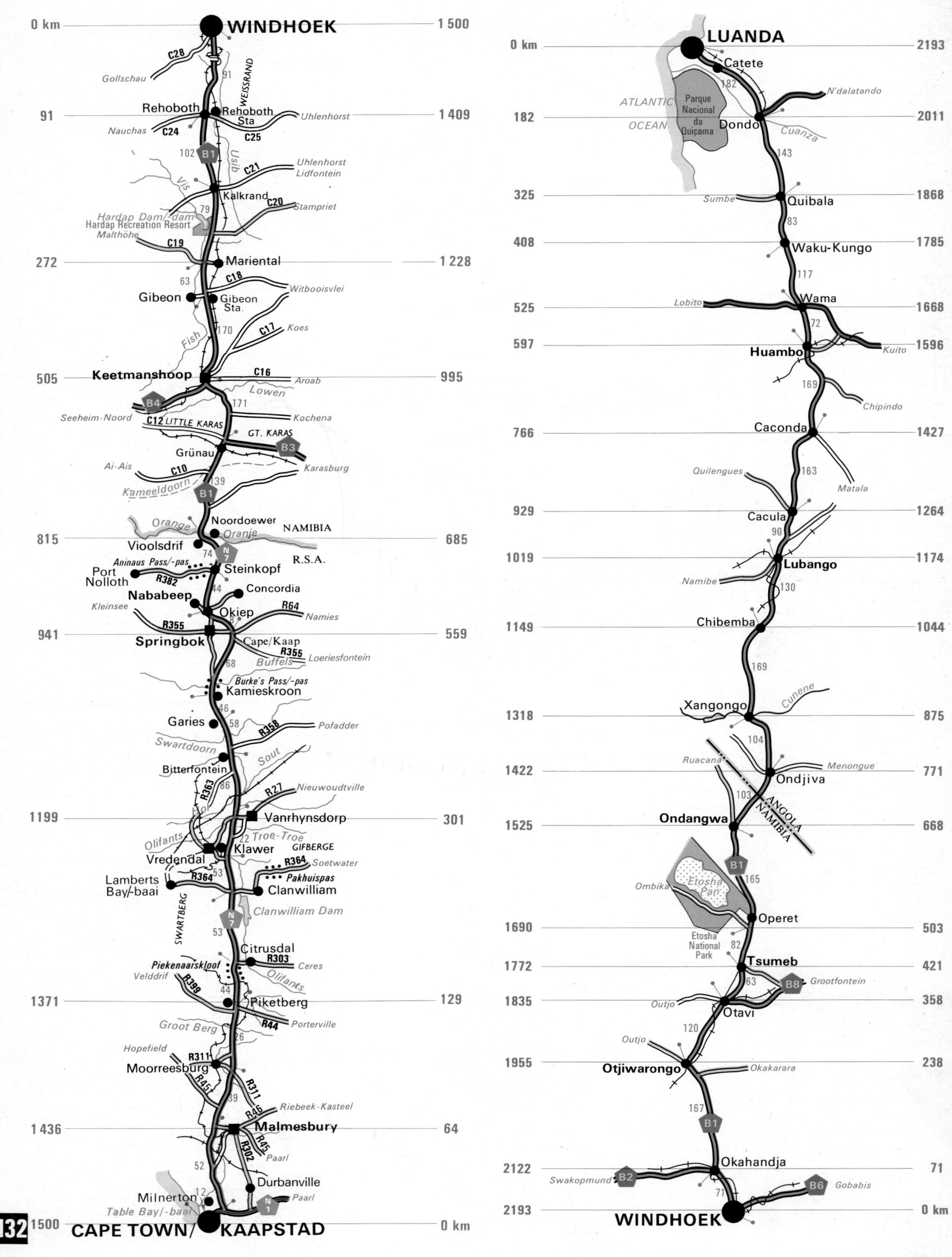

0 km WINDHOEK 1 500
91 Rehoboth Rehoboth Sta 1 409
Kalkrand
Hardap Dam/-dam
Hardap Recreation Resort
272 Mariental 1 228
Gibeon
Gibeon Sta.
505 Keetmanshoop 995
Grünau
Noordoewer
NAMIBIA
815 Vioolsdrif 685
R.S.A.
Steinkopf
Port Nolloth
Nababeep
Concordia
Okiep
941 Springbok 559
Kamieskroon
Garies
Bitterfontein
1199 Vanrhynsdorp 301
Klawer
Vredendal
Lamberts Bay/-baai
Clanwilliam
Citrusdal
1371 Piketberg 129
Moorreesburg
1 436 Malmesbury 64
Durbanville
Milnerton
1500 CAPE TOWN/KAAPSTAD 0 km
0 km LUANDA 2193
Catete
182 Dondo 2011
ATLANTIC OCEAN
Parque Nacional da Quiçama
325 Quibala 1868
408 Waku-Kungo 1785
525 Wama 1668
597 Huambo 1596
766 Caconda 1427
929 Cacula 1264
1019 Lubango 1174
1149 Chibemba 1044
1318 Xangongo 875
1422 Ondjiva 771
ANGOLA
NAMIBIA
1525 Ondangwa 668
Etosha Pan
Etosha National Park
1690 Operet 503
1772 Tsumeb 421
1835 Otavi 358
1955 Otjiwarongo 238
2122 Okahandja 71
2193 WINDHOEK 0 km